Scribes, Theology, and Apologetics

Scribes, Theology, and Apologetics

Assessing Scribal Interference in New Testament Manuscripts

ALAN MUGRIDGE

WIPF & STOCK · Eugene, Oregon

SCRIBES, THEOLOGY, AND APOLOGETICS
Assessing Scribal Interference in New Testament Manuscripts

Copyright © 2024 Alan Mugridge. All rights reserved. Except for brief quotations in critical publications or reviews, no part of this book may be reproduced in any manner without prior written permission from the publisher. Write: Permissions, Wipf and Stock Publishers, 199 W. 8th Ave., Suite 3, Eugene, OR 97401.

Wipf & Stock
An Imprint of Wipf and Stock Publishers
199 W. 8th Ave., Suite 3
Eugene, OR 97401

www.wipfandstock.com

PAPERBACK ISBN: 978-1-4982-9120-0
HARDCOVER ISBN: 978-1-4982-9122-4
EBOOK ISBN: 978-1-4982-9121-7

11/18/24

For Phillip Jensen,
who gave me a Greek New Testament

Contents

Preface		ix
Abbreviations		xi
Introduction		xv
1	Anti-adoptionist Corruptions?	1
2	Anti-separationist Corruptions?	69
3	Anti-docetic Corruptions?	116
4	Anti-patripassianist Corruptions?	157
5	Apologetic for Intellectual Integrity?	171
6	Apologetic for the Person of Jesus?	195
7	Apologetic for the Followers of Jesus?	221
8	Apologetic for Christians in the Roman Empire?	257
9	Conclusion	284
Glossary		297
Bibliography		301
Index		315

Preface

THIS BOOK IS THE companion volume to *Scribes, Motives, and Manuscripts* and is written with the same goal in mind. That is, I aim to assess claims that scribes of NT manuscripts commonly changed the text in the MS they were producing from what they encountered in their exemplar in order to reinforce their own views, counter the views of others, or defend Christians against criticism. Since I argue that the occasions on which this has been shown to be likely are few, this serves to reinforce the general reliability of the text of the Greek NT as given in modern editions such as NA,[28] its revisions, and the *Editio Critica Maior*.

The studies reviewed in *Scribes, Motives, and Manuscripts* were varied, some focusing on major or minor treatments of particular MSS, while others concentrated on parts of the NT such as the Gospels or some of the Pauline letters. In the present book, I review two major studies. First, I offer an assessment of Bart Ehrman's book *The Orthodox Corruption of Scripture*, which is one of the pioneering studies in this field in recent times. In that volume, Ehrman argues that "proto-orthodox" copyists of the NT changed the text of their MSS to support their own views and oppose the views of others in relation to a number of theological issues. The second study reviewed in this volume is *Apologetic Discourse and the Scribal Tradition* by Wayne Kannaday, in which he looks at MSS with texts from the Gospels. He argues that scribes changed the text of their MSS from what they found in their exemplars in order to provide apologetic material for Jesus and his followers in the context of the hostility they faced in the Roman Empire.

Thus, this book too is a review of the work of other scholars and hence could be seen as combative. I hope I have avoided that mindset, even though I argue that the amount of intentional scribal interference in the production of the MSS of the NT is far less than these authors

PREFACE

propose. Nevertheless, my assessment may seem quite negative, as is inevitable in a study such as this, which offers an analysis and assessment of the work of others. I hope they do not take it personally, and I apologize in advance if I have misinterpreted or misconstrued what they or other authors have written. So, I offer this study, like *Scribes, Motives, and Manuscripts*, as a contribution to the field of NT textual criticism, and no doubt it will be given its own assessment in terms of its validity and usefulness in this area of study. I only ask that this be undertaken in the same spirit of scholarly endeavor in which the present volume is written.

I also want to thank the many authors who have contributed to this issue and whose published work I have referred to, although I have also made my own contributions on a number of issues. Again, I hope this study encourages others to study the actual MSS on which the text of the Greek NT is based, which I have found so interesting and fruitful. I also hope that it assists students of the NT by reinforcing the general reliability of the modern editions of the NT, such as NA^{28} and its successors, which have been produced with such care and enormous endeavor over a long period of time.

The Board of Sydney Missionary and Bible College also deserve thanks for study leave granted to me in the first semester of 2018, during which time both *Scribes, Motives, and Manuscripts* and the present volume took shape. Thanks again to family and friends, the staff of the SMBC library, and the faculty members of SMBC who assisted in the final stages.

ALAN MUGRIDGE
Lecturer in New Testament, Sydney Missionary and Bible College, an accredited college of the Australian College of Theology

Abbreviations

THE FOLLOWING WORKS ARE used as sources of abbreviations:
Biblical Studies primary sources and journals, including OT, NT, and early Christian works, follow those in B. J. Collins et al., *SBL Handbook of Style*. 2nd ed. Atlanta: SBL, 2014, or G. W. H. Lampe, *A Patristic Greek Lexicon*, or Liddell, Scott, and Jones' *A Greek-English Lexicon* with revised supplement. Oxford: Clarendon, 1996.

Papyrus volumes follow those in J. F. Oates and W. H. Willis, et al. *Checklist of Editions of Greek, Latin, Demotic, and Coptic Papyri, Ostraca, and Tablets*. (The web edition can be found at papyri.info).

Manuscripts are abbreviated as in NA^{28}.

The date of the production of MSS is provided by Roman numerals indicating a century or centuries, with a few added features, along with the addition of BC or AD. Note that the dating of undated MSS is usually no more precise than fifty to one hundred years.

ca. AD 450	About AD 450 (AD 425–475)
V AD	Fifth century AD (AD 400–500)
Early V AD	Early in the fifth century AD (about AD 400–450)
Mid-V AD	Middle of the fifth century AD (about AD 425–475)
Late V AD	Late in the fifth century AD (about AD 450–500)
V/VI AD	The period around AD 500 (about AD 450–550)
V–VI AD	Any time in the fifth or sixth centuries AD (AD 400–600)

OTHER ABBREVIATIONS

AB	Anchor Bible
AJT	*Asia Journal of Theology*
ANRW	Temporini, Hildegard, et al., eds. *Aufstieg und Niedergang der römischen Welt*. Berlin: de Gruyter, 1972–.
AUSS	*Andrews University Seminary Studies*
BBR	*Bulletin for Biblical Research*
BDAG	Bauer, Walter, et al. *Greek-English Lexicon of the New Testament and Other Early Christian Literature*. 3rd ed. Chicago: University of Chicago, 2000.
BDF	Friedrich Blass et al. *A Greek Grammar of the New Testament and other Early Christian Literature*. Chicago: University of Chicago, 1961.
BETL	Bibliotheca Ephemeridum Theologicarum Lovaniensium
Bib	*Biblica*
BICS	*Bulletin of the Institute of Classical Studies*
BSac	*Bibliotheca Sacra*
CBQ	*Catholic Biblical Quarterly*
CH	*Church History*
CP	*Classical Philology*
CRBR	*Critical Review of Books in Religion*
CSNTM	Center for the Study of New Testament Manuscripts
CTR	*Criswell Theological Review*
EC	*Early Christianity*
ECM	Editio Critica Maior
ETL	*Ephemerides Theologicae Lovanienses*
ExpTim	*Expository Times*
FN	*Filologia Neotestamentaria*
GELS	Muraoka, Takamitsu. *A Greek-English Lexicon of the Septuagint*. Leuven: Peeters, 2009.
GNT^5	Aland, Barbara, et al. *The Greek New Testament*. 5th ed. Stuttgart: United Bible Societies, 2014.
HBT	*Horizons in Biblical Theology*
HTR	*Harvard Theological Review*
ICC	International Critical Commentary
IGNTP	International Greek New Testament Project
INTF	Institut für neutestamentliche Textforschung

ABBREVIATIONS

JBTC	*Journal of Biblical Textual Criticism*
JBL	*Journal of Biblical Literature*
JBRec	*Journal of the Bible and its Reception*
JECS	*Journal of Early Christian Studies*
JETS	*Journal of the Evangelical Theological Society*
JGRChJ	*Journal of Greco-Roman Christianity and Judaism*
JIBS	*Journal of Inductive Biblical Studies*
JR	*Journal of Religion*
JSNT	*Journal for the Study of the New Testament*
JSOT	*Journal for the Study of the Old Testament*
JTI	*Journal of Theological Interpretation*
JTS	*Journal of Theological Studies*
LSJ	Liddell, Henry George, Robert Scott, Henry Stuart Jones. *A Greek-English Lexicon*. 9th ed. with revised supplement. Oxford: Clarendon, 1996.
LSTS	Library of Second Temple Studies
LXX	Septuagint
MM	Moulton, James H., and George Milligan. *The Vocabulary of the Greek Testament Illustrated from the Papyri and Other Non-Literary Sources*. London: Hodder and Stoughton, 1930.
MS, MSS	Manuscript, manuscripts
MT	Masoretic Text
NA^{28}	Nestle, Eberhard, et al., *Novum Testamentum Graece*. 28th ed. Stuttgart: Deutsche Bibelgesellschaft, 2012.
Neot	*Neotestamentica*
NIDNTTE	Silva, Moisés, ed. *New International Dictionary of New Testament Theology and Exegesis*. 5 vols. Grand Rapids: Zondervan, 2014.
NICNT	New International Commentary on the New Testament
NIGTC	New International Greek Testament Commentary
NovT	*Novum Testamentum*
NT	New Testament
NTS	*New Testament Studies*
NTTS	New Testament Tools and Studies
NTTSD	New Testament Tools, Studies, and Documents
OCD	*Oxford Classical Dictionary*
OL	Old Latin
OT	Old Testament

PGL	Lampe, G. W. H. *A Patristic Greek Lexicon*. Oxford: Clarendon, 1961.
PSB	*Princeton Seminary Bulletin*
Presb	*Presbyterion*
RB	*Revue biblique*
SBJT	*Southern Baptist Journal of Theology*
SEÅ	*Svensk exegetisk årsbok*
SR	Singular reading
SSG	Muraoka, Takamitsu. *A Syntax of Septuagint Greek*. Leuven: Peeters, 2016
StPatr	*Studia Patristica*
SwJT	*Southwestern Journal of Theology*
TDSA	Testi e documenti per lo studio dell'antichità
Th	Theodotion (version of the Greek NT)
THGNT	Dirk Jongkind et al., eds. *The Tyndale House Greek New Testament*. Cambridge: Cambridge University Press, 2017.
TynBul	*Tyndale Bulletin*
VC	*Vigiliae Christianae*
vid	*ut videtur*, meaning "apparently"
WBC	Word Biblical Commentary
WTJ	*Westminster Theological Journal*
WUNT	Wissenschaftliche Untersuchungen zum Neuen Testament
ZNW	*Zeitschrift für die neutestamentliche Wissenschaft und die Kunde der älteren Kirche*

Where volumes comprise collections of previously published material, unless otherwise indicated, I refer only to the page numbers in the collected edition, in which details of previous publication may be found.

Introduction

LIKE THE COMPANION VOLUME, *Scribes, Motives, and Manuscripts*, this book is also a review of studies focusing on the role of the copyists of the MSS of the NT that conclude that the copyists wanted to make their MSS more supportive of their own views and less able to support the views of others. Again, I want to weigh the arguments, as well as the evidence adduced in support, which attempt to show that we can establish the intents of those copyists and show that their intent was to reinforce what later became "orthodox" theology in the church or to counter criticism levelled at Jesus or his followers in the Roman Empire by removing the grounds for that criticism in NT MSS.

The groundwork for this study is the same as in *Scribes, Motives, and Manuscripts*, so I do not include again the material covered in chapters 1 and 2 of that volume. The first of these chapters offered some reflection on a range of Greek works—classical Greek texts, Jewish texts, and Christian texts outside the NT. I noted that modern editors aim to produce an edition of those texts as close as possible to the original, and that the MSS on which they are based are generally far fewer and much later than those on which the text of the NT is based. Thus, students of the NT text can similarly aim to produce its text as like the original text as they are able without being criticized for doing the impossible or wasting their time.

The second chapter of the previous volume entailed a review of NT textual criticism, basically reinforcing the general approach that is common in this discipline. However, I voiced some cautions about various matters including assumptions commonly made about the NT, such as the widely accepted "solution" to the Synoptic problem and the role it sometimes plays in establishing the text of the NT. There seems to be little to limit the role that intentionality plays in this study, for after all

INTRODUCTION

we are attempting to locate changes made in MSS with a certain agenda in mind, however conscious that agenda was. I do not repeat this material in the current volume, so I refer the reader to *Scribes, Motives, and Manuscripts* on these two matters.

In this book, I first offer an assessment of Bart Ehrman's book *The Orthodox Corruption of Scripture*, following his chapters in order. So, in chapter 1, I review variant readings said to have been created to oppose adoptionist theology, according to which Jesus the man was adopted into the Godhead. In chapter 2 I assess arguments that certain readings were inserted to counter "separationist" theology which attempted to create a distinction in some way between the human and divine natures of Jesus. Chapter 3 is a review of readings that are proposed to have been opposing docetism, according to which Jesus only seemed to be a human being. Finally, chapter 4 is a short discussion of variants that might be seen as offering opposition to any form of patripassianism, which so identified Jesus with God the Father that God was then said to have suffered and died on a cross. At the end of this chapter, I offer a summary of my conclusions regarding Ehrman's work.

The second part of this study is a review of Wayne Kannaday's volume *Apologetic Discourse and the Scribal Tradition*. So, in chapter 5, I review his discussion of variants that he maintains were inserted with the apologetic motive of showing that Christianity was an intellectually credible faith. Chapter 6 offers an assessment of readings Kannaday argues were created to stand against views about Jesus himself as weak, foolish, seditious, low-class, a deceptive magician, and bad tempered. In chapter 7 I discuss readings that are said to defend Christians against charges that they were fanatics, fools, or mainly foolish women and children, and I also review relevant aspects of the various endings of Mark's Gospel in that context. Chapter 8 is an assessment of Kannaday's arguments that certain variants were placed in NT MSS to defend Christians against the slur of being disloyal and disturbing citizens of the Roman Empire, and I conclude with a summary of my assessment of Kannaday's work as a whole.

Finally, chapter 9 summarizes my assessment of both Ehrman's and Kannaday's studies with an eye to the implications of this for NT textual criticism. This is not dissimilar to the conclusions drawn in *Scribes, Motives, and Manuscripts* about scribal "tendencies" in NT MSS or the level of scribal interference evident in them. Again, this final chapter reflects on a number of common assumptions regarding the NT documents themselves as well as the way in which they were reproduced in the following centuries. I also mention perspectives on NT textual criticism that should be treated as doubtful and highlight the crucial role that literary, linguistic, religious, and social context, as well as careful and thorough exegesis, should play in evaluating variants.

I emphasize again that I cast doubt on conclusions based on the assumption that early copyists were generally Christians and usually unskilled. I also conclude that the number of variant readings in NT MSS that can be shown to be the result of the theological views or apologetic aims of copyists is minimal, at least compared to the number of those proposed in the studies examined. Indeed, most can be more easily explained as the product of scribal carelessness, tiredness, or the like, so that, while the trend in NT textual criticism to highlight the views of copyists and the role they played in passing on the text of the NT does contain an element of truth, on the whole its conclusions are exaggerated or doubtful.

PRELIMINARY NOTES

As in the companion volume, a few matters deserve comment, in order to help readers navigate through this volume. The reader will observe that, in order to avoid needless repetition, the variants are usually dealt with in only one place, even though they could fit in several places. It has not always been possible to follow this procedure consistently, but the index of passages will guide the reader to the relevant discussions. In most cases, the texts are dealt with in canonical order, but I have sometimes followed the order given by the author of the work under review.

I have chosen not to use upper case Greek, even though that would be more appropriate for early MSS, because it would be visually confronting in the context of a predominantly lower-case Roman font. However, I have deliberately refrained from using punctuation and diacritical points in Greek (except when citing published texts), since they were only rarely and inconsistently employed in MSS in the early centuries, and I use a lunate sigma (ϲ) as was common in early times. In this way, readers will be able to appreciate the text in early MSS in a more "authentic" way. I have also sometimes used original spelling instead of the classical spelling. I have, however, refrained from writing the Greek text in *scriptio continua* (without spaces between words) since that might be too challenging altogether. Some compromises are inevitable. Where relevant, I also indicate the presence of *nomina sacra* in the MSS with a superscript line.

When variants are being discussed, I persist with using MS (MSS) for "manuscript" ("manuscripts"), although "witness" ("witnesses") might be more appropriate at times. The issues arising in relation to versional evidence, especially in "back-translation" from Syriac, Latin, and Coptic are well known, but I do not deal with this in any detail, although the subject does arise from time to time. The MS evidence for variants almost never cites even the limited list in NA^{28}, as this would be both tedious and unnecessary, so only a sample of the significant MSS is usually cited. I use "etc." to indicate that further MSS, even in N^{28}, support a reading in addition to those cited.

MS citation usually follows that in NA^{28}, although I use "*Byz*" as in NA^{28} for the Catholic Epistles and also for the Majority text elsewhere (instead of M), even though this is somewhat inexact.[1] When citing a discussion of a variant or text by a modern author, I do not always provide the page reference for each and every reference or quotation, so that the reader can focus on the argument at hand without being overloaded with footnote references, but the reference does appear somewhere in the footnotes to that section. For dates, I continue to use BC and AD, as is common in many disciplines. The terminology I use varies, but it includes "scribal habits," "scribal practices," and "scribal acts," as well as "scribal tendencies," "scribal intentions," and "scribal bias," in line with the theme of the present study. For lexical matters, besides BDAG, LSJ and *PGL*, I make extensive use of Takamitsu Muraoka's *Greek-English Lexicon of the Septuagint* (*GELS*) because the Septuagint is a mine of Koine Greek and was widely used in early Christian circles. Although "Western" is questionable as a label for a group of MSS for several reasons and is commonly placed in quotation marks, I generally omit the quotation marks as this would be tedious for the reader.

---

1. See NA^{28}, 59*–60*, for an explanation of the distinction in that edition between M and *Byz* (in the Catholic Epistles, since the ECM has appeared for these).

1

Anti-adoptionist Corruptions?

COPYISTS AND THEOLOGY

IN THE FIRST FOUR chapters of this volume, I examine suggestions that variant readings in NT MSS were designed to support or oppose certain theological beliefs, reviewing Ehrman's approach, particularly in his book *The Orthodox Corruption of Scripture*. I follow his fourfold division—anti-adoptionist, anti-separationist, anti-docetic, and anti-patripassianist "corruptions"—as well as their subdivisions, but within these sections I treat the texts in canonical order for ease of reference.

There are several points to make before beginning this review. First, I have discussed the issue of how conscious copyists were of their own "intentions" in *Scribes, Motives, and Manuscripts*, so I do not repeat that here, except to say again that for variants to be created in response to a current debate there must have been some kind of intention, whatever level of consciousness was involved, for a copyist to make the copy of the text he was reproducing different from that in his exemplar.[1] Ehrman portrays copyists engaging in a kind of "interpretation" of their texts by means of altering the readings, just as readers "interpret" texts when they read them. So, by rewriting them they were not "corrupting" the texts at all. This would mean that they were not "forging" readings but simply reading texts differently and hence not intentionally corrupting the text

---

1. Ehrman discusses this issue in *Orthodox Corruption*, 32, 51n110, 337–41.

Scribes, Theology, and Apologetics

of the NT.[2] Yet it is hard to see how some level of scribal intentionality can be avoided, if readings were created in response to a current dispute. Instead of suggesting that copyists made changes for certain "reasons," Ehrman says that he means that the readings could "*function* in theological ways," since they would be "amenable to the proto-orthodox cause."[3] I observe, however, that even if a reading would have been amenable to a cause, it might not have been created to support that cause.

Second, in order to set the discussion in context, Ehrman begins his book with a review of debates in the second and third centuries among people calling themselves Christians with different views on certain theological matters.[4] He sketches various beliefs held by people claiming to be Christians, and he argues that scribes (copyists) changed the readings from those in their exemplar to those in the copies they made in order to support beliefs that later came to be labelled "orthodox" or to make texts less serviceable by those later called "unorthodox." This assumes that all copyists of Christian MSS were Christians, but in view of the normal practice of employing scribes to have MSS reproduced in the Roman imperial period and the variety of scribes who did so, it is questionable that they were all Christians, unless a MS provides clear evidence that this was the case.[5]

Third, in his introductory chapter Ehrman clearly outlines the range of views held by Christians in the first few centuries. By "proto-orthodoxy" he means views held by early church writers who espoused beliefs later championed and defined as "orthodox." As his starting point he takes Eusebius, implying that his views were somewhat optimistic and misleading, although deriving from earlier writers. However, as noted in *Scribes, Motives, and Manuscripts*, the perception of Christianity in the early centuries in sociological terms in line with the work of Walter Bauer, which Ehrman claims has replaced the earlier "orthodoxy and heresy" model, has not been accepted by all. Indeed, there are good reasons to cast doubt on Bauer's reconstruction and hence also on a thesis that depends upon it. Although few would wish to endorse Eusebius's version of early church history in all its details, it does not follow that he gave a grossly distorted portrayal of events. There certainly were tensions and disputes in the early church, even in its first decades (cf. Acts

2. Ehrman, *Orthodox Corruption*, 33–36, esp. 35–36.
3. Ehrman, *Orthodox Corruption*, 121n55.
4. Ehrman, *Orthodox Corruption*, 3–54.
5. Mugridge, *Copying*, 144–54.

ANTI-ADOPTIONIST CORRUPTIONS?

15:37–41; Gal 2:11–21), but they seem to have been resolved, and variety of expression is not necessarily evidence of differing theology. Indeed, outside influences also affected theological views in Christian churches, and the NT itself attests to issues arising from the surrounding culture rather than simply originating from different interpretations of the words of Jesus and the apostles. There is no reason to think that this was any less the case in later centuries as well. Different theology among those calling themselves Christians, then, was not necessarily simply an alternative "Christian" view but might well have been a distortion of original Christian theology stemming from outside influences.

Fourth, the portrayal of the copyists of early Christian texts as "by and large private individuals, not paid professionals,"[6] also stands in need of reassessment in light of the handwriting evident in those MSS. Although mistakes were made, copyists often corrected their work, such as in P^{66} with its extensive corrections by the scribe. Further, to describe these copyists as "warm-blooded Christians, living in a world of wide-ranging theological debates" or to say that "most scribes were surely cognizant of these debates, and many were surely participants,"[7] is to go beyond the evidence. Indeed, it is contrary to the evidence of the care taken by many copyists of the extensive early papyri, which demonstrate their concern for accuracy. The picture of the text of the NT as "in a state of flux" and only "standardized" in the fourth century is clearly true to an extent, as the more regular texts of Byzantine MSS show. However, the description of the early period as "the period of relative creativity" in contrast to the later period of "strict reproduction" gives the impression that earlier copyists did not wish to reproduce the texts in their exemplars with accuracy but felt free to exercise a certain amount of inventiveness.[8] In the Roman imperial world, however, scribes were the usual ones to reproduce MSS, and evidence would need to be provided to show that the copyist of a NT MS was not a "professional" scribe simply attempting to reproduce his exemplar.

Fifth, it is also quite difficult to know if a copyist changed the reading in his exemplar to a different reading in his copy, or whether he was simply reproducing the text in his exemplar. Thus, we cannot often be sure that the copyist of a MS was responsible for a reading, unless there is clear evidence, such as a pattern of SRs. So, it is difficult to prove that

---

6. Ehrman, *Orthodox Corruption*, 29.
7. Ehrman, *Orthodox Corruption*, 29.
8. Ehrman, *Orthodox Corruption*, 32–33.

Scribes, Theology, and Apologetics

a MS was newly provided with a reading at the time it was copied. It follows that a variant in a MS might not have arisen at the time it was produced. Instead, it could have been present in the exemplar used to produce that MS and then reproduced faithfully by the copyist, or it was there in the exemplar of the exemplar, and so on. Therefore, since a variant reading might not have derived from the period in which a copyist produced his MS, it is difficult to be certain that it arose in response to a theological issue current at that time.

Sixth, while most NT textual variants may well have arisen in the second and third centuries, we cannot assume that variant readings occurring only in later MSS *must* have arisen in the early period. Late variants may simply have arisen in later times, even if they are not as common.

Thus, the portrayal of early copyists of Christian texts altering the texts in the MSS they produced to make them more "orthodox" or less able to be used by "heretical" opponents stands in need of review due to a number of unwarranted assumptions. With all these points in mind, I now examine Ehrman's work in relation to the variant readings he draws upon to demonstrate "the orthodox corruption of Scripture," firstly looking at proposed "anti-Adoptionist corruptions."[9]

In chapter 2 of his book Ehrman gives an account of adoptionism in the early church, and then anti-adoptionist polemics by early church writers, including an allusion to Eusebius citing a document alleging that some Roman adoptionists changed NT MSS to support their own views (*Hist. eccl.* 5.28).[10] He then provides a good coverage of the views of the Ebionites, Theodotus and his followers, and Paul of Samosata, insofar as they exhibit various adoptionist viewpoints. He goes on to propose that there are signs that "orthodox" copyists tampered with their NT MSS in order to support their own views and stop adoptionists gaining support for theirs. I do not discuss the suggestion that adoptionist views were present in "preliterary traditions" that were modified when incorporated into NT documents,[11] since this lies outside the scope of the present work and clear evidence is lacking on the issue.

---

9. Ehrman, *Orthodox Corruption*, 55–139.
10. Ehrman, *Orthodox Corruption*, 55–63.
11. Ehrman, *Orthodox Corruption*, 56–58. Cf. Ehrman, "Divine Man," 363–65.

ANTI-ADOPTIONIST CORRUPTIONS?

Jesus' Virgin Birth

Ehrman examines a number of texts, arguing that certain MSS manifest a change from an earlier reading to reinforce the theology of the virgin birth, showing that an "orthodox" (or "proto-orthodox") copyist was wishing to make an adoptionist view less tenable, thus "tampering" with the text.[12]

Matthew 1:16

Some MSS of this text, after mentioning τον ιωσηφ, instead of continuing τον ανδρα μαριας εξ ης εγεννηθη ιησους, read ω μνηστευθεισα παρθενος μαριαμ εγεννησεν ιησουν, now explicitly calling Mary παρθενος and saying that she was "betrothed" to Joseph, rather than calling him her "husband/man" (ανηρ). Although παρθενος could just mean "young woman," in Christian circles it came to mean "virgin" and probably did so for those responsible for this reading. Yet, the earliest MS listed in its support (sy^s) has this reading "apparently through carelessness,"[13] and other supporting MSS are generally quite late—Θ (IX AD), ƒ[13] (XI AD or later), ℓ 547 (XIII AD), OL (IV–XII / XIII AD). It seems clear, then, that the reading referring to Mary being a virgin engaged to Joseph is not original in Matthew 1:16, although its presence in the OL shows that it could have arisen as early as the fourth century. It *might* have been designed to support Mary's virginity when pregnant with Jesus and thus could be an "orthodox corruption,"[14] but it could also have been created to harmonize with 1:18, where it is explained that Jesus was not Joseph's physical son.[15] Or perhaps it was a harmonization to 1:25, where it is stated that the couple did not have intercourse until after Jesus was born, or to Luke 1:27 where μνηστευομαι and παρθενος both occur.[16] So, it is impossible to be certain that the variant originated in the second or third centuries in response to a christological debate in order to support the doctrine of the virgin birth.

---

12. Ehrman, *Orthodox Corruption*, 63–72.

13. Ehrman, *Orthodox Corruption*, 64, 68. Globe argues, however, that the Syriac readings were "translation variants" ("Doctrinal Variants," 63–65).

14. Ehrman, *Orthodox Corruption*, 68–69, 123n71; Ehrman, *Misquoting*, 96–97; Globe, "Doctrinal Variants," 66.

15. Metzger, *Textual Commentary*, 6; Davies and Allison, *Matthew*, 1:183–84, 84n71; Head, "Christology," 116–17; France, *Matthew*, 28n7.

16. Nolland, *Matthew*, 65–66.

Scribes, Theology, and Apologetics

Luke 2:22, 27, 33, 41, 42, 43

I take these passages together, because they occur in close proximity and bear some relationship to one another. In contrast to the implied reference to Joseph and Mary in ανηγαγον αυτον, where "*they* took him [Jesus] up" to Jerusalem (2:22), some late MSS add οι γονεις αυτου (of Jesus), perhaps suggesting more clearly that he had "parents" and was not born by divine fiat through a virgin. So, this might have been an adoptionist reading.[17] In 2:42, Codex Bezae and a few OL MSS support the secondary reading ανεβησαν οι γονεις αυτου instead of the original αναβαινοντων αυτων, again explicitly referring to Jesus' "parents" and perhaps supporting adoptionist Christology.[18] Ehrman comments, however, that, at least in D, this variant reading was probably not designed to support an adoptionist view but to make it clear that Jesus went with Joseph and Mary (adding εχοντες αυτον) so that the rest of the account would make sense—Jesus went too. Anyway, οι γονεις αυτου are mentioned in v. 41 as the antecedent of αναβαινοντων αυτων in v. 42, so adding οι γονεις is only repetitive, not engaging in interpretation or theological clarification.

On the other hand, some readings might have been intentionally anti-adoptionist. So, in 2:27 the reference to the parents (τους γονεις) of Jesus is changed in some later witnesses to Tatian's Diatessaron and omitted altogether in a few late NT minuscules (X–XIII AD),[19] perhaps to avoid the idea that Joseph was Jesus' physical father. In relation to Jesus, the original reading of 2:33 called Joseph ο πατηρ αυτου, but a number of MSS read (ο) ιωσηφ instead, again possibly to avoid the thought that Joseph was Jesus' biological father, despite the fact that this is clarified earlier in 1:26–38.[20] Instead of οι γονεις αυτου in 2:41, MS 1012 (XI AD) and the OL tradition avoid γονεις and read instead ο τε ιωσηφ και η μαρια(μ) conceivably to avoid the same unorthodox adoptionist implication.[21] Likewise, in 2:43, the original οι γονεις αυτου appears as ιωσηφ και η μητηρ αυτου in some MSS, possibly with the same aim in mind.[22]

---

17. Ehrman, *Orthodox Corruption*, 121–22n59. Cf. Globe, "Doctrinal Variants," 60–61.

18. Ehrman, *Orthodox Corruption*, 121–22n59.

19. Ehrman, *Orthodox Corruption*, 66, 121nn58–59.

20. Ehrman, *Orthodox Corruption*, 65, 121n52. Cf. Ehrman, *Misquoting*, 158; Metzger, *Textual Commentary*, 111–12.

21. Ehrman, *Orthodox Corruption*, 66, 121n57; Metzger, *Textual Commentary*, 112; Fitzmyer, *Luke I–IX*, 439.

22. Ehrman, *Orthodox Corruption*, 66, 121n56. Cf. Ehrman, *Misquoting*, 158;

ANTI-ADOPTIONIST CORRUPTIONS?

These readings present a range of references to Joseph and Mary, some original readings calling Joseph Jesus' "father" and referring to Jesus' "parents" and some variants possibly introduced to avoid the view that Joseph was Jesus' biological father. However, none of the MSS with the supposed anti-adoptionist reading were copied earlier than the fourth century, so there is little firm evidence that those readings were created in the second and third centuries to support an anti-adoptionist viewpoint in relation to debates at that time.

Further, when individual MSS are examined in these six passages, many of them do not show a uniform pattern of readings with a "theological tendency."[23] When there appears to be a secondary "anti-adoptionist" reading in certain MSS—2:27 (245), 2:33 (A X 245 c), 2:41 (c), 2:43 (A X 245 c)—this is only carried through consistently once in 2:47 (MS 245, XII AD), and is contradicted in other MSS by the inclusion of possibly "adoptionist" readings—2:22 (X) and 2:42 (D c). Thus, the variety of readings said to support an anti-adoptionist view more likely indicates a "stylistic preference" on the part of the copyists rather than a theological viewpoint, because the MSS in question show elsewhere that Joseph was not Jesus' biological father.[24] So, these variant readings were probably just expressions of style, not indications of theological views.

Luke 2:48

This passage portrays Mary rebuking Jesus for the heartache he had caused her and Joseph by staying behind in Jerusalem, concluding that ο πατηρ cου καγω οδυνωμενοι εζητουμεν cε. Ehrman mentions MSS (C[vid] β e) reading οι cυγγενειc cου καγω (NA[26]) as a variant that removes any mention of Joseph as Jesus' father,[25] which could be seen as an anti-adoptionist reading, but NA[27/28] now have the presumably corrected reading for those MSS (οι cυγγενειc και ο πατηρ cου και εγω).[26] So, this secondary reading adds the mention of relatives (cυγγενειc) but retains ο

Metzger, *Textual Commentary*, 112; Bovon, *Luke 1*, 104n57.

23. Wasserman, "Misquoting?"

24. Wasserman, "Misquoting?," 332–33. Wachtel also notes the lack of consistency in the secondary variants: most MSS have οι γονειc αυτου in 2:41 (except 1012 it) and ο πατηρ cου καγω in 2:48 (with the mixed reading οι cυγγενειc και ο πατηρ cου και εγω in a few MSS, and the whole phrase omitted altogether in others). ("Kinds of Variants," 89).

25. Ehrman, *Orthodox Corruption*, 65.

26. Cf. American and British Committees, *St. Luke*, 55.

πατηρ, so these MSS cannot be seen as possibly serving anti-adoptionist apologetics.

Luke 3:22

In Luke's account of Jesus' baptism, instead of the traditional reading where the heavenly voice says cυ ει ο υιoc μoυ ο αγαπητoc εν coι ευδoκηca, D, the OL tradition, and a small number of Greek and Latin fathers have a reading seemingly derived from Ps 2:7, υιoc μoυ ει cυ εγω cημερoν γεγεννηκα cε. Ehrman argues that the second ("Western") reading is "virtually the only reading that survives" from "witnesses of the second and third centuries," and he proposes that this was the reading of "the ancestor of codex Bezae and the Old Latin text of Luke."[27] He cites Justin (*Dial.* 88) referring to Ps 2:7 and suggests that this was the reading Justin had, as well as Clement of Alexandria (*Paed.* 1.25.2; *sic.* 1.6.2), the Gospel According to the Hebrews (in Jerome *Comm. Isa.* 11.12), the Didascalia 93.26, and the Gospel According to the Ebionites, Origen, and Methodius, as well as some later writers and texts.[28]

However, the citation in Epiphanius's *Panarion* (30.13.7–8) referring to the Gospel of the Ebionites includes both readings. Further, the reference to Origen (*Comm. Jo.* 1.32) should be questioned because there is nothing in the context to suggest that he was referring to Luke 3:22, although he was clearly citing Ps 2:7.[29] Moreover, just prior to the citation in *Dial.* 88.8, Justin speaks about the events at Jesus' baptism as "proof" of his Sonship, just as his triumphal entry into Jerusalem was "proof" that he was the Christ (*Dial.* 88.6). Thus, his words at 88.8 were not necessarily aiming to counter adoptionism, even though it does appear that his text of Luke 3:22 included the words from Ps 2:7 (cf. *Dial.* 103.6).

Ehrman also points out that early support for the traditional reading is limited to P[4] (III AD). However, P[4] has been reliably dated to the second century,[30] and it is also supported by later MSS, ℵ and B (IV AD), A and W (V AD), and many others. Further, Clement of Alexandria has a conflated reading including αγαπητoc, and Augustine says the Western

---

27. Ehrman, *Orthodox Corruption*, 73–74. Cf. Ehrman, "Divine Man," 365–71.
28. Ehrman, *Orthodox Corruption*, 125–26, 126nn87–92.
29. Wasserman, "Misquoting?," 336.
30. Orsini and Clarysse, "Early New Testament," 470. Cf. Charlesworth, "T. C. Skeat."

ANTI-ADOPTIONIST CORRUPTIONS?

reading was not in the most ancient Greek codices (*Cons.* 2.14).[31] So, both readings seem to have been known in the first three centuries and "are very early."[32]

Several NT texts connect Ps 2:7 with Jesus (e.g., Acts 13:33, Heb 1:5, 5:5), and some later sources connect it more specifically with his baptism, but it is unclear where other books such as the Gospel According to the Hebrews derived their readings from, and Justin (*Dial.* 88) and the Gospel of the Ebionites include strange additions like fire coming from the Jordan.[33] Ehrman concludes that the Western reading (γεγεννηκα cε) was original, but because it was "offensive doctrinally" since it spoke of God "having begotten" (γεγεννηκα) the Son, it was dropped by copyists and replaced with a reading that harmonized with Mark 1:11 and was more theologically acceptable (cυ ει ο υιοc μου ο αγαπητοc εν coι ευδοκηcα). So, the Western reading virtually faded out after appearing in D in the fifth century.[34]

However, there might not have been any perception in the early centuries of a theological problem at all, even if γεγεννηκα cε could have supported a view "that became anathema" in later Christian centuries. Further, the evidence that the Western reading was doctrinally offensive due to its apparent support for an adoptionist theology is drawn from Justin and Augustine, who offer clarifying remarks as to the significance of the words of the heavenly voice in the Western reading. Indeed, it is unclear that Justin saw it supporting adoptionism, nor was Augustine necessarily responding to adoptionist theology. Hence, the evidence that the Western reading was original and caused embarrassment, so that copyists changed it to the traditional one, is far from compelling.

It has also been suggested that a copyist (or reader) might have felt a conflict between Jesus being referred to as the Son of God to be born of a virgin (1:35) and then later addressed by the voice of God saying εγω cημερον γεγεννηκα cε (3:22), so a similar quotation was sourced instead from Ps 2:7 in order to avoid this conflict.[35] However, it is also possible that, in order to resolve this issue (if it was felt), a copyist might have

---

31. Augustine, *Cons.* 2.14 (CSEL 43.132), quoted in Wasserman, "Misquoting?," 335n28.

32. Wasserman, "Misquoting?," 335.

33. Epiphanius, *Pan.* 30.8.7, quoted in Wasserman, "Misquoting?," 336. Wasserman also refers to Ps 2:7.

34. Ehrman, *Orthodox Corruption*, 74.

35. Ehrman, *Orthodox Corruption*, 79.

harmonized Luke 3:22 with Mark 1:11 since it is closer than Ps 2:7. Yet, it is difficult to know which reading the copyist was more conscious of, especially as Ps 2:7 was one of the most prominent OT texts in the early church.[36]

Also, since the secondary reading, whichever it was, had to arise somehow, in view of the similarity between the opening phrases (cυ ει ο υιοc μου and υιοc μου ει cυ) it would be best to be hesitant about stating what prompted someone to make the change.[37] A copyist might just have completed the sentence from memory with a well-known phrase that began with almost identical wording.

As relevant background, Ehrman examines the whole of Luke-Acts to see how Luke's Christology is expressed, and he concludes that his terminology is not always consistent. He notes how Jesus was said to be born as the Christ (Luke 2:11), and he contrasts this with the reference to his baptism in Acts 10:37-38 (εχριcεν αυτον ο θεοc πνευματι αγιω και δυναμει), taking this to mean that Jesus *became* Christ at his baptism. He also refers to Acts 2:36, where God is said to "have made" him κυριον και χριcτον at his resurrection and exaltation.[38] But, while these different moments seem to be presented as various times when Jesus became the Christ, in antiquity a baby could be proclaimed king at birth and later confirmed as such. So, Joash is called "the King's son" (2 Kgs 11:4) and "the king" (vv. 7-8, 11), and then proclaimed King and anointed (v. 12), and from then on hailed as king (vv. 12, 14, etc.). Indeed, Ps 2 was probably a coronation psalm, with the declaration in v. 7 as the official confirmation of a status already held in anticipation. Similarly, Jesus' baptism was portrayed as an official "anointing" (cf. Acts 10:38), presumably to mark the beginning of his public ministry. Hence, it would be consistent that Jesus was called God's Christ and Son in his kingdom from the time when his birth was announced (Luke 1:32-33, 35), and he was seen as being granted his full status "officially" (Acts 2:30-36) when he endured the suffering that it was necessary for him to undergo (Luke 24:26, 46). The same applies to the use of κυριοc (Luke 2:11, 10:1; Acts 2:38), cωτηρ (Luke 2:11; Acts 5:31; 13:23-24) and υιοc (του) θεου (Luke 1:32-35; 3:23-38; 8:28; 9:35; Acts 13:33). These titles are not indications of a varied Christology but expressions of a subtle and complex one, which should make us cautious about accepting that certain readings were not original

---

36. See the index of quotations, allusions, and parallels in GNT[5], 858, 871.
37. Fitzmyer, *Luke I-IX*, 485.
38. Ehrman, *Orthodox Corruption*, 126n97.

ANTI-ADOPTIONIST CORRUPTIONS?

because they seem to be in tension with Luke's use of christological titles elsewhere.[39] His vocabulary of Christology and the titles he used are quite varied.

Ehrman examines how Jesus' baptism is dealt with elsewhere in Luke, arguing that it is portrayed not so much as a simple moment of identification (cυ ει ο υιος μου ο αγαπητος) but as an occasion when God *did* something (εγω cημερον γεγεννηκα cε).[40] However, this contrast is somewhat misleading, because *both* readings in 3:22 include identification (υιος μου ει cυ, D), with the contrast in the second half—εν coι ευδοκηcα (most MSS) or εγω cημερον γεγεννηκα cε (D, etc.)—a declaration of endorsement vs. a conferral of status.

So also, in the account of the heavenly voice at Jesus' transfiguration (Luke 9:35), God is said to confirm that Jesus is his elect son (ο υιος μου εκλελεγμενος). But this need not presuppose the D reading at 3:22, for, although the verb εκλεγομαι refers to choosing one from among many and hence might imply a newly conferred status (cf. Sir 45:4),[41] it can also refer to someone who already *has* a unique status, especially if a perfect participle is used. Indeed, the adjective εκλεκτος can mean "*chosen, selected* for a task or destiny," or in a transferred sense "*of top quality, choice*," referring to the resultant status, not the process by which someone or something came to have that status.[42] To put it otherwise, εκλεκτος could mean (sometimes) "pertaining to being considered best in the course of a selection, 'choice,' *excellent*."[43] Thus, there is no reason to think that the traditional reading of 3:22, according to which Jesus is addressed as God's Son and endorsed as pleasing to him, stands in conflict with the divine declaration at his transfiguration in 9:35. So, the Western reading at 3:22 was not necessarily original and the basis of the pronouncement of Jesus' divine sonship in the account of his transfiguration.

With reference to the report of Jesus' crucifixion in Luke, Ehrman notes the use of εκλεκτος, which is semantically equivalent to the perfect participle εκλελεγμενος, where Jesus is mocked as ο χριστος του θεου ο εκλεκτος (23:35), and he observes the virtual equivalence of the terms χριστος and εκλεκτος, as the king is hailed in the OT as God's "anointed" or "chosen" one. After all, the anointing of the king was designed to

---

39. Cf. Wasserman, "Scribal Alterations," 309–10.
40. Ehrman, *Orthodox Corruption*, 77–79.
41. *GELS*, 211.
42. *GELS*, 212 (italics original).
43. *BDAG*, 306 (italics original).

officially confer royal status on God's chosen king, so it is not surprising that Ps 2:7 is often cited in the NT as foreshadowing Jesus having a similar, though more exalted, status. But it does not follow that this official recognition, as seen in Ps 2:7, is "the point at which he becomes God's elect."[44]

Nor does an argument based on how Luke *must* have edited his sources carry conviction, because the widely accepted "solution" to the Synoptic problem is not a fact to be built upon, so we do not know how Luke has crafted material from his sources. Moreover, the aorist tense verb εχρισεν in Jesus' citation from Isa 61:1–2 (εχρισεν με, 4:18–19) was not composed anew by Luke but derives from the LXX text of Isaiah. Further, verbs in the aorist tense do not necessarily refer to past events, even though they often do,[45] so εχρισεν need not refer to a past event there either. Two other uses of the verb χριω (χριζω) are relevant here. In Acts 4:27, Peter refers to God having anointed (εχρισας) Jesus, apparently drawing on his citation of Ps 2:1–2 immediately beforehand (4:25–26). And in Acts 10:38, Peter says that God εχρισεν αυτον with the Holy Spirit and power, which is probably a reference to Jesus' baptism because of the mention of the Holy Spirit and the note that this occurred after John's ministry of baptism (10:37). However, that does not mean that the events following Jesus' baptism signified God "making Jesus the Christ" or the time when he was "chosen to be the Son of God,"[46] as if this supports the proposal that the Western reading of Luke 3:22 is original. It does not follow, then, that Luke's Christology was adoptionist and supports the originality of the Western reading at 3:22.[47]

Therefore, the traditional reading at Luke 3:22 is most likely original, not one designed to counteract adoptionist Christology implied in the Western reading, even if we could prove that it arose in a period when this issue was current,[48] and even if Justin was aware of the issue—and even that is uncertain. Indeed, *P. Oxy.* 405 implies that Irenaeus did *not* yield to the temptation to change the text of the parallel passage in Matt

---

44. Ehrman, *Orthodox Corruption*, 78.

45. The matter of verbal aspect and the significance of the tenses in NT Greek is a matter that has been under discussion for a long time. The notion that an aorist tense verb in Greek, even in the indicative mood, must always refer to one past event has long been abandoned.

46. Ehrman, *Orthodox Corruption*, 78.

47. Cf. Ehrman, "Divine Man," 365–71.

48. Marshall, *Gospel of Luke*, 154–55; Nolland, *Luke 9:21—18:34*, 161–62.

ANTI-ADOPTIONIST CORRUPTIONS?

3:16–17 so that it would be less liable to support an adoptionist theology.[49] So, there is no compelling evidence that there is a "theologically motivated alteration" of the text here.[50] It is also possible that the citation of Ps 2:7 in the Western reading arose by harmonization, perhaps quite accidentally, to the text of Acts 13:33, where it is used to describe how God "raised up" Jesus to perform his work ως και εν τω ψαλμω γεγραπται τω δευτερω. Indeed, Barrett suggests that, since Jesus' resurrection is mentioned in 13:34, v. 33 is a reference to God "raising up" Jesus to accomplish his purpose (cf. Luke 1:69, Acts 3:22),[51] although this is unlikely in view of the strong link with v. 34.[52] Or, perhaps someone harmonized a number of sources, including apocryphal elements like the fire (or light), as is more common in Western MSS. Indeed, the Western reading might even have originated from adoptionist writers wishing to make a link with Ps 2:7 and to inject the notion of Jesus being "adopted" as God's Son by a reference to him being "begotten" at the beginning of his ministry.[53] The traditional reading, then, appears to be original, not an anti-adoptionist variant.[54]

Luke 3:23

This verse forms the introduction to Luke's version of Jesus' genealogy (3:23–38), stating that Joseph was only "thought" to be Jesus' father. But the whole genealogy does not appear in two Greek MSS (W 579), with only one difference between them. Ehrman speculates that copyists might have omitted the genealogy in these MSS because it seemed to be incongruous to trace Jesus' ancestry back to Adam when Joseph was not his father.[55] However, this does not explain the function of the genealogy in Luke's Gospel, nor does it explain how it can go back to Adam and then to God. These are clearly not easy questions to answer, but it would be idle to speculate why it was omitted in these MSS without ascertaining what the significance of the genealogy was in the first place

---

49. Rodgers, "Irenaeus," 51–54.
50. Cf. Hutchison, "Orthodox Corruption," 35–37.
51. Barrett, *Acts*, 645. Cf. Bruce, *Acts*, 309.
52. Bovon, *Luke 1*, 129.
53. Wasserman, "Misquoting?," 336–37.
54. Wasserman, "Scribal Alterations," 310–11.
55. Ehrman, *Orthodox Corruption*, 66.

and how it came to be passed on almost universally in the MSS of Luke's Gospel when there are significant questions about its meaning. I do not engage with these issues here, but without discussing them, it is best not to speculate as to why two MSS omit it, one of them (W) from the fifth century and the other (579) from the thirteenth.[56]

Luke 4:22

In Luke's account of events in the synagogue at Nazareth and the crowd's question (ουχι υιος εςτιν ιωςηφ ουτος;), two Greek minuscules modify the text, either by omitting the question altogether (13, XIII AD) or modifying it to read ουχι υιος εςτιν ιςραηλ ουτος; (1200, XII AD). Ehrman states that "the function of both corruptions is clear," that is, someone found it embarrassing to record the crowd in Jesus' home village uttering such a human estimate of his person.[57] He also supposes that most copyists were content to leave this reading alone despite its faulty estimate of Jesus, because it had already been made clear that Jesus was only Joseph's son ως ενομιζετο (3:23). So, the villagers only *thought* they knew who Jesus was. Since a purely human view of Jesus had already been laid to rest in 3:23, there was no need to adjust the text to avoid it in 4:22.

It is far from obvious, however, why the question was omitted in MS 13, but it could have been left out by a skip from και(ελεγον) (v. 22) to και(ειπεν) (v. 23). It might also have been easy for the copyist of MS 1200 to write the similar word ιςραηλ instead of ιωςηφ, if his or her attention wavered, while copying an extensive MS of two hundred and seventy-nine pages. In any case, these two MSS were produced long after adoptionism was an issue, so there is no reason to adopt a christological intention for these variant readings when simpler explanations are available.

John 1:13

This verse occurs in the prologue of John's Gospel where the overwhelming majority of MSS read οι ουκ εξ αιματων . . . εγεννηθηςαν (v. 13), stating that the "birth" of "those who believe in his name" (1:12) does not stem from a human origin but from God (cf. 3:5–8). Ehrman points out

---

56. Cf. Fitzmyer, *Luke I-IX*, 488–505; Nolland, *Luke 18:35—24:53*, 166–74; Bovon, *Luke 1*, 133–37.

57. Ehrman, *Orthodox Corruption*, 66–67.

ANTI-ADOPTIONIST CORRUPTIONS?

that Tertullian (II/III AD) accused his Valentinian opponents of changing the text from the singular (εγεννηθη, referring to Jesus) to the plural (εγεννηθησαν, referring to believers) (*Carn. Chr.* 19), emphasizing that εγεννηθη would affirm Jesus' birth without the normal means of sexual intercourse but still a physical birth.[58] Ehrman asks, then, if Tertullian's reading (εγεννηθη) could have originated as an anti-adoptionist reading, so that Jesus was not born of "blood," that is, not with a human origin. In support, he notes that Tertullian later referred to this reading to oppose Ebion (*Carn. Chr.* 24), just as Irenaeus (*Haer.* 3.16.2; 3.19.2) and the *Epistula Apostolorum* (ch. 3) had done somewhat earlier, although the latter is less explicit.

However, in view of the strength of the external evidence, the plural reading was surely original in the context,[59] and there are a number of ways in which εγεννηθη might have arisen other than being an anti-adoptionist variant. It could have been caused by a desire to make John's Gospel contain a reference to the virgin birth, or under the influence of αυτου immediately beforehand,[60] or a copyist's eye "involuntarily" relating the Latin *qui* to the preceding *eius*,[61] or Christians could have easily assumed that the threefold statement did apply to Jesus.[62] So, the reading with the singular εγεννηθη was used to serve "orthodox" theology and might have been an "orthodox corruption," as Ehrman suggests, just as Tertullian tried to prevent the Valentinians from using the plural reading to support a reference to their members by taking the singular reading as the original referring to Jesus. Even so, we do not know where Tertullian got his reading from nor whether he was working from a MS or from memory. In summary, it cannot be confirmed conclusively that the secondary variant here (εγεννηθη) was created to refute adoptionist Christology and support orthodox theology.

---

58. Donaldson notes that accusations that opponents had changed texts were not limited to Scripture. So, Rufinus claimed that Origen's *Against Celsus* had been tampered with by his opponents. She also observes that translators of patristic works sometimes inserted readings, and it is difficult to know when this happened if they fit the context ("Explicit References," 17n38).

59. Metzger, *Textual Commentary*, 168–69; Brown, *John I–XII*, 11–12; Barrett, *John*, 164; Pryor, "Virgin Birth." *Pace* McHugh, *John 1–4*, 107–10.

60. Metzger, *Textual Commentary*, 169.

61. Bultmann, *John*, 59–60n5.

62. Barrett, *John*, 164.

Scribes, Theology, and Apologetics

John 6:42

In the context of a discussion about Jesus as "the bread of life" (6:35) where he made that claim so unpalatable to his hearers, 6:41–51 focuses on the identity of Jesus' father. In 6:42, some MSS (ℵ* W b sy^{s,c}) omit και την μητερα, which might "heighten[s] the irony of the passage" by stating more strongly the contrast between the crowd's claim to know Jesus' earthly father and his claim that his father was God.⁶³ But it is difficult to see how this change makes the contrast any stronger, and a scribal leap from πατερα to μητερα is the likely reason for this omission. It is probably not a case of a variant reinforcing the "correct" understanding of the passage but almost certainly just a scribal mistake.⁶⁴

Acts 2:30

Acts 2 contains a report of Peter's speech (2:14–36), during which he appeals to Ps 16:8–11 (15:8–11 LXX) as having foretold the resurrection of Jesus (2:25–28). Based on a paraphrase of Ps 132:11 (131:11 LXX) and appealing to the prophetic voice of the psalmist David, he alluded to Jesus being εκ καρπου της οσφυος αυτου (2:30). But D* has the SR εκ καρπου της καρδιας αυτου. Other Western witnesses (gig p r sy^p Ir^{lat}) support κοιλιας (instead of οσφυος), presumably deriving from the use of κοιλιας in Ps 132, which Luke paraphrased using οσφυος.⁶⁵ Ehrman takes the variant reading καρδιας as possibly setting aside the notion of Jesus as one of David's physical descendants ("from his loins") and replacing it with the idea that he was simply *like* David ("from his heart").⁶⁶ He proposes that a scribe, knowing that Jesus was not literally "one of David's line," removed the reference to Jesus' (physical) descent from David so as not to contradict a doctrine of the virgin birth. However, coming "from David's heart" makes little sense, and a more likely scenario presents itself as the origin of this reading. Since κοιλιας appears in some MSS, clearly coming from Ps 132:11 but for which Luke used οσφυος, καρδιας in D* is probably also a corruption of the original κοιλιας (in Ps

---

63. Ehrman, *Orthodox Corruption*, 122n65.
64. Wasserman, "Misquoting?," 333–34.
65. Bruce, *Acts*, 126; Fitzmyer, *Acts*, 258. Cf. Pervo, *Acts*, 83n78.
66. Ehrman, *Orthodox Corruption*, 71–72.

132), perhaps via D's parallel Latin text (d) being similar in sound and metaphorical meaning,[67] and hence a likely error for a copyist to make.

1 John 5:6

John's "first" letter was written to a church in turmoil because of teachers who were urging particular doctrines regarding who Jesus was and what being one of his disciples entailed. In 5:6 Jesus is described as "having come," δι υδατος και αιματος, with four main variant readings in the MSS (and some variation in the cases), which may be roughly presented as:

1. δι υδατος και πνευματος — 8 minuscules
2. δι υδατος και πνευματος και αιματος — P (IX AD) 6 minuscules arm eth
3. δι υδατος και αιματος και πνευματος — ℵ A 5 minuscules sy[h]cop[sa,bo]
4. δι υδατος και αιματος και πνευματος αγιου — 4 minuscules

Some suggest that the first variant arose as a harmonization to John 3:5 (εαν μη τις γεννηθη εξ υδατος και πνευματος, ου δυναται), with the other readings being various mixtures of this with the original. Ehrman points out, however, that the third variant has both early and strong MS support, even from the third century (Origen), and could have been created from the original reading just by adding και πνευματος. So, it might have been the earliest variant, added to highlight the view that Jesus' birth was not by normal means but through the Spirit of God.[68]

However, Origen does not actually attest this reading.[69] Further, the meaning of the whole verse is also not easy to determine, even though the author was clearly wishing to highlight that Jesus came δια . . . αιματος, not just δι υδατος. Was he wanting to highlight Jesus εν σαρκι εληλυθοτα (4:2), referring to his incarnation? Clearly, the opponents agreed that he came εν τω υδατι (5:6b), but what else did the author hope to affirm by further adding και εν τω αιματι as well (5:6)? One interpretation is that the water is a reference to Jesus' baptism, when a symbol of the Holy Spirit alighted on him and he was commissioned as the Christ (e.g., Luke 3:21–22), and the blood is a reference to his death, so that Jesus was the

---

67. Metzger points out that *praecordia* meant both "belly" and "heart" (*Textual Commentary*, 259).

68. Ehrman, *Orthodox Corruption*, 70–71.

69. Wasserman, "Genealogical Method," 211–12.

Christ at his baptism and his death. Perhaps this was a response to early gnostic beliefs that the Christ left Jesus before his death—hence the dual phrase ιησου χριστου.[70] The mention of το αιμα ιησου in 1:7 and Jesus having come εν σαρκι (4:2) would fit with this suggestion, and it is the most likely interpretation. The study of the textual variants here clearly requires a discussion of the meaning of the emphatic contrast in ουκ εν τω υδατι μονον αλλ εν τω υδατι και εν τω αιματι (5:6).

Further, the addition of και πνευματος need not have a theological motivation, since after the second phrase, which resembles the one under discussion (εν τω υδατι και εν τω αιματι, 5:6b), the text continues και το πνευμα εστιν. And in 5:8 the same three nouns in the third variant occur again, το πνευμα και το υδωρ και το αιμα, albeit in a different order and case. Thus, if a copyist was familiar at all with this letter, it would have been easy for him to add και πνευματος after δι υδατος και αιματος in 5:6a as a harmonization to the context.

So, it is possible that the third variant listed above was original and the others came from harmonizing it to John 3:5.[71] But it is also possible that the traditional reading was original, and the copyist added και πνευματος in an attempt to deal with his difficulty in understanding the whole passage rather than feeling that there was a theological issue in his exemplar that needed to be resolved. Indeed, the variant seems to have arisen "several times independently," which implies repeated intrusion from John 3:5 or the immediate context.[72] There is certainly no clear case to show that any variant mentioning the Spirit was added to oppose adoptionist Christology by affirming Jesus' virginal conception.

The "Adoption" of Jesus

The second group of texts in Ehrman's study relate to the suggestion that copyists created readings to support the view that Jesus was always God's Son rather than being "adopted" as such, or at least to make their MSS less susceptible to that interpretation.

---

70. Painter, *1, 2 and 3 John*, 302–7.
71. Metzger, *Textual Commentary*, 646; Smalley, *1, 2, 3 John*, 272–73nb; Wasserman, "Criteria," 603–4; Brown, *Epistles of John*, 573; Strecker, *Johannine Letters*, 183n9.
72 Wasserman, "Genealogical Method," 212–13.

Luke 9:35

This text occurs in the account of Jesus' transfiguration and what the divine voice said to him on that occasion. The best MSS support the traditional reading that describes Jesus as ο υιος μου ο εκλελεγμενος, and this is almost certainly original. Other readings using αγαπητος or εκλεκτος instead of εκλελεγμενος appear to be harmonizations to Mark 9:7 (ο υιος μου ο αγαπητος), Matt 17:5 (ο υιος μου ο αγαπητος εν ω ευδοκησα) or Luke 23:35 (ο εκλεκτος).[73] Ehrman suggests, however, that, while εκλεκτος is virtually equivalent to εκλελεγμενος, the use of αγαπητος shows a desire "to eliminate the potentially Adoptionist overtones of the text" by avoiding the notion that Jesus was "chosen" (adopted) as God's Son and replacing it with the mention of Jesus just being "loved" by God.

Yet this assumes a significant difference in meaning between εκλελεγμενος (or εκλεκτος) and αγαπητος when εκλεκτος and αγαπητος could be quite similar in meaning. While αγαπητος did literally mean "loved, beloved,"[74] it could also have meant "prized, valued" or "only, only beloved";[75] and εκλεκτος did mean "chosen, selected" but could also mean "of top quality, choice, excellent."[76] Indeed, in the Septuagint εκλεκτος was used to render a variety of Hebrew words related to בחר (choose) but also others such as חמדה (desirable) and צבי (splendour).[77] So, it could describe "choice (youths)" (Jer 31:15), "choice (hearts)" (Prov 17:3), "choice (men)" (Lam 5:14), "a decent (man)" and God as "decent" (Ps 17:27), and perhaps Israel as God's "chosen one" (Isa 42:1). In certain contexts, then, these two words could be virtually equivalent. Thus, it was a natural semantic transition from "chosen" to "special" or "beloved," so referring to Jesus as God's αγαπητος Son is not necessarily different in meaning from referring to him as God's εκλελεγμενος (= εκλεκτος) Son.[78] Therefore, the proposal that the use of αγαπητος was due to a desire to avoid an adoptionist view possibly implied by εκλελεγμενος (= εκλεκτος) is unlikely, since it is based on too stark a distinction between εκλελεγμενος and αγαπητος in the minds of copyists of NT MSS. Indeed,

---

73. Ehrman, *Orthodox Corruption*, 79; Metzger, *Textual Commentary*, 124. Pardee suggests harmonization to Mark 9:7 in P[45] (*Scribal Harmonization*, 160).

74. BDAG, 7, ἀγαπητός 1; GELS, 4, ἀγαπητός a.

75. BDAG, 7, ἀγαπητός 2.

76. BDAG, 306, ἐκλεκτός 3; GELS, 212, ἐκλεκτός b.

77. Silva, *NIDNTTE*, 2:147. Cf. Muraoka, *Greek-Hebrew/Aramaic*, 37.

78. Marshall, *Gospel of Luke*, 388.

the meaning of εκλεκτος (= εκλελεγμενος) as "choice" or "excellent" was still current in the patristic period, when the majority of the MSS with this reading were produced.[79] If it is unlikely, then, that copyists might have perceived εκλελεγμενος as implying the notion of Jesus being "adopted" as God's Son, it is also improbable that they changed their copies of NT MSS in order to avoid this thought. Rather, the variant readings are probably due to harmonization to the similar passages in the other Gospels.

Luke 23:35

The account of Jesus' crucifixion records the taunts of "the rulers," as they mocked Jesus as ο χριστος του θεου ο εκλεκτος. Although certain MSS add υιος at various points in this passage, only two later MSS omit ο εκλεκτος or its equivalent.[80] Ehrman suggests that, while ο εκλεκτος might have been taken to imply an adoptionist Christology, it was generally left unaltered because it was clear to scribes that "the rulers" did not know the truth.[81] This assumes that copyists did "modify" the text elsewhere, including Luke 9:35, in order to avoid εκλεκτος because it could support adoptionism. However, I have shown cause to doubt this, so there is no reason to think that the *lack* of variants for ο εκλεκτος here was due to copyists allowing for the fact that the speakers knew no better. Indeed, ο εκλεκτος (του θεου) might have been a messianic title similar in meaning to ο αγιος του θεου (Mark 1:24), which expressed an exalted Christology, so it would not have been an adoptionist title to be avoided anyway.

John 1:34

John the Baptist is here credited with testifying about Jesus that ουτος εστιν ο υιος του θεου. Ehrman proposes that a reading in which ο εκλεκτος occurs instead of ο υιος is more likely to be original, citing the "early and significant" MSS with that reading (P^{5vid} ℵ* b e ff^{2*} sy^{s,c}),[82] with other MSS

79. *PGL*, ἐκλεκτός B.
80. Parker, *Living Text*, 162.
81. Ehrman, *Orthodox Corruption*, 80.
82. Ehrman cites P^5 (*P. Oxy.* 208 + 1781) as apparently (*vid*) supporting this reading (*Orthodox Corruption*, 81), but it is a reading reconstructed based on the spacing of letters in the line since the papyrus itself only contains part of the final sigma (of υιος or εκλεκτος). While the editors of the volume on John in *The New Testament in*

supporting both υιος and εκλεκτος (a ff²ᶜ sa). He rightly points to the early attestation of this reading in one (now two?) third century Alexandrian papyri (P⁵ᵛⁱᵈ P¹⁰⁶ᵛⁱᵈ), as well as the original reading of Codex Sinaiticus, which is Western in complexion in this part of John's Gospel. He suggests that it would be virtually impossible to explain the reading ο εκλεκτος if ο υιος were original, while it would be understandable for a copyist to change the unusual ο εκλεκτος into ο υιος, since it frequently refers to Jesus in John's Gospel. Moreover, he asserts that the use of εκλεκτος could have been seen as support for an adoptionist Christology, especially since it occurs so close to the account of Jesus' baptism (1:32–33)—he was only "chosen" to be God's Son on that occasion. If so, then the original reading of John's Gospel stated that Jesus was God's εκλεκτος, a reading that some take to imply an adoptionist Christology,[83] and Ehrman suggests that copyists found this reading "potentially offensive" and changed ο εκλεκτος into the "standard Johannine usage" of ο υιος in order to avoid supporting that Christology.[84]

As noted above, however, the expression ο εκλεκτος could be virtually equivalent to ο αγαπητος and was probably one of a number of ways of designating Jesus, who was believed to be ο χριστος, ο υιος του θεου.[85] Its occurrence on the lips of the Jewish authorities in Luke 23:35 in apposition to ο χριστος του θεου, as well as the use of the perfect passive participle εκλελεγμενος in Luke 9:35 alongside ο υιος μου, shows that it meant more than that Jesus was just a man "chosen" by God. He was God's "Chosen One." Thus, there is no reason to think that ο εκλεκτος was the original reading rejected in favor of the more orthodox ο υιος out of a desire to avoid adoptionist Christology.[86] Rather, the "age and

---

Greek originally suggested the reading υιος in P⁵ (American and British Committees, *John*, 29), the online edition now restores the reading εκλεκτος proposed in the *editio princeps* of P⁵. Interestingly, the INTF website reads υιος, apparently on the grounds that εκλεκτος is too long. The IGNTP website suggests εκλεκτος, although with only one letter certain. Wasserman notes that the evidence of P⁵ is ambiguous ("Scribal Alterations," 311–12). The damaged state of P¹⁰⁶ (P. Oxy. 4445) also makes its reading only "apparent" (vid). In both cases, significant doubt remains.

83. Watson, "John's Christology Adoptionist?."

84. Ehrman, *Orthodox Corruption*, 82.

85. Wasserman shows that ο εκλεκτος is consistent with christological terminology in the Fourth Gospel ("Scribal Alterations," 313).

86. Skinner argues that narrative criticism should tip the balance in favor of ο εκλεκτος as original ("Son of God"), but such considerations are secondary to traditional external and internal textual evidence. Quek accepts ο εκλεκτος as original but maintains that harmonization to Synoptic baptismal accounts or common Johannine

diversity" of the MSS reading ο υιος show that it was original,[87] and the variant ο εκλεκτος could then have arisen due to familiarity with Isa 42:1 (ισραηλ ο εκλεκτος μου),[88] especially if both terms were equivalent messianic designations.[89] Finally, it now appears that P[75] originally read ο υιος ο εκλεκτος, with ο εκλεκτος later corrected to του θεου, and that full reading with both variants (and without του θεου) might just have been original.[90] The issue as to which reading was original and why the other one arose is a complex one.

Acts 10:38, 37

During Peter's address to Cornelius and his household recorded in Acts 10, he said about Jesus, ως εχρισεν αυτον ο θεος πνευματι αγιω και δυναμει prior to engaging in his ministry. Ehrman notes that the use of ως to introduce a noun clause in parallel to the following relative clause (ος διηλθεν . . .) was probably slightly awkward, so it might have caused copyists to change the first clause from ως εχρισεν αυτον to ον εχρισεν, as in D* and the OL, Syriac, and Middle Egyptian traditions. This would certainly help the grammar in Greek, but Jesus is still the object of God's anointing (with the Holy Spirit and power). It is true that the reading with the relative clause "identifies Jesus as the one God anointed to do good."[91] But so does the reading with αυτον, so there is no real change in the meaning of the text by the use of ον εχρισεν instead of ως . . . αυτον.[92] Hence, the variant ον εχρισεν rather than ως εχρισεν αυτον is probably just a grammatical "secondary improvement."[93]

Ehrman also notes the omission of a reference to John's baptism in the original text of 10:37 in Codex Vaticanus, with κηρυγμα replacing

---

usage are likely explanations for the alternative reading, rather than it being a response to adoptionism ("Text-Critical Study"). McHugh opts for ο εκλεκτος being original but suggests that it was changed to ο υιος to harmonize this account of Jesus' baptism with those in the Synoptic Gospels (*John 1–4*, 141–43).

87. Metzger, *Textual Commentary*, 172. Pace Brown, *John I–XII*, 57; Barrett, *John*, 178.
88. Haenchen, *John 1*, 154.
89. *Pace* Wasserman, "Scribal Alterations," 313–14.
90. Flink, "Son and Chosen"; Flink, "New Variant Reading." Rodgers accepts an original reading including all the variants (not by conflation) based on tracing several OT passages in the background ("John 1:34").
91. Ehrman, *Orthodox Corruption*, 80–81.
92. Barrett, *Acts*, 524.
93. Pervo, *Acts*, 263nkk.

βαπτιcμα. He suggests that this is another case of making a distinction between John's baptizing and Jesus' ministry, so that it would be "less susceptible to an Adoptionist use" by loosening a link between the events surrounding Jesus' baptism and his being endowed with the Spirit. But this distinction is far too subtle and cannot really support the proposal that the change was made to avoid Jesus' endowment with the Spirit being associated with a particular time and place. A scribal error adding κηρυγμα before ο εκηρυξεν is a more plausible explanation.

Acts 13:33

The account of Paul's speech in the synagogue in Pisidian Antioch (Acts 13:16–41) includes a quotation from Ps 2:7, υιοc μου ει cυ εγω cημερον γεγεννηκα cε, as testimony to what God had done by raising Jesus from the dead. Ehrman suggests that this text "survived the pens of the orthodox scribes virtually unscathed," because the idea that Jesus was appointed as God's Son at the time of his resurrection and exaltation was not a current one, so copyists did not take too much notice of what might otherwise have been seen as "problematic."[94]

As we have seen, however, there was no contradiction between the use of γεγεννηκα and later orthodox (or proto-orthodox) theology, because the language of Ps 2:7 and the theme of Jesus' appointment is widely used in the NT—appointed for his role at his baptism, confirmed at his transfiguration, and appointed finally as "Lord and Christ" with all authority at his resurrection and exaltation, having accomplished his assigned mission (Acts 2:36, Matt 28:18). The separation of Jesus' resurrection and exaltation at the moment of his appointment as the Son of God does not do justice to this wider perspective evident in the NT documents. Rather, it is portrayed as the "crowning moment" when his messianic status was finally confirmed and celebrated.[95] Perhaps the reason that there is so little significant variation in the MSS at Acts 13:33 is not because copyists did not identify the proposed interpretation with a current "heresy" but because they appreciated this broader view, or perhaps they did not feel at liberty to alter the words at all and did not make mistakes here when copying, apart from some MSS (D vg^mg sy^hmg

---

94. Ehrman, *Orthodox Corruption*, 84.
95. Cf. Barrett, *Acts*, 646; Fitzmyer, *Acts*, 516–17.

mae) including further material from Ps 2:8, perhaps to highlight the mission to the gentiles (εθνη).[96]

Romans 1:3–4

The opening of Paul's letter to the Romans describes Jesus having descended from David κατα capκα (1:3) but του οριcθεντοc υιου θεου εν δυναμει, and this occurred κατα πνευμα αγιωcυνηc εξ αναcταcεωc νεκρων (1:4). Ehrman is surprised at Paul speaking of Jesus being "appointed" as God's Son at the resurrection, presumably because this might seem to contradict a static view that since Jesus was God's Son beforehand, he did not need to be "appointed" as such later on. However, the proposal that Paul added εν δυναμει to a previously existing creed has no supporting evidence, so the notion that this was Paul's way of adapting an "adoptionist" creed to the shape of his theology has no basis.[97] As with Acts 13:33 above, it should be remembered that the categories in use for this modern discussion are probably much more rigid than those in mind in the first century. Paul elsewhere wrote about Jesus becoming human (e.g., Phil 2:6–8, Gal 4:4, 2 Cor 8:9), but he also spoke about his death as the climax of his mission (Rom 8:3), followed by his resurrection and exaltation to the highest authority (Phil 2:9–11).[98] The fact that we may find it difficult to hold all of these together in a consistent Christology is no indication that Paul could not. Nor is there any reason to attribute to Paul an adjustment to an ancient creed, since Jesus' resurrection from the dead and exaltation as the Christ is portrayed as a momentous (εν δυναμει) event, no less than in Acts 13:33.

1 John 5:18

The final passage in this section is from 1 John, where the author is addressing the matter of sin in the life of πας ο γεγεννημενος εκ του θεου, saying that each such person ουχ αμαρτανει. The reason given for this is that ο γεννηθεις εκ του θεου τηρει εαυτον (NA[28]). Ehrman was working from NA[27], in which αυτον was the primary reading and εαυτον in

---

96. Barrett, *Acts*, 646–47.

97. Johnson gives an account of this passage without antithetical parallelism ("Romans 1:3–4").

98. Cf. Whitsett, "Son of God"; Jipp, "Romans 1:3–4"; Bates, "Christology."

the footnotes, and he notes their different meanings—Jesus keeps the believer (αυτον) *or* the believer keeps himself (εαυτον).[99] He also points out that instead of ο γεννηθεις εκ του θεου, some MSS have η γεννηcιc του θεου. Where did these readings come from, and which was original?

Ehrman observes that there is little to commend η γεννηcιc as original in view of its slim MS support (1852 latt sy[h] bo),[100] so the original final clause was ο γεννηθεις εκ του θεου τηρει εαυτον (or αυτον). He argues that αυτον is original and that Christ is the one in view as ο γεννηθεις εκ του θεου, and he suggests that this might have created an issue for some copyists (or readers) who would ask *when* Christ was "born from God." Adoptionists would have responded that this happened when Jesus was chosen by God and anointed with his Spirit at his baptism, and Ehrman proposes that the reading η γεννηcιc was created to remove this question by making it clear that there was no reference here to Christ at all. Rather, it is "birth from God" that keeps a believer. Similarly, the use of εαυτον instead of αυτον would serve this purpose by referring the clause to the believer, not to Christ—he or she keeps himself or herself (εαυτον).

Although εαυτον enjoys strong support (ℵ A[c] P Ψ 33 81 1739 *Byz Lect* Or), Ehrman concludes that it is not original, based on its occurrence elsewhere in 1 John with γενναω in the perfect tense, not the aorist (γεννηθεις here), when it refers to believers. He proposes that αυτον also makes sense of the verse, so that the believer (ο γεγεννημενος εκ του θεου) does not sin, for Christ (ο γεννηθεις εκ του θεου) keeps him from sin and ο πονεροc ουχ απτεται αυτου. Thus, Ehrman accepts αυτον as original, and suggests that η γεννηcιc and εαυτον were attempts to remove any possible adoptionist reading referring to Christ as "having been born from God" *at some time*.

However, John 1:13 is a parallel text (εκ θεου εγεννηθηcαν), and γενναω is not used elsewhere in 1 John to refer to Christ.[101] Further, there are parallels with 3:6 and 3:9 (referring to believers in παc ο γεγεννημενοc εκ του θεου and describing a believer in εκ του θεου γεγεννηται), so it is difficult to imagine Christ being in view as ο γεννηθεις εκ του θεου.[102] Indeed, major editions of the Greek NT accept εαυτον as original, not a

---

99. Ehrman, *Orthodox Corruption*, 82–83.

100. Ehrman, *Orthodox Corruption*, 128n120.

101. Wasserman, "Misquoting?," 339.

102. *Pace* Painter, who concludes that, because of the parallel with John 17:11, 13, and 15, "somehow 1 John 5:18 means that God keeps the believer" (*1, 2 and 3 John*, 324).

Scribes, Theology, and Apologetics

secondary reading designed to support a theological agenda.[103] Wasserman also points to the comparable use of εαυτον in πας ο εχων την ελπιδα ταυτην επ αυτω αγνιζει εαυτον (1 John 3:3).[104] So, the reasons proposed for changing αυτον to εαυτον are not compelling, and the context of the passage supports a reference to the believer keeping himself or herself (εαυτον) rather than Christ keeping them (αυτον).[105]

Moreover, the two variant readings (η γεννησις and εαυτον) are related, since, if εαυτον was original, reading η γεννησις was probably the reason for changing it to αυτον, since birth (η γεννησις) keeping itself (εαυτον) would make little sense. And, since η γεννησις is rejected, αυτον should also be rejected because the MSS reading η γεννησις are seemingly unreliable (1852 latt sy^h bo). So, the only significant MSS remaining in support of αυτον are A* and B.[106] Further, αυτον could have been intended to mean εαυτον anyway, since breathings are not present to decide which was in mind, and εαυτον sometimes appears as αυτον with a rough breathing assumed. The remaining problem is to decide what αλλ(α) is doing here. What was the intended contrast? Most likely, the contrast is between what happens (ουχ αμαρτανει) and how that can be true (ο γεννηθεις εκ του θεου τηρει εαυτον).

However, the meaning of much of 1 John is not easily determined, so it would be wise to refrain from a firm conclusion as to the original reading here. The variants might just have been due to copyists wishing to clarify an ambiguous and difficult text.[107] Indeed, in the context of 1 John, mention of Jesus as the one to keep the believer safe when threatened by "the evil one" would be more appropriate in meaning, so αυτον might be original after all, despite the evidence discussed above. But, even if αυτον was replaced by εαυτον, it could still have been an attempt to clarify a problematic text rather than being designed to hinder an adoptionist reading of this text. A final decision as to what was the original reading and how the variant arose must await further data.

---

103. Cf. GNT⁵, NA²⁸, ECM and *THGNT*. Contrast Metzger, *Textual Commentary*, 650.

104. Wasserman, "Misquoting?," 339.

105. *Pace* Smalley, *1, 2, 3 John*, 293ne; Strecker, *Johannine Letters*, 208–9.

106. Wasserman, "Misquoting?," 337–38.

107. Metzger, *Textual Commentary*, 650.

Jesus Before His Baptism

Based on the adoptionists' claim that Jesus became the Son of God at his baptism, the next variants are discussed in the light of possible anti-adoptionist "corruptions" which sought to specify that he was the Son of God prior to that time, so that "his coming into this world was not his coming into existence."[108]

Matthew 1:18

The most likely original reading of this text, based on "the earliest and best manuscripts," is του δε ιησου χριστου η γενεσις ουτως ην (P¹ ℵ B C W f¹ etc.), but for γενεσις other MSS have γεννησις (K L Γ f¹³ etc.). Despite the phonetic similarity between the two words and the possible slipup on the part of copyists, Ehrman suggests that the use of one word rather than the other cannot have been accidental, since both readings are widely attested.[109] While the MS evidence suggests that γενεσις is original, support cannot be drawn from the occurrence of γενεσις at Matt 1:1, since that could well have caused a copyist to wrongly use γενεσις at 1:18 instead of an original γεννησις. Nevertheless, γενεσις was probably original, with γεννησις substituted later in view of the following narrative of Jesus' birth. Ehrman goes on to propose that, since γενεσις can mean "coming into being" as well as "birth," copyists (or someone) substituted γεννησις for it to make sure that any notion of Jesus coming into existence at the time of his birth was circumvented. Only his birth is mentioned, not his origin. Thus, Jesus' pre-existence could not be challenged based on this verse, since it had now suffered an "orthodox corruption."

Yet, copyists were apparently happy to leave γενεσις in 1:1 (βιβλος γενεσεως ιησου χριστου), which would be strange if they were concerned to stifle adoptionist Christology by changing it in 1:18. Indeed, since γενεσις meant "genealogy" in 1:1, copyists might have been led to substitute a more specialized word (γεννησις) in 1:18 to clarify its meaning there.[110] Second, since both words could mean "birth" in current usage,[111] it would not be difficult for a change to be made by mistake. Third, the context clearly concerns Jesus' birth, and the following narrative is replete with

---

108. Ehrman, *Orthodox Corruption*, 88.
109. Ehrman, *Orthodox Corruption*, 89.
110. Metzger, *Textual Commentary*, 7.
111. BDAG, 192, γένεσις 1; 194, γέννησις; GELS, 127, γένεσις 1; 128, γέννησις 1.

related vocabulary, with γεννάω occurring multiple times in 1:1–16. So, the use of γεννησις could easily be a harmonization to the context using a more common and specific word,[112] rather than an attempt to remove a possible theological misinterpretation. Indeed, at Luke 1:14 there is a similar variation in the MSS with regard to the birth of John the Baptist (γενεϲει, γεννηϲει), and since copyists might have harmonized the noun γενεϲις to the verb γεννάω in Luke 1:13, this is surely possible in Matt 1:18 as well.[113] Fourth, papyri from the Koine period attest Greek orthography, including cases of gemination, so single consonants, including ν, were sometimes doubled without the writer intending any difference in meaning;[114] a copyist might have written γεννηϲιϲ for γενεϲιϲ (with an ε–η vowel exchange)—or *vice versa*. For all these reasons, a simple error on the part of a copyist or a mistaken doubling of the consonant with a vowel exchange could easily have produced the reading γεννηϲιϲ, and the fact that γενεϲιϲ was left unchanged in 1:1 implies that copyists did not change γεννηϲιϲ to γενεϲιϲ at 1:18 to subvert a reading that might seem to support adoptionism.

Mark 1:1

Most MSS (including ℵ¹ B D W *f*¹,¹³ and the Latin, Syriac, and Coptic traditions) have the reading αρχη του ευαγγελιου ιηϲου χριϲτου υιου θεου, but a few omit υιου θεου.[115] This might have been omitted by homoioteleuton (ιυ χυ υυ θυ),[116] but support for the omission is not inconsiderable—ℵ*, Origen (*Comm. Jo.* 1.14, 6.14; *Cels.* 2.4), and a small number of MSS from the Alexandrian (and Caesarean?) families.[117] The wide spread of the MSS with the shorter reading might suggest that the absence of υιου θεου was not accidental,[118] since a number of copyists would have had to

---

112. Hagner, *Matthew 1–13*, 14na.

113. Wasserman, "Misquoting?," 339–40.

114. Gignac, *Grammar*, 1:154–65, esp. 158 (c, d). He also notes the tendency in Coptic to confuse single and double consonants (154–55, 155n5).

115. Head observes that an amulet (*P. Oxy.* 5073, III/IV AD) also omits υιου θεου ("Additional Greek Witnesses," 442).

116. Metzger, *Textual Commentary*, 62; Guelich, *Mark 1–8:26*, 6nc.

117. Ehrman, *Orthodox Corruption*, 85, 129n132. Wasserman presents the full textual evidence and then reviews the readings in three amulets, two of which attest the long reading ("Son of God," 22–23). Cf. Wright, "Jesus as ΘΕΟϹ," 244n70.

118. Head shows the wide attestation for the shorter reading, including the limited Greek MS support ("Text-Critical Study," 624–26).

ANTI-ADOPTIONIST CORRUPTIONS?

make the same omission, presumably by parablepsis, although it would just have been copied by later scribes. Ehrman states that the phrase was not omitted by later copyists in the Byzantine tradition, so it would be an unlikely mistake to make, but it is now clear that a number of Byzantine MSS *do* omit it.[119]

Ehrman observes that this "omission" occurs almost at the very beginning of the Gospel of Mark and asks whether such a mistake is likely to have occurred at the beginning of the book as opposed to the middle or end.[120] He rightly cautions against drawing a hasty conclusion since we know so little about how copyists actually worked, but he speculates that after copying Matthew a copyist would have taken a break and come to the task of copying Mark "with renewed strength and vigor."[121] However, while copyists were indeed generally more accurate at the beginning of documents,[122] we do not know anything about how the copyists in question performed their task. Ehrman also refers to the way in which the copyists of ℵ and Θ decorated the end of Matthew's Gospel as evidence that they saw Mark's Gospel as a new beginning.[123] But again little is known about how copyists worked, and some scribes did accidentally omit passages from the beginning of books.[124] Ehrman argues that the omission or addition was deliberate,[125] but many copyists would just have been copying their exemplar, and if the change occurred early on, it was simply copied with the changed text by later scribes from then on. In fact, apart from Sinaiticus, the supporting Greek MSS for the shorter reading are much later—Θ (IX AD), 28 (XI AD), ℓ 2211 (X AD)—with one Sahidic MS (P. Palau Rib. inv. 182; V AD) and citations in Origen (II/III AD), along with Irenaeus and Epiphanius, both of whom also omit

---

119. Wasserman, "Misquoting?," 335n24.
120. Ehrman, "Text of Mark," esp. 149–54. Cf. Head, "Text-Critical Study," 629.
121. Ehrman, *Orthodox Corruption*, 86.
122. McReynolds, "Establishing," 103.
123. Codex Sinaiticus includes a small coronis at the end of Matthew, and then Mark begins in a new column. Codex Koridethi (Θ) has a clear break between the two Gospels with some intervening material.
124. Wasserman, "Son of God," 47.
125. Ehrman, *Orthodox Corruption*, 86.

ιησου χριστου.¹²⁶ The reading in Sinaiticus is also corrected.¹²⁷ Thus far, the shorter reading has not been shown to be original.¹²⁸

Ehrman reviews arguments for ιησου χριστου being original based on the theology or structure of the Gospel, rightly dismissing them as inadequate. So, he determines that copyists deliberately added υιου θεου to 1:1 in order to avoid an adoptionist reading of Mark whereby Jesus *became* the Son of God at his baptism (cf. 1:11). Now, he was already the Son *before* his baptism.¹²⁹ However, the full reading does not necessarily indicate that he *was* the Son of God then. An adoptionist could reply that this is just a heading, and that is what Jesus is now, but it need not mean that he was the Son of God *then*, before his baptism—a literary, not an ontological, reference.¹³⁰ Moreover, Mark 1:11 has been characterized as a declaration of status (cυ ει . . . εν cοι ευδοκηcα), not a change of status, as in the use of Ps 2:7 in some MSS of Luke 3:22 (cημερον γεγεννηκα cε), so it might not have been as attractive to adoptionists as we imagine.

Hence, although both readings have early and widespread support,¹³¹ attestation for the shorter reading is not nearly as strong as that for the longer one. Since there is reason to think that the original υιου θεου was omitted accidentally by parablepsis,¹³² it was probably omitted later—this shorter finding its way into the original Codex Sinaiticus and other later MSS, as well as the copy of Mark used by Origen, with an even shorter reading appearing in works by Irenaeus and Epiphanius.¹³³ Such

---

126. For a review of the patristic evidence see Head, "Text-Critical Study," 624–26; Wasserman, "Son of God," 26–34. Wasserman also examines the versional evidence ("Son of God," 34–39).

127. Malik, "Myths," 164–66.

128. Internal evidence can be highly inconclusive, although Wasserman maintains that intrinsic evidence favors the longer ending here ("Son of God," 41–44). Epp notes that textual criticism needs to engage with the exegesis of a text and its context, referring to this text and its variants as a case in point ("Textual Criticism," 463–65). France gives a brief but balanced discussion (*Mark*, 49–53).

129. Ehrman, *Orthodox Corruption*, 87–88.

130. Cf. Gundry, *Mark*, 39; Wasserman, "Son of God," 49.

131. Wasserman, "Son of God," 41.

132. Head argues that omission by parablepsis (or homoioteleuton) is unlikely because *nomina sacra* were "designed to draw attention to and protect the highlighted terms" ("Text-Critical Study," 628). However, the origin and purpose of *nomina sacra* are by no means certain. Wasserman also points out places where the copyist of ℵ did indeed omit words and phrases, as he *might* have done here ("Son of God," 45, 45n117).

133. Wasserman, "Son of God," 46. He also points out that the correction by which υιου θεου was added in ℵ¹ was done by the copyist himself or an early corrector, perhaps against a different exemplar. Cf. France, *Mark*, 149.

a scenario is much more likely than the phrase being omitted by "proto-orthodox" copyists in order to bolster an anti-adoptionist Christology.[134] Even if it were deliberately added, however, the longer reading could have simply been the result of piety rather than doctrinal concern.[135]

Luke 2:43, 3:21

An exalted reference to Jesus prior to his baptism in the Gospel accounts is the description of Jesus at the age of twelve in the Palestinian Syriac text (ca.VI AD) in Luke 2:43 as ο παις ο κυριος ιησους, instead of the original ιησους ο παις.[136] There is also a reading of Luke 3:21 in the Greek-Coptic diglot MS 0124 (VI AD) where, instead of the original ιησου, Jesus is called κυριου (κυ) when he was baptized. Ehrman implies that such variant readings attest this tendency to exalt Jesus prior to his baptism, in order to stave off any thought of adoptionist Christology.[137]

However, both of these MSS were produced around the sixth century, so they are not directly relevant to disputes in the second and third centuries. Second, this might be a case of altering the text if we knew that the copyists of the two MSS were responsible for the readings, which cannot be firmly established, and they might only have been created out of piety, not in response to adoptionist Christology. Third, since it is common Lukan usage to refer to Jesus as "the Lord," even in authorial narrative (e.g., 1:76; 2:11; 7:13, 19; 10:1; etc.), whoever was responsible for these readings might have just been harmonizing to this wider usage in Luke. Fourth, with regard to 2:43, the Syriac versions in general sometimes use *maran* ("our Lord") for (ο) ιησους, and (ο) ιησους is normally rendered by *mare isus* ("the Lord Jesus") according to "Syriac ecclesiastical idiom" in the Palestinian Syriac version.[138] Therefore, it is unlikely that

---

134. Wasserman, "Son of God," 49–50. He also discusses reasons for copyists omitting the phrase ("Son of God," 47–49). *Pace* Collins, *Mark*, 130na; Marcus, *Mark 1–8*, 141. Cf. Hutchison, "Orthodox Corruption," 37–48; Botner, "Transcriptional Probability"; Jongkind, "Make a Difference," 41–43.

135. Head concludes that the shorter reading was original, noting that adding material "fits what we know of scribal habits and the tendency of the gospel traditions," perhaps out of piety ("Text-Critical Study," 629). Collins concludes that υιου θεου was added "either out of piety or to combat too human an understanding of Jesus" (Collins, "Establishing").

136. Wasserman provides references for the MS evidence ("Misquoting?," 340n47).

137. Ehrman, *Orthodox Corruption*, 88.

138. Wasserman, "Misquoting?," 341. Cf. Metzger on Rom 3:26 (*Textual Commentary*,

these two readings were anti-adoptionist corruptions, largely because of the character of the Syriac version at 2:43, but also because there are a number of other factors that cast doubt on the suggestion in general, and piety rather than doctrinal purity could also have played a part in both.

John 9:33, 35

In the context of a discussion about Jesus after he healed a blind man, the crowd refers to him in 9:33 as ουτος in the phrase ει μη ην ουτος παρα θεου. Some MSS, however, add ο ανθρωπος after θεου (P⁶⁶ Θ N 1241). In Jesus' question to the blind man in 9:35, some of these same MSS (not P⁶⁶), along with most others, read τον υιον του θεου instead of τον υιον του ανθρωπου, the latter most likely being original due to its early and strong support.[139] Ehrman suggests that in both cases "Jesus proceeds to identify himself as the proper object of belief," although it is the crowd speaking in 9:33. His point is that the readings in Θ and N (and 1241) have incorporated testimony to Jesus as both human (ανθρωπος, v. 33) and divine (τον υιον του θεου, v. 35), affirming by this double testimony the orthodox theology of Jesus as human and divine, an "orthodox corruption" to reinforce orthodox theology.[140]

Yet, N (Codex Purpureus Petropolitanus) does not include John 9:35, so the MSS with both readings are reduced to two—Θ (IX AD) and 1241 (XII AD)—both of which are too late to be relevant to anti-adoptionist debates in the early centuries. Second, it is impossible to be certain that the copyists of these MSS intentionally inserted these readings contrary to the text of their exemplars, although someone clearly created them at some point. The second variant is the almost universal reading in later MSS, so it is understandably present in Θ and 1241. As for the addition of ο ανθρωπος in 9:33, this could well be a harmonization to 9:16, which reads ουκ εστιν ουτος παρα θεου ο ανθρωπος,[141] or just an alternative reference to Jesus since ανθρωπος is applied to him elsewhere in John's Gospel (4:29, 8:40) and occasionally it just refers to "someone" (5:7, 7:51, 18:14). Thus, there are numerous reasons to account for these

---

449).

139. Metzger, *Textual Commentary*, 194.
140. Ehrman, *Orthodox Corruption*, 134–35n186.
141. Willker, "TCG," 4:227.

Ephesians 4:9

In Eph 4:8, Paul cites Ps 68:18 (67:19 LXX), then, parenthetically drawing on that citation in 4:9, expands the implications of Jesus having "ascended" (ανεβη). That is, he must also have "descended" (κατεβη εις τα κατωτερα [μερη] της γης). Ehrman rejects the view that κατεβη was a reference to a descent into hell,[142] arguing instead that this was an "orthodox" reference to the preexistent Jesus descending to earth at his incarnation before ascending to heaven at his ascension and exaltation.[143] He then refers to readings in certain MSS (ℵ², VI–VII AD; C³, IX AD; etc.) that insert πρωτον to qualify κατεβη, making it plain that the passage refers to Jesus' incarnation. Since this reading with πρωτον occurs as a correction in ℵ² and C³, presumably seen as an "improvement," Ehrman takes this apparent clarification also as an indication of "an orthodox desire" to highlight Jesus' incarnation, emphasizing that he was the Son of God beforehand. However, πρωτον also occurs in Vaticanus, as well as the Syriac and Sahidic traditions, which shows that it was an early reading, even if not original.[144] So, if we assume that the incarnational interpretation of the original text is more likely, then the addition of πρωτον might have been a way of "reinforcing" this interpretation to emphasize Jesus' preexistence against an adoptionist theology.

Yet it could have been a way of simply "elucidating" the original text,[145] because the original text could have been taken in various ways, as the extensive discussion of this passage in modern literature shows. Ehrman's point, then, is possible, but there are other reasons for the insertion of πρωτον that are just as likely.

---

142. Ehrman, *Orthodox Corruption*, 131n147. Cf. Best, *Ephesians*, 383–86.
143. Ehrman, *Orthodox Corruption*, 89–90.
144. Harris takes πρωτον to be secondary ("Ascent and Descent," 201–2).
145. Metzger, *Textual Commentary*, 536. Cf. Lincoln, *Ephesians*, 223–24nd; Best, *Ephesians*, 383; Hoehner, *Ephesians*, 531.

Scribes, Theology, and Apologetics

Against a Low Christology

In this section, Ehrman deals with variants he suggests were added to highlight Jesus as divine, more than a mere man, and indeed divine along with God the Father from eternity, not from some point in his earthly lifetime.[146]

Mark 1:3

In the opening section of Mark's Gospel, several OT texts are cited, concluding in 1:3 with an adapted version of Isa 40:3, first leading into John's ministry as φωνη βοωντος εν τη ερημω and then referring to his role of preparing την οδον του κυριου and making straight τας τριβους αυτου. Some MSS, however, seem to make it explicit that Jesus is God himself so that, whereas Mark modified Isa 40:3 LXX by reading τας τριβους αυτου instead of τας τριβους του θεου ημων, now του θεου ημων is restored so that John will prepare for "our God" and the κυριος in view in the previous line is now Jesus, as elsewhere in Mark (e.g., 2:8, 11:3). Thus, Ehrman suggests that the copyists of the MSS which replaced αυτου with του θεου ημων (D (it) sy^hmg) wished to read Jesus' divinity into the text by conforming it exactly to the LXX, so that it would affirm Jesus' divinity "even before his baptism" in a context in which that doctrine was at stake.[147] Ehrman sets aside the idea that this was "a thoughtless reversion to the LXX" by noting that D has υμων instead of ημων, implying that this change means that the person responsible was not just writing the LXX from memory. This point loses some force, however, when we remember the υ-η vowel exchange in the papyri,[148] so a copyist might not even have been aware of the change in the vowel. Hence, a copyist of the quotation might have simply remembered the OT text and completed it here in the way he knew it to be (in the LXX), the same word order indicating its origin, without having any theological motive for doing so. Further, the MSS that support this reading derive from the fourth century onwards, so they are not necessarily relevant to debates in the second and third centuries.

Ehrman notes that the other Gospels have similar changes, but only a small number of MSS contain this reading. He points to the same

---

146. Ehrman, *Orthodox Corruption*, 90–102.
147. Ehrman, *Orthodox Corruption*, 97; Ehrman, "1 John 4.3," 148–49.
148. Gignac, *Grammar*, 1:262–65.

ANTI-ADOPTIONIST CORRUPTIONS?

reading in MSS at Matt 3:3 (OL b, sy^c and Irenaeus) and Luke 3:5 (OL r¹ sy Diatessaron MSS), and he observes that John 1:23 (OL e) has this whole last line added (in the LXX form).[149] Were these theologically motivated additions or just rare cases of copyists from III/IV AD onwards copying from memory, conforming to a known OT text? It is impossible to know, so we cannot be certain that they were designed to support the divinity of Jesus prior to his baptism. Also, they just imply that Jesus was divine without making any explicit claim that he had been so from eternity.

Mark 1:10

In Mark's account of Jesus' baptism, the Spirit descended ως περιστεραν . . . εις αυτον. Support for εις αυτον is impressive (B D f¹³)—combining Alexandrian and Western witnesses—but clearly limited, so it is difficult to know why it is accepted as the original reading in NA²⁸ and GNT⁵, as opposed to επ αυτον. Perhaps the editors took επ αυτον as a harmonization to the parallel accounts in Matt 3:16 and Luke 3:22, or thought of εις αυτον as the harder reading, given the possible difficulty of εις meaning "to" or "into." Ehrman takes εις αυτον to be original, but he suggests that copyists changed it to επ αυτον, thus conforming their MS to that of Matthew and Luke and removing any possible gnostic interpretation of this text according to which "Christ" came *into* "Jesus" at his baptism.[150]

However, if Mark's original reading was εις αυτον, the meaning was probably little different from επ αυτον followed by a noun in the accusative case, since εις could mean "on, upon, at," as Mark uses εις with that meaning elsewhere (cf. Mark 4:5, 8; 11:8; 12:14; 13:3).[151] Second, in Luke 3:22, D does not have επ αυτον but the SR εις αυτον, perhaps indicating a preference for that phrase as a description of Jesus' baptism in D, which would lessen the force of the textual evidence for εις αυτον at Mark 1:10. Third, whichever preposition was original, it is the Christ, not the Spirit, who would be needed to support the proposal of an anti-gnostic reading. Further, επ αυτον may have arisen by harmonization to John 1:33 (εφ ον

---

149. Ehrman, *Orthodox Corruption*, 97.

150. Ehrman, "1 John 4.3," 148. Dixon takes εις as expressing the language of a god descending "into" a person ("Descending Spirit").

151. BDAG, 289, εἰς 1a.γδ. Cf. *GELS*, 196–97, εἰς 3, 5, 8; LSJ, 491, εἰς I 2; Marcus, *Mark 1–8*, 160. Botner points to Mark using εις and επι interchangeably in 4:8, 20 ("How Do the Seeds Land?," 549–51).

Scribes, Theology, and Apologetics

αν ιδης το πνευμα καταβαινον και μενον επ αυτον).[152] Thus, if εις αυτον is original, there is no conclusive evidence that someone changed the reading to επ αυτον in order to remove or forestall a possible gnostic interpretation of the text.[153] The proposal is both unproven and unnecessary.

Mark 3:11

Mark's Gospel gives a summary of Jesus' early ministry in Galilee, describing how evil spirits responded to him, including their confession, cυ ει ο υιος του θεου. Ehrman points to a reading in MS 69 (XV AD), which reads cυ ει ο θεος ο υιος του θεου, noting the addition of the divine title (ο θεος).[154] However, since this variant occurs in a very late MS, it provides no evidence that early copyists had a desire to remove a possible adoptionist interpretation. Further, even if the reading originated earlier than MS 69, it might just have been a pious exaltation of the person of Jesus, although admittedly still a "corruption" of the text.

Mark 5:19

After recounting Jesus healing a demon-possessed man, Mark's Gospel records him telling the man to go home and inform his family about οσα ο κυριος σοι πεποιηκεν και ηλεησεν σε. The person in view as ο κυριος on Jesus' lips is most likely the Lord God, but some MSS (D 1241) make this explicit by reading ο θεος instead of ο κυριος. Ehrman notes the possibility that ο θεος is a harmonization to the parallel ο θεος in Luke 8:39,[155] but instead he suggests that it is an "orthodox corruption" designed to highlight the divinity of Jesus (as ο θεος), as if he were the κυριος in view.[156]

Yet, the change is more likely a slip to an alternative word since the κυριος in mind in the text is clearly God (cf. ιησου υιε του θεου του υψιστου, 5:7) described in Septuagintal style as ο κυριος. The ensuing reference to the man proclaiming οσα εποιησεν αυτω ο ιησους (5:20) is then to be understood as proclaiming what the Lord (God) had done through Jesus his Son (cf. 5:7). Thus, while it is possible that the reading in D (V AD)

---

152. Pardee, *Scribal Harmonization*, 339.
153. *Pace* Collins, *Mark*, 133–34nh.
154. Ehrman, *Orthodox Corruption*, 100.
155. Cf. Collins, *Mark*, 265nm.
156. Ehrman, *Orthodox Corruption*, 135n189.

and 1241 (XII AD) was inserted to highlight Jesus' divine status, it could just have been a slip to an alternative title for ο κυριος, the God of the OT, or a harmonization to the parallel in Luke.

Luke 1:15, 17, 76; 2:26

The birth narratives in Luke's Gospel have variant readings that could have been motivated by a desire to emphasize that Jesus was divine even as a baby. At Luke 1:15, the angel Gabriel assures Zechariah that his son John will be μεγας ενωπιον [του] κυριου. Ehrman suggests that the person in view here as κυριος is Jesus, before whom Zechariah's son will go (προελευσεται ενωπιον αυτου, 1:17a), and presumably also prepare a people "for the Lord" (κυριω, 1:17b). On this basis, he proposes that the variant reading θεου (θυ) in 1:15, instead of the original κυριου (κυ), is "more than accidental," wishing to refer to "not the Lord Jesus, but the God Jesus."[157] Clearly, θεου is secondary, as its MS support is quite late—Θ (IX AD), Ψ (IX/X AD), f^{13} (IX–XV AD), 700 (XI AD), 1424 (IX/X AD)—but it is not obvious that the motive for its insertion was to highlight the divinity of Jesus. The context indicates that the κυριος in view in 1:15 is not Jesus but the Lord God,[158] and being μεγας ενωπιον [του] κυριου is an echo of an OT phrase referring to being "great" in someone's estimation (2 Kgs 5:1; Sus 1:64 Th). In 1:16 John's task of turning "many of the sons of Israel" επι κυριον τον θεον αυτων plainly refers to "the Lord their God," and in 1:17, with its echoes of Mal 3:1 and 4:4–5 (3:22–23 LXX), John is the one who will prepare the people for "the Lord (God)" (κυριω) when προελευσεται ενωπιον αυτου (1:17).

Later in the chapter, Zechariah's song confirms this theocentric reading since John will be προφητης κυριου and προπορευση ενωπιον κυριου ετοιμασαι οδους αυτου (1:76; cf. Mal 3:1). The fact that the focus in 1:17 is on John "going before" God and preparing "his way" is consistent with how closely Jesus' own life and ministry was seen as the means of God's coming to his people without necessarily implying that Jesus was divine. Thus, the reading θεος instead of κυριος in a few MSS in 1:15 was merely stating what Luke intended, not a divine claim for the person of Jesus and hence not an orthodox corruption of the text. Thus, the variant του θεου in 1:15 does not highlight Jesus' divine status but affirms

---

157. Ehrman, *Orthodox Corruption*, 99.
158. Fitzmyer, *Luke I–IX*, 325; Bovon, *Luke 1*, 36, 36n50.

Scribes, Theology, and Apologetics

with another word what Luke intended by του κυριου in accord with Septuagintal usage.[159] Later Christians *might* have understood the "Lord" in view here as Jesus in view of later theological formulation, but it is uncertain how many did.

This implies, then, that in 1:17, where some MSS read ενωπιον κυριου (Δ, IX AD; Didymus) or ενωπιον θεου (Persian Diatessaron, XIII AD; Georgian MSS, V AD) instead of ενωπιον αυτου, they are merely clarifying the original meaning, not emphasizing Jesus' divinity.[160] Even in 1:76, the κυριοc in view is still the Lord God, so the Palestinian Syriac MS, which reads "before your God," is only rephrasing the original meaning, not referring to Jesus' divine status.[161] Again, the proposal of a reading provided to confirm Jesus' divine status is unproven and, in view of the context, it is unlikely that anyone would have created the reading with that connotation in mind.

The case of Luke 2:26 is different, however, since, instead of Simeon being promised that he would see "the Christ of the Lord" (τον χριcτον κυριου), the OL MS ff² (V AD) reads that he will see "Christ, namely God."[162] This is certainly a case of "corruption" in this MS—although it might also have sprung from piety rather than being designed to oppose an adoptionist Christology, and it is attested only from the fifth century.

Luke 7:9

In response to a centurion's faith, Luke records, ακουcαc δε ταυτα ο ιηcουc εθαυμαcεν αυτον, but MS 124 (XI AD) reads ο θεοc in place of ο ιηcουc. This is also clearly a corruption,[163] but the MS is quite late, so the copyist is unlikely to have been responding to an adoptionist Christology in the early centuries. Rather, it is more likely the product of over-zealous piety or a careless slip in a late MS.

---

159. Fitzmyer, *Luke I–IX*, 327.
160. *Pace* Ehrman, *Orthodox Corruption*, 99.
161. *Pace* Ehrman, *Orthodox Corruption*, 100.
162. Ehrman, *Orthodox Corruption*, 100.
163. Ehrman, *Orthodox Corruption*, 100.

ANTI-ADOPTIONIST CORRUPTIONS?

Luke 8:28

Luke's Gospel has an account of Jesus' encounter with a demoniac, who responded to his words of exorcism by addressing him as ιησου υιε του θεου του υψιστου. However, MS 124 (XI AD) omits υιε so it reads instead ιησου του θεου του υψιστου, which might then be understood to mean "Jesus, the Highest God," thus highlighting Jesus' divinity.[164] While this might make sense, it is an awkward reading because, despite the endings being identical, ιησου is clearly in the vocative case (cf. υιε) but both του θεου and του υψιστου are in the genitive. This awkwardness stands against the suggestion that someone created the reading to align Jesus with "the Most High God," unless their knowledge of Greek was minimal. Like the previous variant, it is probably just a careless omission (of υιε). Still, even if it were a "corruption" highlighting Jesus' divine status, it is a SR in a late MS without any indication of its purpose, so it has little relevance to what might have been written in the second and third centuries in response to adoptionist Christology.

Luke 8:40

The narrative in Luke 8:40 records a crowd welcoming Jesus since they had been waiting for him (ησαν ... προσδοκωντες αυτον). Codex Sinaiticus originally had the SR προσδοκωντες τον θεον, and Ehrman implies that this was an expression of orthodox theology on the part of the copyist, perhaps in response to adoptionist Christology.[165] However, since the text was corrected early on, possibly even before it left the scriptorium, it is more likely just a scribal error. While it is difficult to account for the origins of this reading, confusion and inattention are likely factors in its creation. So, τον θν (τον θεον) was written instead of αυτον perhaps by an inattentive copyist or out of piety, so it is clearly a "corruption" of the text, but not necessarily designed to oppose an adoptionist Christology.

Luke 9:20

In Luke's account of Peter's confession of Jesus as τον χριστον του θεου, some Bohairic MSS read "Christ, God," which could have originated

---

164. Ehrman, *Orthodox Corruption*, 100.
165. Ehrman, *Orthodox Corruption*, 100.

from a desire to emphasize the divine status of Jesus by changing the original reading, thus forming an "orthodox corruption."[166] However, it could just as well have sprung from piety, or perhaps it was an error based on an unclear exemplar. At this point in time, it is difficult to assign a cause for this variant.

Luke 20:42

Toward the end of Jesus' ministry, Luke records his response to some of the Jewish authorities, asking how they could say that τον χριcτον ειναι δαυιδ υιον (20:41). He then quotes from Ps 110:1, including ειπεν κυριοc τω κυριω μου. Here the Psalmist refers to "the Lord" (God) addressing someone as "my Lord" (τω κυριω μου) in this messianic psalm. The Persian Diatessaron (XIII AD), however, reads, "God said to my God," which might indicate an emphasis on Jesus' divine status ("my *God*"), perhaps anti-adoptionist in design.

Yet, again, this is a very late MS and the habits of the Persian Diatessaron would need to be examined to ascertain the nature of this reading in that version before drawing conclusions about its origins or the motives of the copyist. Clearly, it cannot be used as evidence for what copyists were hoping to achieve in their MSS in the second and third centuries. Further, since both instances of "Lord" in ειπεν κυριοc τω κυριω μου are replaced with "God" the reading retains some of the enigmatic nature of the original and hardly provides support for the view that someone wished to describe Jesus as "God," unless the MS also had "God" for "lord" in "David calls him lord" (20:44), which does not appear to be the case.[167]

John 1:18

In an extended discussion of the variant readings here, Ehrman argues that the original reading is ο μονογενης υιος ο ων εις τον κολπον του πατρος, not (ο) μονογενης θεος, as in NA[28], the latter being an "orthodox corruption" on the part of copyists wishing to affirm the deity of Christ.[168] He

---

166. Ehrman, *Orthodox Corruption*, 100.

167. Messina, *Diatessaron*, 267.

168. Ehrman, *Orthodox Corruption*, 92–96 (cf. 131n157); Ehrman, *Misquoting*, 161–62.

rightly dismisses other readings with minimal MS support as almost certainly corruptions of more fully attested readings, leaving only two viable readings: ο μονογενης υιος and (ο) μονογενης θεος.[169]

Ehrman acknowledges the strength of the MS support for (ο) μονογενης θεος, including uncials (א B C*) and early papyri (P[66] P[75]), but he minimizes the significance of the papyri because their discovery has not significantly altered "the documentary alignments," since it was already known that the Alexandrian tradition predominantly had this reading.[170] However, the dates of the papyri (c. AD 200, early III AD) provide much earlier evidence than the uncials of the fourth and fifth centuries, so they should be given due weight in this discussion. Ehrman maintains that "virtually every other representative of every other textual grouping" has the reading ο μονογενης υιος, but the existence of the Caesarean family is doubtful, and the Byzantine family represents the text of the NT after it became standardized from the fourth century onwards. So, if the Alexandrian family represents an early tradition of the NT text, it should not be lightly dismissed, especially since its reading goes back to papyri from around AD 200. The occurrence of ο μονογενης υιος in "secondary Alexandrian witnesses" (C³ Ψ 892 1241 etc.) does not add much support since, despite sharing some characteristics with early Alexandrian MSS, the third corrector of C (probably IX AD), Ψ (IX/X AD), 892 (IX AD), and 1241 (XII AD) are all quite late. In order to show that (ο) μονογενης θεος can be dated as early as the papyri, Ehrman suggests that there is no other explanation for "its predominance in the Greek, Latin and Syriac traditions," and it occurs in some MSS of Clement, Didymus, and perhaps Origen, although it is not quite predominant in the Syriac tradition since only sy^p sy^hmg read θεος.[171] Finally, Ehrman notes that Irenaeus and Clement attest both readings, but he maintains that they only used θεος because of its "theological usefulness," so he concludes that both readings were early.[172]

Ehrman then argues that intrinsic arguments support ο μονογενης υιος being original.[173] He contends that ο μονογενης θεος is highly specific, with the article reinforcing the notion of uniqueness already carried by

---

169. Ehrman, *Orthodox Corruption*, 131–32n158.

170. Ehrman, *Orthodox Corruption*, 92–93.

171. Ehrman, *Orthodox Corruption*, 131–32n158.

172. Ehrman, *Orthodox Corruption*, 132n162. Wright provides a good review of the external evidence, agreeing that both readings are early, but leaning toward θεος as original due to the weight of the MS evidence ("Jesus as ΘΕΟΣ," 242–47).

173. Ehrman, *Orthodox Corruption*, 93–96.

the word μονογενης,[174] but the presence of an article does not necessarily make the noun definite. Ehrman comments that the adjective μονογενης itself means "unique" or "one of a kind,"[175] and he argues that to assert that Jesus is the "only God" would be awkward in John's Gospel, where God the Father is constantly mentioned, and even in this verse Jesus is said to be εις τον κολπον του πατρος. This difficulty would be overcome if the other reading (ο μονογενης υιος) were original, since it would conform to other occurrences of μονογενης with υιος in Johannine literature (John 3:16, 18; 1 John 4:9).[176] It may be that ο μονογενης θεος is the harder reading, and that it was changed to the easier ο μονογενης υιος, but it is uncertain that it *was* perceived to be harder. Even if it is the harder reading, there comes a point when a harder reading is just too hard. Ehrman notes that Jesus is spoken of as having parity with God (10:30, 33) and is sometimes referred to as God (20:28; 1:1) but not as "the only God," so he proposes that the reading ο μονογενης θεος is almost impossible to fit into Johannine theology.

In response to suggestions that retain ο μονογενης θεος as the original reading but invest it with a meaning different from the obvious one, some take μονογενης as implying the notion of sonship and the whole expression to mean "the only Son who is God." But Ehrman argues that μονογενης never means "only son" elsewhere, not even in the NT,[177] and since it is normally used with υιος, it is unlikely that it implied sonship on its own. Others maintain that (ο) μονογενης is a substantive, so that the whole refers to "the unique one, God, who is close to the Father,"[178] but if this were the meaning, it would be difficult to explain why others changed the reading to ο μονογενης υιος. Ehrman also states that μονογενης is never used as a substantive when followed by a noun agreeing with it in gender, number, and case, so this would be an almost impossible construction in

---

174. Ehrman observes that P[75] includes the article and P[66] does not (in line with its common omission of short words and phrases), so he concludes that the article was the original Alexandrian reading, despite its slightly weaker MS attestation (*Orthodox Corruption*, 132n163). Royse confirms that P[66] tends to omit words, but he also notes that most omissions were corrected by the copyist (*Scribal Habits*, 511–14).

175. Cf. BDAG, 658; Coutsoumpos, "Difficulty."

176. It is also implied in John 1:14 where υιος precedes παρα πατρος.

177. Cf. LSJ, 1144; GELS, 467. It is used without a noun to describe Isaac in Heb 11:17, but this probably derives from Gen 22:2 where both MT and LXX mention "son" in the context, although LXX used αγαπητος and Symmachus used μονος to translate יחיד. See Bruce, *Hebrews*, 301n135.

178. McHugh, *John 1–4*, 69–70, 110–12.

ANTI-ADOPTIONIST CORRUPTIONS?

Greek, and while this claim might be a little too absolute, the proposed meaning would certainly be odd.[179]

Ehrman concludes, then, that intrinsic probabilities suggest that ο μονογενης υιος is original since ο μονογενης θεος would not have made sense in its immediate and wider context and ο μονογενης υιος is just as likely on the grounds of external MS evidence. It seems, then, that ο μονογενης υιος is probably original, despite the strength of the MS support for ο μονογενης θεος.[180]

However, Ehrman's proposal as to why the original ο μονογενης υιος was changed to ο μονογενης θεος is not as compelling. He notes that ancient authors, both orthodox and gnostic, who support ο μονογενης θεος "attest a 'high' Christology," and they stand apart from the adoptionists who maintained that Jesus was merely a man adopted by God to divine status. He points out that Origen certainly condemned the belief that Christ was not divine (Origen, *Dial.* 128), and he also referred to the Ebionites saying that Christ was born of a man and a woman, so he was human (*Hom. Luc.* 17.4).[181] Thus, Ehrman concludes that ο μονογενης θεος was created in order to stand apart from adoptionists who maintained that Jesus was not divine, referring to him as "the unique God," although still distinct from the Father, and therefore it is an "orthodox corruption" introduced to oppose adoptionist Christology. However, "orthodox" writers were not as uniform in their appeal to ο μονογενης θεος as Ehrman suggests, nor is there comprehensive use of ο μονογενης υιος by Arians or adoptionists.[182] He asks why this is the only place in John where ο μονογενης υιος was changed in this way, suggesting that someone thought that the importance of this passage in the prologue was a crucial place to ensure correct Christology.[183] But, since the immediate context already contains a high Christology even apart from ο μονογενης θεος, it is difficult to see how this change would have achieved much in the setting of the whole prologue.[184]

---

179. Wallace argues that such cases of a substantive exist in the NT, but he does not find all the proposed parallels convincing, and the proposed meaning ("the unique/only one, himself God") would still be strange in the context ("According to Bart," 344–45).

180. Cf. Beasley-Murray, *John*, 2–3ne; Birdsall, review of *Orthodox Corruption*, 461. *Pace* Wasserman, "Misquoting?," 343.

181. Ehrman, *Orthodox Corruption*, 133n173.

182. Edwards, "Orthodox Corruption?"; Burkholder, "Considering the Possibility."

183. Ehrman, *Orthodox Corruption*, 133n175.

184. Wasserman, "Misquoting?," 342.

Further, there are other explanations for the origin of ο μονογενης θεος. The reading might have been *able* to be used for the purposes Ehrman proposes, but this does not prove that it was *designed* for that purpose.[185] Indeed, θεος might have arisen as "a primitive, transcriptional error in the Alexandrian tradition (ΥC/ΘC)."[186] The argument that the *nomina sacra* forms of υιος are not attested as early as θεος might seem to counter this point,[187] but the origin and development of the *nomina sacra* are unclear, so they cannot be used as the basis of a conclusion here. Thus, as a simpler conclusion in accord with the realities of MS production at the time, it would seem more likely that the reading with υιος (υc) was original and θεος (θc) was simply a copyist's mistake, perhaps arising from pious inattention,[188] but not necessarily wishing to make a christological point against adoptionism.

John 12:41

In the portrayal of the closing stages of Jesus' public ministry in John's Gospel, the author refers to two texts from Isaiah having foreshadowed how the nation would respond to him (12:37–40), and he goes on to explain how Isaiah could have written this—because ειδεν την δοξαν αυτου και ελαλησεν περι αυτου. But, instead of ειδεν την δοξαν αυτου, some MSS read ειδεν την δοξαν του θεου (Θ f^{13} sy sa (pbo) bo) or ειδεν την δοξαν του θεου αυτου (D), and Ehrman concludes that scribes responsible for the first variant "altered the text" to refer to Jesus as "God" in order to further an anti-adoptionist view.[189]

Clearly, του θεου is secondary, in view of its limited MS support, but how did that reading arise? Perhaps the clue is that the quotation in 12:40 is taken from Isa 6:10, which occurs in the context of Isaiah reporting a vision of God in his throne room, including seraphim praising him and saying that πληρης πασα η γη της δοξης αυτου (12:3). The vision, then, was certainly one of God in *his* glory (6:1–4), which stood in stark contrast to the fruitless ministry to which Isaiah was commissioned (6:9–13)

185. Wallace argues that a *possible* conclusion is here made into a *probable* one without sufficient evidence ("According to Bart," 347). Cf. Chapa, "Contribution," 117–18.

186. Allen Wikgren, quoted in Metzger, *Textual Commentary*, 170.

187. Wright, "Jesus as ΘΕΟΣ," 248.

188. Cf. Brown, *John I–XII*, 17; Barrett, *John*, 169; Maloney, *John*, 46; Morgan, "Legacy," 112n98; Miller, "Least Orthodox Reading," 72–77; Kristianto, "Evaluating."

189. Ehrman, *Orthodox Corruption*, 99.

and which John had in mind in 12:37–40 as a description of the lack of positive response to Jesus' ministry. It would not be hard to imagine the context of the quotations from Isa 6 coming to mind if a reader or copyist was a Christian, so that he wrote ειδεν την δοξαν του θεου instead of ειδεν την δοξαν αυτου, perhaps even recalling the text of a Targum that mentions seeing "the glory of the Lord" in Isa 6:1 and "the glory of the *shekinah* of the Lord" in 6:5.[190] Thus, rather than tracing the variant reading to a copyist's "theological intention," it could easily have arisen due to the influence of the context of the quotation from Isa 6 if the copyists of these late MSS were aware of that. Or, since the theme of God's "glory" or "majesty" in his heavenly palace/temple is common in the OT, especially in the Psalms (e.g., Ps 96:6), this also might have been in a copyist's mind as he produced his MS, and later copyists simply followed suit.

John 18:32

In John's account of Jesus' trial before Pilate, he adds a comment that Jesus' impending crucifixion would be in fulfillment of his earlier words (18:32), presumably referring to his reference to Jesus being "lifted up" (12:32–34). This was in relation to the words of "the Jews" that they had no right to execute anyone, implying that they wished Pilate to have him executed (18:31), most likely by crucifixion. However, instead of saying that events would be in accord with Jesus' previous pronouncement (ο λογος του ιησου πληρωθη ον ειπεν), some MSS (L Δ pc) read ο λογος του θεου πληρωθη ον ειπεν. Ehrman proposes that scribes "understood that when Jesus spoke, God spoke," thus reading their high Christology into the text where it had not been beforehand.[191]

Yet, the expression ο λογος του θεου was common in the LXX and occurs previously in John's Gospel, so it would have come readily to mind for a copyist who slipped into using this expression, especially in a context where it is said that this λογος was going to be fulfilled (πληρωθη) (cf. 12:38; 13:18; 15:25; 17:12; 18:9; 19:24, 36). The suggestion, then, that this reading was motivated by a scribe's theology is unnecessary, since it could easily have arisen by association with other Johannine phraseology.

---

190. Brown, *John I-XII*, 486–87. Cf. Barrett, *John*, 432.
191. Ehrman, *Orthodox Corruption*, 134n183.

John 19:40

John's account of Jesus' burial by Joseph of Arimathea and Nicodemus includes the note that ελαβον ουν το cωμα του ιηcου. Codex Alexandrinus (V AD), however, has the SR το cωμα του θυ [θεου]. Ehrman suggests a number of ways in which this reading could have "functioned" for orthodox Christians, such as countering Docetism or certain varieties of Gnosticism, but he emphasizes that it expresses the orthodox notion that Jesus is God in the flesh.[192] Clearly, this reading is not original, but it does refer to Jesus as God, perhaps accidentally (θυ for ιυ), or out of piety, or from a desire to highlight the deity of Jesus. It is impossible to know which of these was the cause of this variant, but noting how it *could* "function" only indicates that it *might* have been designed to achieve something without any certainty about why the person responsible *did* create it. Ehrman concedes that the reading might have been created unconsciously but states that "one would still need to ask what kind of scribe might have been likely to make it, and how, having done so, he might have understood it."[193] Yet this might be crediting a scribe's understanding of the text with too great a role in producing his MS. Further, a recent study concludes that this SR was accidental but that it would also have had significance for those who had experienced the Nestorian controversy not too long before Alexandrinus was produced.[194] So, it is still uncertain that this was an "orthodox corruption."

Galatians 2:20

In a section of his letter to the Galatians devoted to the role of the OT Law in the life of a believer, Paul wrote, "I live by faith" τη του υιου του θεου του αγαπηcαντοc με και παραδοντοc εαυτον υπερ εμου (2:20). Some important MSS (P[46] B D* F G), however, have the secondary reading τη του θεου και χριcτου instead of τη του υιου του θεου,[195] and MS 330 (XII

---

192. Ehrman, *Orthodox Corruption*, 98.
193. Ehrman, *Orthodox Corruption*, 134n180.
194. Hixson, "Body of God."
195. Wright notes that this is an early reading attested by both Alexandrian and Western MSS. He agrees that του υιου του θεου is most likely original but perhaps not with the degree of certainty implied by the A rating in GNT[5] ("Jesus as ΘΕΟΣ," 254–56). Wasserman maintains that του θεου και χριcτου is original due to its strong external support in Alexandrian and Western MSS, as well as the fact that it is the more difficult reading ("Short Textual Commentary," 360–62).

AD) also omits και χριcτου so it refers to God "who loved me and gave himself up for me." Ehrman notes Metzger's view that an early copyist omitted του υιου by parablepsis (του . . . του . . .) and then, since the resulting text was seen as misleadingly referring to God giving himself up (παραδοντοc εαυτον) for Paul, added και χριcτου at the end, thus creating "faith in God and/even Christ who . . ." Indeed, he suggested that another copyist added the correct του υιου at the end, so creating τη του θεου του υιου, "(faith) in God the Son."[196] Ehrman endorses Metzger's view that the traditional text is original despite the strength of the support for the reading with και χριcτου at the end, partly because the other readings would be highly unusual phrases from Paul's pen.[197] However, he also suggests that it could be construed as "orthodox," since the phrase του θεου και χριcτου has only one article, thus "equating the two names" and hence referring to Christ as God.[198] But the use of the article with two nouns following one another is not uniform in the NT,[199] so the issue is not easily decided. The proposal is that this is an "orthodox corruption" from the third century and that it might have arisen earlier if it was present in the exemplar of P[46]. This last suggestion is speculative, however, so it cannot be used as the basis of this proposal. While this reading is intriguing, it is uncertain that it betrays "orthodox" motives on the part of the copyist or reader, and could easily have arisen from parablepsis with further adjustments made to fix the mistake.[200]

1 Timothy 1:1

The opening of 1 Timothy has the original reading indicating that Paul's apostolic status was κατ επιταγην θεου cωτηροc ημων και χριcτου ιηcου τηc ελπιδοc ημων. But some MSS (42 51 104 234 327 463 fu eth[ro]) omit και, so they read κατ επιταγην θεου cωτηροc ημων χριcτου ιηcου τηc ελπιδοc

---

196. Ehrman, *Orthodox Corruption*, 132n192. Cf. Metzger, *Textual Commentary*, 524.

197. Wright notes that expressions like these occur in the Pastorals (1 Tim 5:21, 2 Tim 4:1; cf. 1 Tim 6:13. ("Jesus as ΘΕΟΣ," 255). However, Ehrman would probably not count these as Pauline.

198. Ehrman, *Orthodox Corruption*, 101–2 (cf. 135n193, referring to BAGD, ὁ II.10.β; καί I.1.a).

199. Turner, *Syntax*, 181–82; BDF §276; Wallace, *Greek Grammar*, 286–88.

200. Cf. Longenecker, *Galatians*, 82nb. Burton called it a "Western corruption" without specifying its origin (*Galatians*, 139). Betz suggests that it was "due to later theology" but does not elaborate (*Galatians*, 125n104).

ημων.²⁰¹ The MSS with this reading stem from the eleventh to the sixteenth century, so this is a very late reading, but Ehrman suggests that it was designed to highlight the deity of Christ.²⁰² Although it is difficult to know why και was omitted, it could have been due to inattention or it might have sprung from someone's piety, but in view of the late date of its supporting MSS, it is unlikely that it was produced to support anti-adoptionist Christology in the second or third centuries.

1 Timothy 3:16

There is a variant reading in certain MSS (ℵ³ Aᶜ C² D² K L P Ψ etc. Byz vgᵐˢ) here, which have θεος instead of the relative pronoun ος in ος εφανερωθη εν capxi.²⁰³ Ehrman allows that this might have been accidental since the *nomen sacrum* θc would have been almost identical to ος in upper case letters (ΘC for OC), where a copyist might well have assumed that ΘC (ΘΕΟC) was intended and added a superior *makron* to indicate a *nomen sacrum*. However, Ehrman proposes that this change was deliberate since (1) in ℵ A C and D it only appears in corrections, which are clearly intentional—although those responsible for the corrections might have made the assumption mentioned above, even if it initially arose by accident;²⁰⁴ and (2) this reading provides a strong affirmation of the deity of Jesus, which Ehrman implies was a welcome one.²⁰⁵ Given the early attestation of this variant reading "from the fourth century on," Ehrman takes it as a purposeful variant stressing the deity of Christ.

However, although the corrected readings are clearly intentional, it is difficult to place them earlier than the fifth or sixth century, which makes this reading later than the earlier attested ος in ℵ* (mid-IV AD). Further, quotations in church fathers date from the last third of the fourth century (Gregory of Nyssa, Apollinaris, and John Chrysostom), well after the Council of Nicaea. Moreover, the fact that there is no record of this reading being used in the first stages of the Christological and Trinitarian controversies implies that it was not known at that time.²⁰⁶ Thus, θεος is

---

201. Ehrman, *Orthodox Corruption*, 136n195.
202. Ehrman, *Orthodox Corruption*, 102.
203. Ehrman, *Orthodox Corruption*, 91–92; Ehrman, "Divine Man," 371; Ehrman, *Misquoting*, 157.
   204. Cf. Wasserman, "Misquoting?," 344.
   205. Cf. Mounce, *Pastoral Epistles*, 214nd.
   206. Wasserman, "Misquoting?," 344–45.

probably a late reading originating as an accidental corruption, rather than being designed to support a high Christology.[207]

2 Timothy 1:10

In 2 Tim 1:10 Paul refers to salvation having been made known (φανερωθεισαν) δια της επιφανειας του cωτηροc ημων χριcτου ιηcου, but MS I (V AD) reads θεου instead of χριcτου ιηcου, which might have been intended to highlight the divine status of Jesus.[208] Since it is unlikely that "being made known" (φανερωθεισαν) and "appearance" (επιφανεια) applied to God the Father, especially as the text goes on to speak of his having destroyed death (καταργηcαντοc μεν τον θανατον) and revealed ζωην και αφθαρcιαν "through the gospel," these are allusive but clear references to the effects of Jesus' death and resurrection. Hence, with Jesus clearly in view, perhaps in this one fifth-century MS there is a clear case of an "orthodox corruption," even if it is uncertain that it was designed to oppose adoptionist Christology by replacing χριcτου ιηcου with θεου.

Titus 3:6

A similar case occurs toward the end of the Letter to Titus, where the original reading δια ιηcου χριcτου του cωτηροc ημων is changed to δια ιηcου χριcτου του θεου ημων in certain lectionaries. Since lectionaries derive from the seventh century onwards, however, this is clearly a late reading, perhaps not an accidental error but the result of pious devotion to Christ, highlighting his divine status. So, it could be an "orthodox corruption," but again there is no evidence that it arose in the second or third centuries to counter adoptionist Christology. Moreover, since the subject of the sentence is "God our savior" (v. 4), God is the one who "poured out" the Spirit δια ιηcου χριcτου (v. 6). So, changing του cωτηροc ημων to του θεου ημων is something of a nonsense reading, and it is an understandable error in view of the copyist having recently written του σωτηρος ημων θεου just beforehand in v. 4.

---

207. Metzger, *Textual Commentary*, 573–74; Marshall, *Pastoral Epistles*, 505.
208. Ehrman, *Orthodox Corruption*, 102.

Scribes, Theology, and Apologetics

Hebrews 13:20

The doxology at the end of the Letter to the Hebrews describes Jesus as τον κυριον ημων ιησουν, but one OL MS (d, V/VI AD) refers instead to "our God Jesus." If deliberately created, it might have arisen out of piety or perhaps to support the doctrine of the divinity of Jesus, but since the MS was produced well after the third century it is doubtful that it was created as a response to adoptionist Christology. Thus, this variant would be an "orthodox corruption" but perhaps only due to a careless error or pious thought.

1 John 3:23

After assuring his readers that they can be certain that their prayers will be heard if they heed God's commands (1 John 3:21–22), John writes that his primary command is ινα πιστευcωμεν τω ονοματι του υιου αυτου ιησου χριστου (3:23), where "his" (αυτου) refers to God (cf. v. 21). But several MSS (A 1846 vg^{mss}) omit του υιου, so the text reads πιστευcωμεν τω ονοματι αυτου ιησου χριστου. This could be entirely accidental with so many words ending in ου (του υιου αυτου ιησου χριστου), but Ehrman argues that someone omitted this phrase to highlight Jesus Christ as the subject of "*his* name," that is, "the name *of God*."[209] Jesus would then be "God." However, this interpretation is problematic, because it would refer to "*his* [God's] name, Jesus Christ," where Jesus would then be God's name, and the meaning would be unclear. More likely, a copyist became confused in a context where a number of nouns end in ου, and it would not have been difficult then for him to omit του υιου accidentally since he might have written τω ονοματι του, glanced up to copy the next phrase, thought that he had already written του υιου, and then continued with ιησου χριστου—thus omitting υιου αυτου. This is certainly possible and perhaps more likely than a deliberate elevation of Jesus' status in the context of copying MSS in antiquity when the proposed deliberate omission resulted in a text that would be difficult to understand. Further, the earliest MSS supporting this variant come from the fourth/fifth century, so they cannot confirm someone's intention in the second or third century.

---

209. Ehrman, *Orthodox Corruption*, 98.

ANTI-ADOPTIONIST CORRUPTIONS?

The Exchange of Predicates

In this section, Ehrman deals with variant readings that seem to predicate things of Christ that would naturally belong to God, or vice versa, mentioning examples from church fathers such as "the blood of God" or "the passion of God," or speaking of God being "crucified" or "murdered," without actually identifying the divine Christ with God the Father.[210] For example, he notes that Tertullian spoke of "God" being crucified (*Carn. Chr.* 5.1–2), even though Tertullian made fun of Praxeas for "crucifying the Father" (*Prax.* 1).

Acts 20:28

Acts 20 contains an account of Paul's farewell address to the elders of the Ephesian church, in which he urges them ποιμαινειν την εκκληcιαν του θεου ην περιεποιηcατο δια του αιματοc του ιδιου (20:28). Ehrman examines several variant readings he argues were designed "to circumvent different misconstruals." He argues that "the original form of the passage" was την εκκληcιαν του θεου, which he (God) obtained by means of "the blood of his own [Son]" (του αιματοc του ιδιου).[211] He refers to the reading την εκκληcιαν του κυριου in some MSS (P[74] A C* D E Ψ etc.) but dismisses this as a corruption on the basis that "church of the Lord" occurs nowhere else in the NT while "church of God" appears frequently in Paul's letters and την εκκληcιαν του θεου is supported by important Alexandrian witnesses such as ℵ and B.[212] He also suggests that την εκκληcιαν του κυριου might have been created in order to avert any thought of "the blood of God," if του αιματοc του ιδιου was taken to mean "his own blood." He thus proposes that orthodox scribes "changed the text to make it refer instead to Christ"—"the church of (the Lord) Christ," not "the church of God." In the final words of the verse, many MSS read του ιδιου αιματοc (instead of του αιματοc του ιδιου), so the reference is to "his own (blood)," the blood of God, which cannot be original. Thus, Ehrman maintains that this reading was meant to speak of Christ in divine terms—his blood shed (v. 28b), so he is the God referred to in "the church *of God*" (v. 28a).

---

210. Ehrman, *Orthodox Corruption*, 102–7.
211. Ehrman, *Orthodox Corruption*, 103.
212. Cf. Barrett, *Acts*, 976.

51

In the final phrase of the verse, most commentators take του αιματος του ιδιου to be original and understand του ιδιου as an instance of the substantival use of ο ιδιος, comparable to its use in certain papyri as "a term of endearment to near relations,"[213] as Ehrman understands the meaning of the original reading του αιματος του ιδιου—"the blood of his own [Son]." In the Hellenistic period ιδιος was coming to be used with little more force than a possessive pronoun, such as in the LXX, but it could still have the stronger meaning of "one's own."[214] Other commentators have also understood the phrase in this way,[215] so the meaning might be "the blood of his own" if the background was the OT use of יחיד or LXX αγαπητος, εκλεκτος and μονογενης.[216] It is nonetheless possible that it means "his own blood,"[217] since the LXX apparently provides no parallel use of the substantive masculine singular but does have uses virtually equivalent to a possessive pronoun.[218] So, the "natural" reading of του αιματος του ιδιου is probably "his own blood," but it would have been a clumsy expression on Luke's part, who clearly wished to refer to the church of God and the blood of Christ.[219] Thus, if the original reading was the less explicit του αιματος του ιδιου, rather than του ιδιου αιματος, its meaning was unclear.

As for the first variant, while την εκκληcιαν του θεου is the more common Pauline-sounding phrase, Paul does refer to αι εκκληcιαι του χριcτου (Rom 16:16), which provides some parallel to την εκκληcιαν του κυριου. Further, while (η) εκκληcια (του) κυριου does not appear in the NT, it does occur in the LXX (e.g., Deut 23:2–4, 1 Chr 28:8, Mic 2:5), and since the MS evidence for both readings is balanced, internal evidence must decide the issue.[220] Metzger notes that while a change either way might have occurred, if του αιματος του ιδιου was understood by a reader to mean "his own blood," there would have been a good reason to

---

213. Moulton, *Grammar*, 90. Cf. MM, 298. Fitzmyer notes that ιδιος occurs as a substantive plural (των ιδιων) in 1 Tim 5:8 (*Acts*, 680). Cf. τα ιδια and οι ιδιοι in John 1:11.

214. Turner, *Syntax*, 191–92; Silva, *NIDNTTE*, 2:499–500.

215. Cf. Pervo, *Acts*, 523. However, Fitzmyer describes it as "a last-ditch solution for this text-critical problem" (*Acts*, 680).

216. Bruce, *Acts*, 434. Johnson describes this as only "just possible" (*Acts*, 36).

217. BDAG, 467, ἴδιος 2.

218. *GELS*, 336–37.

219. Barrett, *Acts*, 977.

220. Cf. Wright, "Jesus as ΘΕΟΣ," 249–50.

change θεου to κυριου earlier in the verse, in order to remove a patripassian interpretation in the latter part of the verse, even if not intended by Luke.[221] On the other hand, if την εκκληcιαν του κυριου were original, the more natural meaning of του αιματοc του ιδιου ("his own blood") might have been Luke's intent—"the Lord's [Jesus'] blood." Indeed, the THGNT adopts the reading την εκκληcιαν του κυριου, which would mean that κυριου was changed to θεου at some time.

It is difficult to come to a decision about both places where there are variant readings in this verse, but if Ehrman is right about the original, as most commentators agree, then Luke composed a difficult text, which later readers or copyists tried to clarify by changing the readings in their MSS. If so, it would appear that there has been a "corruption" of the original text that was not easy to understand (την εκκληcιαν του θεου ην περιεποιηcατο δια του αιματοc του ιδιου).[222] Yet, if the original reading was την εκκληcιαν του κυριου ην περιεποιηcατο δια του αιματοc του ιδιου and later copyists changed κυριου to θεου, this might count as an "orthodox corruption," with Jesus as "the Lord" changed to referring to him as "God." As we have seen, scholars continue to find these issues challenging,[223] because the direction of the changes and the reason for the creation of the variant readings are difficult to determine. In either case, however, there could have been a "corruption"—with "God" changed to "Lord" (20:28a) or with "Lord" changed to "God," and adjustments made to the final phrase—but clarifying a somewhat ambiguous original was probably the reason for the secondary readings rather than a desire to support or oppose a theological viewpoint.

Romans 14:10

In an exhortation to the church(es) in Rome, Paul urged them not to judge their "brothers," παντεc γαρ παραcτηcομεθα τω βηματι του θεου, but some MSS (ℵ^c C² Ψ 048 0209 etc.) read τω βηματι του χριcτου instead of τω βηματι του θεου. Ehrman points out that this variant reading cannot be accidental in the two MSS that correct the original to this second reading, although it could be a harmonization to 2 Cor 5:10 where Paul says that τουc γαρ παντας ημας φανερωθηναι δει εμπροσθεν του βηματαοc

---

221. Metzger, *Textual Commentary*, 425–47.
222. Cf. Metzger and Ehrman, *Text*, 32–33; Pervo, *Acts*, 523–24.
223. Cf. Keener, *Acts*, 3:3037–40.

του χριστου.²²⁴ He adds, however, that, in the OT text cited in support of this statement in v. 11 (Isa 45:23), bowing the knee εμοι in the first line corresponds to confessing τω θεω in the second, and he concludes that, by changing του θεου to του χριστου, scribes have used the OT text to interpret "God" in the OT text as "Christ" in the NT. Now Christ is God.

Several points may be made in response to this. First, it is only in two of the MSS cited that the original reading has been corrected to read χριστου, so, while a number of MSS have that reading, it is only in those two MSS that the reading is clearly not accidental. Second, the citation in v. 11 is not a straightforward quotation of Isa 45:23 but a pastiche made up from that passage (εμοι καμψει παν γονυ και εξομολογησεται πασα γλωσσα τω θεω) and Isa 49:18 (ζω εγω λεγει κυριος). Third, the statement that the new reading about Christ ensures that it is he "whose deity every tongue will confess" is certainly consistent with the context of Isa 45:23— εγω ειμι ο θεος και ουκ εστιν αλλος (45:22 LXX)—but neither corrector of ℵ or C changes τω θεω to τω χριστω in v. 11 or adds τω χριστω at the end of v. 12 as the one to whom they will give account (if τω θεω is original). It would be strange if a copyist deliberately changed 14:10 ("Christ" instead of "God") but then allowed "God" to remain in the conclusion in 14:11 (and perhaps 14:12). This might only reinforce the point that Christ is given divine titles, but the change to του χριστου in 14:10 could just be an expression of piety drawn from a parallel text in 2 Cor 5:10. Thus, while the reading *might* have been changed to support the divinity of Christ, there are other possibilities, so it is quite uncertain that an "orthodox corruption" has occurred here. The text has clearly been changed in some MSS and appears unchanged in others, but perhaps this only derived from piety or as a harmonization to 2 Cor 5:10.²²⁵

1 Corinthians 10:9

Paul issued warnings to the church in Corinth based on certain events recounted in the OT. In 10:9 he alludes to Num 21, adding an exhortation not to act as Israel did. Most MSS read μηδε εκπειραζωμεν τον χριστον, but instead of τον χριστον, some MSS read τον κυριον or τον θεον

---

224. Ehrman, *Orthodox Corruption*, 106–7.

225. Metzger, *Textual Commentary*, 468–69; Cranfield, *Romans*, 2:709n4; Moo, *Romans*, 834n29; Jewett and Kotansky, *Romans*, 830–31nm; Longenecker, *Romans*, 989–90.

ANTI-ADOPTIONIST CORRUPTIONS?

(A 81 ℓ883).²²⁶ Here, τον χριστον occurs in P⁴⁶ (ca. AD 200) as well as most Western and Byzantine MSS, and τον κυριον appears in the best Alexandrian MSS (ℵ B C 33).²²⁷ Ehrman suggests that if copyists found τον χριστον in their exemplar and thought it odd that Christ was acting in the OT era, they might have changed it to τον κυριον to allow for a different interpretation. Or (with the reading τον θεον) it might have been meant to require it.²²⁸ However, Ehrman notes that many early Christians had little trouble thinking of Christ at work in OT times, so there is no firm basis for accepting this as a motive to remove τον χριστον. He refers to two ancient sources citing this passage against Paul of Samosata to show that Christ was alive in OT times and hence not a mere man,²²⁹ and since this was such a common belief, he concludes that it is more likely that copyists changed the original reading (whatever that was) to τον χριστον to support their belief.

Ehrman concludes then that τον χριστον is secondary, but that it occurs as early as the time of Clement of Alexandria (ca. AD 150–215) and a presbyter cited by Irenaeus (*Haer.* 4.27.3). God would then be in view and τον κυριον would be original, especially as the context of this verse has God in view as the one who was displeased with them and brought disaster upon them in the wilderness (v. 5). Ehrman takes this as a more compelling link than a reference to ο χριστος sustaining the nation (v. 4), although Osburn suggests that χριστον was changed to κυριον by an Eastern writer based on an Antiochene literal interpretation.²³⁰ Ehrman concludes that the original reading was τον κυριον, referring to God, but that copyists changed this to τον χριστον because they believed that "Christ" existed in OT times "exercising divine prerogatives."²³¹ This would then be an intentional "orthodox corruption," aiming to specify who τον κυριον was in opposition to adoptionist

---

226. Ehrman, *Orthodox Corruption*, 105–6.

227. Ehrman, *Orthodox Corruption*, 136–37n211.

228. Metzger, *Textual Commentary*, 560.

229. The sources appear to be a scholion in the margin of MS 1739 that referred to Origen's *Stromateis*, as well as the *Epistle of Hymenaeus* citing τον χριστον from this text in support.

230. Osburn, "1 Corinthians 10:9," 208, 211–12. He also refers to the focus on Christ in vv. 14–22, once using κυριος (v. 21), with God (θεος) also mentioned (v. 20) ("1 Corinthians 10:9," 208n29).

231. Ehrman, *Orthodox Corruption*, 106.

Christology. It would also contrast with the reading in NA[28], although the *THGNT* opts for τον κυριον.[232]

However, there are several reasons why these changes might have occurred, apart from someone's desire to further their theological views.[233] First, there might have been some confusion between the words as *nomina sacra* (κν, χν), or someone wished to clarify which κυριος was in view, or lectionary usage resulted in a MS harmonized to a customary text. Wasserman argues that some such changes in MSS are due to "a free and unreflected attitude" by scribes "to interpret what is already implied in the text," as Ehrman suggested about the variants in Jude 5.[234] The variations among MSS in Jude 5, 1 Cor 10:5, and 1 Cor 10:9 show that there was no consistent pattern in such variations either among text-types or in individual MSS, so that "mind slip," rather than "theological intention," is more likely their cause. Indeed, τον χριστον might just have been original.[235]

2 Corinthians 5:6, 8

In this section of 2 Corinthians, Paul was highlighting the contrast between living life now (ενδημουντες εν τω cωματι but εκδημουμεν απο του κυριου) and his preference to depart this life (εκδημηcαι εκ του cωματος και ενδημοucαι προς τον κυριον). Ehrman proposes that, instead of του κυριου . . . τον κυριον, the MSS that have the secondary readings του θεου . . . τον θεον clarify that believers will be "with God" and also stand εμπροcθεν του βηματος του χριστου (5:10), thus implying that Christ is God.[236] This depends, however, on the notion that only one divine personage (θεος) is to be present in the heavenly court, which does not fit with portrayals of the heavenly realm elsewhere with multiple beings present (e.g., Isa 6, Rev 4). It would also require someone having this description of Christ as God in mind. The variant readings here, then, cannot serve as examples of "orthodox corruption" since they do not clearly exalt Jesus to divine status.

---

232. The reading τον θεον is unlikely to be original in view of its limited MS support.

233. Wasserman, "Misquoting?," 346–48.

234. Wasserman, "Misquoting?," 347–48, referring to Ehrman, *Orthodox Corruption*, 100.

235. Fee, *First Epistle*, 504n515; Thiselton, *First Epistle*, 740.

236. Ehrman, *Orthodox Corruption*, 137–38n21.

Jesus as No Ordinary Human

In this section, I discuss certain variant readings said to have been created to remove any possibility of supporting the view that Jesus was merely human.

Matthew 24:36

Matthew 24 contains a series of Jesus' sayings in response to the disciples' question about his "coming" and "the end of the age" (24:3). During this discourse, Jesus emphasizes that no one knows when that will be, ουδε οι αγγελοι των ουρανων ουδε ο υιος ει μη ο πατηρ μονος. However, ουδε ο υιος is missing in certain MSS ($\aleph^{2a}$ K W etc. *Byz*), although it is present in early and reliable MSS in both the Alexandrian and Western traditions ($\aleph^*$ $\aleph^{2b}$ B D Θ f^{13} etc.).[237] Since the shorter text is attested by Origen and most of the early versions (vg sy co), it must have existed quite early on. Ehrman refers to the argument that the phrase was added to Matt 24:36 as a harmonization to Mark 13:32 since the words are secure there, thus showing that copyists had no theological issue with that reading. In response, however, he notes that, even in Mark 13:32, a few MSS (X vg^{ms}) do omit ουδε ο υιος and also that, if this phrase were not original in Matthew, in view of Matthew's popularity in comparison with Mark, we would expect copies of Mark to be harmonized to Matthew (and therefore leave it out)—which did not generally occur. Further, ουδε ο υιος stands as the second element in a pair (ουδε . . . ουδε . . .), which might sound odd if the second element were missing, although there are cases where Matthew does have a single ουδε.[238] Ehrman observes that in Sinaiticus the phrase was originally present but was removed by a corrector and then resupplied by a later corrector, so he suggests that it was omitted at an early date because it seemed to support the view that the Son of God was not omniscient, which might support adoptionist Christology.

However, although the phrase was probably original in Matthew in view of its MS support, it is not clear that it was omitted to subvert adoptionist Christology, since adoptionists believed that Jesus was adopted as God's Son at his baptism, and this is referring to a situation well after that, when, even on adoptionist grounds, Jesus was the Son of God and *should*

---

237. Ehrman, *Orthodox Corruption*, 107–8. Cf. Ehrman, "Text and Transmission," 333; Ehrman, *Misquoting*, 203–4.

238. Messer, "Patristic Theology," 135n32. Cf. Powell, "Textual Problem."

have had divine attributes. Perhaps this phrase was omitted because it seemed strange that, as the Son of God, Jesus was not omniscient,[239] but it was not necessarily omitted to remove a weapon from the adoptionist arsenal. Indeed, if proto-orthodox copyists removed the offending phrase from Matt 24:36, why were they happy to preserve ο πατηρ μονος at the end of the sentence, as well as leave ουδε ο υιος in Mark 13:32?[240] Some MSS actually emphasize the fact that the Son did not know as the Father did.[241] If the omission was deliberate, the person responsible might have had pious or theological motives, and as such it would be an "orthodox corruption," but not to counter adoptionism.

On the basis of a thorough examination of the patristic evidence, it appears that Sabellian or Praxean groups in the West would have benefited most from removing the phrase, if it were original, but Messer argues that the patristic evidence suggests that it was not original, and he disputes the claim that Origen knew of the shorter text.[242] Further, if the phrase was not original, its addition could have derived from certain "unorthodox" sources.[243]

Whether the phrase was original or not, given the varieties in belief from an early period in the history of the church, it is always possible to think of a "heresy" that might benefit from a variant, but that does not necessarily imply that the reason for its creation was to counter that heresy. Thus, in the context and in view of the MS evidence, ουδε ο υιος was probably original and omitted at some point due to pious sensibilities, perhaps a genuine "corruption" but not one to oppose adoptionist Christology.[244]

---

239. Head, "Christology," 121–22.

240. Wallace, "Lost in Transmission," 45–49.

241. Head, "Christology," 120–21.

242. Messer, "Patristic Theology," 171, 179–82. Cf. Marcello, "Myths," 223–24. Wallace concludes that ουδε ο υιος was not original, but he argues that μονος was meant to suggest the same thought in a softer way ("Son's Ignorance").

243. Messer, "Patristic Theology," 173.

244. Metzger, *Textual Commentary*, 51–52; Hagner, *Matthew 14–28*, 709nj; Davies and Allison, *Matthew*, 3:377n22; Luz, *Matthew 21–28*, 213n22; Pardee, *Scribal Harmonization*, 244–45. Cf. Miller, "Least Orthodox Reading," 68–72.

ANTI-ADOPTIONIST CORRUPTIONS?

Luke 2:40

In the first two chapters of the third Gospel, Luke sums up Jesus' boyhood years, saying that ηυξανεν και εκραταιουτο πληρουμενον σοφια και χαρις θεου ην επ αυτου (2:40). However, some MSS (A K N Θ Φ Ψ $f^{1,13}$ etc. *Byz* aur f q r¹ sy^{p.h} bo^{mss}) include πνευματι after εκρατοιουτο. Ehrman interprets this to mean "he increased and grew *in spirit*," and he argues that it was original but copyists omitted it because it implied that Jesus "underwent spiritual development."[245] He acknowledges the strength of the MS support for πνευματι not being original, but notes that some secondary Alexandrian MSS, a small number of Western MSS, and the bulk of later Byzantine MSS all include the phrase, so that both readings are possible based on the external evidence.

As for internal factors, he points out that the same phrase including πνευματι is used to describe John (1:80) and some scholars have argued that the longer text in 2:40 might be a harmonization to that.[246] On the other hand, the phraseology of ηυξανεν και εκραταιουτο in 1:80 and 2:40 is identical, so, if πνευματι was not original in 2:40, Jesus would be described as growing up as well as increasing in (physical) strength while John grew up and also increased in spiritual strength (πνευματι), and this could be taken as an insult to Jesus. Hence, someone might have inserted it so that Jesus would not appear spiritually inferior to John. Ehrman also points out that Luke's Gospel has an emphasis on the activities of the Holy Spirit (1:35; 2:25–35; 3:16, 22; etc.), so he suggests that mentioning Jesus growing "in spirit" or "in Spirit" would fit with Luke's emphasis elsewhere, so πνευματι could have been original in this description of Jesus' boyhood but then omitted to avoid a slight on Jesus as if he needed "spiritual" development.

Thus, it depends what people might have thought about the reading, and good reasons can be given both for omitting the phrase if it was original or for inserting it if it was not. The argument can go both ways. However, despite Ehrman's estimate regarding the MSS supporting the variants, the strength of the external MS evidence supporting the absence of πνευματι (ℵ B D L W lat sy^s co; Or^{lat}) indicates that it was not original, and its insertion by harmonization to fit with the description of John the Baptist in 1:80 is just as likely as its insertion for theological reasons. The case for "orthodox corruption" here must remain unproven.

245. Ehrman, *Orthodox Corruption*, 108–10 (italics added).
246. Cf. Fitzmyer, *Luke I-IX*, 432.

Scribes, Theology, and Apologetics

John 19:5

At the beginning of an account of Jesus' trial, Jesus is mockingly provided with royal garb and Pilate announces, ιδου ο ανθρωπος (19:5). However, P66* omits και λεγει αυτοις ιδου ο ανθρωπος, as do other unrelated MSS (it ly). Since there is no obvious reason for the omission, Ehrman argues that it must have been omitted deliberately, and he suggests why someone might have done so. He points out that Codex Vaticanus has a SR here, omitting the article before ανθρωπος (so, ιδου ανθρωπος), and then concludes that the original meaning "Behold the man" has then become "Behold a man," or "See, he is mortal." He proposes that this reading "once had a wide currency," so that copyists who were then troubled by this, according to which Jesus was "a mere mortal," just cut out the entire sentence, as in P66* etc.[247]

Yet, it is doubtful that a Christian copyist would have been troubled by what Pilate said, even if his words did not include the article, and it is difficult to believe that anyone took the phrase to mean that Jesus was a "mere mortal." Pilate was, after all, a doubtful guide to truth, and he was not dealing with anyone suggesting that Jesus was anything other than a real human being. The whole proposal is doubtful. First, the page of P66 that bears John 19:5 is quite fragmentary toward the lower edge and, while the sentence is clearly missing, it is "possible that there is a corrector's insertion symbol here" (between the final nu of [ιματι]ον and οτε in 19:6).[248] So, there may well have been a correction in the lower margin adding the missing phrase, perhaps now only partially visible under the κ of [ε]-κρ[αυγασαν] (v. 6). Hence, it would be unwise to build an argument on the omission of this sentence when it could well have been inserted in the missing lower margin as a correction by the original copyist. Indeed, it would be difficult to confirm a conscious motive since he regularly omits (and corrects) material. Further, ανθρωπος is used for Jesus throughout P66, which shows that the copyist had no hesitation in having Jesus described as such.[249] While this does not account for the OL and Lycopolitanic versional MSS, these are all much later.[250]

---

247. Ehrman, *Orthodox Corruption*, 110–11. Cf. Comfort and Barrett, *Text of the Earliest*, 384.

248. Royse, *Scribal Habits*, 448n278 (cf. 514–15n614). Cf. Malik, "Myths," 162–63.

249. Head, "Scribal Behaviour," 69–70.

250. Cf. Royse, *Scribal Habits*, 459–60.

Moreover, the meaning attributed to the singular omission of the article in Codex Vaticanus is doubtful. As noted previously, the omission of an article in Greek does not necessarily make a noun indefinite and, in this case, certainly not with the meaning "He is mortal." Indeed, Panackel understood the meaning of the expression *with* the article to be referring to Jesus' humanity,[251] which, even if unlikely, should alert us to the false distinction being made. Moreover, Codex Vaticanus is the only MS to omit the article, so it was probably just a mistake. It is unlikely, then, that copyists deleted the inarticular reading by removing the whole sentence to avoid speaking about Jesus as a mere man.[252]

1 Corinthians 10:4–5

While delivering warnings to the church in Corinth based on events related in the OT, Paul said that Israel επινον γαρ εκ πνευματικης ακολουθουςης πετρας, and then adds the clarifying remark that η πετρα δε ην ο χριστος (10:4). The claim that Paul's argument was based on Moses having struck the rock on several occasions so it must have followed them around is not evident from the passage,[253] but instead of the original reading in v. 5 (ουκ εν τοις πλειοςιν αυτων ευδοκηςεν ο θεος) a few MSS and other witnesses (Clem Iren^pt) omit ο θεος, so the subject of this sentence becomes ο χριστος, taken from 10:4. Thus, Christ would be the one who was not pleased with them so they were "laid low" in the wilderness. Ehrman argues that this reading would then be extending the christological focus from 10:1–4, not just asserting that Christ as η πετρα brought sustenance (v. 4) but also judgment (v. 5), thus highlighting Christ's role as divine—bringing both salvation and judgment.

However, it is simpler to explain the omission of ο θεος as a pious mistake, perhaps by "mind slip" in a context where the divinity of Christ was assumed. Indeed, an accidental copying mistake is much more likely than the proposal of a rather subtle theological point as the purpose of this variant reading, since the Greek MSS cited for omitting ο θεος are 81 (AD 1044), 257 (XIV AD), and 1610 (AD 1463), and the MSS of the

---

251. Panackel, ΑΝΘΡΩΠΟΣ, 336–37.

252. Chapa, "Contribution," 119–20. Royse also notes that the omission of about twenty letters might have been a complete line in the exemplar of P^{66}, which could explain the omission of such a long section *(Scribal Habits*, 459–60).

253. Ehrman, *Orthodox Corruption*, 104–5.

works of Clement and Irenaeus are neither early nor extensive.[254] There is little reason, then, to suppose that this reading was an early one deriving from a time when the adoptionist controversies were current, so the proposal that it was an "orthodox corruption" remains unproven, and there is at least one simpler and more likely explanation for its origins.

1 Corinthians 15:45

First Corinthians 15 is a chapter dealing with the issue of resurrection, including a citation from Gen 2:7 (εγενετο ο πρωτος ανθρωπος αδαμ εις ψυχην ζωσαν) and then a comparison with Jesus as ο εσχατος αδαμ who became πνευμα ζωοποιουν (15:45). Some witnesses (B K 326 365 Iren[lat]) omit ανθρωπος as a description of the first Adam, and Ehrman suggests that this might have been done to remove any parallel with Christ, who would have been referred to as a (created) ανθρωπος.[255] However, it is hard to believe that anyone would have seen this significance in the two occurrences of ανθρωπος, especially since, even omitting the first one, Jesus is still called ο εσχατος αδαμ in comparison to ο πρωτος αδαμ. Further, it is also open to question that this reading was generated "at least by the beginning of the third century," because it depends on the dating of Iren[lat], none of whose MSS derive from the early centuries. His works might have included this reading, but due to their late MS attestation they cannot be used to bear the sole weight of the argument. Perhaps ανθρωπος was omitted because "it appears to replicate" αδαμ.[256]

1 Corinthians 15:47

A little later in the same chapter Paul asserts that Adam, ο πρωτος ανθρωπος, came εκ γης χοικος, while Christ, ο δευτερος ανθρωπος, came εξ ουρανου (15:47). However, ο δευτερος ανθρωπος has been changed in certain MSS to read:

1. ο δευτερος ανθρωπος ο κυριος   ℵ² A D¹ K L P Ψ 075 *Byz* sy
2. ο δευτερος ο κυριος   630 Marcion^A

---

254. Zuntz, *Text*, 232. Fee calls the patristic evidence "tenuous at best" (*First Epistle*, 487n436).

255. Ehrman, *Orthodox Corruption*, 111.

256. Thiselton, *First Epistle*, 1281. Cf. Fee, *First Epistle*, 870n321.

3. ο δευτερος ανθρωπος πνευματικος   P⁴⁶

4. ο δευτερος ανθρωπος ... ο ουρανιος   F G latt

Ehrman suggests that all four readings emphasize the difference between Adam and Christ, so that Christ is not just a man created by God, but (1) the second man, ο κυριος; (2) the second one, ο κυριος; (3) the second man, πνευματικος; or (4) the second man, ο ουρανιος. He concludes that all of these variants betray "an orthodox tendency to portray Jesus as far more than human."[257]

While this is true of the addition of ο κυριος, the notion of Christ as πνευματικος in P⁴⁶ is prepared for in 15:45, where he is said to have become πνευμα ζωοποιουν. Hence the third variant is presumably a harmonization to the immediate context. Further, the addition of ο ουρανιος in the fourth variant comes immediately after describing Christ as having come εξ ουρανου, so it is probably a harmonization to that.[258]

Thus, we are left with the task of explaining the origin of the first two variants. MS support for the second (630, XII/XIII AD) is very late,[259] and the reference to Marcion's text is dependent on citations in Tertullian (II/III AD) and Adamantius (early IV AD). However, even if those citations are accurate,[260] ανθρωπος could simply have been omitted because it seemed superfluous or repetitive,[261] with ο κυριος being a pious addition (cf. v. 31). The first variant only dates from the fifth century, the date of the earliest MSS in Syriac with this reading (syr^(p,h,pal)), but the *reason* for the insertion of ο κυριος in the first variant is unclear. Fee suggests "reasons of piety" and Ehrman proposes "an orthodox tendency to portray Jesus as far more than human."[262] It is unclear which of these is the more likely cause of this reading.

---

257. Ehrman, *Orthodox Corruption*, 111.

258. Fee describes these two variants as "attempts to balance the first clause" (*First Epistle*, 787n2).

259. NA²⁸ appears to cite 630 for both ο κυριος and ανθρωπος ο κυριος. GNT⁵ cites 1912 and 2200 for ο κυριος (the latter without ο δευτερος).

260. Thiselton accepts Tertullian's reference to Marcion (*First Epistle*, 1285).

261. Fee, *First Epistle*, 787n2.

262. Fee, *First Epistle*, 787n2; Ehrman, *Orthodox Corruption*, 111. Fitzmyer accepts "dogmatic reasons" as the cause (*First Corinthians*, 599). Cf. Metzger, *Textual Commentary*, 501–2.

Scribes, Theology, and Apologetics

Colossians 1:22

In the central part of Col 1, Paul highlights how Christ was and is supreme over the created world.[263] In contrast to believers being previously estranged from God, he says that νυνι δε αποκατηλλαξεν [you] εν τω cωματι της capκoc αυτου δια του θανατου. Some MSS (D* F G b vg^ms etc.) have replaced the aorist active verb αποκατηλλαξεν [sc. υμας] with the aorist passive participle αποκαταλλαγεντες, which Ehrman notes as a shift in focus away from Christ to believers—not "he reconciled [you]" but "[you] having been reconciled." Further, two of these same MSS (F G) omit αυτου and thus refer to "the body of *the* flesh" rather than "the body of *his* flesh," which is a possible shift of focus away from the body of Christ to the bodies of believers. This would then hinder a reference to Christ's "body of flesh," so that he could not be seen as merely human, and it would avoid any association of him with "flesh," which often has a negative connotation in the Pauline corpus.[264]

There are several points to be made in relation to this proposal. First, there are three other variant readings here (αποκαταλλαγητε, αποκατηλλακται, απηλλαξεν), which admittedly enjoy little MS support—the first occurs in P[46] and B, the second in MS 33 (IX AD), and the third in MS 104 (AD 1087). This probably indicates that the syntax of the sentence was unclear.[265] Second, the suggestion that there is a purposeful shift in focus away from Christ is true from a grammatical point of view since believers are now the subject of the verb, but there is still the mention of the *means* of the reconciliation, that is, δια του θανατου, which must refer to Christ's death. Further, the believers' resulting unstained status is still said to be κατενωπιον αυτου, again referring to Christ, which also reduces the proposed shift in focus. Finally, the idea that it is believers' "flesh" that is in view in the variant reading of the text is unlikely, again, because there is a reference immediately afterwards to δια του θανατου, clearly referring to the (physical) death of Christ. This makes it highly unlikely that anyone reading this text in its variant form would have thought of the death of believers as what was being referred to, so it is unlikely that anyone would have created this reading to support that view and to avoid mentioning the humanity of Christ.

---

263. As with the Pastoral Epistles, I find arguments for the non-Pauline authorship of Colossians unconvincing, so I refer to Paul as the author.

264. Ehrman, *Orthodox Corruption*, 113.

265. Metzger, *Textual Commentary*, 554–55.

ANTI-ADOPTIONIST CORRUPTIONS?

Hebrews 1:3

The opening four verses of the Letter to the Hebrews are a compressed christological statement about the superiority of the Son of God as the agent of God's revelation. A part of this exalted description of Jesus is the reference to his work, καθαριcμον των αμαρτιων ποιηcαμενοc (1:3), and most Byzantine MSS add ημων,[266] thus making it clear that it is "*our* sins" that have been cleansed. Ehrman argues that this emphasizes the contrast between Christ and the Levitical priests of the OT, the latter having to sacrifice for *their own* sins before offering a sacrifice for the nation in general.[267] He implies that adding ημων was meant to emphasize that Jesus did not have to sacrifice for *his own* sins.

However, while this point is certainly made later in the letter (7:27, 9:14), it is unclear that the variant in 1:3 was created to emphasize it. It could just as easily have been meant to clarify the original meaning without wishing to oppose a contrary doctrinal stance that might hint at the imperfection of Jesus. Indeed, if this were a concern, the theme in Hebrews of Jesus having "been made perfect" using the verb τελειοω (Heb 2:10; 5:9; 7:28) would have been a far more obvious element to change, and there is no trace of any hesitation or uncertainty regarding this, so the proposed intention to highlight that Jesus did not have to sacrifice for his sins is an unlikely origin for the addition of ημων in 1:3.[268]

Hebrews 2:18

The latter part of Heb 2 is an exposition of the true humanity of Jesus as the basis of an appeal to the readers to trust in him as their high priest. One aspect of this was to assert that he had to be made "like his brothers" κατα παντα (2:17). Then in 2:18 the author refers to Jesus having suffered (πεπονθεν) after being tempted/tested (πειραcθειc). Ehrman suggests that the idea of Jesus being "tempted," if that is how πειραcθειc was understood, "could understandably cause some confusion," so he proposes that one "natural" interpretation of 2:18 is that it was the difficulty that Jesus

---

266. This occurs as either των αμαρτιων ημων ποιηcαμενοc or ποιηcαμενοc των αμαρτιων ημων.

267. Ehrman, *Orthodox Corruption*, 113.

268. Attridge agrees that the variant was "made on dogmatic grounds, to indicate that Christ did not die for his sins," but he adds that it could "simply reflect common language used of the atonement" (*Hebrews*, 35n9).

encountered in withstanding temptation that led to his suffering. Presumably, this is based on the grammatical priority of the aorist participle πειρασθεις, which must refer to action prior to the main verb πεπονθεν. Of course, a causal relationship between the two verbs is a possibility ("because he was tempted . . . he suffered"), and Ehrman proposes that, when the copyist of Codex Sinaiticus omitted πειρασθεις, he did so to remove that potential problem. Subsequently, πιρασθις (πειρασθεις) was supplied in the MS, so it could well have been an accidental omission which was later rectified, but Ehrman calls it an "intriguing" omission because it leaves out any thought of Jesus being tempted, leaving only the mention of his suffering.[269]

Yet, even if the idea is one of temptation rather than testing, temptation in general was not viewed by the early Christians as sinful in itself. Rather, it was "falling into" or "giving way to" temptation that was viewed with disapproval (e.g., 1 Cor 7:5, 10:13; 1 Thess 3:5; Jas 1:13–14). Further, the narratives of Jesus' own temptation in the Gospels (Matt 4:1–11, Luke 4:1–13) were probably well enough known to obviate any need to remove a reference to him being tempted in Heb 2:18. Indeed, Ehrman notes the reference to Jesus being tempted later in Hebrews (4:15), where it is stated explicitly that he did not sin, but he suggests that the copyist of Codex Sinaiticus omitted πειρασθεις in 2:18 to *ensure* that this text could not be used to support any notion of Jesus being tempted (and sinning).[270] However, the "testing" or "temptation" in view in 2:18 seems to be a clear reference to Jesus' temptation in Gethsemane to depart from the will of God (cf. 5:7), a testing of his obedience to God's will. The Gospel narratives end with his accepting that will rather than his own (e.g., Luke 22:42), and Christian readers could hardly fail to be aware of that. Therefore, it is unlikely that the mention of Jesus being tempted or tested was removed as unacceptable by anyone familiar with the NT writings, especially with the Gospel narratives. But it is still unclear why πειρασθεις was absent in ℵ*, unless it was due to parablepsis from sigma to sigma (αυτος . . . πειρασθεις).

Hebrews 10:29

As the author of the Letter to the Hebrews moved from his central doctrinal section into the final exhortatory segment, he began to urge his

---

269. Ehrman, *Orthodox Corruption*, 112.
270. Ehrman, *Orthodox Corruption*, 138n230.

readers to continue in faith. As part of this, he issued one of his most strident warning passages (10:26–39), and within that he included a description of how serious it would be to despise the Son of God, το αιμα της διαθηκης κοινον ηγηcαμενοc εν ω ηγιαcθη (10:29). Codex Alexandrinus uniquely lacks εν ω ηγιαcθη, and there is no obvious reason for a scribal error here, so Ehrman wonders if the copyist of the codex wished to clarify who the subject of the verb was—was the believer or Christ "sanctified"? He notes that the closest personal noun is τον υιον του θεου, so the copyist might have omitted the phrase to remove any possibility of the thought that Christ himself was sanctified or needed to be.[271]

While this is possible, it is also unnecessary since it could have been a simple mistake, as Ehrman observes. Further, the closest personal antecedent is not "the Son of God" but ο . . . το αιμα της διαθηκης κοινον ηγηcαμενοc, so ηγιαcθη would naturally look back to that person, that is, the believer. The grammar is clear enough and certainly not so unclear as to warrant the excision of the final clause to avoid an interpretation which no one would be likely to adopt. Finally, as noted above, Christ being "made perfect" occurs elsewhere in Hebrews, so the idea would not have been difficult anyway.

CONCLUSION

At the end of the chapter dealing with a large number of variants in NT MSS that might have been created to either oppose adoptionist Christology or subvert adoptionists from using texts to support their beliefs, Ehrman summarizes his findings.[272] He maintains that the "orthodox" party, and proto-orthodox scribes in particular, changed the readings from those in their exemplars to the ones in their copies, noting several central doctrines especially in view. Even if a variant has almost no support and that support is quite late, he takes this as evidence for his proposal—the orthodox won the day, so the very fact that only one late MS contains vestiges of this anti-adoptionist "theological tendency" shows how complete the victory of the orthodox was.[273] The fact that such readings are only adopted intermittently is not seen as a problem for this

---

271. Ehrman, *Orthodox Corruption*, 112–13.
272. Ehrman, *Orthodox Corruption*, 113–16.
273. Ehrman, *Orthodox Corruption*, 239n234.

Scribes, Theology, and Apologetics

thesis because copyists apparently felt no need to change every possible text that might be "misconstrued."

Yet the evidence can be read differently. As I have shown, except for a few cases, there are other likely explanations for those variants, and Ehrman's proposals often fail because the surrounding context makes it clear that a reader would be unlikely to see the supposed doctrinal aberration in that text. Further, perhaps the small amount of MS support for a reading is not a sign that all the MSS with that reading were destroyed or lost but an indication that it was never widely current. Often, the proposed difference in meaning of the variant reading from the original text is so subtle that readers are unlikely to have noticed, and therefore no one is likely to have created a variant with the intention of opposing the proposed "unorthodox" theological point. Finally, the apparent inconsistency of the efforts of scribes to remove or obviate "unorthodox" readings might not be a sign of their sporadic efforts but of the insubstantial nature of the evidence. Thus, while some variants might have been created to support orthodox theology, few are finally convincing, and those that might have been created to further a theological point of view were not necessarily made to oppose adoptionist Christology in the second and third centuries, whether consciously intended or almost unconsciously performed. While they are "corruptions," they could just have been the result of the inattention or piety of the copyist.

2

Anti-separationist Corruptions?

CHAPTER 3 OF THE *Orthodox Corruption of Scripture* deals with textual variants said to have been made in response to "separationist" Christologies in early Christianity. Ehrman first outlines the people and beliefs in view, beginning with Cerinthus, who believed that the divine Christ came upon the human Jesus but left him prior to his crucifixion.[1] He then summarizes the beliefs of various gnostic groups, including their view of the God of Israel and the world, as well as the nature of salvation, and therefore how the Christ came but did not really become a part of the created order. Rather, he brought knowledge to humanity by indwelling the man Jesus for a time, usually from the time of his baptism, and then returning to the heavenly realms.

This is the "separationist" Christology being discussed—that is, that Jesus and the Christ were not identical, and that the Christ left the man Jesus before he was crucified. It often included the belief that the divine Christ raised the man Jesus from the dead and then for a time revealed through him the knowledge, or *gnosis*, which would bring salvation. This involved a manner of interpreting the OT and NT that looked beneath or behind the text for other meanings, and it was consistent with the gnostics' belief that they alone possessed the true meaning of the Scriptures. In this chapter Ehrman argues that proto-orthodox scribes modified their copies of the NT texts in order to hinder the spread of such "gnostic" beliefs which separated Jesus from the divine Christ.

---

1. Ehrman, *Orthodox Corruption*, 140–46.

Jesus and Christ the Same

In this first section, Ehrman examines variant readings that seem to oppose views which distinguish between Christ and the person of Jesus.[2]

Matthew 12:30 / Luke 11:23

Matthew 12 includes an extended discourse, presenting Jesus' response to accusations brought against him by Pharisees (12:22–37). In that context, he urged his hearers to maintain their allegiance to him, concluding with ο μη cυναγων μετ εμου cκορπιζει (12:30), and the parallel passage in Luke 11:23 has the same wording. However, some MSS add με at the end of the sentence, both in Matt 12:30 (ℵ 33 sy^h bo) and Luke 11:23 (ℵ* ℵ^{2b} C^2 L Θ Ψ 33 etc. sy^s bo). This variant implies that the person who does not "gather with me" also "scatters me" (cκορπιζει με).[3] This reading is clearly not original, given its limited support in Matthew and divided support in Luke.

Ehrman refers to Metzger's argument suggesting that the addition of με might have been due to someone wishing to add an object to cκορπιζω since it is a transitive verb and to provide a balance to the three previous verbs, which all have qualifying material. But he argues that this cannot stand because the other three verbs are not followed by an "object" but a prepositional phrase.[4] Thus, he suggests that, if balancing the sentence was a priority, a copyist would have added κατ εμου (not με) in line with the first pair of items—μετ' εμου ... κατ' εμου ... μετ' εμου ... [κατ' εμου]. He also notes that the previous verb cυναγω is transitive and yet has no object, so neither would an object be expected after cκορπιζει. However, cυναγω is not always transitive (e.g., Matt 20:28 D),[5] and με refers to a first person (like εμου ... εμου ... εμου), so adding με might have seemed appropriate.[6] Nevertheless, the variant with με is difficult to understand, so the judgment on Luke 11:23 that it is so difficult that it

---

2. Ehrman, *Orthodox Corruption*, 146–60.
3. Ehrman, *Orthodox Corruption*, 159–60.
4. Ehrman, *Orthodox Corruption*, 201n79, refers to Metzger, *Textual Commentary* (1st ed.), 32 (Matt) and 158 (Luke). In the second edition, Metzger dropped any mention of the Matthaean variant, and there are no text-critical notes on Matt 12:30 in GNT^4 and GNT^5.
5. BDAG, 963, συνάγω 5.
6. Nolland, *Matthew*, 503.

ANTI-SEPARATIONIST CORRUPTIONS?

must be "a scribal blunder" could also apply to Matt 12:30.[7] Yet, Ehrman proposes that the implied condemnation of someone who σκορπιζει με derives from an orthodox concern to portray Jesus' enemies as those who "scatter" him or "divide" him up, as gnostics divided him into the Christ and Jesus. Thus, the variant would be an assertion of the unity of Jesus Christ, and this carried through into later MSS.[8]

Can this proposal stand? The verb σκορπιζω usually referred to scattering a group (or gathering) of things or people or dispersing or spreading a substance in various directions, and in patristic times it could mean "divide," i.e., "cause disunity among" *or* "separate."[9] Its intransitive use is unusual, but Jesus often used enigmatic sayings and perhaps unusual constructions, whether in Aramaic or Greek. The original saying was probably referring to a person distancing themselves from him (by not continuing their allegiance to him), the intransitive having a reflexive sense. Perhaps the image in the background was of Israel being scattered like sheep on the hills.[10] What could σκορπιζει με mean? Could "scattering" Jesus refer to dividing him into the divine Christ and the human Jesus? This is unlikely because in the context a reader or copyist could hardly imagine that σκορπιζω με could be a parallel thought to κατ εμου εστιν in the same way that μη συναγων μετ εμου is parallel to μη ων μετ εμου, unless someone had little thought for the context and simply decided to add the thought of not "scattering" Jesus. We may never know how this reading arose because its meaning is unclear. So, perhaps the conclusion about Luke 11:23 does apply to Matt 12:30 as well, and it is just a "scribal blunder" without any apparent rationale,[11] unless it relies on a meaning of σκορπιζω unavailable to us at the present time.

2 Corinthians 11:4

The letter we call 2 Corinthians was probably not the second letter that Paul wrote to the church in Corinth. Since he had left after an extended period of time in the city, certain people whom he characterizes as "super apostles" had gained entry to the church (11:5) and were proclaiming

---

7. Cf. Metzger, *Textual Commentary*, 134.

8. Cf. Ehrman on the spread of this variant (*Orthodox Corruption*, 202n82).

9. BDAG, 931; GELS, 626; LSJ, 1614, rev. suppl. 277; PGL, 1241.

10. Cf. Davies and Allison, *Matthew*, 2:343; Luz, *Matthew 8–20*, 206; Nolland, *Matthew*, 504.

11. Nolland says that the MSS add με "oddly" (*Luke 1—9:20*, 635nj).

αλλον ιηcουν (11:4). Some MSS, however, refer to αλλον χριcτον (F G 4; cf. vg arm etc.), a change which might have come about by an exchange of *nomina sacra* (χν for ιν), as in other NT MSS. This is clearly not a harmonization to another NT passage, so Ehrman observes that the new reading would be a forceful one with which to oppose any suggestion that there were multiple Christs, as gnostics like the Valentinians believed.[12]

However, did anyone use this passage in the context of that debate? The MS evidence only goes back to the fourth century in the Latin West, but Ehrman argues that it existed at an earlier time so it would fit a time when such gnostic views were current.[13] However, its earlier existence is uncertain so the argument is inconclusive, and the suggestion is unlikely anyway because the variant could just as easily have been a pious or scribal slip calling Jesus "(the) Christ," which was common in the early church and therefore would *not* necessarily have been meant to serve the suggested doctrinal purpose.

1 John 4:2–3

The "first" letter of John was written to a church in crisis partly because people had come to the church claiming to be prophets inspired by the Spirit, so John urged the church to "test" those "spirits" (4:1). In explanation, he wrote that παν πνευμα ο μη ομολογει τον ιηcουν εκ του θεου ουκ εcτιν (4:3). However, MS witnesses from the second century onwards, notably the Vulgate, Lucifer, and Socrates, as well as Irenaeus, Clement, and Origen (according to 1739^{mg}), have the reading ο λυει τον ιηcουν instead of ο μη ομολογει τον ιηcουν (in v. 3), although the occurrence of ο λυει τον ιηcουν in the margin of MS 1739 (X AD) adds little to the case for its authenticity.[14] Nevertheless, ο λυει τον ιηcουν is almost universally absent in the Greek MSS, early versions, and church fathers, which is a strong indication that it was not original.[15] Some scholars accept λυει as original in v. 3 because it is the "harder reading," while others ask if the traditional reading (μη ομολογει) could be a secondary harmonization to the use of ομολογει in v. 2.[16]

12. Ehrman, *Orthodox Corruption*, 201–2n81 (presumably referring to Irenaeus, *Haer.* 3.17.4).
13. Ehrman, *Orthodox Corruption*, 202n85.
14. Ehrman, *Orthodox Corruption*, 150–53.
15. Ehrman, *Orthodox Corruption*, 147–49.
16. Ehrman, *Orthodox Corruption*, 147. Cf. Ehrman, "1 John 4.3."

ANTI-SEPARATIONIST CORRUPTIONS?

Since it is unusual for μη to go with an indicative verb (ομολογει), Ehrman suggests that it is unlikely that such a grammatical "anomaly" would have been placed in the text later on, although μη does sometimes accompany a verb in the indicative elsewhere in the NT.[17] So, although both readings (λυει, μη ομολογει) are "difficult" in their own way, the slight grammatical "difficulty" of μη with ομολογει is not nearly as great as the difficulty of assigning meaning to λυει τον ιησουν in the context.[18] So, the harder reading (λυει τον ιησουν) is probably too hard and therefore secondary, and the traditional reading (μη ομολογει τον ιησουν) is likely to be original.

Regarding theological issues, Ehrman argues that in the original context of 1 John the opponents whom John had in mind were denying that Jesus was the Son of God who came in the flesh (cf. 4:2, 1:1–3) and shed his blood (cf. 5:6).[19] He concludes that those who left the church were more likely of a Docetic stamp, holding the kind of beliefs Ignatius condemned somewhat later (*Smyrn.* 1.1–2, 3.1–2, 4:1–2, 5.2; *Trall.* 9.1–2), especially that Jesus only *appeared* to suffer (*Smyrn.* 1.1, 2.1–2, 6.1; *Trall.* 10.1), which is consistent with the view alluded to in 1 John (1:7, 2:2, 5:6).

Among the Greek fathers, Socrates refers to this reading (λυει) εν ταιc παλαιαιc αντιγραφαιc, treating it as original and intended to condemn those who would "separate" the divine Christ from the human Jesus (*Hist. eccl.* 7.32). Irenaeus also refers to it in opposing Valentinian Gnostics who divide Christ up by saying that Christ descended into the man Jesus and left him before he was crucified (*Haer.* 3.16.8). Origen knew both readings, citing this verse to show that his own "dividing up" of Jesus was not in error (*Comm. Matt.* 65, *Hom. Exod.* 3.2). Clement also seems to have been aware of the reading.[20] Thus, the variant λυει τον ιησουν was known by the end of II AD and was cited in christological disputes to refute any "dividing up" of Christ. The Latin reading is attested by Tertullian (*Marc.* 5.16.4), Priscillian (*Tract.* 1.31.3; cf. *Tract.* 2.42.4–5;

---

17. BDAG, 646, μή 4b; Ehrman, *Orthodox Corruption*, 197n32.

18. Painter compares Pauline thought albeit in a different idiom (*1, 2 and 3 John*, 254–55). Strecker doubts that λυει can mean "divide" here, and he proposes that it must mean "destroy" or "annul" in accord with its use in 3:8 (*Johannine Letters*, 136).

19. Ehrman, *Orthodox Corruption*, 153–57.

20. Clement, "About the Pasch," according to 1739[mg], quoted in Brown, *Epistles*, 494.

2.52.27-29) and later Latin witnesses.[21] So, although most of these authors knew both readings, they used the secondary one (παν πνευμα ο λυει τον ιηcουν εκ του θεου ουκ εcτιν) to refute any thought of dividing up Christ's natures; so they did at least attribute meaning to it, using it to debate with those who divided Jesus from the divine Christ, from the Creator God, or from true Deity. Ehrman asks what someone might have meant by "loosing" Jesus, and he argues that it must have meant what those who used it took it to mean, that is, dividing the divine Christ from human Jesus.

Ehrman's concluding suggestion is that the variant reading, which some early fathers found useful in confuting gnostic Christologies, arose in the context of disputes with gnostics in the second century, was copied in some NT MSS, and finally included in the Vulgate. Thus, it can be fairly described as an "orthodox corruption," which not only changed the text but did so in order to support an orthodox theological position.[22] This seems reasonable,[23] if λυει can mean "separate" or "divide," despite normally meaning "untie, set free, release" or even "destroy, abolish."[24]

Yet, it is also possible that the patristic authors simply used a reading that served their ends, even if it hadn't been created with those ends in mind. And λυει could have originally meant "destroys" or "annuls" rather than "divides," referring to removing the power and significance of Jesus, unless it was just a mistake without any viable meaning at all.[25] So, while Ehrman's proposal as to the origin of this variant is possible, it is not without its difficulties, and there are other possibilities for its origin and original meaning that are just as likely.

The Birth of Christ

In this section, I review a small number of variants that are said to have been created to oppose gnostic beliefs and support the view that Jesus was already the Christ at his birth, as Irenaeus affirmed (*Haer.* 3.16.2).[26]

21. Ehrman, *Orthodox Corruption*, 199n49.
22. Ehrman, *Orthodox Corruption*, 157-58. Cf. Ehrman, "1 John 4.3"; Ehrman, *Misquoting*, 173-75.
23. Cf. Metzger, *Textual Commentary*, 644-45; Marshall, *Epistles*, 207-8n11; Smalley, *1, 2, 3 John*, 214-15nc.
24. BDAG, 606-7; GELS, 437.
25. Brown, *Epistles*, 494-96.
26. Ehrman, *Orthodox Corruption*, 160-65.

ANTI-SEPARATIONIST CORRUPTIONS?

Matthew 1:16

At the end of the genealogy in Matt 1, there is a note about Mary, εξ ης εγεννηθη ιηcουc ο λεγομενοc χριcτοc (1:16). Some MSS (64 [d] k sy^c etc.) omit ο λεγομενοc, so it then reads εξ ης εγεννηθη ιηcουc χριcτοc, which is clearly a secondary reading with little MS support.[27] Ehrman alludes to Tertullian's reference to this verse (*Carn. Chr.* 20), in which he omits any indication of "who is called," and he concludes that an orthodox copyist must have wished to "improve" the text by omitting ο λεγομενοc.[28] Thus, Jesus was born as the Christ rather than being imbued with the Christ later.

It is possible, however, that the phrase was omitted accidentally, moving from ιηcουc to χριcτοc, particularly if these were written as *nomina sacra* (ιc . . . χc). Further, the omission could have simply been an abbreviation without any perceived difference in meaning. Indeed, does the shorter reading actually achieve what is proposed? Jesus is called ο χριcτοc, but there is no clear statement that he was the Christ at birth, even if Tertullian thought this reading useful to support that doctrine. Hence, the proposal about why ο λεγομενοc was dropped out is doubtful because the textual issues are complex, involving different Syriac versions of the verse.[29] Even if the new reading was found useful by "orthodox" writers, its origins can be accounted for by a loose parablepsis from similar-sounding words (ιηc*ουc* . . . λεγομεν*οc*), since the papyri contain instances of the ου–ο vowel exchange.[30] Or it might have been a confusion of *nomina sacra* without any theological purpose in view. We simply do not know how this variant reading arose.

Matthew 1:18

Soon after the previous passage, the traditional text reads that του δε ιηcου χριcτου η γενεcιc ουτωc ην, but there are variant readings for του δε ιηcου χριcτου, namely (1) του δε ιηcου (W 4 74 270 pc), (2) του δε χριcτου ιηcου (B), and (3) του δε χριcτου. Manuscript support for the first two is too limited for them to be original, so both appear to be adaptations of the traditional text. However, the third variant (του δε χριcτου) occurs in

---

27. Metzger maintains that only sy^c has this reading (*Textual Commentary*, 3–6). *Pace* Ehrman, *Orthodox Corruption*, 161.
28. Ehrman, *Orthodox Corruption*, 161.
29. Metzger, *Textual Commentary*, 2–6; Nolland, *Matthew*, 65–66nf-f.
30. Gignac, *Grammar*, 1:211–14.

some Western MSS (it vg sy). The use of ιηcου χριcτου in the traditional reading could be original, looking back to Matt 1:1, but Ehrman argues that it would be more natural to expect χριcτου to be original, matching 1:17 (εωc του χριcτου), which was then later harmonized with 1:1 to read του ιηcου χριcτου.[31]

When Irenaeus refers to this event, and possibly this passage, he takes the occurrence of του χριcτου to be proof refuting those who say that Jesus was born of Mary and the Christ came upon him from above (*Haer.* 3.16.2). However, while this shorter text certainly proved valuable in refuting gnostic beliefs, and hence might have been an orthodox corruption originating in the second century, Irenaeus's reference could just as easily be abbreviated, simply noting the significance of χριcτου to denote the one who was born, so there is little gain to be made from that.

Thus, opinions vary as to what was original and what was secondary, but there is no final certainty that the original text was ιηcου and χριcτου was added as an "orthodox corruption" to support Jesus as the Christ from the time of his birth. Indeed, Ehrman observes that του ιηcου χριcτου is attested by all families of Greek MSS, including P[1] (III AD) ℵ B *f*[1] and sy[h] and not one Greek MS attests the shorter του χριcτου. So, the MS evidence for του δε ιηcου χριcτου is almost overwhelming and it is most likely original, not a variant created to oppose gnostic Christology.[32]

Luke 1:35

In Luke's version of events surrounding the birth of Jesus, the original text contained the angel's words to Mary, that το γεννωμενον αγιον κληθηcεται υιοc θεου (1:35), but some MSS insert εκ cου after γεννωμενον. Clearly this addition is secondary given its weak MS support (C* Θ *f*[1] 33 etc.), and there is no clear reason why it would have been omitted if it were original. It might have arisen from a desire to balance the previous two expressions using the second person singular (επι cε . . . cοι) with a third (εκ cου),[33] or to harmonize with the thought of Matt 1:20 (το . . . εν αυτη γεννηθεν). Ehrman refers, however, to Irenaeus and Tertullian opposing Valentinus's view that Jesus, the Christ of the demiurge, did not come *from* Mary but

---

31. Ehrman, *Orthodox Corruption*, 161–63. Cf. Davies and Allison, *Matthew*, 1:198n3.

32. Cf. Metzger, *Textual Commentary*, 7; Nolland, *Matthew*, 88nb.

33. Cf. Metzger, *Textual Commentary*, 108–9.

ANTI-SEPARATIONIST CORRUPTIONS?

through her (*Val.* 27; cf. Irenaeus *Haer.* 1.7.2), urging instead that he came *from* Mary so that he was fully human (cf. *Haer.* 5.1.2).[34]

Yet, while it is true that Irenaeus wished to highlight the true humanity of Jesus, including his true human birth, could this variant have served that purpose? If Valentinus himself could use the longer text, including εκ cου,[35] it appears that he did not see the variant reading being created for that reason. Is the longer text an instance of what someone *wished* it to achieve but failed to do so, or is it a scribal expansion, as Metzger suggested, to balance out the account of a half-poetic text uttered by an angel? Whatever its origins, it is not a definite case of an "orthodox corruption."

Jesus as Christ at His Baptism

The next few variant readings relate to accounts of Jesus' baptism, which is highly significant because a number of "separationist" Christologies focused on that moment as the occasion when the divine Christ entered into the man Jesus. In contrast, the NT accounts say that it was the Holy Spirit who came upon Jesus at that time, as Irenaeus was keen to emphasize (*Haer.* 3.17.1). Ehrman examines the three accounts in the Synoptic Gospels to see if variants bear traces of alterations to the text designed to counter such "separationist" beliefs.[36]

Matthew 3:16

In Matthew's account of Jesus' baptism, the Spirit comes down like a dove επ αυτον, but some MSS read προς αυτον. Ehrman takes this as having been designed to remove any thought that the Spirit "empowered" him and, by using "the still less ambiguous πρός," to make it clear that the Spirit "simply comes 'to' Jesus."[37] Yet, επι was a widely used preposition with a broad semantic range depending on the following case and the noun it governed,[38] so it is often difficult to specify its meaning, and προc

---

34. Ehrman, *Orthodox Corruption*, 163–65.

35. According to Hippolytus, *Haer.* 6.30, cited in Ehrman, *Orthodox Corruption*, 204n104.

36. Ehrman, *Orthodox Corruption*, 165–68.

37. Ehrman, *Orthodox Corruption*, 166.

38. Cf. BDAG, 363–67; GELS, 263–67.

also had a wide range of meaning.[39] Hence, the use of προc instead of επι cannot be cited as a clear case of eradicating one meaning and replacing it with another so that the Spirit "simply comes 'to' Jesus." Both readings required interpretation, and to characterize one as justifying a picture of the Spirit "empowering" Jesus and the other just "coming to" him does not consider the difficulty of assigning a meaning to both variants.

Another variant here is the use of ωcει περιcτεραν to describe the descent of the Spirit rather than ωc περιcτεραν.[40] Since we do not *know* that Matthew was editing Mark as his source, it is uncertain that Matthew substituted ωcει for Mark's ωc. Further, ωc and ωcει were virtually synonymous in the early centuries,[41] although Ehrman states that ωcει is usually "less definite and more hypothetical." The evidence for this is taken from LSJ,[42] but the only evidence cited is when ωcει is used with a verb in the optative or subjunctive mood. That is not the case here, so whoever was responsible for ωcει here might have seen no difference in meaning at all between the two. Hence, the conclusion that Matthew or a later copyist might have been attempting to remove any notion that the Spirit took the actual form of a dove has no firm basis.

Ehrman refers to Irenaeus's description of the Marcosian understanding of the dove's descent (*Haer.* 1.14.6, 1.15.3), Jesus receiving the fullness of deity. He proposes that both Mark 1:11 and Luke 3:22 *could* be read in that way, so the variant reading with ωcει might well have been inserted to subvert this possible interpretation, as ωcει would make the identification of the Spirit with a dove less certain. Yet, considering the uncertainty regarding any difference in meaning between ωc and ωcει, as well as the interpretation of what that difference might have involved in Christology, there is little reason to see the use of ωcει here as an attempt to forestall an unorthodox theological understanding of the significance of Jesus' baptism.

---

39. Cf. BDAG, 873–75; GELS, 588–91.

40. Ehrman, *Orthodox Corruption*, 166–67.

41. BAGD, 905, referred to in Ehrman, *Orthodox Corruption*, 204n115. Cf. BDAG, 1106.

42. Ehrman, *Orthodox Corruption*, 205n116.

ANTI-SEPARATIONIST CORRUPTIONS?

Mark 1:10

Mark's Gospel also has an account of Jesus' baptism, concluding with a heavenly voice proclaiming, cυ ει ο υιος μου ο αγαπητος εν coι ευδοκηca (1:11). Ehrman states that Mark's version of events does little to avoid a gnostic understanding of what transpired, that is, that the divine Christ (in the form of a dove) came down from heaven, entered Jesus, and empowered him for his ministry. Thus, Irenaeus asserted that those who "separate Jesus from the Christ" used Mark's Gospel alone (*Haer.* 3.11.7).[43] The original text was most likely το πνευμα ωc περιcτεραν καταβαινον εις αυτον (1:10), despite its slim MS support (B D f^{13} 2427 *pc*), and not επ αυτον (for εις αυτον), as in most MSS, partly because it is the reading most unlike the parallels in Matt 3:16, Luke 3:22, and John 1:32.[44] In support of this, Ehrman states that the reading εις αυτον occurs "in the earliest and best representatives of the Alexandrian and Western traditions," presumably a reference to B and D, and he goes on to show that επ αυτον occurs in the majority of Byzantine manuscripts. But επ αυτον also occurs in ℵ (Alexandrian), W (Western in this section of Mark), and the Syriac tradition, so the score on MS grounds is fairly even. Ehrman argues that εις αυτον would have been liable to gnostic interpretation, a divine being descending "into" Jesus, but gnostic beliefs focused on the Christ, not the Spirit, entering Jesus. He implies that Matthew and Luke also felt the difficulty and so changed Mark's εις to επι,[45] but since it is not certain that they used Mark, it would be unwise to adopt this line of argument. Indeed, the original meaning of εις αυτον was probably no different from επ αυτον, since in Koine Greek εις can be equivalent to επι, as in Mark 4:5, 8; 11:8; 12:14; and 13:3.[46]

Ehrman argues that the reading επ αυτον in Mark 1:10 probably arose in the second century given its widespread and early attestation, and he suggests that scribes changed εις to επι to subvert gnostic Christology since we know that gnostics appealed especially to Mark's Gospel. However, the MSS supporting επ αυτον are no earlier than the late third century, and we do not know that gnostics used εις in this passage, so copyists might just have substituted επι with the same meaning, but in time επι came to be the dominant reading, even if not original. It is thus

---

43. Ehrman, *Orthodox Corruption*, 165.
44. Ehrman, *Orthodox Corruption*, 165–66. Cf. Collins, *Mark*, 133–34nh.
45. Ehrman, *Orthodox Corruption*, 166.
46. Collins, *Mark*, 160. Cf. BDAG, 289, εἰς 1αγδ; GELS, 196, εἰς 3a.

Scribes, Theology, and Apologetics

not certain that επ αυτον is an "orthodox corruption," even though it is clearly secondary.

Luke 3:22

MS 579 omits the whole of το πνευμα το αγιον cωματικω ειδει, which Ehrman proposes might have been done to undercut a possible gnostic reading of the text—no Spirit descending, so no divine Christ entering Jesus. Perhaps this is a case of "orthodox corruption," but it is still unclear what it achieves.

Jesus Crucified as Christ

In this section Ehrman deals with variants that might have been created to oppose the gnostic belief that the Christ left Jesus prior to his crucifixion, as Irenaeus outlines (*Haer.* 3.17.4) and counters by asserting that the same one who died was both Christ and Son of God (*Haer.* 3.16.9).

Matthew 16:21

Almost immediately after Peter's confession about Jesus, cυ ει ο χριcτοc ο υιοc του θεου του ζωντοc (Matt 16:16), Matthew's Gospel has an account of Jesus speaking to the disciples—ηρξατο ο ιηcουc δεικνυειν . . . οτι δει αυτον . . . και πολλα παθειν . . . και αποκτανθηναι (16:21). Some significant MSS (ℵ* B* sa^mss bo), however, read ιηcουc χριcτοc instead of ο ιηcουc. Ehrman accepts that these MSS offer limited support for this variant, and he notes that the readings in both ℵ* and B* have been corrected later, and since this double title is unusual in Matthew, he argues that it was not original.[47] He also refers to Irenaeus's apparent reference to this passage, where he makes it very clear that "Christ" is the one who suffered.[48] However, it is unclear that this was based on the addition of χριcτοc at this point in Matthew's Gospel. Further, a copyist might well have added χριcτοc out of habit since ιηcουc χριcτοc was a common title for Jesus in early Christian circles, so it could just be the result of "scribal inadvertence."[49] So the variant might not have been connected

---

47. Cf. France, *Matthew*, 630n2.
48. Ehrman, *Orthodox Corruption*, 180, 208n157.
49. Metzger, *Textual Commentary*, 42–43. Hagner maintains that while the fuller

with Irenaeus's concerns at all—although it would have been useful in supporting them—and might simply show an early "tendency to expand with names and titles of Jesus."[50]

Mark 14:65 / Luke 22:64 / Matthew 26:68

Another collection of variant readings center around the account of Jesus' trial. The description of the guards blindfolding Jesus and then saying προφητευcον (Mark 14:65) was clearly meant to portray their joke, asking him to say who hit him (14:65a) since they had heard that he claimed to be a prophet. In Luke 22:64, this account reads more explicitly, προφητευcον τιc εcτιν ο παιcαc cε; and in Matt 26:68, there is an even longer account, προφητευcον ημιν χριcτε τιc εcτιν ο παιcαc cε. Ehrman suggests that the later MSS of Mark and Luke that add χριcτε were emphasizing that it was Christ who experienced this treatment and that this addition was deliberate in order to subvert a gnostic understanding of the crucifixion of Jesus by emphasizing that the divine Christ did not leave the human Jesus when he was crucified.[51] Only a few MSS are cited as adding χριcτε at Luke 22:64 (X 131 g² l) and more at Mark 14:65 (W Δ Θ f^{13} sy^h sa^{mss} bo etc.), but none of these are earlier than the third century and most, much later. But even if they were early readings, it is far from certain that they were intended to score a theological point against the gnostics. Later copyists tended to harmonize their copies to parallel texts, especially in the Gospels (here to Matthew),[52] and there is no proof that these variants had any other origin than an unconscious reference to the "real passion" of Jesus as the Christ.[53] Harmonization to Matthew, then, or a pious multiplication of names for Jesus are just as likely to account for these variants as the suggestion that they were created to promote a particular theological view or to forestall another.

---

reading might have been original, the addition of χριcτοc was probably influenced by the previous verse and pericope (*Matthew 14–28*, 476na). Cf. Luz, *Matthew 8–20*, 380n1; Davies and Allison, *Matthew*, 2:655n10.

50. Nolland, *Matthew*, 684na.

51. Ehrman, *Orthodox Corruption*, 180.

52. Metzger, *Textual Commentary*, 97; Evans, *Mark 8:27—16:20*, 439np; France, *Mark*, 597; Marcus, *Mark 8–16*, 1009; Collins, *Mark*, 969–97nf.

53. Ehrman refers to such almost unconscious "intentionality" (*Orthodox Corruption*, 208n159), but if only done out of habit or piety, it cannot easily be an "orthodox corruption" to oppose Gnosticism.

Scribes, Theology, and Apologetics

Mark 15:34

Toward the end of Mark's account of Jesus' crucifixion, he records Jesus' words in transliterated Aramaic and then Greek, the latter as a citation from Ps 22:1 (21:2 LXX), omitting προϲχεϲ μοι (ο θεοϲ μου ο θεοϲ μου ειϲ τι εγκατελιπεϲ με;).[54] Ehrman suggests that the variants here were intended to subvert the gnostic notion of Jesus being "left behind" by Christ before his death, using the literal sense of the verb εγκαταλειπω ("leave behind") rather than its figurative one ("abandon, forsake").[55]

In order to establish that this interpretation of Jesus' words was current, Ehrman refers to the Gospel of Philip 68,[56] a work known to some church fathers (Epiphanius, *Pan.* 26.13.2), where this verse is cited along with the comment "for it was there that he was divided," where the notion of "division" lends credence to the idea that this gnostic text spoke about the Christ leaving Jesus based on Mark 15:34 (or Matt 27:46). A recent edition of this text translates the passage "for he had departed from that place," which Ehrman takes to be equally applicable to this issue.[57] Other editions also concur with this revised translation.[58] However, the meaning of the text in the Gospel of Philip is unclear, and the context is of little assistance. Certainly, Jesus must be the one who uttered the quoted words "on the cross," but when an explanation is provided ("for he . . .") it is natural to read that as referring to Jesus as the one who spoke ("he . . . he"). Thus, the meaning of this passage in the Gospel of Philip is quite difficult to determine, so it would be unwise to use it as evidence for the existence of this gnostic notion at that point.

The Gospel of Peter has a similar allusion to these words from the cross (frag. 1.19), "My power, my power, why have you left me," which might be a reference to the divine Christ leaving the human Jesus, but it could also be a free paraphrase of Mark 15:34 or the other Gospel texts

---

54. There is a slight change from current texts of the LXX, using ειϲ τι instead of ινα τι, but with no real difference in meaning.

55. Ehrman, *Orthodox Corruption*, 168–71. Cf. Ehrman, "Text of Mark," 147–48; Ehrman, "Text and Transmission," 328–29; Ehrman, *Misquoting*, 172–73; Haines-Eitzen, *Guardians*, 118–19.

56. "*Gospel of Philip* 68" refers to p. 68 of the codex, where the passage occurs on lines 26–29.

57. Isenberg, "Gospel of Philip," 151, quoted in Ehrman, *Orthodox Corruption*, 205n124.

58. Cf. "for he [had] withdrawn from that place" (Layton, *Gnostic Scriptures*, 342 [64.26–27]); "for he had left that place" (Meyer, *Nag Hammadi Scriptures*, 174).

ANTI-SEPARATIONIST CORRUPTIONS?

without appreciable difference in meaning, except that God is now called "my power." The ensuing narrative in the Gospel of Peter ("and having said this, he was taken up") might also be a summary way of referring to Jesus' return to God the Father without being read in an explicitly gnostic manner. The context is of little help in being any more specific, although the citation of this passage by Irenaeus (*Haer.* 1.8.2) regarding the beliefs of the Valentinians certainly refers to an interpretation of this passage that might have been in line with gnostic Christology.

The major variant to which Ehrman draws attention here (ο θεος μου ο θεος μου εις τι ωνειδιςας με;) occurs in a small number of witnesses (D c i k* sy^h; Porphyry).[59] This variant is clearly not original, but it is not easy to account for it, since ονειδιζω normally means "reproach, revile, reprimand."[60] How could it have been included when it is offered as a translation of the Aramaic *sabachthani*, which certainly does not mean "you *reviled* me." Ehrman suggests that, in order to stop anyone drawing a gnostic interpretation of Jesus' cry (εις τι εγκατελιπες με;), which might be taken to imply that the Christ had left Jesus to die on his own, someone substituted ωνειδιςας for εγκατελιπες, now also using the text to show that Jesus had borne the reproach of God as part of bearing the judgment of his people.[61] This interpretation is certainly interesting, both in terms of why εγκατελιπες might have been omitted and also how ωνειδιςας could have served in its place, but it is difficult to see how it would fit the context. If the Christ was to avoid suffering and death, at what point did he leave Jesus? He was at least still present to be addressed from the cross as Jesus suffered.[62]

Further, perhaps there was not as much reason as we might think to omit εγκατελιπες to avoid a gnostic interpretation. The new reading can hardly be accidental, but it need only have been motivated by a feeling of awkwardness at the notion of the Father "abandoning" the Son.[63] So, perhaps substituting ωνειδιςας for εγκατελιπες was an intentional corruption of the NT text, but the reasons for its creation are unclear. On the

---

59. Cf. Wasserman, "Scribal Alterations," 323–24.

60. BDAG, 710; LSJ, 1230.

61. Cf. Marcus, *Mark 8–16*, 1055.

62. Hence, the views of Cerinthus, as cited by Irenaeus (*Haer.* 1.26.1) and Epiphanius (*Haer.* 28.1.5-7), do not quite fit, for it seems they believed that the Christ departed *and then* Jesus suffered. Pace, Haines-Eitzen, *Guardians of Letters*, 182n61.

63. Metzger, *Textual Commentary*, 100; Evans, *Mark 8:27—16:20*, 497nk; France, *Mark*, 649.

other hand, attributing the use of ωνειδιcαc to a doctrine of God treating Jesus with disdain may account for this word being used as a substitute,[64] because ονειδιζω could mean "cause and subject to public humiliation,"[65] perhaps a handy word to use to avoid the idea of God abandoning his Son. In conclusion, the origin of the variant ωνειδιcαc is uncertain.[66] It might have come from someone wishing to forestall the gnostic notion that the Christ abandoned Jesus at his crucifixion, but it could also have been drawn from the context, given the various words used to describe various people's contempt for Jesus at that time: βλαcφημουν (15:29), εμπαιζοντεc (15:31), and ωνειδιζον (15:32).[67]

John 1:36

After the prologue, the first chapter of the Fourth Gospel contains several accounts of people interacting with Jesus in the early stages of his ministry. Among these, John the Baptist is described as standing with two of his disciples and proclaiming about Jesus, ιδε ο αμνοc του θεου. Some MSS, however, insert ο χριcτοc before ο αμνοc του θεου (G 039 124 sy^c etc.). Ehrman proposes that this variant arose when someone wished to emphasize that Christ, not just the human Jesus, would be God's (sacrificial) Lamb, in order to highlight that the one who died on the cross was not just the human Jesus but the one person Jesus Christ.[68]

However, in view of the frequent interchange between the three titles (Jesus, Christ, and Jesus Christ) in the Gospels, including the Fourth Gospel, the case is not a strong one. Indeed, χριcτοc is used twice to refer to Jesus in the immediate context, once by the author (1:17) and once by Andrew (1:41), so it would not be surprising if a copyist made the substitution unconsciously, without having any intention of emphasizing that the Jesus later crucified was also the Christ.

---

64. Cf. Porter and Pitts, *Fundamentals*, 125.
65. *GELS*, 497–98.
66. Collins, *Mark*, 731ng.
67. Wasserman, "Scribal Alterations," 325–26.
68. Ehrman, *Orthodox Corruption*, 180.

ANTI-SEPARATIONIST CORRUPTIONS?

Romans 8:34

In Rom 8 Paul highlights the new life of believers, empowered by the Spirit, as well as their future hope, whatever difficulties their present existence might entail. At 8:34 he refers to χριστος ιησους ο αποθανων, μαλλον δε εγερθεις ος και εστιν εν δεξια του θεου. Some MSS (B D etc.), however, do not have ιησους, and there is an even balance of MSS that support its inclusion or omission.[69] If ιησους were absent, Ehrman argues, this would be a favorable text to support gnostic beliefs about the Christ being exalted to the pleroma without dying (cf. Irenaeus., *Haer.* 3.17.4), although this would need the first part to be a question ("Is Christ the one who died?") and the second a contrasting statement ("No, rather he is the one who was exalted"). Thus, he suggests that ιησους was added later and the question changed into a positive statement, so that "Christ" and "Jesus" were united both in death and exaltation.[70]

The punctuation of this verse is difficult, however, whatever the original reading, but in light of the flow of the argument, God is said to be on the side of believers as the one who justifies them (8:31–33). Then Paul seems to affirm that neither will Christ (Jesus) condemn them, given what he has done for them already as well as his present intercession on their behalf (8:34–35).[71] In this context, the proposal that ιησους was inserted into the first clause to head off a gnostic reading of the passage needs it to be a question, but this cannot be verified in view of the lack of punctuation in early MSS. Further, the fact that Irenaeus used the longer reading of this passage to oppose the gnostics (*Haer.* 3.16.9) is no proof that gnostics used the shorter one. On balance, the proposal is interesting but lacks certainty, and even if ιησους was secondary, it could simply have been a pious addition out of habit.

Later in the verse, εκ νεκρων is inserted after εγερθεις in some MSS (ℵ* ℵ²ᵇ A C Ψ etc.), and Ehrman proposes that this was designed to make it clear that the Christ *did* die, since he came εκ νεκρων, in contrast to gnostics who believed that he was raised/exalted as one event without dying. He also argues that the addition of και after μαλλον δε in

---

69. Ehrman, *Orthodox Corruption*, 177–79. Cf. Metzger, *Textual Commentary*, 458; Dunn, *Romans 1–8*, 497nb; Longenecker, *Romans*, 743.

70. Jewett and Kotansky accept the shorter text as original, noting Ehrman's view as a possibility (*Romans*, 531nd).

71. Cf. Dunn, *Romans 1–8*, 496, 503–4. Jewett and Kotansky do not follow Ehrman's understanding of the text, despite accepting his claims about why "Jesus" was inserted (*Romans*, 530).

certain MSS was meant to show that Christ *did* die *and moreover* (μαλλον δε και) was raised. If it is true, however, that the first point above is not proven, this second suggestion is weakened. If a gnostic reading of the first part of the verse was never an issue and the text affirmed that χριϲτοϲ [ιηϲουϲ] died (ο αποθανων), then the insertion of εκ νεκρων only clarifies by a minor expansion the sense that was already present,[72] thus forming a more common phrase (e.g., 4:24; 6:4, 9; 7:4; 8:11; 10:9).[73] The addition of και only emphasizes what was already implied.[74] Thus, the proposal that these variants were designed to oppose gnostic theology remain unproven, and the last variant is probably just an expanded description of Jesus' resurrection (εγερθειϲ).[75]

2 Corinthians 4:10, 5:15; 1 Corinthians 11:27; Galatians 5:11, 6:17

In 1 Corinthians the apostle Paul was not writing to the church in Corinth for the first time, and it is likely that the letter we know as 2 Corinthians was not the second letter he wrote to them.[76] In 2 Cor 4 Paul is elaborating on his and his companions' weakness in this present life (perhaps implying that this was true of all believers) as he continued his apostolic ministry, a weakness which reflected the weakness of την νεκρωϲιν του ιηϲου. But in some MSS, this reads την νεκρωϲιν του χριϲτου (D^p F G). Ehrman refers to Tertullian (*Res.* 44) mentioning the "death of Jesus Christ" as evidence that Tertullian wished to show that Christ has real flesh like the rest of humankind.[77] But in the same chapter Tertullian also adds "Jesus" to "Christ" in citing 2 Cor 4:6, as in a number of Western MSS (D F G 1739* lat etc.), which implies that the double title was simply an alternative. Similarly, at 2 Cor 5:15 υπερ παντων απεθανεν has χριϲτοϲ as its subject in certain MSS (F G etc.), although this is clearly not original, and other MSS include the even fuller title "the Lord Jesus Christ." Further, when writing about the Lord's Supper in 1 Cor 11:27, some MSS (A etc.) read του ϲωματοϲ και του αιματοϲ του χριϲτου rather than the original reading του ϲωματοϲ και του αιματοϲ του κυριου. When

---

72. Longenecker, *Romans*, 743–44.

73. Dunn, *Romans 1–8*, 497nb.

74. Cranfield suggests that και might have been added "due to assimilation to the following clause" (*Romans*, 438n6).

75. Pace, Jewett and Kotansky, *Romans*, 531nnd-f.

76. Cf. Thrall, *Second Epistle*, 49–74.

77. Ehrman, *Orthodox Corruption*, 208n160.

writing to the churches in Galatia, to the original reading το cκανδαλον του cταυρου (Gal 5:11), some MSS (A C etc.) add του χριcτου.

On the basis of these variants, Ehrman proposes that scribes, wishing to highlight that it was the one person, Jesus Christ, who died, added χριcτοc to these passages in order to support this and thus head off any gnostic interpretation that insisted that only the human Jesus died, not the Christ.[78] He also adds one of an apparent multiplicity of such examples, where Paul, in describing his own ministry, makes the metaphorical statement that he bore "the marks of Jesus" (τα cτιγματα του ιηcου) in his own body (Gal 6:17), presumably referring to his sufferings being like the marks of Jesus' own death, so closely did the apostle identify his ministry with the Lord whom he served. Some MSS, however, refer to τα cτιγματα του χριcτου (P Ψ etc.), or even more elaborately τα cτιγματα του κυριου (ημων) ιηcου χριcτου (ℵ D* F G it).[79]

However, the suggestion as to the motive, however unconscious, of the persons responsible for those readings is open to question. The addition of "Christ" to such texts might simply have been the result of piety, common usage, or conformity to previous titles, with a reader or copyist seeing little distinction between the original text and the newly created one with the addition of "Christ," even in the fuller "Lord Jesus Christ." In 2 Cor 4, for example, Paul himself had already spoken of "the glory of Christ" (4:4), "Jesus Christ (as) Lord" (4:5), and "the face of Christ," and later mentioned "the Lord Jesus" (4:14) and "Jesus" (4:14); so, clearly Paul referred to Jesus in various ways, including when mentioning his death and resurrection.[80] In Gal 6:12 there is mention of "the cross *of Christ*," so a copyist familiar with this kind of phraseology might well have added του χριcτου in 5:11, and this could have been true at 6:17 as well.[81] Further, none of the MSS that include these readings are early, all being from the fourth century onwards when the Empire was more "Christian" in tone so such changes could have been created more easily. So, these additions need not have sprung from a desire to affirm that "the Christ" died in opposition to gnostic thought, but simply from a habit of

---

78. Ehrman, *Orthodox Corruption*, 181.

79. Ehrman, *Orthodox Corruption*, 208n162.

80. Furnish notes that in Paul's letters he commonly used the fuller title when referring to Jesus' death (e.g., 2 Cor 1:5) and resurrection (e.g., Rom 6:3, 1 Cor 2:2, Gal 3:1) (*II Corinthians*, 256).

81. Metzger refers to various "edifying" readings in MSS (*Textual Commentary*, 530). Cf. Longenecker, *Galatians*, 286ng.

referring to Jesus more fully or from similar language in the immediate or broader context of Paul's letters.

Hebrews 1:3

In the opening paragraph of the Letter to the Hebrews, the author offers an exalted description of Jesus as the Son of God. In 1:3, just before asserting that καθαρισμον των αμαρτιων ποιησαμενος, some MSS add δι εαυτου. Among the MSS with this variant, P⁴⁶ (δι αυτου) is early and 1739 is quite significant, and Western and Byzantine families of MSS are also represented (D *Byz* a b sy co). MSS without δι εαυτου have αυτου, which is usually taken with the previous phrase—so, τω ρηματι της δυναμεως αυτου. Ehrman takes the reading with δι [ε]αυτου as original, suggesting that it was omitted because it might have been understood to imply that Jesus accomplished καθαρισμον των αμαρτιων "by his own effort," and this could then be understood to imply that "the divine element had left him prior to its consummation." Thus, by copyists omitting the offending phrase, and leaving the bare αυτου, which would be taken with the previous line, such a gnostic interpretation could be averted.[82]

First, however, the issue of which reading is original is not easily resolved. The argument based on meter put forward by Zuntz is not a strong one,[83] since it is not certain that this section was meant to adhere to classical meter. Nor is it clear that the section is making use of a text prior to this letter being written. On the other hand, the inclusion of αυτου at the end of the previous line would be an adequate translation of an analogous Hebrew phrase like "mountain of his holiness" (Pss 48:1, 99:9) meaning "his holy mountain,"[84] so the sense of the reading without δι εαυτου would be "his word of power" or "his powerful word." Others suggest that it is more likely that δι εαυτου was added to "clarify the meaning" or "enhance the force" of the middle voice participle ποιησαμενος.[85] Finally, the MS evidence of Codex Dᵖ is a little complicated because, according to NA²⁸, the original δι αυτου (D*) was corrected to αυτου (D¹) and then later to δι εαυτου (D²). Nonetheless, whichever reading

---

82. Ehrman, *Orthodox Corruption*, 176–77.

83. Zuntz, *Text*, 43–45.

84. Cf., for example, εξ ορους αγιου αυτου (Ps 3:5).

85. Metzger, *Textual Commentary*, 592; Attridge, *Hebrews*, 35n8; Lane, *Hebrews 1–8*, 5nf.

was original at this point in the text, it would be difficult to derive the proposed gnostic meaning attached to δι εαυτου, whereby Jesus accomplished καθαρισμον των αμαρτιων by himself without divine assistance, so it is hard to see anyone wishing to avoid that meaning by removing δι εαυτου. On balance, the reconstructed intention for someone removing it to hinder a gnostic reading of the text is unlikely.

Hebrews 2:9

In an interpretive exegesis of much of Ps 8:4–6, the author of Hebrews refers to Jesus as human and fulfilling the words of the psalm, so δοξη και τιμη εσταφανωμενον (2:9; cf. 2:7; Ps 8:6 LXX). Most MSS go on to relate that the purpose of this was οπως χαριτι θεου υπερ παντος γευςηται θανατου, but some MSS read χωρις θεου instead of χαριτι θεου. The reading χωρις θεου is cited as occurring in only three Greek MSS, two from the tenth century (0243 1739*) and one from the eleventh but later corrected (424$^{c\,vid}$).[86] Ehrman refers to the late minuscule 1739 having been copied from a fourth century MS, although the claim that its text is at least as old as P[46] is exaggerated. A better date would be late in the fourth century.[87] However, Origen referred to these two readings in NT MSS (*Comm. Jo.* 1.35 (40), 28.18 (14), 32.28),[88] so both must have been current in the first half of the third century. Ehrman also alludes to χωρις θεου occurring in MSS known to Ambrose and Jerome and cited by writers up until the eleventh century, as well as the Latin (vg^G) and the Syriac Peshitta.[89] On the whole, however, although it was known from the third century, the reading χωρις θεου virtually faded out of existence. Yet, since it is the harder reading by far, due to its uncertain and possibly difficult meaning, Ehrman concludes that it is more likely to have been original, with χαριτι θεου secondary despite having far superior MS attestation.[90]

86. Ehrman, *Orthodox Corruption*, 171–76. Cf. Ehrman, "Text and Interpretation," 320–24; Ehrman, "Text and Transmission," 327–28; Ehrman, *Misquoting*, 144–48, 171–72.

87. Zuntz, *Text*, 69, cited in Ehrman, *Orthodox Corruption*, 206n133. Ehrman cites Zuntz in support of his opinion, but a date "toward the close of the fourth century" is more likely (Metzger and Ehrman, *Text*, 91). Cf. Metzger, *Manuscripts*, 112–13.

88. Ehrman, *Orthodox Corruption*, 206n134. Cf. Donaldson, "Explicit References," 99, 531–32; see also 533–36 for other authors with similar readings.

89. Parker notes the versional MSS and early church writers supporting this reading (*Introduction*, 277–78).

90. Elliott suggests that χωρις was the original reading based largely on the style

Scribes, Theology, and Apologetics

Assuming that χωρις θεου was original, Ehrman asks whether the substitution of χαριτι θεου for χωρις θεου was deliberate, arguing that explanations of the secondary reading, whichever one it is taken to be, as a simple scribal blunder are unlikely because the meanings of the two readings are so different. However, scribes *did* make mistakes, sometimes without noticing or correcting them, and this could be a case in point. The fact that a number of papyri contain an α–ω vowel exchange certainly makes this possible (χωρις–χαρις).[91] Nevertheless, Ehrman assumes that the change must have been deliberate.

He goes on to suggest that, since χαρις is used more frequently than χωρις in the NT, the direction of change is more likely to have been from χωρις to χαριτι. But the person first responsible might not have had a complete NT or been overly familiar with all of it, and such word statistics prove little anyway. Ehrman also proposes that, since χωρις θεου is the "harder" reading, this would support χωρις being original and χαριτι θεου secondary. But the "typical" change from a difficult reading to an easy one does not always apply because "harder" readings are sometimes just too hard.

Ehrman refers to the suggestion that someone, perhaps a copyist, had 1 Cor 15:27 in mind (παντα υποτετακται ... εκτος του υποταξαντος αυτω τα παντα) and therefore wished to make the same kind of exception statement here—all things *except for* God (χωρις θεου) were subjected to Christ—and so put this in the margin of a MS. It then found its way into the text of a MS of Hebrews at a later date.[92] Although he disagrees with this suggestion and says that a copyist with 1 Cor 15:27 in mind would have used εκτος, not χωρις, this is not necessarily the case. Who can say what a copyist *would* have written? Still, it is a rather complicated solution, as he notes, despite Paul alluding to Ps 8:6 in that very passage (1 Cor 15:27–28). Word statistics and "usual" constructions in such a short text as Hebrews are inconclusive here, with only four uses of χαρις in Hebrews.[93]

---

of Hebrews and proposed links with Jesus' words about being abandoned by God (Ps 22:1), and he suggests that copyists "found the idea that Jesus was 'without God' puzzling" ("Apart from God").

91. Gignac, *Grammar*, 1:286–89.

92. Cf. Metzger, *Textual Commentary*, 594; Bruce, *Hebrews*, 70–71; Attridge, *Hebrews*, 76–77; Lane, *Hebrews 1–8*, 43ng.

93. *Pace* Elliott, "Epistle," 72–74, esp. 74.

ANTI-SEPARATIONIST CORRUPTIONS?

The argument that χωρις θεου is consistent with the theology of the letter is also unpersuasive. Since the presentation of Jesus' fully human death in Hebrews as emphasizing that he died a "shameful death, totally removed from the realm whence he came, the realm of God," and hence "apart from God," does not fit the context of the letter. Although Ehrman appeals to Jesus' "loud cries and tears" (5:7) and his scorning the "shame" of death (12:2), as well as reading 13:12 as referring to Jesus' death (he suffered εξω της πυλης) "in the realm of shame and reproach" apart from God's favor,[94] these do not support that interpretation. With regard to 13:12, for example, the author's description of Jesus' death "outside the gate" is followed by an exhortation for his readers to be willing to follow him "outside the camp" (εξω της παρεμβολης, 13:13), which is not an exhortation to leave the realm of God's favor but to be willing to sever their ties with official Judaism, if need be, "bearing the disgrace he bore" from that same source. Nor does this usage of χωρις fit with its use in the Septuagint,[95] although it could match some uses in the NT.[96] In support of seeing χωρις θεου as a description of death "apart from God," Elliott refers to Sheol as "a realm outside God's control," appealing to Isa 38:18 and Ps 6:5,[97] and thus as background to Jesus being "apart from God" in his death. Indeed, these texts do refer to those in Sheol as distant from the presence of God and to this extent might provide a parallel. His appeal to Jesus' cry of dereliction (e.g., Matt 27:46) citing Ps 22:1 as what might have been in mind here is also possible, since χωρις (with a noun in the genitive) can refer to being "separated from someone" without implying hostility or the like (Eph 2:12; John 15:5; 1 Cor 4:8, 11:11; Heb 11:40).

However, it is also possible that the author was focusing on the "gracious" help provided for Jesus to endure το παθημα του θανατου, just as the readers are later urged to "approach the throne of grace [χαρις]" to find "mercy and grace [χαρις]" to help in their time of need (4:16). Their model is Christ who pursued the path of suffering and was finally vindicated (4:14; cf. 2:5–9), so he can sympathize with them in their suffering and give them hope that their suffering is not the end of the story. This might, then, be an example of the author's common practice of providing a hint of a theme and enlarging on it later in the letter. If so, the

---

94. Ehrman, *Orthodox Corruption*, 175, 207n141.
95. *GELS*, 740, χωρίς, where the meanings are (1) "besides, in addition to" and (2) "except, not including."
96. BDAG, 1095, χωρίς 2aα.
97. Elliott, "Epistle," 73.

author might well have had the similar idea in mind in 2:9, with Jesus himself enabled to tread the path of suffering with determination empowered "by the grace of God" (χαριτι θεου) prior to being δοξη και τιμη εστεφανωμενον. Or perhaps the grace (kindness) of God that made this way of salvation possible was in mind. Hence, while it is true that Jesus' death is presented as fully human (5:7–8; 2:11, 14; 12:3), it is difficult to accept that χωρις θεου was original. The context certainly highlights Jesus' truly human death (2:5–15), along with that being the basis for the author's appeal to the readers to see in Jesus their sympathetic high priest (2:17–18), but the conclusion that, because of this focus on his true humanity, his death was "apart from God" is unwarranted. The quotation from Ps 22:22 in Heb 2:12 does not prove that Jesus' words from that same psalm (22:1) were in mind in χωρις θεου here, with Jesus speaking about God forsaking him.[98]

Thus, the reading χωρις θεου does not enjoy the strong support it is said to have, and the argument that, since the majority reading (χαριτι θεου) was early, it must have been created to counter a gnostic reading of this text does not follow. Gnostics might have been able to take "apart from God" to mean "abandoned by the divine being who had sustained him during his ministry," and it is possible that some did so, but this does not prove that χωρις θεου was original, nor that it was removed to subvert a gnostic interpretation of this text. It is just as likely that an inattentive copyist wrongly inserted χωρις for χαριτι,[99] and that reading then left its mark on later MSS, the similarity of the words accounting for the substitution. So, untidy majuscule script, ΧΩΡΙC and ΧΑΡΙΤΙ, could have occasioned the change. Further, Hartog finds no patristic evidence that this variant was used for the suggested purpose.[100] Hence, neither internal nor external evidence necessitates taking χωρις θεου to be original, and it is more likely that in view of its overwhelming MS support χαριτι θεου is original,[101] rather than a secondary reading designed to avoid χωρις θεου being used to support gnostic theology.

---

98. Pace Ehrman, *Orthodox Corruption*, 175, 207n143.

99. Cf. Miller, "Least Orthodox Reading," 77–81.

100. Hartog, "Hebrews 2:9." Miller refers to a thesis by Krista Miller claiming to show that the patristic evidence weighs in favor of χαριτι θεου (Miller, "Patristic Evidence," referred to in Miller, "Least Orthodox Reading," 79n104).

101. Koester, *Hebrews*, 217–18.

Hebrews 9:26

At the heart of the central doctrinal section of the Letter to the Hebrews there is a depiction of Jesus' death as the fulfilment of OT sacrifices. In 9:26, instead of the original παθειν (πασχω) to describe Christ's death, some MSS use αποθανειν (αποθνῃσκω), and Ehrman proposes that the use of αποθανειν was designed to make it clear that Christ did not just "suffer" but "died" in order to hinder a gnostic interpretation of this text in which "the Christ" did not die.[102]

The proposed distinction is unlikely, however, because the writer of Hebrews frequently uses πασχω elsewhere to refer to Jesus' death, so readers would assume that πασχω referred to Jesus' death even though it could mean suffering more generally.[103] Thus, αποθανειν might not carry the rhetorical flourish that the author intended, but nor does it necessarily convey a different meaning. Further, the constant mention of death in the context—blood (9:7, 12–14, 18–19, 21–22, 25), death (απο νεκρων εργων, 9:14), sacrifices (θυςιαις, 9:23), the metaphor of a will (διαθηκη, 9:16, 17), as well as the mention of "his own blood" (του ιδιου αιματος, 9:12; το αιμα του χριστου, 9:14), his death (θανατου, 9:15, 16), his death as a sacrifice (δια θυςιας αυτου, 9:26), the allusion to humankind having to die (αποθανειν) once (9:27), and then the conclusion, ουτως και ο χριστος απαξ προςενεχθεις (9:28)—would make such a minor change of little consequence. It is also notable that in this one chapter "Christ" is the only way that Jesus is referred to (9:11, 14, 15, 24, 26, 28), and this is followed by "the body of Jesus Christ" (10:10) and "the blood of Jesus" (10:19). It is unlikely, then, that a reader would have perceived αποθανειν to mean anything different from the original παθειν in this context, so it is also improbable that anyone would have made this change to achieve an anti-gnostic interpretation. Rather, the variant is easily understood as a simple alternative by an inattentive scribe.

1 Peter 2:21, 3:18, 4:1

In these passages in 1 Peter, references to Jesus' suffering using πασχω have secondary variant readings using αποθνῃσκω. So, χριστος επαθεν is replaced by χριστος απεθανεν in 2:21 (P⁸¹ ℵ Ψ syᵖ). Also, there are a

---

102. Ehrman, *Orthodox Corruption*, 181–82.
103. Lane, *Hebrews 9–13*, 233nll. Cf. BDAG, 785, πάσχω 3aα.

number of variant readings for χριστος . . . επαθεν at 3:18, with απεθανεν replacing επαθεν as one of the main variants (P⁷² ℵ* ℵ² A C*ᵛⁱᵈ C² syᵖ saᵐˢˢ). In 4:1 ℵ* has the SR χριστου . . . αποθανοντος instead of the original text χριστου . . . παθοντος. Ehrman points out that, while there is some variation in the MSS when πασχω refers to Christ, there is no such variation when it is used to describe the suffering of believers, and on this basis he suggests that this early variation was designed to counteract any possibility of a gnostic reading of these texts by highlighting that the (divine) Christ did not just *suffer* but *died*.[104] We have seen above, however, that while πασχω could mean "suffer" it was commonly used to refer to Jesus' death more generally, so the distinction does not really hold.

Further, while πασχω *can* just refer to suffering,[105] in 1 Peter πασχω was probably used to refer to Jesus' death because Peter wished to draw a parallel between his death and the readers' probable coming suffering (5:10).[106] So, in 2:21 the way Christ suffered was to be an example (υπογραμμος) for them, with their sufferings mentioned in 2:19, 20, and 23. In 3:18 Christ's suffering for their sins is mentioned in the context of their suffering for what is "right" (3:14) or "good" (3:17; cf. 4:15, 19), again hailing Christ's willingness to suffer as an example for them to emulate. In 4:1 Christ's sufferings are to inspire the readers to have την αυτην εννοιαν (4:1). With this purpose in mind, the author highlights the physical suffering of Christ that he had in mind with this verb by the addition of cαρχι (3:18, 4:1), and indeed Christ dying (θανατωθεις, 3:18). It seems clear, then, that the verb πασχω was used to describe Christ's physical sufferings and death to make a link with the readers' potential sufferings, with his death clearly in view considering the firm reading θανατωθεις in 3:18.

Further, the use of αποθνησκω for πασχω to refer to Christ's death in the three cited instances is not a stark contrast with the lack of variants for πασχω for believers suffering because in all but two cases referring to believers (in 2:19–20, 23; 3:14, 17; 4:15, 19; but not in 4:1, 5:10) the verb is in the present tense, such as πασχων (2:19), which was unlikely to be altered into a present tense form of αποθνησκω, unlike the aorist forms referring to Christ—επαθεν (2:21, 3:18) and παθοντος (4:1). Hence, the accidental use of an aorist form of αποθνησκω (απεθανον, etc.) instead of

---

104. Ehrman, *Orthodox Corruption*, 181–82.
105. BDAG, 785–86; GELS, 538.
106. Achtemeier, *1 Peter*, 239n1; Elliott, *I Peter*, 524–25, 640, 711–12.

an aorist form of πασχω (επαθον, etc.), when the meaning is unchanged, is the likely reason for the occurrence of these variants,[107] rather than an intention to distinguish between the sufferings of believers and the death of Christ or to make sure that Christ was said to have died to counter gnostic theology. It may be that other passages with similar wording, such as 1 Cor 15:3 and Rom 5:8, were in the mind of a copyist who made this change,[108] but this is uncertain. Thus, there are more probable reasons to account for these variants than their being anti-gnostic in design,[109] especially in view of the author's clear preference for πασχω to refer to Jesus' death in relation to the readers' imminent danger of suffering, as well as the similar verb forms.[110]

1 John 1:7

In the opening section of his "first" letter, John urged his readers to live ("walk") εν τω φωτι, and he stated that one of the results of that would be that το αιμα ιησου του υιου αυτου καθαριζει ημας απο πασης αμαρτιας (1:7). The MS support for this reading clearly shows that it was original, but some versional MSS (t w z vg^(cl,ww) sy^(h**)) and almost the entire Byzantine tradition read το αιμα ιησου χριστου rather than το αιμα ιησου. There are also two other poorly attested variants. Ehrman takes this as another example of copyists inserting the word "Christ" to ensure that any gnostic notion that the human Jesus died (but the divine Christ did not) could not be read from this text.[111]

This is unlikely, however, in view of the double title "Jesus Christ" in the immediate context—in 1:3 (του υιου αυτου ιησου χριστου) and 2:1 (ιησουν χριστον δικαιον), as well as him being the ιλασμος περι των αμαρτιων of the whole world (2:2), surely linked to the mention of his "blood" (1:7). Thus, a reader could hardly be supposed to notice any difference, given the context, so a copyist could not expect to make a difference by adding χριστου in 1:7. It is unlikely, then, that the addition

---

107. Michaels argues that the variant απεθανεν is probably an accommodation to more common usage in the early church (cf. John 11:5–51; Rom 5:6–8, 14:15; 1 Cor 5:14–15; 1 Thess 5:10) (*1 Peter*, 134nf; cf. 195na). Cf. Achtemeier, *1 Peter*, 189n9, 239n1.

108. Wachtel, "Towards a Redefinition," 109–12.

109. Wachtel, "Towards a Redefinition," 112.

110. Metzger, *Textual Commentary*, 622–23.

111. Ehrman, *Orthodox Corruption*, 179–80.

of χριστου was motivated by theological intentions, with either habit or piety the more likely cause of this later reading.

Jesus Christ Raised from the Dead

In this section Ehrman alludes to the gnostic belief that the divine Christ left the human Jesus before he died and notes that, as well as the orthodox group emphasizing that "Christ" died, it would have been consistent also to highlight that Christ or Jesus Christ, not just Jesus, was raised *from the dead*—for then he must have *died* beforehand—which would entail his unity as divine and human. In relation to this issue, Irenaeus provides a description of the gnostic view and a statement of the "orthodox" doctrine (*Haer.* 1.30:13, 3.16.9).

Matthew 28:7

The final chapter of Matthew's Gospel recounts events surrounding Jesus' resurrection and his appearances to his disciples. In 28:7 angels tell the women to inform the disciples that ηγερθη απο των νεκρων, but some MSS (D 565 it sy^s) lack απο των νεκρων.[112] Ehrman acknowledges that the MS support for the shorter text is minimal, but he doubts that απο των νεκρων was omitted because a copyist was just following the wording of 28:6 where it is absent after ηγερθη.[113] Despite the minimal MS support, he argues that the shorter reading was original and orthodox copyists inserted απο των νεκρων to make sure that the text would imply that the Christ had been raised *from the dead*.

However, there is no mention of χριστος in Matt 28, the last reference to "Christ" being in 27:22, so a gnostic adherent could have argued that the divine Christ was not in view here and the person responsible for inserting απο των νεκρων would have achieved very little in opposing Gnosticism and would then be unlikely to have done so for that reason. Hence, without a feasible rationale, the MS evidence should carry the weight of any textual conclusion, so that απο των νεκρων was probably original and the proposal regarding the original text and the reason for the suggested addition are both unlikely.

---

112. Ehrman also cites the support of Origen for this reading (*Orthodox Corruption*, 186).

113. Pace Metzger, *Textual Commentary*, 59–60; Hagner, *Matthew 14–28*, 867nf.

Matthew 28:17

In the closing section of Matthew's Gospel, there is an account of Jesus meeting his disciples on a mountain in Galilee, και ιδοντες αυτον προσεκυνησαν. Since there is no explicit mention of who "they worshipped"—God or the risen Jesus—it has been suggested that the MSS that add the secondary readings αυτω or αυτον betray a desire to make sure that the text specifies that Jesus was an object of worship and hence divine.[114] Yet, since προσκυνεω includes the idea of prostrating oneself before someone (e.g., Matt 4:9),[115] the context would surely imply that they "worshipped" Jesus whom they saw (αυτον), so the alleged ambiguity does not really exist and a copyist is unlikely to have inserted αυτον or αυτω in order to remove it. Further, Jesus is mentioned in v. 16 and is the natural antecedent to αυτον in v. 17, as well as the implied object of προσεκυνησαν. Moreover, the verb προσκυνεω was previously used to describe the disciples' response to Jesus (14:33), and his divine status is made clear in the following passage by linking him with the Father and the Holy Spirit (28:19). So, the proposed theological intention for the variant readings is unlikely, and the variants are more easily explained as expansions of the implied meaning of the text, possibly wishing to add an object to the verb or just to complete an abbreviated phrase.

Mark 16

The final chapter of Mark's Gospel presents a number of challenges for the textual critic, and there have been various proposals as to whether any of the various "endings" in the MSS (after 16:8) are original. If not, did the Gospel originally finish at 16:8 or did it continue on with the last part having been lost at an early stage? In 16:7, the angelic messengers are said to have told the women to inform the disciples that προαγει υμας εις την γαλιλαιαν, but a few MSS (f^1 pc) add ηγερθη απο νεκρων και ιδου before that. Ehrman proposes that this has been added to make it clear that Jesus is the one who has been raised απο νεκρων, an expression occurring nowhere else in Mark, so that someone felt that it needed to be emphasized here.[116] Yet, the addition might also be an echo of earlier

---

114. Ehrman, *Orthodox Corruption*, 186.
115. BDAG, 882–83; *GELS*, 596.
116. Ehrman, *Orthodox Corruption*, 185–86.

passion and resurrection references, such as οταν ο υιος του ανθρωπου εκ νεκρων αναστη (Mark 9:9),[117] which is reechoed in the following note that the disciples wondered τι εστιν το εκ νεκρων αναστηναι (9:10). Thus, Mark did mention Jesus' resurrection "from the dead" elsewhere, despite the slightly different phraseology (εκ νεκρων), so it is unlikely that someone would have felt the need to include it here for emphasis.

A similar suggestion has been made with regard to 16:19 in the "longer ending." Most MSS that include this ending refer to ο . . . κυριος ιησους being taken up to heaven and sitting at God's right hand. Ehrman points out, however, that many MSS do not include ιησους, thus only referring to ο . . . κυριος and avoiding any possible distinction between Jesus and Christ. Also, a few MSS read ιησους χριστος as the ascending one. He infers, then, that both later readings were meant to bolster the view that Jesus was not only human but also divine by simply calling him κυριος (omitting ιησους) or by adding χριστος. The first suggestion is rather subtle, and it is unlikely that a reader or copyist in antiquity would have appreciated the distinction. Moreover, the use of κυριος on its own is probably a later development.[118] The second suggestion is possible, but it is also possible that habit, piety, or simple inattention was the cause of such a minor change.

It is appropriate at this point to discuss briefly the ending of Mark's Gospel in general.[119] Ehrman notes that the various endings to Mark in the MSS are all suspect and probably not original, so all we have of the original Gospel is up to the end of 16:8. He suggests that "scribes thought the ending was too abrupt," so they concocted endings to round it off, and others agree that the "longer ending" was composed in the second century, drawing on material in Matthew, Luke, and John, and adding other material as well.[120] Irenaeus (d. AD 202) referred to this longer ending (*Haer.* 3.10.5), so it clearly originated early on. Ehrman mentions the view that "the last page" was lost, but he maintains that Mark intended to end his Gospel at 16:8 with a high degree of subtlety and irony, shocking the reader into wondering what happened next.

---

117. Evans, *Mark 8:27—16:20*, 530ne.

118. Metzger, *Textual Commentary*, 107.

119. Ehrman, *Misquoting*, 65-68. Cf. Metzger, *Textual Commentary*, 102-7; Evans, *Mark 8:27—16:20*, 540-51; France, *Mark*, 685-88; Collins, *Mark*, 802-18; Marcus, *Mark 8-16*, 1088-96.

120. Head, "Early Text," 110-11.

ANTI-SEPARATIONIST CORRUPTIONS?

There are probably two factors, however, that influenced how the Gospel of Mark was passed on, including its latter portion: (1) "improvements" to the text, whether historical or theological; and (2) harmonization to the other Gospels.[121] In my view, the interpretations which accept 16:8 as the intended ending are improbable in view of the final γαρ,[122] so it is most likely that the last column(s) of a roll or last page(s) of a codex was (were) lost before many copies were made, and certain people composed endings later to finish the Gospel "properly."[123] Nevertheless, rounding off a perceived truncated Gospel would surely count as a "corruption," albeit not necessarily "orthodox," so if this is correct, it is a classic instance of material inserted not only to complete the narrative but also, in the case of the longer ending, to make Mark's Gospel fit a certain theological view that held with snake handling and drinking poison. The Freer Logion in Codex W adds another theologized dimension.[124] Parker provides a balanced and detailed discussion of the originality of the various endings and their MS support,[125] although I do not agree that 16:8 was the intended ending. Nevertheless, he rightly asserts that the intermediate ending comes from "a later and orotund theologian" and that the long ending has "a determined polemical slant."[126] In chapter 7, we review Kannaday's suggestion that the endings were designed to serve apologetic interests.

Acts 3:13

In Luke's account of a speech by the apostle Peter to those who had seen a crippled man healed, Peter assured them that God εδοξαcεν τον παιδα αυτου ιηcουν (3:13), probably with Jesus' resurrection and exaltation in mind as the mode of that glorification (3:15; cf. 2:32-33). Ehrman alludes to D and some Ethiopic MSS adding χριcτοc to form the double

---

121. Head, "Early Text," 111.

122. *Pace* Iverson, who argues that it is illegitimate to argue for intentional or accidental ending theories and that the issue is not resolved by the occurrence of γαρ at the end of 16:8 (Iverson, "Further Word"). Croy argues that Mark's Gospel lost *both* its original ending *and* its beginning (Croy, *Mutilation*). Cf. Focant, "Silence"; Moore, "Enigmatic Endings."

123. Metzger, *Textual Commentary*, 102-6, esp. 105n7. Cf. Elliott, "Last Twelve Verses," 80-102.

124. Cf. Parker, *Introduction*, 341-42.

125. Parker, *Living Text*, 124-47.

126. Parker, *Living Text*, 138, 140-41. Cf. Metzger and Ehrman, *Text*, 322-26.

title "Jesus Christ," and he proposes that this was intended to make it clear that God had glorified "Jesus Christ," not just "Jesus," by raising him εκ νεκρων (3:15).[127] He suggests that such a variation did not occur in 2:32 because 2:31 mentioned της αναστησεως του χριστου, so it was not needed.[128] On the other hand, it might show that copyists were not preoccupied with this issue.

Still, Ehrman's proposal is that this would then be a theologically motivated variant to oppose gnostic Christology and support "orthodox" Christology—Christ was raised, so he had also died. However, χριστος could also have been added out of habit or piety. Ehrman suggests that although it might have felt "natural" to make the addition, that was only because of the passage of time—D from the fifth century and the Ethiopic MSS were also late.[129] But if so, the addition was not made at a time when Gnosticism was a live option. Indeed, D regularly uses the double title in Acts,[130] showing not only the secondary nature of the variant but that this was a "habit" of the copyist or someone at an earlier stage, so the proposal may be set aside as doubtful.

Acts 4:33

In a similar way, the original description of the apostles' testimony της αναστασεως του κυριου ιησου (Acts 4:33) is extended by the addition of χριστου in slightly different places in certain MSS as an epithet to κυριου, sometimes with ημων.[131] Ehrman notes that the variant with χριστου added is clearly secondary,[132] but it does not follow that it must have been added in order to oppose gnostic Christology, as Ehrman suggests. Indeed, this addition was made in a number of other MSS, including ℵ, A, and 1739, but none of these are earlier than the fourth century. Habit or piety, then, might just as easily have been the reason for its inclusion, and no MS prior to the fourth century has it, so it is unlikely that χριστου was added to make the proposed theological point in the early centuries of the church.

---

127. Ehrman, *Orthodox Corruption*, 183.
128. Ehrman, *Orthodox Corruption*, 209n168.
129. Ehrman, *Orthodox Corruption*, 209n171.
130. Bruce, *Acts*, 111, 140.
131. Metzger, *Textual Commentary*, 283–84.
132. Ehrman, *Orthodox Corruption*, 183.

ANTI-SEPARATIONIST CORRUPTIONS?

Acts 13:32-33

Luke reports that during Paul's address to the members of the synagogue in Pisidian Antioch, he affirmed that God had at last fulfilled his promises, "having raised Jesus" (αναςτας ιηcουν) in accordance with the words of Ps 2:7 (13:33). Bezae adds the word χριςτον making the whole phrase τον κυριον ιηcουν χριςτον. Ehrman argues that this highlights that "Christ" was raised and hence that the variant reading arose to counter the insistence of a form of Gnosticism according to which Jesus only *became* Christ at his resurrection—he was already Christ when he was raised. Further, the gnostic belief that Christ returned to the pleroma before Jesus' death was also subverted. Perhaps the mention of the Lord's χριςτος in Ps 2:2 provided some feasibility for the change.[133]

This reading in D is clearly secondary, since it is the only MS including it, while other MSS (614 sy[h**] (mae)) read τον κυριον ημων ιηcουν. If the point depends on the insertion of χριςτον, this reading is another SR in D, so it might not have been intentional. Further, the reference in D to the quotation being from the "first" psalm (not the "second"), as well as the addition of much of Ps 2:8 at the end, add to the colorful and quirky nature of this variant in D. Moreover, there is no evidence that this reading existed in the second and third centuries, which implies that it was probably not created to oppose separationist or gnostic Christology. Further, there are other feasible explanations for this variant in D, such as piety or custom. Nor does τον κυριον ημων ιηcουν accord with the proposal, since it does not include an explicit reference to "Christ." Thus, this proposal regarding these two readings is only one possibility among many, but an unlikely one because the MSS supporting it are quite late—D (V AD), 614 (XIII AD), sy[h**] (VII AD onwards), and the Middle Egyptian (mae) (IV-VI AD).

Romans 8:10-11

The opening section of Rom 8 is an exposition of what life is, and should be, for those who are εν πνευματι (8:9). In 8:10 Paul mentions χριςτος εν υμιν and then alludes to the presence of το πνευμα του εγειραντος τον ιηcουν εκ νεκρων in the life of the believer (8:11). Ehrman suggests that this could be taken to support a gnostic theology, with a distinction

---

133. Ehrman, *Orthodox Corruption*, 183-84, 209n172.

being made between the Christ and Jesus, although Paul goes on in 8:11 to refer to God again as ο εγειρας χριστον εκ νεκρων, as Irenaeus observed (*Haer.* 3.16.9). Ehrman also alludes to the fact that the Valentinians, as well as other witnesses, had the reading χριστος, not ο χριστος, at 8:11, and he suggests that they might have taken this as a personal name, not a title for "the Christ," whom they deemed not to have been raised from the dead.[134] However, many MSS lack the article, and this is unlikely to be significant since the presence or absence of the article in Greek did not have this significance and an anarthrous noun is not necessarily indefinite.[135] It is also unlikely that early orthodox copyists inserted the article in their MSS, because it is only present in a number of late MSS. Ehrman also proposes that the insertion of ιησουν in 8:11b, in a variety of ways in numerous MSS (ℵ* A C D sy^p etc.), was another attempt to bind "(the) Christ" to Jesus as raised εκ νεκρων in order to ensure that the person of Jesus Christ could not be divided.

While the mention of this passage by some church fathers is significant, it is not a compelling basis for this argument, and the suggestions are unlikely overall. Ehrman refers to Hippolytus (*Noet.* 40) and Tertullian (*Prax.* 28; *Marc.* 5.14),[136] but they make no use of the proposed "corrupted" readings. Hippolytus's argument refers to "the Son" distinct from "the Father," as Tertullian does, and affirms that Christ had a real body, but he makes no mention of this being Christ *and* Jesus. While some of the proposed scenarios may have led to the creation of these readings, factors such as habit or piety are just as likely to have brought them into being.[137]

1 Corinthians 9:1

Paul puts his own example before the Corinthian believers in 1 Cor 9, and he begins by appealing to having seen ιησουν τον κυριον ημων (9:1). Some MSS here read ιησουν χριστον (D^p E K L P sy^p co etc.) or χριστον ιησουν (F G etc.) as the object of Paul's gaze. Ehrman suggests that this twofold title was an attempt to cement the two together in order to

---

134. Ehrman, *Orthodox Corruption*, 184, 209nn173-75.

135. Longenecker notes that some MSS omit the article with ιησουν, probably as a "stylistic improvement" (*Romans*, 677). Cf. Jewett and Kotansky, *Romans*, 475ng.

136. Ehrman, *Orthodox Corruption*, 209-10n176.

137. Cf. Cranfield, *Romans*, 390-91n6; Jewett and Kotansky, *Romans*, 475nng-h; Longenecker, *Romans*, 677-78.

counter any gnostic suggestion that Jesus and Christ were separate persons.[138] Again, in view of the MSS with this reading generally dating from the fourth century onwards, it is not relevant to the early christological controversies and could easily have come about for a number of other reasons, as we have seen with regard to many of the readings discussed above.

1 Corinthians 15:15

In an extended treatment of the resurrection of Christ and of believers in 1 Cor 15, Paul refers to certain people's assertion that there is no resurrection from the dead, and he says that if that were so it would imply that Christ also had not been raised (v. 13). Further, that would mean that their faith was in vain and Paul and his colleagues would be falsely testifying about God (15:12–15), for they were saying that ηγειρεν τον χριστον. Indeed, he mentioned earlier in the chapter that the foundation of their belief was the apostolic testimony that Christ died, was buried, was raised on the third day, and appeared to many (15:1–8). In 15:15, he refers to the idea that God did not raise Christ, ον ουκ ηγειρεν ειπερ αρα νεκροι ουκ εγειρονται, and Ehrman observes that some MSS (D ar b r vg^{mss} sy^p) omit the whole of ειπερ αρα νεκροι ουκ εγειρονται. Since there is no obvious reason for it being omitted accidentally, many have proposed that it was deliberately left out because it seemed repetitious. Ehrman observes, however, that the phrase ειπερ αρα appears nowhere else in the Pauline letters, so he wonders whether it is a secondary addition. Since gnostics would have accepted that God did not raise Christ from the dead, he suggests that this phrase was added by an orthodox copyist wishing to forestall any interpretation of this verse that might imply Christ has not been raised from the dead (ον ουκ ηγειρεν).[139] Thus, he proposes that by adding ειπερ αρα νεκροι ουκ εγειρονται, the previous statement cannot be taken as a statement of fact but only a supposition.

Yet, the slight MS support for this omission is no earlier than the fourth century, and the explanation that it was omitted because it was thought to be repetitious is just as likely on internal grounds. The fact that Paul does not use ειπερ αρα elsewhere is not a strong point in view of the limited number of his extant letters and the fact that he *does*

---

138. Ehrman, *Orthodox Corruption*, 184.
139. Ehrman, *Orthodox Corruption*, 184–85.

sometimes use ειπερ (Rom 3:30; 8:9, 17; 1 Cor 8:5; 2 Thess 1:6) and makes frequent use of αρα. Not finding them together is likely to reflect our small sample of Pauline letters, the infrequent use of ειπερ, and the somewhat more frequent use of αρα in Hellenistic Greek.[140] The proposal is then unproven, and the repetitious nature of the clause in question is the more likely reason that it was left out of a few MSS. Or, since the following verse begins with an almost identical phrase, it is possible that a copyist's eye slipped from ει(περ αρα νεκροι) to ει (γαρ νεκροι), omitting the text in between.[141]

Jesus Christ, the Son of God

The following variants are cited in support of the proposal that orthodox scribes wished to highlight that Jesus was the Christ, the Son of God, so they altered the text to include that claim.

Mark 1:34

The Gospel of Mark provides a summary of Jesus' early ministry in Galilee (1:32–34) in which Jesus is said to have cast out demons, whom he would not allow to speak οτι ηδεισαν αυτον (v. 34). Some MSS, however, contain an additional phrase, mentioning that they knew αυτον χριστον ειναι, or the like (ℵ² B C W Θ $f^{1,13}$ and some early versions). Ehrman suggests that these secondary additions were designed to support the orthodox view that Jesus was the Christ—one person, not two.[142] Despite the somewhat limited MS support for the shorter reading (ℵ A K Γ Δ and early versions), the longer readings with added material are probably secondary, being the result of harmonization to Luke 4:41.[143] Neither proposal, however, offers a cogent explanation for the variety of variants. Perhaps scribes copied according to sense and just followed the meaning of their exemplar without strict word order, but there is no definitive way of knowing how the variant readings arose on present evidence and

---

140. In the whole LXX, ειπερ occurs twice (Jdt 6:9, Sus (Th) 1:54), αρα, thirty-nine times, and ει αρα, only five times.

141. Thiselton, *First Epistle*, 1218.

142. Ehrman, *Orthodox Corruption*, 187.

143. Metzger, *Textual Commentary*, 64; Marcus, *Mark 1–8*, 197; France, *Mark*, 108; Collins, *Mark*, 175na.; Wasserman, "Variants of Evil," 73–74; Pardee, *Scribal Harmonization*, 254, 441.

hence no way to confirm that they were created to support the theological point of view proposed.

Mark 3:11–12

In another summary of Jesus' ministry, Mark records that demons *did* later speak, falling down and calling out, cυ ει ο υιοc του θεου (3:11). Ehrman refers to Jesus' command to them ινα μη αυτον φανερον ποιηcωcιν (3:12), noting that some OL MSS (b g^{1,2} q) rework this to say that he commanded their silence because "they knew that he was the Christ himself." He also observes that in 3:11 some MSS (C M P sy^p c pc) insert a reference to Jesus as "Christ," reading "You are the Christ, the Son of God." On this basis, these two readings are taken to be "orthodox corruptions."[144] However, again this thesis is by no means proven, and habit, piety, or just following similar titles copied elsewhere are just as likely to account for the additions.

John 1:1

The first verse of John's Gospel is justly famous for its exalted Christology. One MS (L, X AD),[145] instead of reading θεοc ην ο λογοc, includes the article to read ο θεοc ην ο λογοc, which Ehrman construes to mean that now the λογοc is "God," not just "divine." He suggests that this variant derived from the period of the later Arian controversy, so he does not deal with it in this section.[146] However, the function of the article in Greek is not always easy to determine, although its use in this context is clearly a matter for discussion and more could be said about its usage in general.[147] Origen's mention of the absence of the article in John 1:1 (*Comm. Jo.* 2.2.17–18) is also relevant. The early Sahidic and Bohairic MSS attest to the lack of an article in their Greek exemplar, which is good evidence that it was not original,[148] and, since one MS with the article (L)

---

144. Ehrman, *Orthodox Corruption*, 187.

145. Morgan states that W^S also includes this reading, this part of W deriving from the seventh century ("Legacy," 124–26).

146. Ehrman, *Orthodox Corruption*, 210–11n187.

147. Cf. Turner, *Syntax*, 183; BDF, 131–45; Wallace, *Grammar*, 257–59, 266–69; Köstenberger, *Going Deeper*, 49–50.

148. Wright, "Jesus as ΘΕΟC," 235–41.

was produced in the tenth century and the other (W[S]) in the seventh, it is a very late variant in any case.

On the basis of a thorough examination of both the theological climate in the second century and Codex L, it seems that in line with the common scribal habits of the copyist of L, the addition of the article there is almost certainly due to his "sloppy habits." It is unclear how the reading arose in W[S], but piety or habit could have been the cause. Further, the variant reading with the article would be opposed to the attested grammatical norms of the NT documents, where the lack of the article with θεoc is standard usage.[149] The suggestion, then, about the article designed to make Jesus' divinity more explicit is unlikely.

John 10:36

John recounts a growing hostility toward Jesus in certain quarters in the latter part of his public ministry, especially in Jerusalem. In Jesus' response to an attempt to stone him, he refers to an OT text (Ps 82:6), asking why they were accusing him of blasphemy for saying υιoc του θεου ειμι. Ehrman refers to the SR in P[45] (ο υιoc, not just υιoc), implying that the article was added to highlight the claim that Jesus was indeed "*the* Son of God."[150] As noted above, however, the significance of the presence or absence of the article in Koine Greek is not simply that an article makes a noun definite and the lack of one makes it indefinite. Royse notes the construction put on this variant, but he suggests that it was a harmonization to general usage,[151] which appears to be the most likely explanation.

Acts 8:36

Luke provides an account of Philip's encounter with an Ethiopian eunuch in Acts 8:26–40. Toward the end of the account, the eunuch asked Philip what was preventing him from being baptized (8:36), and the original text relates how he had his chariot stopped and was baptized on the spot (8:38). A long addition in some MSS, however, expands on this by including Philip's statement that he could be baptized if he really believed, and the eunuch is then said to utter, πιcτευω τον υιον του θεου ειναι τον

---

149. Morgan, "Legacy," 123–24.
150. Ehrman, *Orthodox Corruption*, 188.
151. Royse, *Scribal Habits*, 129, 194, 194n465.

ιησουν χριστον, or similar (E etc it vg^{cl} sy^{h**} mae; Irenaeus Cyprian).[152] Clearly, Irenaeus found this added text useful in his disputations with the gnostics (*Haer.* 3.12.8), but it does not follow that it was created in order to serve that purpose.[153] Of course, it is clearly secondary, since it is lacking in P^{45} P^{74} ℵ A B C etc., with its earliest MS appearance being in C from the sixth century,[154] but it is not easy to account for its presence in the MSS, and Irenaeus's reference (*Haer.* 3.12.8) shows that it was known as early as the second century. It might be explained on the basis of a formula used in baptismal ceremonies, so it was included in the margin of a MS and subsequently in the body of a copy of that MS,[155] or because of the feeling that Phillip would surely not have left it out,[156] but none of the explanations given is finally provable, so its origins remain obscure.

Romans 15:8

As part of Paul's treatment of division in the Roman church(es), he urged gentile believers to honor their Jewish brothers and sisters, enlarging on how χριστον διακονον γεγενηςθαι περιτομης (15:8). Ehrman suggests that gnostics would have had little difficulty with this if they understood it to mean that the divine Christ came to Jesus for the sake of the elect. However, MSS which read ιησουν χριστον (D E F G OL pc) or χριστον ιησουν (L P vg etc.), instead of just χριστον, would have caused difficulties for them because of the double title, so he proposes that these readings were composed to achieve exactly that result.[157] Such readings, however, only appear in MSS from the fifth century onwards, unless some of the OL support comes from the fourth, so evidence for the variant is not early. Again, habit, piety, or similar titles occurring elsewhere are just as plausible as reasons to account for these readings, so their origins must be left undetermined.

---

152. Ehrman, *Orthodox Corruption*, 210n185.
153. *Pace* Ehrman, *Orthodox Corruption*, 187–88.
154. Pervo, *Acts*, 217–18nm.
155. Metzger, *Textual Commentary*, 315–16; Barrett, *Acts*, 433; Fitzmyer, *Acts*, 414–15.
156. Bruce, *Acts*, 229.
157. Ehrman, *Orthodox Corruption*, 188.

Scribes, Theology, and Apologetics

2 Corinthians 4:10

Paul was describing his ministry as characterized by weakness and insignificance, despite the fact that he and his colleagues were carrying around "the treasure" of the gospel (4:7–9). In fact, so weak was their ministry, it was as though they were carrying around την νεκρωσιν του ιησου, so that η ζωη του ιησου, evident in the gospel and its results, might be manifested (4:10). Some MSS, however, add χριστου, reading η ζωη του ιησου χριστου (D F G etc.), and Irenaeus refers to this (*Haer.* 5.13.4). Ehrman maintains that this was meant to emphasize that Jesus was also the Christ in opposition to gnostic thought.[158] But again, this variant might have arisen out of a copyist or reader's piety or habit, or even from the custom of writing the double title in other parts of the same MS, so the proposal must remain unproven.

Hebrews 3:1

The author of the Letter to the Hebrews addressed his readers as αδελφοι αγιοι (3:1), urging them to fix their attention on τον αποστολον και αρχιερεα της ομολογιας ημων ιησουν. Numerous MSS read χριστον ιησουν (*Byz*) or ιησουν χριστον (C^c D^c E K L etc.) instead of just ιησουν, and Ehrman infers that this is an orthodox highlighting of Jesus as the Christ, intended to subvert a gnostic separation of the human Jesus from the divine Christ.[159] The same comments made above are relevant here—the MSS are quite late and other more mundane explanations for the origins of these variants are just as likely, given that we know so little about how the MSS were actually copied. Further, the context contains references to Jesus as the Christ (3:6, 14), so it would not be surprising if an extra instance slipped in by mistake, and if so, it would probably have passed unnoticed.

1 John 4:15

The latter part of John's "first" letter refers to anyone who confesses that ιησους εστιν ο υιος του θεου, saying that God lives in that person and that person in God, so close is their relationship (4:15). Ehrman refers to the

---

158. Ehrman, *Orthodox Corruption*, 188, 211n189.
159. Ehrman, *Orthodox Corruption*, 188–89.

ANTI-SEPARATIONIST CORRUPTIONS?

reading in Codex Vaticanus (and one Vulgate MS), which reads ιησους χριστος instead of just ιησους, as another suggested "orthodox corruption" designed to support the divinity of Jesus as Christ.[160] Yet, this reading might well have arisen out of habit or piety, or inadvertently following other double titles, such as in 2:1, 3:23, and 4:2.[161] This is quite likely in view of the realities of MS reproduction in antiquity with copyists working by hand, especially in view of the similar title in 4:2 copied so soon beforehand.

1 John 5:5

Somewhat later in 1 John, John explains that overcoming "the world" comes to the one who believes that ιησους εστιν ο υιος του θεου (5:5). Again, a few MSS (33 378 arm) have the reading ιησους χριστος instead of just ιησους, perhaps intended to bolster "orthodox" Christology, according to which Jesus and Christ are one and the same person.[162] However, this reading is clearly secondary with limited MS support, none earlier than the fifth century, so there is no evidence that it was meant to serve as armor against gnostic theology in the early centuries. There are also other possible reasons for its occurrence that are just as viable as that proposed and less dependent on historical reconstructions of the setting in which it arose. The same reasons suggested for many of the variants in this section would apply here too, noting especially that the compound title could well also have been in a copyist's mind from 1:3, 2:1, 3:16, 3:23, and 4:2, and it appears immediately afterwards as well (5:6).

The Unity of "Our Lord Jesus Christ"

In this section Ehrman discusses the presence of variants which have the full title ιησους χριστος ο κυριος ημων, or similar, asking why copyists preferred this and where the tradition began.[163] He rejects the theory that the presence of the full title reflects the supposed bias in the Western Text (or D) against the Jews, highlighting how bad it was for them to reject such a great one, because it gives no context in which that bias might

---

160. Ehrman, *Orthodox Corruption*, 188.
161. Smalley, *1, 2, 3 John*, 234nh; Brown, *Epistles*, 524.
162. Ehrman, *Orthodox Corruption*, 188.
163. Ehrman, *Orthodox Corruption*, 189.

Scribes, Theology, and Apologetics

have arisen. Instead, he cites the rather strident emphasis of Irenaeus on the unity of "Jesus Christ our Lord" (*Haer.* 1.9.2–3; 3.16.6), including his mention that the Valentinians refuse to call Jesus κυριος (*Haer.* 1.1.3). So, he suggests that this predilection for calling Jesus κυριος, especially in combination with ιηcουc χριcτοc, "may well have arisen within the context of anti-Gnostic polemics."[164] It would be good to remember, however, that acknowledging Jesus as "Lord" was a central aspect of Christianity from earliest times (e.g., 1 Cor 8:6, 11:23, 12:3), so this proposal is doubtful from the outset.

Matthew 4:18

Matthew 4:18–22 records Jesus calling his first disciples, and the account begins with a description of the context—περιπατων δε παρα την θαλαccαν (4:18). One MS (sy^c, III/IV AD) begins with περιπατων δε ο κυριος, which might be understood as an attempt to provide ammunition for anti-gnostic polemic.[165] It is certainly unusual for the Gospel writers to call Jesus κυριος in their narrative, although Luke does this several times, so it was presumably a later addition in Matthew. But whether the person responsible had a theological intention to oppose gnostic Christology or whether it sprang out of piety or habit is unknown. Given the period when this MS was produced, either of these would be a feasible explanation to account for it, so the proposed motive is not the only one, and not necessarily the most likely.

Matthew 9:27

In Matthew's account of Jesus healing two blind men, their appeal begins with the address, ελεηcον ημαc υιοc δαυιδ (9:27). Some MSS correct υιοc δαυιδ to υιε δαυιδ, and others read κυριε υιε δαυιδ (N *f*^13 892^c). This second group of late MSS exhibits a secondary reading reflecting how many people addressed Jesus in the Gospels as an exalted personage and how more were addressing him in prayer in later centuries, so habit or harmonization to a similar context in the Gospels are likely to account

---

164. Ehrman, *Orthodox Corruption*, 189–90, 211n192.
165. Ehrman, *Orthodox Corruption*, 190.

ANTI-SEPARATIONIST CORRUPTIONS?

for the reading.[166] Indeed, in view of the late date of the MSS, these are more likely reasons for its origin than anti-gnostic polemic.[167]

Matthew 20:30

In this passage, Matthew records another two blind men being healed by Jesus, their initial appeal beginning with ελεησον ημας [κυριε] υιος δαυιδ. While the word order varies a little in the MSS, Ehrman points out that some MSS (L 892 bo sa^mss etc.) insert ιησου before υιος δαυιδ, which he takes to be a reverse case, where the κυριος being addressed is clearly identified as ιησους.[168] However, since the parallel (or at least similar) passages in Mark 10:47 and Luke 18:38 include ιησου, harmonization to similar or parallel passages is likely to have been the cause of this variant,[169] rather than an anti-gnostic scribal concern.

Mark 10:51

In Mark 10 there is an account of Jesus' encounter with a blind man named Bartimaeus. In response to Jesus' question asking what he wanted him to do for him, Bartimaeus is said to reply, ραββουνι ινα βλεψω. Ehrman alludes to the fact that some MSS (D it) add κυριε before ραββουνι, suggesting this as an example of the tendency to add κυριος to descriptions of Jesus.[170] Clearly this is a secondary reading, but in view of the fact that many people address Jesus using κυριε in the Gospels meaning little more than "Sir" (e.g., Matt 8:2, Mark 7:28, Luke 9:59), it is far from certain that any more than that was intended here, nor is it obvious that it was an anti-gnostic variant. It might simply have arisen from habit, piety, or harmonization to similar contexts in the Gospels, so it is not necessarily a sign of theological proclivities on the part of the copyists of these later MSS.

---

166. Pardee suggests harmonization (*Scribal Harmonization*, 307).
167. *Pace* Ehrman, *Orthodox Corruption*, 190.
168. Ehrman, *Orthodox Corruption*, 190.
169. Metzger, *Textual Commentary*, 43; Pardee, *Scribal Harmonization*, 148–49.
170. Ehrman, *Orthodox Corruption*, 190, 211n195.

Scribes, Theology, and Apologetics

Luke 5:19

Another variant suggested as anti-gnostic is the addition of "Lord" to the name "Jesus" in Luke 5:19 in one sixth century MS (sy^pal).[171] In Luke's Gospel, however, his occasional use of ο κυριος to refer to Jesus (e.g., Luke 7:13, 19; 10:1) is reason enough to explain this variant as a harmonization to his usage elsewhere. Or, if the copyist was a Christian (which is more likely in this late MS), piety or habit could have been the main factor. So, anti-gnostic fervor is far from being a likely explanation for this variant in a sixth century Syriac MS, when Gnosticism had well and truly passed as an option or a threat.

Acts 2:38

This passage records Peter addressing the crowd on the day of Pentecost, calling on them, μετανοησατε και βαπτισθητω εκαστος υμων επι τω ονοματι ιησου χριστου, with some MSS (D E 1739 sy^(h) etc.) inserting του κυριου before ιησου χριστου. It is proposed that adding του κυριου is an example of the tendency to add κυριος to Jesus' titles in order to oppose gnostic Christology.[172] However, there are a variety of titles used in Acts in similar baptismal contexts, including κυριος (e.g., 8:16, 19:5),[173] so a copyist could easily have adapted the present text to one of those. Or it might be an honorific title arising from the piety of a copyist, and it occurs elsewhere in D at 5:42 and 10:48 (cf. 1:21, 7:55, 13:33).[174] Thus, the above proposal for the source of this variant is not the only possibility, and others are just as likely, especially in MSS from the third century onwards.

Acts 7:59

The account of Stephen's speech to the Sanhedrin comes to a climax with him being stoned and uttering his final cry, κυριε ιησου δεξαι το πνευμα μου (7:59), with some MSS (C sy etc.) adding χριστε after κυριε ιησου to form the triple title. In contrast to the explanation of this variant as an

---

171. Ehrman, *Orthodox Corruption*, 190.
172. Ehrman, *Orthodox Corruption*, 191, 211n199.
173. Fitzmyer, *Acts*, 266.
174. Bruce, *Acts*, 129.

attempt to counter gnostic Christology,[175] the reading in these late MSS could easily be the result of habit, piety, or a harmonization to similar titles elsewhere in Acts (11:17, 15:26, 28:31) or the rest of the NT.

Romans 6:11

Paul's exhortation to the Roman church(es) included urging believers to consider themselves "dead to sin and alive to God" εν χριστω ιησου, to which a number of MSS add τω κυριω ημων. Despite the somewhat strong support for this variant (P^{94vid} ℵ (sy^p) bo), it appears to be secondary, since it is omitted from P^{46} A B D G 1739* sy^h sa. As regards its origin, it could be "a liturgical expansion, derived perhaps from ver. 23,"[176] rather than a theologically motivated variant opposing gnostic Christology.[177] Or perhaps it is just "a secondary stylistic improvement that brings v. 11 to a more solemn conclusion, as in 5:21 and 6:23."[178]

Romans 10:9

Paul outlines the confession necessary for a person to be a believer—ομολογησης . . . κυριον ιησουν; but a few MSS (P^{46} a t) add χριστον to read κυριον ιησουν χριστον. Once again, "scribal piety" is a likely explanation for this variant,[179] or perhaps "assimilation" to the use of "Christ" earlier in the chapter (10:4, 6, 7),[180] rather than anti-gnostic polemic.[181]

Romans 16:18, 20

In the closing section of his letter to the Romans, Paul uses the titles τω κυριω ημων χριστω (16:18) and του κυριου ημων ιησου (16:20). Some MSS (L cop arm) support τω κυριω ημων ιησου χριστω (adding ιησου) in 16:18, and in 16:20 others (A C Ψ Byz it sy co) have the reading του κυριου ημων ιησου χριστου (adding χριστου). The contention that these evince

---

175. Ehrman, *Orthodox Corruption*, 191.
176. Metzger, *Textual Commentary*, 453–54. Cf. Longenecker, *Romans*, 608.
177. Pace Ehrman, *Orthodox Corruption*, 191.
178. Jewett and Kotansky, *Romans*, 391nl.
179. Metzger, *Textual Commentary*, 525; Jewett and Kotansky, *Romans*, 622ni.
180. Longenecker, *Romans*, 831.
181. Pace Ehrman, *Orthodox Corruption*, 191.

anti-gnostic bias is possible in earlier MSS,[182] but in these later ones, "scribal piety," habit, or a tendency to "expand liturgical formulations" are more likely explanations.[183]

Revelation 22:21

There are various secondary readings for του κυριου ιησου here—του ιησου χριστου (046 051ˢ Byz syʰ) or του κυριου ημων ιησου χριστου (2067 it sy)—and it has been proposed that they were composed to counter gnostic Christology.[184] Again, scribal piety is a likely explanation for both of these, rather than a theological intention to oppose another christological stance,[185] since many scribes, especially in later times, tended to expand Jesus' titles in the MSS they copied.

CONCLUSION

In this chapter I have reviewed suggestions that textual variants show the influence of a polemic against the various gnostic Christologies current in the second and third centuries on the part of "proto-orthodox" copyists. Ehrman maintains that they were not hoping to convince the gnostics but to stop the defection of their members to the ranks of the gnostics.[186] However, it is also possible that they thought that this was the right way to deal with the text of the NT by copying it accurately, perhaps adding titles derived from their own piety without any thought of using these to combat other christological views. As we have seen, in most cases there are other explanations for the variants that are just as viable to account for them, whether in Greek or versional MSS. Further, many of the variants occur in MSS only from the fourth century onwards, so it is unlikely that the controversy with Gnosticism formed the context for their creation. Habit, piety, harmonization to other similar passages, and other reasons are just as likely to have been the cause of the secondary readings referred to. Indeed, even if a variant *was* current in the period concerned, it is another matter to show that it was *designed* to achieve

182. Ehrman, *Orthodox Corruption*, 191.
183. Metzger, *Textual Commentary*, 476; Dunn, *Romans 9–16*, 901nd.
184. Ehrman, *Orthodox Corruption*, 191.
185. Metzger, *Textual Commentary*, 690; Smalley, *Revelation*, 581.
186. Ehrman, *Orthodox Corruption*, 191–93.

the suggested purpose. In any case, since we do not know whether the copyist(s) of the MSS cited *created* the variant or whether they were following their exemplar, it is virtually impossible to prove that a variant arose at a certain time based on the extant MS evidence. It might have arisen earlier, or it might not have. In general, the proposals remain unproven and mostly unlikely, since there are other simpler explanations for them, especially for MSS from the fourth century onwards when copying was coming to be performed in more controlled settings and executed more generally by pious believers.

3

Anti-docetic Corruptions?

CHAPTER 4 OF THE *Orthodox Corruption of Scripture* is devoted to variants said to have been created in response to docetic Christology. First, Ehrman provides a clear outline of docetism in early Christianity from its roots, even as reflected in responses to it in some of the later NT documents.[1] The basic tenet of docetism was that Jesus Christ only "seemed" to be human and experience suffering, but he was not human at all (cf. Irenaeus, *Haer.* 3.18.6; Hippolytus, *Haer.* 8.1–4; 10:15). The opponents referred to in 1 John, and by Ignatius and others later, were those who propounded this "docetic" Christology, some of which related to Gnosticism. Various other doctrines were related to the person of Christ, but I note these as they arise in relation to the texts discussed below. The main issues reviewed are the docetists casting doubt on the birth of Christ as a man, his real human body, and the reality of his suffering and crucifixion. Ehrman suggests that a number of variant readings attest an orthodox response to the docetists, as scribes (or others) sought to support their own theological point of view and to prevent texts from being used to support docetic Christology.

---

1. Ehrman, *Orthodox Corruption*, 212–19.

ANTI-DOCETIC CORRUPTIONS?

Christ Suffered in the Flesh

The first group of texts highlight the reality of the physical sufferings of Christ, as Ignatius (*Smyrn.* 2.1; *Trall.* 9.1–2) and Tertullian (*Carn. Chr.* 5) testify were issues at the time.

Matthew 17:12–13

After Matthew's account of Jesus' transfiguration, he records Jesus speaking to the disciples about John the Baptist who had suffered, and ουτως και ο υιος του ανθρωπου μελλει πασχειν υπ αυτων (17:12). Apparently, the disciples understood that he had been speaking about John (17:13), presumably implying that Jesus would suffer like him. This original form was adjusted in some Western MSS (D it), so the reference to the Son of Man suffering (v. 12) appears in the text after the mention of the disciples understanding the reference to John in v. 13.[2] This variant might have been motivated by a desire to ensure that the reference to John in v. 13 was clearly understood not to be referring to the previous statement that ο υιος του ανθρωπου μελλει πασχειν (17:12).

However, in view of the preponderance of references to Jesus as "the Son of Man" in the Gospels, it is unlikely that anyone would have thought that ο υιος του ανθρωπου could possibly refer to John. Whoever was responsible for this variant reading *might have* wanted to clarify the meaning of the text, however unlikely that misunderstanding was, but this would not necessarily be due to a wish to emphasize that Jesus' sufferings as the Son of Man were real. So, the proposed motive for the Western variant must remain unproven.

Matthew 20:22, 23

Matthew recounts the request by the mother of the sons of Zebedee that they be granted superior status in Jesus' kingdom. He then adds Jesus' response, asking them if they can πιειν το ποτηριον ο εγω μελλω πινειν (20:22) and then saying that το μεν ποτηριον μου πιεσθε (20:23). The Byzantine tradition, however, adds the parallel clauses το βαπτισμα ο εγω βαπτιζομαι βαπτισθηναι (v. 22) and και το βαπτισμα ο εγω βαπτιζομαι βαπτισθησεσθε (v. 23). The additions are clearly not original and could

---

2. Ehrman, *Orthodox Corruption*, 229–30.

be harmonizations to Mark 10:38–39. However, it would be unusual for harmonizations to go from Mark to Matthew, although "unusual" does not mean impossible. It has been suggested that, since the "baptism" in mind was clearly a metaphor for suffering, as appears in Mark 10 (cf. Luke 12:50; Tertullian, *Bapt.* 16), this *might* have given copyists the opportunity to highlight Jesus' suffering even more than was already implied by the reference to drinking the cup. Hence, the sense, rather than being changed, would just be strengthened by making use of a parallel passage and inserting another reference to Jesus' coming suffering and death.[3] While this is not a "corruption" in the strict sense of the word, because the meaning is unchanged, it could be seen as such in a limited sense. Yet, while this interpretation of the evidence is possible as the motivation for the insertion, the reading might just have been a harmonization to Mark 10:38–39 without any other motivation than scribal memory of a similar passage and the sense of wishing to complete the text in Matthew.[4]

Matthew 27:50

Matthew's account of Jesus' death records that ο δε ιησους . . . αφηκεν το πνευμα (27:50), but some MSS (ℵ B C L sy[pal mss] etc.) add just prior to this, αλλος δε λαβων λογχην ενυξεν αυτου την πλευραν και εξηλθεν υδωρ και αιμα. Despite its rather strong support (ℵ B C vg[mss] mae), this reading is almost certainly derived from the nearly identical wording in John 19:34. Irenaeus referred to this incident in writing against the Ptolemaeans (*Haer.* 3.22.2) and Marcion (*Haer.* 4.33.2),[5] both of whom were docetists, and it appears that docetists did deny the truth of this event (Acts of John 101). Thus, the variant could be an orthodox corruption designed to reinforce the truth of Jesus' suffering in opposition to the docetists' denial.[6] However, Irenaeus and the docetists might not have had this text in Matt 27:50 in mind at all, but the account in John. Indeed, a reader could have written it in the margin of Matt 27, and it could have later found its way into the text, albeit somewhat awkwardly.[7] It is also just possible that the

---

3. Ehrman, *Orthodox Corruption*, 229.
4. Metzger, *Textual Commentary*, 42; Hagner, *Matthew 14–28*, 577nnc-d.
5. Ehrman, *Orthodox Corruption*, 292n64.
6. Ehrman, *Orthodox Corruption*, 228–30.
7. Metzger, *Textual Commentary*, 59; Hagner, *Matthew 14–28*, 842nh; Luz, *Matthew 21–28*, 541–42n5; France, *Matthew*, 1073n4.

phrase was original in Matthew, since its placement is slightly different from that in John.[8]

Luke 22:43-44

Luke's account of events that transpired on the Mount of Olives on the evening of Jesus' arrest includes his prayer not to have to die but also his final acceptance of God's will if that was necessary (22:42). Then many MSS relate an angel coming and strengthening him, και γενομενος εν αγωνια εκτενεστερον προσηυχετο και εγενετο ο ιδρως αυτου ωσει θρομβοι αιματος καταβαινοντες επι την γην (22:43-44). It has been suggested that this was created by second-century scribes wishing to highlight Jesus' real human agony to repudiate docetic Christologies.[9]

The MSS including 22:43-44 are not insignificant (ℵ* ℵ²ᵇ D L Δ* 0170^vid f¹ 565 892*), but these verses do not appear in some of the earliest Greek MSS and much of the Alexandrian tradition (P⁷⁵ A B T W 579). The balance of evidence here is not conclusive, but the incident is reported by Justin, Irenaeus, and early Latin and Syriac witnesses. So, if the verses are secondary, they must have been inserted by the middle of the second century. If original, they must have been deleted in certain MSS by about the same time since they are absent from Clement and other witnesses in the late second and early third centuries.

Clivaz observes that MS 0170 probably includes this reading, as does ℵ*, but there is no evidence from P⁴⁵, so it does not provide any confirmation here either way. Further, P⁶⁹ omits the whole of 22:42-45a (or 22:42, 45a), possibly due to Marcionite editing or perhaps by homoioteleuton (προσευχετο [v. 41] ... προσευχης [v. 45]).[10] It follows then that 22:43-44 is not a strongly Western reading and its absence in some MSS is not Alexandrian. Further, while the reference to Jesus' agony and sweat might be taken to serve anti-docetic purposes, there is still no explanation for the presence of the angel. Parker suggests that the occurrence of these verses after Matt 26:39 (and not in Luke) in most of the MSS in f¹³ "is due to the use of the verses as a lection in the Byzantine

---

8. Davies and Allison, *Matthew*, 3:627n81. Pace Nolland, *Matthew*, 1201nf.

9. Ehrman, *Orthodox Corruption*, 220-27. Cf. Ehrman and Plunkett, "Angel and Agony," 178-95; Ehrman, "Text and Interpretation," 316-20; Ehrman, "Text and Transmission," 326-27; Ehrman, "Christ in the Flesh," 353-54; Ehrman, *Misquoting*, 139-44, 164-65.

10. Clivaz, "Angel and Sweat." Cf. Head, "Christology," 123n76.

Maundy Thursday cycle."[11] In fact, in some MSS (346, 828, 983, 1689) the passage occurs in both Matt 26 and Luke 22, so the evidence of f^{13} is uncertain. Hence, the external evidence supporting the originality of 22:43–44 is considerable, and portraying the passage as an anti-docetic addition does not answer all the textual issues, so the arguments thus far are inconclusive.

As for internal arguments based on syntax and word usage, Ehrman argues that the content of these verses is "intrusive" in Luke, but this is surely due to the uniqueness of the event. The contrast here with the portrayal of Jesus' "calm assurance" throughout the Lukan narrative is clear, but this may only serve to highlight the extreme nature of Jesus' feelings as he approached death. Might not someone be especially troubled in the face of death?[12] Since we do not know how Luke used his sources, we cannot know, apart from the content of his Gospel, what themes he might have wished to highlight—and he *might* have wished to highlight how Jesus, calm though he had been, was extremely troubled at the prospect of crucifixion.[13] These verses might thus be Luke's counterpart to the Markan reference to Jesus' distress (Mark 14:33–35), and "Take this cup from me" (Luke 22:42), a parallel to Mark's statement that Jesus prayed for the hour to pass from him (Mark 14:35). Indeed, the prayer for the cup to be taken away could have been shocking to readers in antiquity who might have expected a noble speech or dignified silence. So, there would be good reason for someone to omit this material rather than add it,[14] although it is difficult to be certain that this is what happened.[15]

Further, it is not certain that recording Jesus praying once for the cup to be removed, including ει βουλει ("if you are willing," 22:42), was any less emphatic *for Luke* than Mark's more vibrant record. Moreover, the description of the drops of sweat καταβαινοντες fits the narrative, since it is in line with Jesus kneeling at the time (22:42).[16] So, despite Luke's more controlled narrative style, this might be the one exception.

---

11. Parker, *Living Text*, 158.

12. Cf. Wasserman, "Scribal Alterations," 317–18.

13. Nolland notes the emotional tone of this passage as an important factor (*Luke 18:35—24:53*, 1080-81nd).

14. Clivaz, "Angel and Sweat," 428–29.

15. Clivaz notes that the statement that every man wished to be calm in the face of death is overdrawn ("New Testament at the Time," 45). Neyrey argues that the picture of Jesus' agony might have been perceived in antiquity as quite extreme ("Absence of Emotions"). Cf. Blumell, "Luke 22:43-44," 33–34.

16. Pope, "Downward Motion."

Luke's more restrained account of Jesus on the road to Golgotha and then on the cross is no argument that he changed the emphasis in his source. Perhaps he just narrated events from a different point of view. Hence, all the elements mentioned can be accounted for by the fact that Luke was a different author, highlighting the positive and hopeful elements of the story, presumably selecting elements from his sources (cf. Luke 1:1–3). As such, the differences between Luke's account and Mark's appear to be exaggerated.

The fact that we can construct a chiasmus without 22:43–44 is of little consequence since Luke might have used this literary feature *but with a difference*, to highlight the element that does not quite fit.[17] We also do not *know* that this account was meant to urge the importance of prayer in response to temptation, as some suggest. Rather, it is a narrative, and any characterization of the *purpose* of a narrative is necessarily speculative. Perhaps the "purpose" might have been to include recounting the events in the Garden. The theory that Luke's narrative portrays Jesus as a model martyr for believers is also only one option, and we do well not to impose that model on the narrative without firm evidence. Even if it were true, however, the narrative shows that in extreme anxiety prayer is appropriate as the best approach to death, though it is still a guess that this was Luke's purpose in including the account. What we know is that Luke recounted Jesus praying, as well as encouraging his disciples to pray in the fact of testing (v. 46). It does not follow that 22:43–44 is secondary. Indeed, Tuckett has argued that, with the arguments inconclusive either way, literary considerations might tip the balance in favor of the disputed verses being original.[18]

Ehrman maintains that the passage is too long to have been accidentally omitted and there is no obvious reason why it might have been. And even if we were to agree that 22:43–44 is not original,[19] it cannot have been inserted by mistake. However, was it inserted to emphasize Jesus' true humanity in suffering such extreme agony? Justin refers to these verses as showing Jesus' true suffering (*Dial.* 103) and Irenaeus used them to oppose docetic themes (*Haer.* 3.22.2), while Hippolytus mentions them to refute patripassianism (*Noet.* 18). The fact that these

---

17. Blumell, "Luke 22:43–44," 32–33.
18. Tuckett, "Luke 22, 43–44," 144.
19. Fitzmyer concludes that the passage was not original (*Luke X–XXIV*, 1443–44). Metzger and Nolland note that it is marked with obeli in certain MSS (*Textual Commentary*, 151; *Luke 18:35—24:53*, 1080nd).

verses were used in these ways does not prove that they were inserted in the narrative as polemic.[20] There are other possibilities, such as someone thinking it was a reliable part of early tradition, "and it might have been."[21] If it was originally part of Luke's Gospel, it might have been omitted because someone felt uncomfortable with Jesus going through suffering.[22] Or the passage might have been omitted in response to outsiders criticizing Jesus for being weaker than he should have been as the Son of God, that is, for apologetic motives.[23] Indeed, it might have been omitted on several unrelated occasions.[24] It is not certain, then, that this reading was secondary or, if it was, why it was introduced.

The Body and Blood of Christ Bring Salvation

In line with Irenaeus's strident emphasis on the reality of Jesus shedding real human blood as the means of salvation (*Haer.* 5.2.2), Ehrman argues that orthodox scribes inserted references to Jesus' blood where it had not been present in the original text in order to highlight this "orthodox" doctrine.

Mark 14:22, 24

Mark's account of the Last Supper recounts Jesus handing around the bread and saying, λαβετε τουτο εστιν το cωμα μου (14:22). One OL MS (a, IV AD), however, adds, "which is broken for many for the remission of sins," which is said to highlight "the salvific necessity of Christ's suffering and death." This construction is also put on a reading in the same MS (as well as W and f^{13}) at 14:24, where the original reading, τουτο εστιν το αιμα μου της διαθηκης το εχχυννομενον υπερ πολλων, is extended by εις αφεcιν αμαρτιων.[25]

---

20. Blumell, "Luke 22:43–44," 34. Pace Parker, *Living Text*, 159.

21. Metzger, *Textual Commentary*, 151. Head concludes that the verses are more likely original ("Christology," 123–26). Cf. Chapa, "Contribution," 108.

22. Bovon, *Luke 3*, 199. Cf. Wasserman, "Scribal Alterations," 319–21.

23. Blumell gives a thorough review of the evidence for the interpretation of this passage in early history, as well as a careful examination of the various proposals regarding the originality of the variants, concluding that, while not certain, it is "a tantalizing possibility" that the passage was omitted for apologetic reasons ("Luke 22:43–44").

24. Blumell, "Luke 22:43–44," 31–32.

25. Ehrman, *Orthodox Corruption*, 147.

Given the extremely limited MS support for both these readings, they are clearly not original. The question arises, however, as to whether they were added in order to counter docetic Christology by highlighting Jesus' real human death (as the means of forgiveness of sins) or whether they derive from someone's piety as a reminder to the reader. There is no proof that the reason for their insertion was a doctrinal one and, in view of the dates of the MSS (IV–XIII AD), they cannot be used to postulate motives of "proto-orthodox" scribes in the second or third centuries. The person responsible for the variant in 14:24 might just have had the parallel passage in Matt 26:28 in mind, where εις αφεcιν αμαρτιων occurs.[26]

Luke 22:19-20

This passage is set in the context of Luke's presentation of the words of Jesus at the Last Supper.[27] After handing the bread around, Jesus is recorded as saying τουτο εcτιν το cωμα μου (22:19a), with most MSS continuing the narrative with το υπερ υμων διδομενον . . . το ποτηριον ωcαυτωc . . . το υπερ υμων εκχυννομενον (22:19b-20). Among the various readings in MSS here, Ehrman rightly dismisses four with far too little MS support to be original,[28] leaving two as possibly original (22:19a; 22:19-20). The shorter text occurs only in D and some OL MSS, so this is plainly a Western reading, although not supported by all Western MSS. Since Western readings are normally longer and this one is shorter, it might be original.[29]

Ehrman first examines intrinsic probabilities.[30] He points out that the central elements of the longer reading—υπερ υμων (22:19b, 20) and αναμνηcιν (22:19b)—occur nowhere else in Luke-Acts, nor does the notion of Jesus' death as an atoning death, so he concludes that they were not original to Luke's Gospel. He dismisses Acts 20:28 as a reference to this idea,[31] noting that its language does not contain explicit soteriological words, although his interpretation of the meaning of the reference to

---

26. Evans, *Mark 8:27—16:20*, 385ni.

27. See Ehrman, *Orthodox Corruption*, 231–45. This is a revised form of Ehrman, "Salvific Effect." Cf. Ehrman, "Christ Come," 354; Ehrman, *Misquoting*, 165–67.

28. Ehrman, *Orthodox Corruption*, 294n72.

29. The issue of "Western non-interpolations" was discussed in chapter 2 of *Scribes, Motives, and Manuscripts*. Cf. Ehrman, *Orthodox Corruption*, 261–65.

30. Ehrman, *Orthodox Corruption*, 233–38.

31. See ch. 2 for a discussion of this passage, as well as the following discussion.

Jesus' blood in Acts 20:28 is somewhat strained. Drawing on the mention of Jesus' blood in Acts 5:28, for which the apostles were accusing the Jerusalem authorities of being responsible, he reconstructs the meaning of 20:28 as, "The blood of Jesus produces the church because it brings the cognizance of guilt that leads to repentance."[32] Ehrman's assertion that "Jesus' death, for Luke, . . . drives people to repentance, and it is this repentance that brings salvation,"[33] might have been true in the context of events immediately after Jesus' death and resurrection, when those responsible were still present. However, it can hardly stand as an ongoing element in Luke's theology of Jesus' death since a later generation or an audience far from Jerusalem would surely feel little force in an argument based on feeling guilty regarding Jesus' death. Nor are other references to "blood" in Luke-Acts relevant because words do not carry worlds of meaning from one context to another.

The reference to Paul not being guilty of the "blood" of the Ephesians (20:26) is hardly relevant, while the suggestion that Paul meant that "only if his hearers repent when confronted with Jesus' blood will they be saved from spilling their own," does not really explain this passage. What would it have meant for the Ephesian elders, already believers, to be "confronted with Jesus' blood"? How would they "be saved from spilling their own"? The issue in interpreting Acts 20:28 is what Paul meant by God (or "the Lord") having "obtained" (περιεποιηcατο) God's church δια του αιματοc του ιδιου. This phrase must refer to the role of Jesus' death in some way, since it refers to his "blood," but no feasible explanation of that has been provided.

The clue to this is found in the several references to Jesus' death "on a tree." The apostles accused the Jerusalem authorities of killing Jesus κρεμαcαντεc επι ξυλου (Acts 5:30). Peter referred to them killing him using the same phrase (Acts 10:39), and Luke's report of Paul was of people taking Jesus down from the cross in καθελοντεc απο του ξυλου (Acts 13:29). Of course, this might just be a reference to the "cross" as a piece of wood; however, in early Christian circles this phrase came to refer to Jesus' death. So also, 1 Peter describes Jesus "bearing our sins in his body on the tree" (ταc αμαρτιαc ημων αυτοc ανηνεγκεν εν τω cωματι αυτου επι το ξυλον), and then continues, "by (his) wound you were healed" (1 Peter 2:24). The death of Jesus is clearly referred to in Acts and 1 Peter

---

32. Ehrman, *Orthodox Corruption*, 237.
33. Ehrman, *Misquoting*, 167.

as having taken place on a "tree" and as the means by which God (or the Lord) obtained the church when Jesus "bore" their sins and believers were spiritually healed. In view of this crossover of language and thought in different strands of early Christianity, it is not too much to suggest that Paul's use of the same language about Jesus becoming "a curse for us" (υπερ ημων καταρα) by being "hung on a tree" (κρεμαμενος επι ξυλου) (Gal 3:13, citing Deut 21:23) belongs to the same world of thought, especially noting the parallel language in the phrase κρεμαcαντεc επι ξυλου in Acts 5:30.[34] So, while the language of atonement does not specifically occur in Acts 20:28, the thought of the role of Jesus' death as the means of forgiveness by taking God's judgment on sin on behalf of his people is clearly present in a number of strands of early Christian thought. This is a viable interpretation of the language of *how* God "obtained" his church in Acts 20:28—by Jesus' death "on a tree."[35]

There is then a notion of "atonement" in Luke-Acts. The absence in Luke's Gospel of a parallel text to Mark 10:45 is hardly significant since it only occurs explicitly once in Mark anyway—and we do not know that Luke "omitted" it, since it is not certain that he had Mark as one of his sources. Perhaps Luke was too faithful to his sources to insert a theme where it was not mentioned, with this theme being rare in all the Gospels. Indeed, what else did Jesus mean by saying that he was ωc ο διακονων among them (Luke 22:27), a statement made only just after the Last Supper in Luke's account? How else did he "serve" the disciples other than by "giving his life as a ransom for many" (Mark 10:45), especially when this is related to the theme of coming "to serve" (διακονηcαι) in Mark 10:45? What else could the words in Luke mean?

The suggestion that Luke would have mentioned this theme in Acts 8 does little to resolve the issue because, while the passage cited there from Isa 53:7–8 does not specifically refer to Jesus' atoning death for sins, neither does it refer to his vindication. It only refers to his death as the fulfilment of the words of the prophet. There is no indication of what else Philip said. We are only told that αρξαμενος απο της γραφης ταυτης ευηγγελιcατο αυτω τον ιηcουν (Acts 8:35). Mention of a lamb "led to the slaughter" (8:32), "deprived of justice," being without descendants, and his life being "taken from the earth" (8:33) seems to refer to the death

---

34. Cf. Marshall, *Luke*, 173. Lust says that in a number of places where the LXX text referred to "tree" or "wood," church fathers traced an allusion to Jesus' crucifixion ("Hang Him," 242–43). Cf. Caneday, "Anyone Hung."

35. Marshall, *Luke*, 169–75; Nolland, *Luke 18:35—24:53*, 1041nc.

of the person in view. What is more, Philip "spoke the gospel to him about Jesus," surely including something about his death. It would be possible to cite other allusions to Isa 53, such as those in Luke 22:37 and 23:32–33 (cf. Isa 53:12), which also contain no reference to an atoning death. Matthew also contains such references (cf. Matt 8:17; Isa 53:4). The allusion to Jesus' death from Isa 53 was not always made explicit, but it is implied in Acts 8.

Ehrman's interpretation of Mark's record of the tearing of the temple curtain is also unconvincing. He bases his interpretation on making a connection between the use of the verb σχιζω in Mark 1:10 (the heavens being "torn") and 15:38 (the temple curtain "torn"), as if two occurrences of the same verb make a connection between the two references in two very different contexts. The centurion's words in Mark 15:39 ("Surely, this man was the Son of God") are clearly a confession of faith, but the claim that this embodies Mark's theology of the cross is premature, since there is no evidence that Jesus' death "was not alien to his divine sonship but was instead constitutive of it."[36] Indeed, it is unclear what that would mean. So, the argument that Luke's narrative puts an entirely different construction on the death of Jesus than Mark's account does relies on an inadequate reconstruction of the meaning of the Markan account as well as the significance of Jesus' death in Luke's. It would be unwise then to conclude that the Gospel accounts are quite different in their theological stance. Nor does it follow that the prolonged darkness now speaks of God's judgment on his people.

The centurion's declaration that Jesus was δικαιος (Luke 23:47), not υιος θεου (Mark 15:39), is not to be set aside lightly, as if it simply meant that Jesus was "innocent." Even if it did, for Luke that might have been only part of the significance of Jesus' death. It is not true that Luke's passion narrative simply portrays Jesus as "a righteous martyr" vindicated by God, however much that might be one aspect of it. Luke's account of the *necessity* of Jesus' death and its being foretold in the OT (Luke 9:22; 18:31–32; 24:25–27, 44–46), as well as Jesus' determination to go through with it (9:51) and final acceptance of it (22:42), surely imply that Luke saw it as having some significance beyond Jesus being a model martyr or an inspiration to give up one's life for the truth. There must have been a connection between Jesus' death and the forgiveness of sins (Luke 24:45–46). There must have been a reason *why* it was necessary. Luke

---

36. Ehrman, *Orthodox Corruption*, 235.

ANTI-DOCETIC CORRUPTIONS?

certainly does not enlarge on this. Nor do any of the Gospels portray Jesus saying much about it during his ministry, because the Gospel writers were faithful to their sources, presumably reflecting the limited extent to which Jesus spoke about it.

The upshot of this rather long digression is that, while Luke-Acts does not have the explicit statement about Jesus' death that occurs in Mark 10:45—and it only occurs in Mark once—the thought of Jesus' death as a sacrifice *is* explicitly there in Acts 20:28; it *is* implied by references to his crucifixion as being "hung on a tree," as well as by his statement at the Last Supper that he came to "serve." The fact that the phrases υπερ υμων and αναμνησιν in Luke 22:19–20 do not occur anywhere else in Luke-Acts, nor do "new covenant" or "in my blood," is no indication that this reading did not originate from Luke. We would not expect these themes to recur with any frequency in the Gospel narratives, since they recount unique events. In any case, Luke's account is clearly more restrained than Mark's. In conclusion, there are no grounds to suspect that Luke 22:19b–20 is not original based on internal probabilities focusing on vocabulary, style, or theology.

Another aspect of intrinsic probabilities concerns the structure of the passage.[37] In response to those who advocate that after a reference to the bread (το cωμα μου), it is almost necessary for something like εν τω αιματι μου, etc., Ehrman suggests that it follows Paul's account in 1 Cor 11:23–25 so closely that it looks as if someone inserted the passage in Luke from their memory of that. He also argues that the structure of 22:15–18 is well suited as an introduction to the shorter reading (without 22:19b–20), and that there is a clear parallelism between 22:19a and 21 and 22:22a and 22b. However, there is a repetitious sequence of cup-bread-cup, which would be alleviated by removing the material in the longer reading. Even without that, there is also a repetitious element in the mention of eating (22:16) and drinking again in the kingdom of God (22:18). Mark's account is brief and clear (Mark 14:20–25), as is Matthew's (Matt 26:20–29). Luke includes repetitious material, but the argument that it would flow better without 22:19b–20 lacks force in an account that is somewhat repetitious anyway. Arguments based on our inability to explain how the other reading occurred (adding or subtracting material) are also inconclusive since in this case either scenario is problematic. But

---

37. Ehrman, *Orthodox Corruption*, 238–42. Cf. Petzer, "Luke 22:19b–20."

it would not be hard to imagine that if the cup-bread-cup sequence were original, someone removed 22:19b–20 to alleviate that difficulty.[38]

Regarding transcriptional probabilities, Ehrman discusses how or why 22:19b–20 might have been omitted and rightly dismisses the logic of certain proposals. The only other suggestion he notes is that the words were original and slipped out accidentally. He dismisses this because it is at odds with the theology of Jesus' death in Luke-Acts and resembles the words of Paul in 1 Cor 11.[39] As we have seen, however, the idea that Jesus' death was "necessary" must have some explanation, and the theme of his death being "for" others is not easily removed from Luke-Acts, even if it is only present to a limited extent. Thus, the reconstruction of Luke's anti-atonement theology is doubtful, so also then is the argument that 22:19b–20 is an interpolation.[40] Even if we were to allow that conclusion, however, the fact that Tertullian refers to this material (in Luke 22:19b–20 or 1 Cor 11:23–26) to speak against Marcion's views (*Test.* 17; *Marc.* 4.40) does not prove that someone inserted the passage to support an anti-Marcionite theological concern. Nor would the fact that Irenaeus also referred to it (*Haer.* 4.33.2, 5.2.2) to refute docetic Christology prove that the material was first included for the same reason.[41] Should the criterion of the harder reading being better (in the shorter text)—if indeed this is the case—take precedence over the weight of the external MS evidence supporting the inclusion of the longer? It is difficult to reach a decision, so it might be best to leave the issue in abeyance. Perhaps this is not what we would wish, but it would be in accord with the evidence. And yet, recent studies support the originality of the longer text,[42] although not all are in agreement.[43] Thus, the argument that Luke 22:19b–20 was not an

38. Metzger, *Textual Commentary*, 148.

39. Ehrman, *Orthodox Corruption*, 242–44.

40. Cf. Green, *Death of Jesus*, 35–42.

41. *Pace* Parker, who concurs with Ehrman's reading of the evidence, especially the theological rationale for the inclusion of 22:19b–20 in a later context (*Living Text*, 151–57).

42. Metzger, *Textual Commentary*, 148–50. Cf. Fitzmyer, *Luke X–XXIV*, 1387–88; Green, *Death of Jesus*, 35–42; Walton, *Leadership and Lifestyle*, 137–39; Bovon, *Luke 3*, 154–56; Billings, "Disputed Words"; Billings, *Do This*. While not necessarily following all of Billings's arguments, I disagree with a number of the contrasting perspectives espoused in Epp, review of "Disputed Words."

43. Hernández accepts the shorter text as original, with 22:19b–20 inserted as an assimilation to Paul's account ("Early Text," 133–34). Martin argues that the shorter Western reading is original ("Defending," 280–85), but his conclusions assume too much about the meaning of the texts and depend too heavily on statistics.

original part of Luke's Gospel is inconclusive, and the contention that it was inserted to include atonement theology must remain unproven. That theology was already present.

Acts 13:29

In Luke's account of Paul's address in the synagogue in Pisidian Antioch, he recounts events surrounding Jesus' death and burial. He describes how οι . . . κατοικουντες εν ιερουσαλημ και οι αρχοντες αυτων (13:27) asked Pilate αναιρεθηναι αυτον (13:28); and he then relates that ως δε ετελεσαν παντα τα περι αυτου γεγραμμενα καθελοντες απο του ξυλου εθηκαν εις μνημειον (13:29). Codex Bezae inserts material after γεγραμμενα describing the further actions of the people of Jerusalem and the Jewish authorities—ητουντο τον πιλατον τουτον μεν cταυρωcαι. Ehrman suggests that this could be an instance of "the orthodox" wishing to highlight Jesus' real death (by crucifixion).[44] However, in view of the reference in 13:28 to the crowd and the authorities already having asked Pilate that Jesus be "strung up" (αναιρεθηναι),[45] this theme is already present, so the extra words add little. Why D (and a few other versional MSS) include this reading is a mystery related to the Western text, where the original seems to use a generalizing plural for several different parties.[46] The addition cannot, then, be attributed to someone wishing to emphasize that Jesus was crucified, but even if it could, their motives would still be unknown.[47]

1 Corinthians 5:7

In the context of a metaphorical use of the absence of yeast in the Passover feast, Paul refers to Christ, saying that το παcχα ημων ετυθη χριcτοc (5:7). A secondary reading in many later MSS inserts υπερ ημων before ετυθη χριcτοc, thus highlighting the death of Jesus as a saving death "for"

---

44. Ehrman, *Orthodox Corruption*, 293n67. Cf. Epp, *Theological Tendency*, 41–51.
45. BDAG, 64; GELS, 40. This verb could be used for any kind of killing.
46. O'Collins, "Buried?," 399–403.
47. Metzger describes the text of vv. 27–29 in D as "ungrammatical and obviously corrupt" (*Textual Commentary*, 360–61). Barrett asserts that the original text of Acts 13:27–29 "was found obscure and unusual and was rewritten in various ways" in the MSS (*Acts*, 1:642–43). Cf. Bruce, *Acts*, 307.

his people.⁴⁸ Clearly, this is a secondary reading. It is another matter, however, to assert that it was designed to counter docetic Christology by underlining his death as a saving death. It certainly does not add anything to the reality of Jesus' death. The theme of Jesus' death as being "*our Passover sacrifice*" is already present, so it is unclear why υπερ ημων was created, except perhaps through habit or to add a more specific reference to its benefactors.

1 Corinthians 11:23-24

Paul provides an account of the Last Supper in 1 Cor 11:23-26, where he relates the words of Jesus, τουτο μου εcτιν το cωμα το υπερ υμων (11:24). Some Coptic MSS, however, include translations of διδομενον (presumably harmonized from Luke 22:19) or κλωμενον (perhaps reflecting εκλαcεν in 11:24a). Again, it is reasonable to see these additions as harmonizations,⁴⁹ and they do add a somewhat vivid emphasis to the passage, but it is difficult to see how they could have been designed to highlight the physical nature of Jesus' passion. While D's use of θρυπτομενον (from θρυπτω, "I break in [small] pieces")⁵⁰ does provide a "graphic emphasis" on Jesus' death, it is only a slightly more vivid word than κλωμενον drawing on the imagery already present in the context (εκλαcεν), and it does not necessarily highlight the reality of Jesus' death in opposition to docetic Christology. More likely, Paul's concise statement was felt to need more explanation, and the MSS reflect various attempts to do that.⁵¹

Colossians 1:14

In Col 1:1-14, Paul relates his prayers for the believers in Colossae and describes how they have been rescued from τηc εξουcιαc του cκοτουc and transferred ειc την βαcιλειαν του υιου τηc αγαπηc αυτου (1:13). He goes on to say that "in him" εχομεν την απολυτρωcιν την αφεcιν των αμαρτιων. Some later MSS add δια του αιματοc αυτου after απολυτρωcιν, probably drawing on that wording in the parallel passage in Eph 1:7.⁵² Ehrman

---

48. Ehrman, *Orthodox Corruption*, 247.
49. Ehrman, *Orthodox Corruption*, 245-46.
50. BDAG, 460.
51. Metzger, *Textual Commentary*, 496; Thiselton, *First Epistle*, 866.
52. Metzger, *Textual Commentary*, 554; Bruce, *Colossians*, 45n26; Barth and Blanke,

points out that Irenaeus uses the language of this addition (*Haer.* 5.2.2), probably with Colossians in mind, so this secondary reading must have been quite early.[53] Yet, it is unwarranted to assert that the person responsible for the added mention of Jesus' blood wished to highlight the reality of Jesus' death in opposition to docetic Christology, even if Irenaeus made use of it for that purpose. This is to turn a possibility into a certainty without sufficient evidence.

The Bodily Resurrection of Christ

Some variant readings are said to emphasize that Jesus' resurrection was a physical one, as a number of early church writers, such as Irenaeus (*Haer.* 4.33.2, *Marc.* 3.8), Tertullian (e.g., *Carn. Chr.* 5) and Origen (*Dial.* 132–34), highlighted in opposition to docetic Christology.

Matthew 28:6

The original text of Matthew's account of the angelic response to the women at the tomb was δευτε ιδετε τον τοπον οπου εκειτο. Many MSS, however, add ο κυριος at the end, Φ (VI AD) has ιησους, and MS 1424 (IX/X AD) has το σωμα του κυριου. On this basis, Ehrman categorizes these secondary variants, particularly the third, as providing an "anti-Docetic stress on Jesus' body."[54] It is difficult to see how the first two variants could be seen in this light, however, since they simply add nomenclature, although το σωμα του κυριου might emphasize the physical reality of Jesus' resurrection. It also does not follow that any of them were *designed* to achieve this end, particularly in response to docetic thought, since they occur in such late MSS. More likely, someone felt that a subject was needed for εκειτο in order to clarify the sentence.[55]

Colossians, 192n93; Dunn, *Colossians*, 67n7.

53. Ehrman, *Orthodox Corruption*, 246–47.

54. Ehrman, *Orthodox Corruption*, 260.

55. Metzger, *Textual Commentary*, 59; Hagner, *Matthew 14–28*, 867ne; France, *Matthew*, 1096n7.

Scribes, Theology, and Apologetics

Luke 23:53

Luke recounts the actions of Joseph of Arimathea, who arranged for Jesus' burial in his own rock-hewn tomb ου ουκ ην ουδεις ουπω κειμενος (Luke 23:50–54). A small number of MSS add words in two different forms (presumably taken from the accounts in Matt 27:60 and Mark 15:46) about a stone being rolled across the entrance to the tomb. Codex Bezae (and 0124 c [sa]) adds even more material about how big the stone was and how difficult it was for people to move it. Ehrman proposes that these variants were inserted by orthodox scribes wishing to oppose docetic Christology and highlight the physicality of Jesus' resurrection by emphasizing the difficulty of him being raised.[56]

Yet, mention of the stone could simply be harmonizing to the similar accounts in Matthew and Mark. Besides, the stone is mentioned later in Luke 24:2–3 anyway, so someone might have wanted to offer an explanation from the other Gospels about what that stone was. The expansive detail supplied in D is characteristic of numerous other details added in that MS,[57] so it is more likely an example of that tendency to expand, rather than an addition by someone with a theological point to make.[58] Thus, the proposals of an anti-docetic purpose for these variants are among several possibilities, with no way of deciding what their real causes were, except for the expanded details in D being in line with its style elsewhere.

Luke 24:12

Luke 24 recounts several incidents relating to the resurrection appearances of Jesus. In this narrative, most MSS of 24:12 refer to Peter's visit to the tomb, although some (D it) omit the whole verse. Because of its Western support, the omission is another "Western non-interpolation," where the variant is shorter, so the expected expansive style of the Western text is unusually absent. Ehrman argues that the shorter reading must have originated in the second century.[59] The dating, however, can be disputed

---

56. Ehrman, *Orthodox Corruption*, 259–60.

57. Metzger, *Textual Commentary*, 156.

58. Cf. Bovon, *Luke 3*, 333n96; Kotansky, "Early Papyri," 271. Parker notes the suggestion that the expansion in D makes use of Homeric cento (*Living Text*, 164–65).

59. Ehrman, *Orthodox Corruption*, 248–54 (cf. 298n130). Cf. Ehrman, *Misquoting*, 168–69.

ANTI-DOCETIC CORRUPTIONS?

since the agreement of D (V AD) and some OL MSS (a b d e l r¹) that originate no earlier than the fourth century does not prove the point. So, other arguments are more central to the discussion.

Ehrman suggests that arguments based on the style of this verse containing elements that are characteristic of Luke's style elsewhere are of little worth because many of the elements cited are common throughout the NT. It is true that the historic present tense of βλεπει is unusual in Luke, but citing uncommon vocabulary like παρακυπτω, τα οθονια, or even απηλθεν προς εαυτον, is not decisive because the first two at least are specialized words that we would not expect to occur much in the Gospel narratives anyway. Luke used cινδων, an alternative word for τα οθονια—if it really is an alternative—in 23:53, but even that appears nowhere else in his narrative. Interestingly, John uses τα οθονια consistently in this same context (John 20:5, 6, 7). This kind of argument, then, is clearly not conclusive, despite the words resembling John 20:5, while the so-called anomalies of Lukan style in 24:12 are not as significant as proposed. As such, intrinsic probabilities are not decisive in supporting the secondary nature of this verse.

However, Ehrman finds transcriptional probabilities conclusive. He notes the similarity to the Johannine account and argues that no valid reason has been given for someone omitting this whole verse. However, the length of the omission carries no weight, since in a text written in *scriptio continua* several lines might well have been omitted at some point in the MS tradition, especially if the same letter or series of letters occurred at line-endings. Moreover, both 24:11 and 24:12 end in a sigma, which might account for the omission, although verses were not included in MSS at that time—but even parablepsis from one sigma to another mid-line could achieve the same result. It follows that an omission need not have been deliberate.

Ehrman discusses other proposals to account for an omission and offers a reasonable rebuttal of most. So, he proposes that this verse was a secondary reading inserted to support the fact of the physical resurrection of Jesus. In particular, he urges that it was created to provide a text to prove that the docetic understanding of Jesus' resurrection as "spiritual," not physical, was without foundation. He cites Origen's words affirming this very event as evidence (*Dial.* 132–33). Yet, the use of the physical event by an apologist does not prove that this was the reason for its creation, especially since there is a parallel account in John's Gospel. Indeed, the arguments for this verse being secondary are not strong.

Finally, the link between (1) ηπιστουν (24:11) and θαυμαζων (24:12) and (2) απιστουντων αυτων . . . και θαυμαζοντων (24:41) is a signal that 24:12 does fit into Luke's literary pattern, suggesting its originality.[60] It is also a "natural antecedent" to the later reference to the tomb in 24:24, so it could easily be original, with the resemblance to John 20 due to dependence on similar traditions.[61]

Therefore, there is no firm evidence that this verse does not fit its context, and its so-called "non-Lukan" features are not as great as proposed. There are also good reasons to suggest that it was original but omitted at an early stage in the transmission of the text, so the further inference that it was inserted to support anti-docetic Christology is unlikely.[62]

Luke 24:36

Jesus' appearance to the disciples while they were talking about his previous appearance to Peter and listening to the two disciples who met him on the road to Emmaus is recounted in Luke 24 (v. 36). In most MSS, Jesus is said to have stood among them και λεγει αυτοις ειρηνη υμιν, although some Western MSS (D it) omit that. Other MSS add, εγω ειμι μη φοβεισθε (P (W) sy$^{p.h}$ bo^{pt} etc.). This last variant is unlikely to be original and was probably a gloss based on John 6:20.[63]

The traditional reading (και λεγει αυτοις ειρηνη υμιν) might have been drawn from John 20:19.[64] Ehrman proposes that it served to clearly identify that this person *was* the one crucified ("It is I"), and he takes the variant as *possibly* dating to mid-II AD, although this is uncertain. He notes the resemblance to John 20:19, but stylized greetings would probably resemble one another anyway (cf. John 20:21, 26; 1 Pet 5:14). He

---

60. Neirynck, "LUKE 24,12," 158. Cf. Neirynck, "Supplementary Note"; Bovon, *Luke 3*, 353-54nn89-92. *Pace* Dauer, "Zur Authentizität."

61. Metzger, *Textual Commentary*, 157-58; Parsons, "Christological Tendency," 466-67; Parsons, *Departure*, 36. Nolland takes the shorter text of D in Luke 24 as due to a desire for conciseness (*Luke 18:35—24:53*, 1177no). Marshall wonders if the verse was left out by people who thought it stood in contradiction to 24:34, which only mentions Peter (*Gospel of Luke*, 888). Cf. Fitzmyer, *Luke X-XXIV*, 1547.

62. Parker takes this verse as a "summary" of the Johannine account (*Living Text*, 167-68). Cf. Hernández, "Early Text," 135-36.

63. Ehrman, *Orthodox Corruption*, 258. Cf. Metzger, *Textual Commentary*, 160.

64. Ehrman, *Orthodox Corruption*, 300n162; Parker, *Living Text*, 168-69. Cf. Hernández, "Early Text," 136; Bovon, *Luke 3*, 390; Fitzmyer, *Luke X-XXIV*, 1575.

also points out that, without the added section, the disciples' fear (24:37) is more understandable since he had only appeared without speaking, but it is less understandable if he had already greeted them (24:36b). But, even with a greeting, it might have been understandably unnerving for someone to suddenly appear in a private gathering.[65] Thus, since the clause is omitted from only a limited portion of MSS, the words are probably original, despite their absence in Western MSS.[66] There could have been eye-skip from the *nu* at the end of αυτων to the *nu* at the end of υμιν, although this is speculative. In conclusion, και λεγει αυτοις ειρηνη υμιν is likely to be original, and Tertullian refers to this very passage showing that Jesus had the same body as he had before his death (*Marc.* 4.53). But even if this variant was secondary, it does not follow that it originated as anti-docetic polemic. It could have simply arisen from someone using the words of the parallel passage in John 20:19.

Luke 24:37

Following the previous passage, instead of the disciples being afraid because they had seen a πνευμα, D has the SR φαντασμα. The more vivid or colorful character of many of the readings in D probably explains the use of this word. Ehrman notes, however, that Tertullian quotes Luke 24:39 and uses the Latin word *phantasma* in refuting certain heretics (*Carn. Chr.* 5), and he suggests that this was another anti-docetic insertion.[67] Thus, the disciples were rebuked for thinking that he was a φαντασμα, so the docetists too should reject any such notion. This is a lot to hang on one word, which had some semantic overlap with πνευμα anyway in referring to disembodied spirits (cf. Acts 12:15, 23:8–9; 1 Pet 3:19; Heb 12:23).[68] Additionally, it might have come from the use of φαντασμα in Matt 14:26 recounting the disciples' reaction when they saw Jesus walking on the water in the dark. This suggestion could thus be left in the

---

65. In John 6:19 the disciples' initial reaction to seeing Jesus walking on the water is εφοβηθησαν prior to him speaking, whereas in Luke 24:37 their response is highlighted even after he spoke (πτοηθεντες δε και εμφοβοι γενομενοι). It is conceivable that a speaking πνευμα might cause alarm, even if speaking with the voice of Jesus. Further, what might appear to be conclusive evidence was not always taken as such in antiquity, as when, even in Matt 28:17, οι δε εδιστασαν.

66. Metzger, *Textual Commentary*, 160; Fitzmyer, *Luke X–XXIV*, 1575; Nolland, *Luke 18:35—24:53*, 1210na-a; Bovon, *Luke 3*, 390 and 390n24.

67. Ehrman, *Orthodox Corruption*, 259.

68. Bovon, *Luke 3*, 390.

realm of speculation, but it is an unlikely reason for the creation of this variant when D *does* use πνευμα two verses later (24:39) to recount Jesus' reference to the disciples' fear mentioned in v. 37.[69]

Luke 24:40

During Luke's account of Jesus' appearance to his disciples, he relates how he urged them to observe his hands and feet and to touch him in order to confirm that he was no πνευμα, since he had capкα και οcτεα (24:38–39). Most MSS then add the note, και τουτο ειπων εδειξεν αυτοιc τac χειρac και τουc ποδαc (24:40). The whole verse, however, is omitted in some MSS (D it sy[s,c]). Ehrman refers to early fathers, such as Ignatius (*Smyrn.* 3.2), Hippolytus (frag. 3), and Tertullian (*Carn. Chr.* 5, *Marc.* 4.43), who mentioned this event as proof of Jesus' physical resurrection. Again, he notes parallels with John 20:20 but emphasizes that this verse might have been added in support of anti-docetic polemic.[70] However, it might also have been omitted from some MSS to support a docetic Christology;[71] or perhaps it was seen as repetitive after 24:39 (ιδετε τac χειρac μου καν τουc ποδαc μου).[72] Or it was drawn from the parallel in John 20:20 but adjusted by changing "side" to "feet."[73] Hence, without conclusive arguments that this variant was inserted to support an anti-docetic agenda, the MS evidence should prevail and this verse be accepted as original to Luke's Gospel but somehow omitted in Western MSS for reasons that are at present unclear.[74]

John 20:30, 21:1

Toward the end of John 20, John comments that Jesus performed πολλα . . . και αλλα cημεια not recorded in his book (20:30). Ehrman asks if these "many other signs" were meant to refer to those Jesus performed

---

69. Matthews rightly argues that Luke himself cannot be placed on either side of a docetic viewpoint ("Fleshly Resurrection").

70. Ehrman, *Orthodox Corruption*, 255–56.

71. Bovon, *Luke 3*, 392.

72. Metzger, *Textual Commentary*, 160–61.

73. Parker, *Living Text*, 169; Hernández, "Early Text," 136.

74. Fitzmyer, *Luke X–XXIV*, 1576. Martin takes all seven variant readings in Luke 24 as additions to support an anti-separationist theology ("Defending," 280–94).

ANTI-DOCETIC CORRUPTIONS?

after his resurrection "to demonstrate its physical reality."[75] If so, he asserts that this has an "anti-Docetic appeal" to it. And since the OL MS e (V AD) adds "after he had been raised from the dead," Ehrman suggests that this is a remnant of an earlier reading. Further, in 21:1 other MSS (G f^{13} 1241 1424 etc.) insert the phrase αυτου εγερθεις εκ νεκρων, which he again takes to be "reasserting the proto-orthodox emphasis on Jesus' resurrection 'from the dead.'"[76] It is clear that these readings are secondary, but it is not certain that they were created to oppose docetic Christology. Indeed, it is unlikely, given the late dates of the MSS concerned. Nor does the omission of the clause from one later OL MS prove that it occurred in earlier MSS when docetism was current. Further, it is far from sure that the clause in 20:30 refers to Jesus' miracles after his resurrection, since this summary statement outlines why the whole Gospel was written, which probably includes its first half, as it certainly focuses on the "signs" Jesus performed.

1 Peter 4:1

Writing to readers facing the prospect of suffering for their Christian faith, in his first letter Peter directed their attention to Christ's sufferings—χριστου ουν παθοντος σαρκι . . . ο παθων σαρκι (4:1). Ehrman points out that a number of MSS and patristic witnesses add υπερ ημων (υμων) to the description of Christ's sufferings here, implying that this emphasis on the salvific nature of Jesus' death betrays an anti-docetic emphasis.[77] It is fairly certain that υπερ ημων is not original, but it is unclear why it was added. It might have been in order "to express the idea more fully," explaining what Jesus' suffering achieved,[78] or perhaps to avoid the idea that Christ had any sin from which he ceased.[79] But it is doubtful that it had an anti-docetic purpose since the verse already includes a reference to Jesus' physical suffering, and this is reinforced by a reference to the readers' probable physical suffering as well. Adding an explanatory purpose phrase hardly strengthens an emphasis on the physical nature of Jesus

---

75. Ehrman, *Orthodox Corruption*, 260–61.
76. Ehrman, *Orthodox Corruption*, 261.
77. Ehrman, *Orthodox Corruption*, 247.
78. Metzger, *Textual Commentary*, 624.
79. Achtemeier, *1 Peter*, 275n1.

and his death, so it is not clear that this variant was anti-docetic. Rather, it appears to show the influence of "familiar traditional formulation."[80]

The Bodily Ascension of Christ

Ehrman also discusses variant readings relating to the physical ascension of Jesus, as reported in the NT documents, especially since it formed a core aspect of Christian belief.[81]

Mark 16:4, 19

In Mark's account of events on the morning of Jesus' resurrection, one OL MS (k, IV/V AD) includes a remarkable addition at the beginning of 16:4. It is clearly not original. It recounts darkness, angels descending, Jesus rising "in the glory of the living God" and ascending with him, and then the darkness passing.[82] Ehrman suggests that this gloss arose in an earlier period than when this MS was produced, but there is little support for this. He also compares 16:19 in the longer ending of Mark, according to which, ο μεν ουν ιησους μετα το λαλησαι αυτοις ανελημφθη εις τον ουρανον και εκαθισεν εκ δεξιων του θεου, an addition containing similar theologically rich material. This second addition appears to be attested in sources as early as Irenaeus, so as part of the longer ending of Mark, it was clearly composed quite early.[83] Ehrman suggests that these two secondary readings reinforce the reality of Jesus' ascension, and therefore that they were designed to counter docetism.

It is true that they provide a greater amount of theological interpretation of Jesus' ascension than the original NT texts, like the graphic account of Jesus' resurrection in the Gospel of Peter.[84] However, while these secondary additions certainly enhance the interpretative element of the rather plain accounts in Luke and Acts, it is only with some difficulty that they can be seen as anti-docetic. They certainly describe the

---

80. Elliott, *I Peter*, 711–12.

81. Ehrman, *Orthodox Corruption*, 265–72, 302n179. Cf. Ehrman, "Christ Come," 354; Ehrman, *Misquoting*, 169–70.

82. Ehrman, *Orthodox Corruption*, 304n197. See Metzger, *Textual Commentary*, 101–2.

83. Ehrman, *Orthodox Corruption*, 272.

84. Metzger, *Textual Commentary*, 101–2; Evans, *Mark 8:27—16:20*, 529–30nc.

ANTI-DOCETIC CORRUPTIONS?

reality of Jesus' ascension; however, they offer imaginative theological interpretation rather than affirmation, and they do not explicitly focus on Jesus' human physicality, so it is hard to imagine that they were inserted for anti-docetic reasons.

Luke 24:51-52; Acts 1:2, 9-11, 22

The traditional ending of Luke's Gospel includes an account of Jesus' ascension—διεcτη απ αυτων και ανεφερετο εις τον ουρανον (24:51)—and then the disciples "worshipped" him (προcκυνηcαντες αυτον) and returned to Jerusalem (24:52). Ehrman notes that και ανεφερετο εις τον ουρανον (24:51) is lacking in Western witnesses (D it sy^s), as well as ℵ*. Nor does προcκυνηcαντες αυτον (24:52) occur in any of these MSS (except Sinaiticus). Without these phrases the end of Luke's Gospel is quite different.

Further, there is an account of a similar event in Acts 1:9-11, where Jesus επηρθη και νεφελη υπελαβεν αυτον απο των οφθαλμων αυτων (1:9), and the apostles were looking εις τον ουρανον πορευομενου αυτου (1:10a), and then ανδρες δυο παρειcτηκειcαν αυτοις εν εcθηcεcιν λευκαις, who told them that they should not be looking εις τον ουρανον, for ουτος ο ιηcους ο αναλημφθεις αφ υμων εις τον ουρανον ουτως ελευcεται ον τροπον εθεαcαcθε αυτον πορευομενον εις τον ουρανον (1:10b-11). It is not easy to reconcile the two accounts in Luke 24 and in Acts 1 as reporting the same event, one apparently on the day of Jesus' resurrection and the other forty days later (Acts 1:3). Moreover, Acts begins by referring to Jesus' actions and teaching αχρι ης ημερας εντειλαμενος τοις αποστολοις . . . εξελεξατο ανελημφθη (Acts 1:2). The latter issue, however, is not as difficult as we might imagine since Acts 1:1-2 is a summary, as is 1:3, and then 1:4-11 is an account of Jesus' final appearance (cf. 1:3) before he was "taken up" (1:2, 9). There is also a reference in Acts 1:22 to Jesus' ascension—της ημερας ης ανελημφθη αφ ημων. In fact, the ending of Luke's Gospel is probably a stylized ending, recounting the event that is also recorded in Acts 1 in order to draw the Gospel narrative to a close, despite an apparent chronological link with the events recounted up to that time on the day of resurrection. In view of the complexity of the issue, Ehrman makes the tentative suggestion that Luke 24:51 is an interpolation

Scribes, Theology, and Apologetics

inserted "to emphasize Jesus' bodily ascension against Docetic Christologies that denied it."[85]

With regard to external evidence, the "Western non-interpolations," of which this is one, might have been original, and Ehrman notes that 24:51 D aligns with ℵ* it sy^s, which adds some support to that. He also refers to the use of αναφερω in Luke 24:51, which does not appear elsewhere in Luke's ascension narratives, nor anywhere else in Luke-Acts, as an argument that it was not original there either. This verdict is not conclusive, however, in view of the limited sample of Luke's extant writing and noting that his vocabulary for the ascension varies significantly anyway, with several words used at times to describe the event. The difference between αναφερω and αναλαμβανω in these contexts is insignificant, however much they have had their own emphases elsewhere.

Ehrman also argues that Acts 1:2 and 1:22 do not necessarily refer back to the account in Luke 24:51, and this may be correct. However, if the ending of the Gospel were a stylized ending, as suggested above, this would not be an issue. These two verses do not both *need* to refer back. Acts 1:2 could refer forwards to 1:4–11, and Luke 24:51 could then stand on its own as an ending constructed to round off the narrative by referring to the events related in Acts 1. Perhaps when finishing his Gospel, Luke had no definite plan to continue with his narrative in Acts, so he finished off the story with a climactic conclusion. This is at least one explanation for the two accounts, which would reduce the likelihood that the original Gospel text was lacking these two phrases, as in those Western MSS.

Ehrman dismisses suggested transcriptional probabilities about scribes adding elements to 24:51–52 because they were needed by Acts 1:2, and likewise the proposal that parts of Luke 24:51–52 were omitted as unnecessary due to the content of Acts 1:2. However, the mention of Theophilus in Luke 1:3 and Acts 1:1 implies that even in antiquity readers would have seen a connection between Luke 24 and Acts 1 and then possibly omitted the "duplicate" material from Luke 24 due to the presence of a similar account in Acts 1, especially if Acts 1:2 was *not* seen as referring "back" to a previous account.[86] Ehrman rejects this argument,

---

85. Ehrman, *Orthodox Corruption*, 266–71.

86. Parsons argues that the word ανελημφθη, included in the account in Acts 1:9–11, refers to Jesus' death, resurrection, *and* ascension, as in Johannine parlance, and to Jesus' exaltation as including his crucifixion ("Text of Acts 1:2"), but this is probably too subtle for Luke's Gospel.

since other material that presents apparent contradictions is hardly ever dealt with by being reworked,[87] while here the material might not have been seen as contradictory but just superfluous.

It is also possible that the phrase in Luke 24:51 was omitted by homoioteleuton, since the letter sequence νκαι occurs at the beginning of the omitted material and at its end. Ehrman rejects this because it would suppose that one MS was the original of the readings in the Western MSS and the original of Codex Sinaiticus.[88] In fact, this might help to explain the variant, for there is no real reason why one mistake might not have spread to other places, were it not for the fact that, except for Sinaiticus, the same MSS that omit the material in 24:51 also omit the phrase in 24:52. Although much of Ehrman's argument is inconclusive, this last point is certainly one to ponder. That the same MSS have the same omission is not surprising, but why was the material omitted from both verses?

Ehrman points out that Codex Bezae omits ανελημφθη at the end of Acts 1:2, as well as επηρθη in 1:9 and εις τον ουρανον in 1:11, but ανελημφθη is inserted elsewhere in 1:2 and απηρθη is used instead of επηρθη in 1:9, so his point is not as strong as it might seem. He concludes, however, that copyists *added* the phrases to 24:51 to highlight Jesus' physical ascension, and that this was done as anti-docetic propaganda. He notes that Irenaeus stressed Jesus' physical ascension against the Marcionites (*Haer.* 4.34.3) and the gnostics (*Haer.* 5.31.1-2) and Tertullian also referred to it (*Res.* 51). None of these, however, prove that this was why this variant reading was created, even if it was secondary.[89]

Yet it is possible that the material was original and then omitted by scribal blunder (homoioteleuton) in 24:51 (νκαι . . . νκαι),[90] and similarly in 24:52 (αυτοι . . . αυτον).[91] Or perhaps someone wished to smooth

---

87. Ehrman, *Orthodox Corruption*, 304n192.

88. Parker notes that the first hand of ℵ tends to omit material by mistake, so it should not be given too much weight in the discussion here (*Living Text*, 170).

89. Metzger notes the suggestion that material implying Jesus' bodily ascension was removed from Acts 1 for theological reasons, and he seems to accept the originality of the longer text there (*Textual Commentary*, 240–41).

90. Porter and Pitts suggest that the first phrase could have been omitted because of the same beginning and ending of two lines of Greek text: (1) και ανεφερετο εις τον ουρανον; and (2) και αυτοι προςκυνηςαντες αυτον. Thus, a scribe could easily have skipped from the beginning of the first to the beginning of the second (και . . . και), especially in a text written in *scriptio continua* (*Fundamentals*, 124).

91. Metzger, *Textual Commentary*, 162–63.

out the tension with the narrative in Acts 1. Or the general tendency of the Western text to be shorter in Luke 24 is evident here.[92] The fact that Luke rounded off his Gospel with a stylized account of Jesus' ascension, and then repeated it in the opening of Acts does not present a problem, then, since when he completed his Gospel he might not have intended to compose a second book and wished to round off the narrative in a significant way. This would seem more likely than the subtle theory of an anti-docetic copyist manufacturing details in the Gospel to further his or her doctrinal cause.[93] On the other hand, if there was a theological motive for the variants, someone might have wished to minimize the physical nature of Jesus' ascension by omitting some words.[94] In this case, the Western text would be a "heretical corruption of scripture."[95] The proposal of an anti-docetic motivation for this variant is, then, far from proven, with its complexity an indication that it is an unlikely interpretation of the data.

Christ's Return in Judgment

The doctrine of the physical return of Christ in judgment is referred to by church fathers of the second and third centuries. Ehrman argues that some MSS bear traces of an orthodox adjustment to make this doctrine clearer, in order to enhance their ability to oppose docetic Christology.

Luke 23:42–43

In the context of a description of Jesus on the cross, Luke records one of the two criminals crucified alongside him making a request of Jesus: μνηcθητι μου οταν ελθηc εic την βαcιλειαν cου (23:42). Ehrman suggests that in general Luke de-emphasized futuristic aspects of Jesus' teaching

---

92. Nolland, *Luke 18:35—24:53*, 1224nb; Fitzmyer, *Luke X–XXIV*, 1590; Bovon, *Luke 3*, 409–10.

93. *Pace* Parker, who concludes that the shorter text is original in both verses, arguing that "mechanical error" is implausible (*Living Text*, 170–72).

94. Epp, "Ascension."

95. Zwiep, "Ascension Narratives," 244. Hernández discusses these variants but offers no conclusion ("Early Text," 137).

about the kingdom of God, citing several texts in support (Luke 9:27; 10:9, 11; 11:20; 17:21), although 21:7–32 does preserve an "end of the age" component. However, since this only amounts to an emphasis on what *has* come, without omitting aspects of Jesus' teaching referring to what *will* come, it is only an emphasis, and a slight one at that. Mark's Gospel also notes that the time of fulfilment *has* come (Mark 1:2–3, 15), so the texts cited from Luke cannot serve as support for a Lukan emphasis on realized eschatology. Nor can the utterance of Jesus on the cross affirming that "today" the criminal would be with him "in paradise" be seen as a replacement of the idea of a future kingdom of God with a present one, "the truly imminent event in which Jesus will enter into that glorious reign of God upon the completion of his task."[96] Rather, the promise to the criminal is better understood by comparison with the description in the parable of the state of Lazarus after death εις τον κολπον αβρααμ (16:22) where he "was comforted" (παρακαλειται, 16:25), in stark contrast to the rich man, υπαρχων εν βαςανοις εν τω αδη (16:23), who described his own state as οδυνωμαι εν τη φλογι ταυτη (16:24). The description of Lazarus's state was probably in the παραδειςος Jesus promised the criminal "today," presumably in contrast to his own hope that at some future time, when the kingdom of God arrived with Jesus as its vice-regent, he would experience salvation. Hence, Luke's Gospel does not omit the future aspect of the kingdom of God, nor did Jesus mean that his glorious kingdom was "imminent" and the criminal would shortly join him in it.

Ehrman alludes to the fact that most MSS read εν τη βαςιλεια ςου, rather than εις την βαςιλειαν ςου, suggesting that the reading εις την βαςιλειαν ςου (P[75] B etc.) is original and that it fits with the proposed realized eschatological interpretation of Luke's theology. This does not follow, however, partly because his explanation of the meaning of Jesus' words in the context of Luke's Gospel is unlikely, and partly because the distinction in meaning between εις and εν was almost non-existent in Koine Greek.[97] So, there is no theological emphasis on the glorious return of Jesus in the secondary variant in contrast to Luke's use of ςημερον (23:43). The fact that D has a SR in 23:42, in which the criminal asks Jesus to remember him εν τηc ημεραc τηc ελευςεωc ςου, is not then an example of the theological tendency to focus on the physical return of Jesus

---

96. Ehrman, *Orthodox Corruption*, 274.

97. BDF, 1n2, §§ 205–6, 218; BDAG, 289, εἰς 1αδ, 1bβ; 327, ἐν 3; GELS, 197, εἰς 8; 233, ἐν 17; Bovon, *Luke 3*, 311.

Scribes, Theology, and Apologetics

in contrast to Luke's minimizing that theme,[98] but the result of someone's correct but expanded account of the criminal's plea in the original. Hence, the proposed significance of the original text is unproven, and the causes of the variant readings were probably just linguistic alternatives and paraphrases.

Acts 28:31

At the end of the book of Acts, Luke describes Paul under house arrest in Rome, "proclaiming the Kingdom of God and teaching" τα περι του κυριου ιηcου χριcτου (28:31). Ehrman refers to the reading in an OL MS (p), some Vulgate MSS, and sy[h], according to which Paul's message is expanded to read "this is Jesus, the Son of God, through whom the whole world is about to be judged."[99] He implies that this is an emphasis on Christ's return in judgment as part of an anti-docetic corruption. However, this is exactly the kind of pious insertion one might expect in later MSS including Vulgate MSS, the Harclean Syriac (VI AD), and an OL MS from the twelfth century,[100] so it has little relevance to the concerns of anti-docetic disputes in the second and third centuries.

1 John 2:28

One of the major themes of 1 John is the exhortation to continue in Christian faith, living, and love—or, to put it as he does, to continue εν αυτω (2:28), that is, "in him [Jesus]." The purpose of thus "continuing" is then given in the following clause: ινα εαν φανερωθη cχωμεν παρρηcιαν και μη αιcχυνθωνεν απ αυτου. Ehrman notes that, instead of εαν, a number of MSS (minuscules and *Byz*) have οταν, which he takes as evidence that someone was wanting to remove any doubt that Jesus would come by replacing εαν ("if") with the more definite οταν ("when"). Based on this, he argues that someone wished to highlight Jesus' physical return by removing any equivocation that could have been read into the text.[101]

---

98. Pace Metzger, *Textual Commentary*, 154; Fitzmyer, *Luke X–XXIV*, 1510.
99. Ehrman, *Orthodox Corruption*, 273.
100. Metzger, *Textual Commentary*, 444–45; Barrett, *Acts*, 1253.
101. Ehrman, *Orthodox Corruption*, 273.

Yet, εαν and οταν can be quite close in meaning in certain contexts, such as Tob 4:3 (B A).[102] Further, both words contain -αν, the "particle of uncertainty," although the uncertain element in οταν does concern when the action will take place. Still, the proposed reason for this variant builds a lot on the difference between these conjunctions, especially when the context indicates that εαν did not contain a notion of uncertainty. In fact, the time reference εν τη παρουcια αυτου (2:28) hardly allows uncertainty. Coupled with this, εαν φανερωθη occurs soon afterward in 3:2, again, with no hint that reflects hesitation, and it is accompanied by the indicative verbs εcομεθα (*bis*) and οψομεθα. Someone might have wished to remove any shadow of doubt as to the reality of Jesus' return. It is hard to imagine, though, that anyone could have read uncertainty into 2:28 or that a copyist with the suggested motive for replacing εαν with οταν left the same phrase intact so soon afterward referring to a definite future event. So, the use of οταν instead of εαν in much later MSS is probably just a stylistic variant, not an attempt to support a theological viewpoint.

Christ, the Real Man of Flesh and Blood

The next group of variants concern the real flesh and blood of Jesus, with Ehrman suggesting that copyists with anti-docetic Christologies were attempting to ensure that the text of their MSS supported that aspect of their theology.

Matthew 8:27

In Matthew's account of Jesus calming the storm (Matt 8:23–27), the response of the disciples is given in the form of a question, ποταποc εcτιν ουτοc οτι και οι ανεμοι και η θαλαccα αυτω υπακουουcιν; (8:27). Codex W, however, inserts ο ανθρωποc after ουτοc, which could be seen as changing the meaning from a question perhaps implying that, whatever (ποταποc) he is, he is not human, to a question just asking who ουτοc ο ανθρωποc is. With this addition, there is then confirmation that Jesus was truly a man.[103] However, ποταποc is used elsewhere in the NT to refer to people without any possible hint that the subject might not be human (e.g., Luke 7:39, 2 Pet 3:11), so adding ο ανθρωποc would make little difference. Of

---

102. BDAG, 268, ἐάν 2; Brown, *Epistles*, 379.
103. Ehrman, *Orthodox Corruption*, 278.

course, the disciples were apparently faced with someone with more than human abilities, so the context might support a reference to their uncertainty but, rather than uncertainty about the reality of Jesus' humanity, the context clearly implies that they were wondering *what else* he might have been apart from being human, or *what kind* of person he was—perhaps a prophet like Moses?[104] Surely, no one could have understood this text to imply that the disciples wondered if he were truly human, and therefore no copyist would have felt the need to make Jesus' humanity more certain. Further, ουτος ο ανθρωπος is a common phrase in the NT (e.g., Luke 14:30; John 9:24, 11:27), as is ο ανθρωπος ουτος (Acts 6:13; 26:31, 32; 28:4). So, ο ανθρωπος was in common use, and its insertion here was likely to have been a slip to this usage on the part of a copyist. It is unlikely, then, that adding ο ανθρωπος had the goal of refuting docetic Christology by affirming Jesus' true humanity.

John 7:46

John 7 contains a series of reactions to Jesus and discussions about his identity. When the chief priests and Pharisees sent temple guards to arrest him (7:32) and they came back empty handed (7:45), the only explanation they could offer was that ουδεποτε ελαλησεν ουτως ανθρωπος (7:46). Ehrman proposes that this might be taken to suggest that Jesus was not human, even though there is no hint in the context that this occurred to anybody. He refers to the reading of P[66*], ουδεποτε ουτως ανθρωπος ελαλησεν ως ουτος λαλει ο ανθρωπος—and other MSS, including Sinaiticus, have variations of this. He then infers that there is an emphasis on Jesus' humanity in this variant with an added ανθρωπος, which was not present in the original.[105]

While this is possible, two factors argue against it. First, the variant with its second instance of ανθρωπος is quite awkward. If the emphasis is present, it is very slight indeed and only emphasizes something already present ("as this man speaks").[106] Second, the variant is probably a conflation of two readings. Indeed, in P[66] at least, the reading has been

---

104. BDAG, 856; *GELS*, 579. France suggests that the question might have meant, "How wonderful!" as in Mark 13:1 and 1 John 3:1 (*Matthew*, 331n6). Pace Davies and Allison, *Matthew*, 2:76.

105. Ehrman, *Orthodox Corruption*, 278.

106. Beasley-Murray, *John*, 103no. Pace Barrett, *John*, 331.

corrected.¹⁰⁷ So the textual situation is not as simple as might appear at first glance. It is also possible that the longer variant is original and some elements have dropped out by homoioteleuton.¹⁰⁸ Even in Sinaiticus, the original reading has been corrected, so, apart from anything else, it would be unwise to cite this variant as evidence for a copyist having a theological purpose, when it is difficult to know if the copyist was combining other readings and what the corrections were designed to achieve. So, the idea that ανθρωπος was inserted to confirm the humanity of Jesus must remain unproven and, in view of the readings being conflated, it is an unlikely interpretation of their intention.

Romans 5:19

In Rom 5:12–21, Paul was elaborating on the significance of Christ, couched in terms of the deleterious effects of the disobedience του ενος ανθρωπου (Adam) for the whole of humankind and contrasting this with the similarly universal but beneficial effects of the obedience του ενος (Jesus, 5:19). Some MSS (D* F G), however, insert ανθρωπου after του ενος referring to Jesus. Ehrman concedes that this word is already understood as part of Paul's meaning in 5:19, as is clear from its use in 5:15 referring to Jesus. He goes on to suggest, however, that ανθρωπου was supplied in 5:19 by scribes wishing to make it more explicit that Jesus is truly human, as Irenaeus argued based on this passage (*Haer.* 3.18.7).¹⁰⁹

Irenaeus was certainly emphasizing Jesus' human nature, but it has not been shown that someone added ανθρωπου to make this point. Moreover, it is more likely that ανθρωπου was added as a stylistic change, however unconsciously, since we know it was the intended meaning (cf. 5:15), and in 5:17 Adam and Christ are both designated by the phrase του ενος. So, in view of such fluctuation in the original text and the occurrence of του ενος ανθρωπου in 5:19a, it would be natural for someone to slip in ανθρωπου referring to Christ in 5:19b¹¹⁰ without necessarily wishing to emphasize Jesus' true humanity. Indeed, ανθρωπου is inserted

---

107. Royse, *Scribal Habits*, 455–56, 484.

108. Royse, *Scribal Habits*, 467n376.

109. Ehrman, *Orthodox Corruption*, 278–79.

110. Longenecker suggests a desire to highlight the parallelism (*Romans*, 577). Cf. Dunn, *Romans 1–8*, 271ne; Jewett and Kotansky, *Romans*, 370nq.

after δι ενος referring to Adam in ℵ* in 5:18. Thus, the proposal of an anti-docetic motivation for this variant is unfounded.

Ephesians 5:30

Paul was writing about the mutual responsibilities of husbands and wives in Eph 5:22–33 and, as part of his explanation as to why husbands should love their wives, he draws a parallel between Christ and the church. Within this parallel he offers the parenthetic remark regarding believers, οτι μελη εσμεν του σωματος αυτου (5:30). A number of MSS, however, probably under the influence of Gen 2:24 cited immediately afterwards (5:31), add an extended comparison based on Gen 2:23—εκ της σαρκος αυτου και εκ των οστεων αυτου (or similar). The MSS with these readings are not earlier than the fifth century, but the readings became prominent in later times.[111] Referring to Irenaeus (*Haer.* 5.2.3), Ehrman argues that support for this group of variants originated in the second century.[112] He notes that it is difficult to know why the words were inserted at this point but suggests that their reference to the church as the flesh and bones of Christ must be taken to imply something about Christ's own body—"that it comprised flesh and bones."[113]

However, while Irenaeus did make use of this text for that reason, since we do not know why someone added this phrase in the first place, it would be best to be cautious about attributing motives to the person responsible.[114] It might simply have been inserted to highlight the force of the link between Christ and the church, perhaps with the following quotation from Gen 2:24 (and 2:23) in mind, where σαρκα occurs in the LXX, and wishing to emphasize the subject matter of 5:31–32.[115] That Irenaeus used this variant reading in the second half of the second century shows that it existed then, but that does not tell us why it was created, so the proposal is still to be confirmed.

---

111. Best, *Ephesians*, 550–51; Robinson, *Ephesians*, 302.

112. Hoehner accepts the longer reading as original on both external and internal grounds (*Ephesians*, 769–70n3).

113. Ehrman, *Orthodox Corruption*, 276–77.

114. Lincoln accepts the influence of the quotation in v. 31 as the origin of the variant, but he agrees that it might have been anti-docetic in the first place (*Ephesians*, 351nd).

115. Metzger, *Textual Commentary*, 541.

ANTI-DOCETIC CORRUPTIONS?

Hebrews 2:14

After an opening comparison between God's revelation through Jesus and his revelation of the OT law through angels (Heb 1:1—2:4), the author of Hebrews, using Ps 8:4-6 in support, proceeds to describe Jesus being made human ("a little lower than the angels") before being "crowned... with glory and honor." He enlarges on Jesus' true humanity, including his death, stating that the purpose of his death was to free his people from "their fear of death" and to be a faithful high priest on their behalf (2:5–18). In this latter section, he refers to humanity sharing αιματος και σαρκος and therefore Jesus likewise μετεσχεν των αυτων, presumably referring to "blood and flesh." Ehrman points out that some Western MSS (D* b (t)) insert παθηματων after των αυτων, creating the new meaning that Jesus shared "in the same sufferings" or "the same experiences." He suggests that the person responsible for this variant did not have Jesus' death in view because "the same sufferings" is a more neutral reference to the limitations of human experience, so the variant would then be highlighting Jesus' true human experience in general.[116]

However, while the author was clearly emphasizing Jesus' true humanity ("lower than the angels," 2:9), his focus is on the consequences of that, for Jesus endured το παθημα του θανατου (2:9) and has been made the perfect Saviour δια παθηματων (2:10). Indeed, he "shared in them" (blood and flesh), ινα δια του θανατου he might destroy τον το κρατος εχοντα του θανατου (2:14) and free those held captive φοβω θανατου (2:15). Further, the purpose of being made like his brothers κατα παντα was εις το ιλασκεσθαι τας αμαρτιας του λαου (2:17). While his true human nature made it possible for him to empathize with his people in their temptations, it was his overcoming the temptation to veer from his Father's will and avoid death that was such a powerful model for them to follow (2:18, 4:15). If need be, they were called to "follow him" outside "the camp," just as he "suffered" (επαθεν) outside the city of Jerusalem, rejected by official Judaism (13:12–13). So, although the addition of παθηματων in 2:14 is certainly a corruption,[117] and indeed a slight alteration of the author's meaning, it is not an emphasis on Jesus' true humanity for its own sake or as a theological proposition, but an indication that it was only as a true human being that he could suffer death for his people and be their great high priest. The emphasis is clearly on his true humanity, as the context

---

116. Ehrman, *Orthodox Corruption*, 276.
117. Attridge, *Hebrews*, 78n6.

of 2:14 implies; however the focus is on his death as the relevant aspect of his humanity, not as an alternative to it. Thus, the variant reading adding παθηματων merely makes the original text slightly more explicit but does not change its general thrust, so it is unlikely to have been an attempt to highlight Jesus' true humanity in order to oppose docetism.

1 John 5:9

In the context of this passage, John was emphasizing obeying the commands of God as the expression of love for him but especially that "command" to believe in Jesus his Son (5:1–5). He highlights Jesus' true humanity, and then refers to God's testimony about his Son (5:9), with some MSS adding "whom he sent as a savior on earth. And the Son bore witness on earth by fulfilling the Scriptures; and we bear witness because we have seen him, and we proclaim to you that you may believe for this reason." The MSS supporting this reading are some Vulgate and Armenian MSS (derived from the Latin), along with Beatus of Libana (VIII AD).[118] Ehrman notes the emphasis on the connection between Christ and the OT and his having been "seen" (cf. 1:1–4) and suggests that this long addition "appears to magnify an anti-Docetic emphasis that the orthodox could claim was already present" in the text.[119]

This long reading seems to reuse themes from the prologue of the letter (1:2), combined with elements of John 20:31.[120] It is uncertain, however, that it was created for the purpose of opposing docetic Christology, since its MS support is much later than the time when this was an issue. Certainly, it is a pious addition to this anti-docetic letter, and clearly not accidental; however it is unlikely that the addition was motivated by a desire to oppose docetic Christology in the second or third century.

1 John 5:20

The final part of 1 John comprises a number of summary statements of the author's message. In 5:20, after οιδαμεν δε οτι ο υιος του θεου ηκει, some Vulgate MSS add "and [that he] was clothed with flesh for our sake

---

118. Ehrman, *Orthodox Corruption*, 305n208.
119. Ehrman, *Orthodox Corruption*, 276.
120. Brown, *Epistles of John*, 589; Strecker, *Johannine Letters*, 193n48.

and suffered and arose from the dead. And he took us to himself."[121] Since this variant existed in two different versions in the fourth century, Harnack reconstructed a Greek text and suggested that it originated in the late second or early third centuries,[122] and was then interpolated into texts of 1 John, serving to highlight themes in a letter that was already anti-docetic.[123] The steps in this argument should be questioned, however, since Harnack's text is only reconstructed and his dating was based on when it would have been relevant. Hence, the conclusion with regard to its setting was already assumed. Further, the dates of the Vulgate MSS are quite late, so with such uncertainties the implication drawn that this was deliberately anti-docetic in motivation is unwarranted.

Christ Born Human

With the issue of Jesus' true humanity being a major source of contention between docetists and the orthodox, writers like Irenaeus affirmed his true human birth (e.g., *Haer.* 4.33.2; cf. Tertullian, *Marc.* 3.11). Ehrman notes two passages where he suspects that orthodox scribes had been at work emphasizing Jesus' human birth to counter docetic Christology, since church writers made use of such passages in their controversies.

Romans 1:3-4

The opening part of Paul's letter to the Romans highlights his apostleship and the gospel he proclaimed, which concerned God's Son (Rom 1:1–5). In a description of the Son, he describes his human descent (του γενομενου εκ cπερματος δαυιδ κατα capκα), with some MSS (sy[pal] Byz[mss] it[mss acc to Aug]), as well as Origen, reading γεννωμενου rather than γενομενου, perhaps emphasizing Jesus being born (γενναω), as well as coming from David's "seed" κατα capκα. Ehrman takes this as evidence of someone tampering with the text in order to highlight Jesus' true human birth and oppose any docetic doctrine that he was not born as a human being.[124] However, gemination (the doubling of consonants—e.g., νν for ν) and its opposite (a single for a double consonant) were not uncommon in

---

121. Metzger, *Textual Commentary*, 650.
122. Cf. Strecker, *Johannine Letters*, 209n52; Brown, *Epistles*, 623.
123. Ehrman, *Orthodox Corruption*, 275.
124. Ehrman, *Orthodox Corruption*, 280.

Koine Greek,[125] and the o-ω vowel exchange also occurs in the papyri.[126] So, this variant could easily have been accidental and then transmitted to versions in other languages. Further, it should be added that γινεcθαι is sometimes used to refer to human birth,[127] so a copyist could have meant γενομενου, even though he wrote γεννωμενου. Since the origin of this variant is easily explained by contemporary linguistic phenomena, there is no need to propose a theological motive as the reason for its creation.[128] The fact that Tertullian used this text to affirm Jesus' true human birth (*Carn. Chr.* 22; cf. Irenaeus, *Haer.* 3.22) is no reason to attribute its creation to someone with the same purpose in mind, since an accidental corruption is not a purposeful one, even if the new reading was later used to support orthodox Christology.

Galatians 4:4

As in the previous example, Paul describes God's Son as γενομενον εκ γυναικος (4:4). Ehrman notes that coming "from a woman" was a phrase used by Irenaeus (*Haer.* 3.22.1) and Tertullian (*Carn. Chr.* 20) to prove the true humanity of Jesus in opposition to the gnostics, as it was used by Irenaeus against the docetists (*Haer.* 5.21.1). As well as this, some OL MSS read "born of a woman" not "come from a woman," with certain Greek MSS reading γεννωμενον rather than γενομενον (K *f*¹ etc.).[129] However, Greek MSS might have had this reading by linguistic accident, as in the previous example, and OL MSS followed them. Whether the church fathers used this variant is unclear, but it could easily have arisen as a copyist's error or an equivalent reading.[130] Indeed, γινομαι could be used as "a quasi-passive" of γενναω (1 Esd 4.16, Tob 8:6, Wis 7:3, Sir 449, John 8:58).[131] There is no clear proof, then, that the variant arose due to someone intending to highlight a doctrine that is plainly implied by the text anyway—Jesus having "come" εκ γυναικος.

---

125. Gignac, *Grammar*, 1:154–65.

126. Gignac, *Grammar*, 1:275–77.

127. BDAG, 197, γίνομαι 1; GELS, 130, γίνομαι 2b. Cf. Cranfield, *Romans*, 1:59.

128. Longenecker suggests that this reading arose as "an error in hearing or from later Christological speculation" (*Romans*, 46). Cf. Jewett and Kotansky, *Romans*, 95nb.

129. Ehrman, *Orthodox Corruption*, 279–80.

130. Dunn proposes that the variant was to make the meaning of γενομενον more precise (*Romans 1–8*, 4nc).

131. Bruce, *Galatians*, 195; Betz, *Galatians*, 207n49; MM, 126.

Christ and the Old Testament God

This final section of variants that Ehrman suggests derive from a desire to oppose docetic Christology deals with variants emphasizing that Jesus came from the God of the OT, the Creator God, not a different God, as Marcion alleged. In contrast to Marcion, orthodox writers highlighted that there is only one God, the Creator, and that he is also the God of Israel, who gave them the OT Scriptures and sent his Son to fulfill the promises he had made in them. Ehrman cites examples that he suggests show orthodox scribes either having adjusted the text in their copies in order to affirm orthodox theology more clearly or having inserted readings that supported their theology when it was not originally present.

John 10:7–8

Jesus is portrayed teaching about himself as the good shepherd in John 10, so Ehrman proposes that orthodox Christians "must surely have been puzzled" to read that παντες οcοι ηλθον προ εμου κλεπται ειcιν και λῃcται (John 10:7-8), for they might have thought that it meant that *all* the Israelites living before Jesus, such as those mentioned in the OT, were wicked. Hippolytus indicates that some gnostics understood these words like that (*Haer.* 6.30), and Ehrman suggests that this led to the omission of παντες in Western MSS (D b), so that not *all* of Jesus' predecessors are said to be wicked.[132] This does not follow, however, since the statement is almost as damning if the reference was only to οcοι ηλθον προ εμου being wicked. The addition of παντες adds little to οcοι. In any case, it clearly refers to people in positions of leadership in Judaism before Jesus' day (and at that time?), as his reference to himself as "shepherd" shows (cf. vv. 2, 11, 14, 16). As such, it would be difficult to base a case for scribal bias on this reading.

Ehrman also suggests that the reading without προ εμου in some important MSS (P[45vid] P[75] ℵ* lat sy[s,p,pal] sa ly etc.) arose out of a desire to stifle the strength of this saying, making the saying now quite difficult to interpret—παντες οcοι ηλθον κλεπται ειcιν και λῃcται.[133] Metzger agrees that this variant arose due to a desire to avoid condemning "all Old Testament

---

132. Brown suggests that this interpretation might have seemed too "drastic" (*John I–XII*, 386).

133. Ehrman, *Orthodox Corruption*, 281.

worthies,"[134] and this may be true. If so, whoever was responsible created a very difficult text. Who are "they"? When did they "come"? When did "the sheep" not listen to "them"? What did Jesus mean? Again, however, an accidental omission, even if we cannot account specifically for its origin, is a better explanation for this variant than a deliberate change that created a nonsense reading. Surely, the OT images of the leaders of Israel as shepherds who did not care for the flock of Israel (e.g., Ezek 34) would be the natural OT background of the original text. Hence a past reference would only be expected, especially in view of the aorist tense of ηκουcαν. A natural meaning accidentally confused by omission is surely easier to accept than an "orthodox corruption" resulting in nonsense.

Romans 9:5

The context of this passage is Paul's lengthy treatment of the issue of God's faithfulness to the nation of Israel in Rom 9–11. At the beginning of this section, Paul affirms the privileges bestowed on Israel (9:3-4), and in 9:5 he asserts that οι πατερεc belong to the nation και εξ ων ο χριcτοc το κατα cαρκα. Ehrman points out that orthodox writers such as Irenaeus referred to this passage to affirm Christ's relationship to Israel and its God (e.g., *Haer.* 3.16.3), noting that some MSS (F G f g etc.) omit και, so the expression εξ ων ο χριcτοc now ties back Christ's ancestry "more unequivocally" to "the Jewish ancestors" (οι πατερεc). This reading was mentioned by Hippolytus (*Noet.* 2.5) and therefore must have existed at least early in the third century.[135]

Its significance and implications, however, are not transparent. It is true that, without και, the relative pronominal expression εξ ων is more logically taken as referring to οι πατερεc. Is this connection any more significant, however, than if και were present and εξ ων referred to the ιcραηλιται mentioned in v. 4 as the antecedent, as in the original? While οι πατερεc are presumably the OT "patriarchs," and this certainly makes a connection with the OT, Paul has just noted that οι πατερεc belong to the ιcραηλιται (9:5a), presumably including contemporary Israelites. So, coming "from" οι πατερεc physically (το κατα cαρκα) is surely little different from coming from ιcραηλιται physically. Although the antecedent

---

134. Metzger, *Textual Commentary*, 195. Cf. Beasley-Murray, *John*, 164-65nc. Brown does not support this suggestion unequivocally (*John I-XII*, 386).

135. Ehrman, *Orthodox Corruption*, 281-82.

of the relative pronoun ων has changed, in the context the meaning is no different—from the Israelites to whom "the fathers" belong *or* from "the fathers" who belong to the Israelites. Hence, the proposed motivation has little to commend it when the passage with the variant is viewed in context.[136] A reader would have noticed no difference, so a copyist would have had no reason to create it deliberately to reinforce a christological point.

Galatians 3:16, 17

In his letter to the Galatians Paul was dealing with the issue of the OT Law and its place in the life of Christian believers. Referring to the promises given to Abraham, Paul notes that they were given και τω σπερματι αυτου, which he took as a reference to one σπερμα, ος εστιν χριστος (3:16). Clearly, Paul was stating that there is a strong link between Christ and the promises of God to Abraham; however two MSS (F* G) read ου instead of ος, thus creating the meaning "of whom is the Christ." Ehrman takes this to mean that Christ is referred to as being "of" Abraham, supposedly tying Christ more tightly to the OT and the God of Israel.[137] The relative pronoun, however, cannot refer to Abraham because σου in το σπερμα σου refers to Abraham, and Abraham's σπερμα is still the origin of Christ instead of "being" Christ. If anything, the link between Christ and Abraham is made more distant by this reading in these two ninth-century MSS. Probably, the variant was a simple mistake of one letter.

Further, after referring to the covenant being ratified υπο του θεου (3:17) the same two MSS (and D it sy etc.) add εις χριστον, which is also understood to imply a similar strengthening of the association between Christ and the OT covenant and the God of Israel. This variant is clearly not accidental, and it does seem to refer to Christ as the σπερμα in 3:16. However, no MS earlier than the late-third century supports it, so its origin is not necessarily earlier than that. Further, it might not have been created with the aim of supporting a theological position but simply to clarify Paul's argument.[138] Thus, it is not necessarily an "orthodox corruption," even though it is clearly a "corruption" of the original.

136. Cf. Birdsall, review of *Orthodox Corruption*.

137. Ehrman, *Orthodox Corruption*, 282.

138. Metzger suggests that it was apparently added as a reference to Christ, who was mentioned in 3:16 (*Textual Commentary*, 525). Longenecker traces the influence of 3:24–28 (*Galatians*, 125nb). Cf. Burton, *Galatians*, 183; Betz, *Galatians*, 158n43.

CONCLUSION

In this chapter dealing with variants alleged to have come from an orthodox desire to stress anti-docetic Christology in a variety of ways, I have argued that most variants can be explained more easily. Many of them were likely to have been scribal slips due to current pronunciation, inattention, or harmonizing the text to the immediate context or to a similar context in a different part of the NT. Some of them probably stemmed from piety and a high view of the status of Christ, and others seem to have derived from a desire to clarify the text. The fact that church fathers used these variant readings in their disputes with docetists of various hues does not prove that the readings were created with this purpose in mind but simply that the fathers found them useful in that way.[139] In fact, many of the variants cited cannot be firmly dated to the second and third centuries, the time period in question. Coupled with this, although the text was much more controlled after the fourth century, there are many more MSS from that period, and there was also a temptation for "orthodox" copyists in that later period to add theological enhancements to the copies they were making for a variety of reasons.

Further, we do not know what reading was on the exemplar that a copyist was using, so it is fruitless to ascribe a variant to the copyist of a particular MS unless it is clearly part of a pattern of his or her scribal behavior. Prior to the fourth century, copies were beginning to be made in monasteries and churches, but in those first centuries when Christian texts were being copied there is every likelihood that the usual means of book production were commonly used, where copyists were paid to reproduce Christian MSS, without there being any necessity for them to be Christians themselves. For all these reasons, the case for a slew of textual variants created to support anti-docetic Christology, or to stop readings being used by docetists, remains unproven. Indeed, there are generally other more likely reasons to account for most of the variants discussed, particularly when we consider the realities of how MSS were reproduced by hand and all that this entailed in terms of the kinds of errors that commonly occurred.

---

139. Cf. Wasserman, "Scribal Alterations," 307–8.

4

Anti-patripassianist Corruptions?

PATRIPASSIANISM FOCUSED ON THE unity of God and then took this to imply that Christ was in fact identical with God the Father, but in human flesh.[1] Chapter 5 of Ehrman's book contains discussions of variants said to show the hand of "orthodox" scribes in opposition to patripassianist views they deemed "heretical." Ehrman provides an account of patripassianist theology and its advocates, such as Noetus, against whom Hippolytus directed his refutation (*Noet.* 1), or Praxeas, whom Tertullian opposed (*Prax.* 1). On this view, God the Father became a man, suffered, and died. Despite its popularity in certain quarters, even in certain "orthodox" circles, patripassianism was not a major issue in the second and third centuries, so Ehrman proposes only a small number of variants as having been designed to counter patripassianist Christology.

Mark 2:7

Mark provides an account of Jesus healing a paralyzed man (Mark 2:1–12). In response to him also declaring the man's sins forgiven, some Jewish scribes were apparently thinking that he had no right to do so and alleged that he was blaspheming. Surely, τιc δυναται αφιεναι αμαρτιαc ει μη εις ο θεος; (v. 7). Ehrman takes the reading in D (V AD), which omits εις, as an indication that a scribe modified the text to allow for an

---

1. Ehrman, *Orthodox Corruption*, 307–9.

Scribes, Theology, and Apologetics

orthodox interpretation of the text. Thus, Christ can still be divine (ο θεος) but not identical to the Father.[2]

Yet the text need not be understood in as potentially "unorthodox" a way as proposed. While the Jewish scribes clearly thought that Jesus was arrogating to himself the prerogative of God, Jesus' response did not necessarily imply his divinity. He was declaring the man's sins forgiven, which need only have been on behalf of God, just as OT prophets spoke on God's behalf. So, Mark's narrative records that the onlookers "praised God" (2:12), clearly not referring to Jesus. Hence, there is no reason to think that a reader or copyist might have thought that there was a danger of a patripassianist finding support from this text, because even with ειc the scribes' rhetorical question implies that *only God*—not referring to Jesus—had the right to declare sins forgiven,[3] and there is no reason to think that omitting ειc would change that. However, Jesus is portrayed as speaking on behalf of God as the exalted "Son of Man" with divine authority (v. 10), but not necessarily more than that. So, given the whole context, the person responsible for this omission probably thought that he or she was omitting an unnecessary word without changing the meaning rather than creating a text less liable to be misconstrued by patripassianists.

Mark 12:26

Mark relates a discussion between some Sadducees and Jesus on the topic of the resurrection of the body (12:18–27), during which Jesus is said to have cited Exod 3:6 in support—εγω ο θεος αβρααμ και [ο] θεος ιcααk και [ο] θεος ιακωβ (12:26). Ehrman notes that "orthodox" writers sometimes interpreted these words as having been spoken by Christ before his incarnation, as Tertullian probably implies (*Prax.* 16). As such, he suggests that the MSS that omit the three articles before θεος (D W), and the one that contains the first but omits the other two (B), testify to a desire to have Christ speaking not as ο θεος but only as θεος, thus avoiding a simple identification of Christ and God the Father.[4]

However, we do not know how widely it was believed that these words were spoken by Christ in the OT era. Also, as noted previously, the presence or absence of the article in Greek does not necessarily

---

2. Ehrman, *Orthodox Corruption*, 312.
3. Cf. Marcus, *Mark 1–8*, 217; Collins, *Mark*, 185n24.
4. Ehrman, *Orthodox Corruption*, 312.

correspond to a noun being definite or indefinite, so the lack of articles in this variant reading says little about how definite the word θεοc was meant to be. In Mark 10:27, for example, both θεοc and ο θεοc are used for the one person, God (the Father)—παρα θεω and παρα τω θεω. It would be unlikely, then, for anyone to think that by omitting an article he was referring to "a god" as distinct from "the God." Further, θεοc was used in Jewish circles to refer to the God of Israel, and in Christian circles θεοc was used both with and without the article to refer to the God of Israel or to the God and Father of Jesus Christ. And, since even the text being cited (Exod 3:6) lacks the article in those three instances in the LXX—except for Alexandrinus, where it occurs with the first instance and not the others, as in B in the text under discussion—it is much more likely that Mark was following a Greek OT text and that any fluctuation between including the article or not in subsequent copies had no special significance.[5] Thus, while the textual situation as to which reading was original is unclear,[6] there is no evidence that these variants betray an anti-patripassian tampering with the text.

Luke 7:16, 8:39

Luke's Gospel relates how Jesus raised a widow's son from the dead (Luke 7:11–17). In response to this amazing event, the onlookers said that επεcκεψατο ο θεοc τον λαον αυτου (7:16), where some MSS (f^1 aur c l) read ο κυριοc instead of ο θεοc. The same substitution occurs in some MSS at 8:39 (C* 2643 b sy^c), with MS 213 reading ο ιηcουc. Further, in 7:17 the news that spread was περι αυτου (i.e., about *Jesus*), despite the crowd saying that *God* had come to help his people, while in 8:39b the man went around saying what *Jesus* had done for him, although he was told to say how much *God* had done for him (8:39a). Ehrman notes that some MSS delete 8:39b altogether, and others use θεοc instead of ιηcουc, perhaps to avoid the problem.[7] Thus, he proposes that θεοc has been changed to κυριοc in order to avoid the identification of Jesus with God, assuming that ο κυριοc would more easily refer to Jesus.

---

5. France, *Mark*, 470. Pardee discusses this text with regard to harmonization to parallel passages in Luke 20:37 and Matt 22:32 (*Harmonization*, 263). Evans suggests that the phrase from Exod 3:14 (εγω ειμι ο ων) was behind the variant here (*Mark 8:27—16:20*, 251nf), but this is doubtful.

6. Metzger, *Textual Commentary*, 93–94.

7. Ehrman, *Orthodox Corruption*, 318n36.

Scribes, Theology, and Apologetics

The context of the variants, however, shows that this was an unlikely construction for anyone to put on them and hence an unlikely reason for someone to create them with the proposed purpose in mind. In relation to 7:16, the narrative is clear that the crowd εδοξαζον τον θεον, but their praise of God was because προφητης μεγας ηγερθη εν ημιν. Thus, on a plain reading of the text, the crowd distinguished between God and Jesus, describing Jesus as a "great prophet." It was for sending such a one that they said that "God has come to help his people." Hence, there would seem little need to clarify any confusion by altering θεος to κυριος. On the lips of the crowds ο κυριος would most naturally refer to the God of Israel in view of the widespread use of ο κυριος in the LXX to refer to God. So also, later MSS that read ο κυριος instead of ο θεος in 8:39 were also presumably referring to the God of Israel, in accord with Septuagintal usage. The proposal, then, that these variants were created to counter an identification of Jesus with God and stave off a patripassianist reading is doubtful in the context. The one MS (213) with ο ιησους for ο θεος at 8:39 might show that someone wanted to make the verse consistent in its reference to who was responsible for raising the boy, but it was produced in the eleventh century, so it can have had little to do with an anti-patripassianist motivation in the early centuries.

John 1:18

At the end of the prologue of John's Gospel, some MSS describe Jesus with the article before μονογενης θεος (P^{75} ℵ^1 33), while others omit it (P^{66} ℵ* B C* L sy; Irenaeus Origen).[8] Ehrman suggests that the original text included the article,[9] and that it was removed in some MSS to counter a patripassian identification of Jesus, the Son, with God the Father, *the* one and only God. The date of the reading without the article is clearly quite early since it occurs in P^{75} (early III AD), although its significance is not as obvious. It is suggested that the short variant is secondary, showing that a text that initially could have been taken as identifying Jesus with God the Father had now been changed, so that "the identification is less exalted: he is uniquely God, but less explicitly 'the' one and only God."[10]

---

8. Metzger notes that some MSS read ο μονογενης υιος, although he suggests that this is likely to have been an assimilation to John 3:16, 3:18, or 1 John 4:9 (*Textual Commentary*, 169-70). Cf. McHugh, *John 1-4*, 100-112; Haenchen, *John 1*, 121.

9. Cf. Allen Wikgren, in Metzger, *Textual Commentary*, 170.

10. Ehrman, *Orthodox Corruption*, 311.

ANTI-PATRIPASSIANIST CORRUPTIONS?

Despite the fact that the patripassianists did use John's Gospel to support their views, we cannot be certain that this variant was created to oppose them. Indeed, it is debatable that it would have done so, since, as noted above, an anarthrous noun in Greek, even θεoc, is not necessarily indefinite. It depends on the context, and the context here indicates that "the only God" (or "the only Son" in some MSS) is both God and distinct from God, since he is close to him and made him known (1:18; cf. 1:1). Since omitting an article would not significantly change the meaning, it is unlikely that someone would have done so to avoid an unwanted meaning being based on this particular text.[11] Indeed, adding the article (if it were not original) could have resulted from "a scribal tendency to conform" to this phrase in the three (of four) other uses of μονογενης in Johannine writings (John 3:16, 18; 1 John 4:9).[12] The variant with the article (ο μονογενης θεος) is, however, probably original, and it is unlikely that the article was omitted to counter patripassian Christology.

John 14:9

In response to Philip's request, κυριε δειξον ημιν τον πατερα (John 14:8), Jesus is said to have given the enigmatic reply τοcουτω χρονω μεθ υμων ειμι και ουκ εγνωκαc με, Φιλιππε; ο εωρακωc εμε εωρακεν τον πατερα (14:9). Ehrman notes that Noetus apparently referred to this passage to support his view that Jesus was God himself (Hippolytus, *Haer.* 7.4; cf. Tertullian, *Prax.* 20) but also that Hippolytus appealed to the context to show that the Son is clearly differentiated from the Father (*Haer.* 7.5-7). Ehrman then suggests that a copyist, instead of arguing from the context like Hippolytus, changed the reading by inserting και after εωρακεν, thus referring to the person who has seen Jesus having "also" seen the Father and creating a distinction between the two persons. The MSS with this reading are not weighty (P[75] lat ly bo[mss]), so it is clearly secondary, and Ehrman takes this to be an orthodox corruption, for the variant now makes it clear that "Christ and God are two persons, and Christ reveals the Father."[13]

Yet, the variant reading could be used to support the same patripassianist interpretation that it was supposedly designed to avoid, for it

---

11. Marcello, "Myths," 224-27.
12. Brown, *John I-XII*, 17.
13. Ehrman, *Orthodox Corruption*, 310.

could be argued that seeing Christ is *also* seeing the Father, since he *is* the Father. Further, this addition was probably just imitating the thought of 14:7 (ει εγνωκατε με και τον πατερα μου γνωcεcθε).[14] The variant, then, does not avoid the issue, nor do we know that the person responsible for creating it wished to avoid a patripassian interpretation of the original.

John 20:28

Another passage in John's Gospel where an article was omitted in some MSS is John 20:28. Where Thomas addressed Jesus as ο κυριος μου και ο θεος μου (20:28) in the original, some MSS omit the article before θεος. It is proposed that this was done to counter any possibility of patripassian Christology finding support from this text.[15] The MSS cited in support of this variant reading are "the predecessor of codex Bezae and other Gospel manuscripts."[16] It is clear, however, from the transcription on the IGNTP and the image on the Cambridge University Library website, that the copyist of D* wrote ο κc και ο θc μου, which he then corrected to ο κc μου και θc μου. It is difficult to know why the copyist inserted a second μου after ο κc and omitted the article before ο θc μου, although he did have a predilection for omitting articles.[17] As noted previously, the presence or absence of the article cannot be used to support the proposed distinction, particularly with the possessive pronoun μου following. The context determines whether an anarthrous noun is definite or not. So here, where Jesus is addressed as ο κυριος μου, as well as θεος μου, whatever Thomas originally intended and whatever John understood him to mean, removing an article would have made no difference. So, someone would hardly have been likely to omit the article to create a different meaning.[18] Thus, there is no reason to think that this variant was an "orthodox corruption," since even with the article omitted Jesus is still called θεος with divine import.

14. Brown, *John XIII–XXIV*, 622.
15. Ehrman, *Orthodox Corruption*, 311–12.
16. Ehrman, *Orthodox Corruption*, 312.
17. Yoder, "Language," 245.
18. Moule comments that even the article in front of θεος "may, therefore, not be significant" (*Idiom Book*, 116). Cf. Wright, "Jesus as ΘΕΟC," 249–50.

ANTI-PATRIPASSIANIST CORRUPTIONS?

Acts 16:34

This verse occurs in an account of events in Philippi, where Paul and Silas were imprisoned (Acts 16:16–40). Because of an earthquake, they could have made their escape, but they remained where they were and, as a result, the jailer believed "in the Lord Jesus" (16:31–33). Paul and Silas had previously urged him, πιϲτευϲον επι τον κυριον ιηϲουν (16:31), with Luke's account relating that the jailer (and his family) believed—πεπιϲτευκωϲ τω θεω (16:34). Ehrman suggests that the MSS that read τω κυριω instead of τω θεω in 16:34 show someone's desire to remove the apparent identification of Jesus with God—believing in τον κυριον ιηϲουν (16:31) and then τω θεω (16:34). The MSS in question are a number of Greek minuscules and lectionaries, as well as OL d and the Sahidic version.[19]

Again, using κυριω instead of θεω does not necessarily avoid the issue since ο κυριοϲ was the standard way of referring to God in the Septuagint, the traditional OT text of Greek speakers. So, despite "the *Lord* Jesus" being mentioned in 16:31, "the *Lord*" in 13:34 would naturally be taken as referring to "the *Lord* God," as Jesus is not mentioned there. So, a copyist would hardly be likely to have made the change with the intention of hindering Jesus being thought of as God if there was little appreciable difference in meaning. Further, we do not *know* if such a thought occurred to anyone, and there is no proof that the variant was created to avoid that thought. Indeed, the context surely implies a reading of 13:34 in which they believed in "God" (the Father), just as they had believed in "the Lord" (Jesus) as the Savior.

Acts 20:28

Ehrman previously suggested that the original reading την εκκληϲιαν του θεου was changed to την εκκληϲιαν του κυριου. As we noted, however, the textual situation is not simple and perhaps it was the other way around. Nevertheless, he suggests that θεου was changed to κυριου to avoid any thought that God (the Father) shed "his own blood," proposing that the reading του κυριου was created some time in the third century.[20] However, since it is not clear which reading was original, it would be unwise to build an argument on the new reading being του κυριου. If του θεου were

---

19. Ehrman, *Orthodox Corruption*, 313.
20. Ehrman, *Orthodox Corruption*, 309–10.

original, it might well have been changed to avoid the strange sounding "blood of God."[21] So, the proposal that the reading του κυριου was created to avoid referring to Jesus as God and to support patripassian Christology remains doubtful.

Ephesians 5:5

In Eph 5 Paul describes those whose lives show that they have no inheritance εν τη βασιλεια του χριστου και θεου (5:5). Some MSS have the more common phrase εν τη βασιλεια του θεου (P[46] Tertullian) or εν τη βασιλεια του θεου και χριστου (F G bo[ms]), and there are other later readings—"the kingdom of the Christ of God" (1739* eth etc.), "the kingdom of Christ" (38* 90), or "the kingdom of the Son of God" (1836). Whatever the reasons for these readings, Ehrman suggests that in the original Christ seems to be accorded a priority over God, presumably by being mentioned first, and that the various changes were intended to avoid that.[22]

However, it is not clear that the original reading was meant to portray Christ as superior to God, even on the basis of prior mention, nor is it apparent that it was understood like that in the early centuries.[23] No doubt, those responsible for the various readings had their reasons for creating them, whether intentional or not. That they were deliberately designed, however, to avoid a patripassian reading with Christ identified with God the Father is less certain. We do not need to account for idiosyncratic readings in later MSS because our concern here is with the earlier centuries when patripassian Christology was an issue. However, since the common phrase in the Gospels was η βασιλεια του θεου, it would not be difficult to imagine someone omitting του χριστου και or writing the common phrase, realizing their mistake, and then adding και χριστου back in afterwards. There is then no final proof that the suggested reasons for the creation of these readings were the actual reasons of real people. Rather, scribal oversight (copying τουχυκαιθυ) or the predominant phraseology in the Gospels are more likely explanations for their formation.[24]

21. Metzger, *Textual Commentary*, 427. Walton accepts του θεου as the original reading, and he suggests that the reading του κυριου arose out of a desire to clarify that it was "the Lord" (Jesus) who shed his blood, not God (*Leadership and Lifestyle*, 94–98).

22. Ehrman, *Orthodox Corruption*, 315, 319n42.

23. Best, *Ephesians*, 482.

24. Metzger, *Textual Commentary*, 539.

Philippians 2:9

In the "hymnic" material comprising Phil 2:6–11, Christ is said to have been highly exalted by God, και εχαρισατο αυτω το ονομα το υπερ παν ονομα (2:9). A number of MSS (D F G *Byz* etc.) do not have the article before the first ονομα, which Ehrman suggests shows that those responsible wished to avoid the thought that Christ was given *the* name above all, that is, the name of God (the Father).

It is possible that this might have been a slip, since εχαρισατο also ended in το, which could have led to the omission of the article το before ονομα.[25] This, however, fails to account for the fact that αυτω was not omitted. Rather, omitting το before ονομα does not change the meaning, since ονομα is then defined by το υπερ παν ονομα. Omitting the initial article hardly changes the sense—"*a* name, the one above every name" is no different from "the name, the one above every name." How many names can there be υπερ παν ονομα? In any case, the "name" in question is surely "Lord" (2:11), and the distinction between Christ as Lord and God the Father is stated explicitly in 2:11. Further, it was God who gave him that name (2:9). Therefore, the variant omitting the article was probably a scribal slip,[26] not a theologically motivated change that would not do justice to the meaning of the variant itself in the context. The variant reading is thus easily explained as accidental, rather than intentional.[27]

Colossians 2:2

In a section describing Paul's laboring for the church (Col 1:24—2:5), he elaborates on his purpose that believers would be encouraged and have a full appreciation του μυστηριου του θεου χριστου (2:2). Probably due to the unusual syntax of this phrase, there are many variant readings. Ehrman suggests that the readings arose partly in response to a possible interpretation along patripassian lines, where Christ could actually be identified with God.[28] However, it is likely that the readings are just "scribal attempts to ameliorate the syntactical ambiguity," so there is no need to propose more complex theological motivations.[29] If the text in NA[28] is

---

25. Metzger, *Textual Commentary*, 546.
26. Fee, *Philippians*, 218n1.
27. Cf. Rodgers, "Textual Commentary," 191–93.
28. Ehrman, *Orthodox Corruption*, 313.
29. Metzger, *Textual Commentary*, 555. Cf. Bruce, *Colossians*, 89n3; Barth and

original, unless an error occurred very early on, a reader's or a copyist's difficulty in understanding the text is an adequate explanation for the origin of this variant.

Hebrews 1:8

The catena of quotations in Heb 1:5-14 was designed to show the superiority of Christ to the angels, and hence the superiority and finality of God's revelation through him in comparison to the revelation delivered through angels in the OT Law (cf. 1:1-4, 2:1-4). Part of the catena is a quotation from Ps 45:6-7 (44:7-8 LXX), where God is said to have addressed the Son as ο θεος (1:8; cf. 1:5-7)—ο θρονος cου ο θεος εις τον αιωνα του αιωνος. Although this could mean "Your throne is God," this is highly unlikely in a Jewish or Christian text since it would imply that the addressee was seated on God.[30] It is much more likely that ο θεος was meant to be understood to function as a vocative.[31] So, a hyperbolic address to the king in divine terms (in its OT setting)[32] has thus been used as an exalted address to Christ who rules forever, without necessarily addressing the issue of the relationship between God and Christ, although this was probably assumed to be of a "subordinationist" nature.[33] Ehrman draws attention to the reading αυτου instead of cου at the end of the verse (P[46] ℵ B), which changes the meaning from a reference to the kingdom of the addressee (Christ) to one referring to "his kingdom," presumably the kingdom of God.

However, the inference that now the throne in 1:8a must refer to God's throne, and mean "God is your throne forever," is unwarranted and clearly unlikely. Ehrman suggests that the variant reading was composed "to resolve a problematic feature" in this verse, so that Christ would not be identified as God himself (ο θεος) but "made subordinate to him: 'God [himself] is your throne.'"[34] Even if this were possible, however, it is still

---

Blanke, *Colossians*, 280-81; Dunn, *Colossians*, 128n3; MacDonald, *Colossians*, 86; Metzger and Ehrman, *Text*, 334-35; Wilson, *Colossians*, 185-86.

30. Metzger, *Textual Commentary*, 592-93. Pace Ehrman, *Orthodox Corruption*, 310-11.

31. Ehrman, *Orthodox Corruption*, 317n17, refers to Attridge, *Hebrews*, 58-59.

32. On this psalm, see Craigie, *Psalms 1-50*, 335-41. He entitles it "A Royal Wedding Song."

33. Harris, "Translation and Significance."

34. Ehrman, *Orthodox Corruption*, 311.

ANTI-PATRIPASSIANIST CORRUPTIONS?

the wrong way around, since he would then be seated *on God*, hardly a subordinate position. Nor does this follow from the reading αυτου in those MSS, because a change from addressing Christ in the second person (ο θρονος cου) to referring to him in the third person (της βαcιλειας αυτου) could easily reflect such changes in Hebrew poetry as occur frequently in the Psalms—indeed in Ps 45 itself (44:10, 16 LXX).[35] Thus, reading αυτου instead of cου is probably just a transcriptional error,[36] or a failure to realize that the text was a direct second person address,[37] so the proposed reason for these variants as anti-patripassian in intention cannot be sustained.[38]

2 Peter 1:1, 2

In the opening section of 2 Peter, the author refers to "the righteousness" του θεου ημων και cωτηρος ιηcου χριcτου (1:1). It would be natural to understand this as a description of Jesus Christ as "our God and Saviour." Ehrman, however, refers to MSS (א Ψ pc vg[mss] sy[ph] sa) that read κυριου instead of θεου, so that now the whole expression (του κυριου ημων και cωτηρος ιηcου χριcτου) can easily be referred to Jesus, "our Lord and Saviour."[39] Similarly, in 1:2, there is a reference to "the knowledge" του θεου και ιηcου του κυριου ημων, where P[72] omits και, resulting in the reading του θεου ιηcου του κυριου ημων and implying that "Jesus our Lord" *is* God[40]—although this would not necessarily be an identity statement, as noted earlier. This second modification might have been theologically motivated as a way of referring to Jesus as God, although some MSS simply read του κυριου ημων, which Ehrman suggests was a variant designed to avoid patripassian Christology by leaving out any mention of God. However, it could just as easily have arisen by parablepsis (του ... του).[41] Or, someone might just have been trying to simplify a difficult passage. Thus, in 1:1, replacing του θεου by του κυριου would be a pious slip for a Christian copyist. Omitting και in 1:2, however, could well have been due

---

35. Ellingworth, *Hebrews*, 122–23.
36. Lane, *Hebrews 1–8*, 21nf. Cf. Attridge, *Hebrews*, 59.
37. Koester, *Hebrews*, 194.
38. Cf. Wright, "Jesus as ΘΕΟC," 256–61.
39. Ehrman, *Orthodox Corruption*, 312, 318n38.
40. Bauckham, *Jude, 2 Peter*, 165nc.
41. Metzger, *Textual Commentary*, 629.

Scribes, Theology, and Apologetics

to a desire to refer to Christ as God, and omitting του θεου και ιηcου (P Ψ etc.) is likely to have been caused by parablepsis (του ... του). So, one variant might have been due to a desire to speak about Christ as God, whereas the other two are more likely to be the result of a pious slip (or a desire to clarify a passage with complex syntax) and parablepsis.[42] Other motives for these readings have been suggested, such as harmonizing the text to a more common usage in the NT out of habit,[43] but it is quite unlikely that a desire to oppose a patripassian interpretation lay behind any of them.

1 John 5:10

Toward the end of 1 John, the author is dealing with faith in Christ. He refers to the person who believes εις τον υιον του θεου (5:10a), and contrasts this with the person who does not believe τω θεω (5:10b). Some MSS (A 81 vg sy[hmg] etc.) read τω υιω for τω θεω, thus conforming the second part of the verse to the first and removing any mention of God.[44] Ehrman suggests that this might have been motivated by a desire to avoid an actual identification of "the Son of God" with "God," thus creating an anti-patripassian orthodox corruption.[45] Yet, it is also possible that it was a pious slip, so the supposition that it was done in order to avoid identifying the Son with God (the Father) must remain unproven.

GENERAL CONCLUSION

In the previous four chapters, I have examined a number of variant readings cited as evidence that proto-orthodox scribes included readings intended to support their theological viewpoint in the context of four christological controversies in the second and third centuries. These controversies were related to adoptionism, "separationism," docetism, and patripassianism, so the viewpoints proposed as motivating the scribes, however unconsciously, were anti-adoptionism, "anti-separationism," anti-docetism, and anti-patripassianism.

---

42. Metzger, *Textual Commentary*, 629.
43. Bauckham, *Jude, 2 Peter*, 165nb; Wright, "Jesus as ΘΕΟΣ," 261–64.
44. Metzger, *Textual Commentary*, 649; Smalley, *1, 2, 3 John*, 273–74nh; Strecker, *Johannine Letters*, 194n55.
45. Ehrman, *Orthodox Corruption*, 313.

However, for several reasons only a small number of these proposals are convincing. First, although a number of variants are usually understood to be secondary, it is asserted that they are original. We have seen little reason, however, to accept these suggestions in general. Second, when variant readings are clearly secondary, only a few have been found to be convincing cases of being intentionally created, rather than due to the normal range of scribal slips that occurred while producing copies by hand in antiquity—eye-skip, tiredness, inattention, and the like, or (especially in later times) harmonization to the immediate context or parallel passages, especially in the Gospels. Third, among the few intentionally created variants, only a small proportion show signs of being motivated by theological designs, especially regarding the controversies referred to. Even if a variant *was* used by an early church writer in that context, it does not follow that it was *created* with that purpose in mind.[46] Rather, other motives, such as the piety of a copyist or natural liturgical habit, are probably behind many of the variants cited, and, although they are "corruptions," it has not been shown that they were intended to further a theological agenda. They might simply have been due to a desire to clarify the text or to do honor to Christ or God. Fourth, there are variant readings whose origins are obscure, and their "motivations," if they existed, are unknown. This should be acknowledged, rather than engaging in subtle interpretations of variants and attributing certain grammatical features, such as the insertion or removal of an article, to the biases of highly engaged and sophisticated copyists. Thus, variants that *might have* been theologically useful are often taken without sufficient warrant as having been created *in order to* perform that function.[47]

Another issue is that the variants cited are often attested only in MSS from a later period and then projected back into the second and third centuries without firm evidence that they were in existence at that time. Indeed, if a MS has a variant reading, it is not certain that the copyist of that MS was the one responsible for it. It might have been present in his exemplar, or the exemplar of his exemplar, etc. The issue of timing is a crucial one, because a variant reading must have arisen in the relevant

---

46. Fee refers to many of Ehrman's cited cases as unconvincing examples of his thesis regarding the *reasons* for variant readings (review of *Orthodox Corruption*, 204). Cf. Wasserman, "Misquoting?," 348–50.

47. Cf. Houghton, "Recent Developments," 256–57. Birdsall alludes to "much forcing of the evidence, and failure to see other possible lines of argument" (review of *Orthodox Corruption*, 460). Chapa observes that many of the examples cited involve a high degree of speculation ("Contribution," 115–25).

Scribes, Theology, and Apologetics

time for it to have been created in order to oppose a particular "heresy" when it was current. It is often uncertain that a variant *was* created in that period. For these and other reasons discussed above, Ehrman's approach generally lacks proof, and most cited instances are unlikely,[48] while the explanation given of texts is also sometimes improbable. Further, there are good reasons to doubt Bauer's portrait of the history of the early church, including the characterization of the "orthodox" group, as well as early church writers like Eusebius, Epiphanius, and others as "heresiologists." The suggestion that they distorted history, as well as assumptions about what "orthodoxy" involved, weakens the argument in many cases.[49]

Again, if we take the context of the variants into account—that is, in the rest of the verse, chapter, or book in question—it is often unlikely that a reader or hearer would have noticed the change with its supposed theological import. Hence, it is unlikely that a copyist could have imagined someone noticing. For that reason, it is improbable that he would have created the variant to forestall a particular "heretical" viewpoint being derived from his MS or to support his own view. Finally, the argument is often based on the whole range of MSS, instead of features of individual MSS exhibited by SRs that might more certainly be attributed to a copyist, which has sometimes skewed the reading of the textual evidence.[50] Some MSS could also exhibit quite opposing tendencies, such as docetic and anti-docetic viewpoints, so it is difficult to know who would have been responsible for them.[51]

In summary, while Ehrman's work has been well received in a number of quarters,[52] and it certainly raises many fruitful questions, I hope to have provided a new appraisal, while also gathering together the responses of others.

---

48. Miller reviews Ehrman's apparent criterion that "the least orthodox reading" is the preferable one, and he offers a general critique of this methodology ("Least Orthodox Reading," esp. 84–86).

49. Cf. Hernández, *Scribal Habits*, 35–40, esp. 40.

50. Cf. Chapa, "Contribution," 129–33.

51. Cf. Wasserman, "Scribal Alterations," 307.

52. E.g., Attridge, review of *Orthodox Corruption*; Countryman, review of *Orthodox Corruption*; Elliott, review of *Orthodox Corruption*; Metzger, review of *Orthodox Corruption*; Parker, review of *Orthodox Corruption*; Petersen, review of *Orthodox Corruption*; Silva, review of *Orthodox Corruption*; Price, review of *Orthodox Corruption*.

5

Apologetic for Intellectual Integrity?

COPYISTS AND APOLOGETICS

IN THE NEXT FOUR chapters I continue to examine variant readings related to the settings of copyists, but now the readings are said to be motivated by a desire to defend Christians and the Christian faith against the criticism of opponents—that is, it has been suggested that these variant readings were created for "apologetic" reasons, to respond to current criticisms of Christ or the Christians or to charges made against them in pagan society. The study reviewed here is Kannaday's *Apologetic Discourse and the Scribal Tradition.*

Kannaday begins his book with a discussion of pagan writers who criticized Christianity in the early centuries of the church,[1] which sometimes posed a real danger to Christians, especially when combined with popular hostility or suspicion, or the actions of governing authorities. Criticism also came from Jewish authors who denounced the new "sect" (Justin Martyr, *Dial.* 69; cf. *b. Sanh.* 43a). Kannaday's focus is on the responses of Christians, as they defended themselves and their faith. Thus, Christian "apologists" responded to criticism by Celsus, Marcus Aurelius, and others, as well as to satires by writers such as Lucian and Apuleius. Kannaday reviews the rise of anti-Christian literature in the

---

1. Kannaday, *Apologetic Discourse*, 1–5. Cf. Benko, "Pagan Criticism"; Hargis, *Against the Christians*; Engberg et al., *Defence of Christianity.*

second half of the second century, notably by Celsus and Porphyry, along with widespread hostility toward Christians. He observes that Celsus referred to the Christians' sacred texts (Origen, *Cels.* 2.74; cf. 1.12; 2.77), as Origen noted (*Cels.* 1.63–64), and that Porphyry also had access to Christian works.[2]

Kannaday concludes his portrayal of hostility and opposition by suggesting that Christian scribes had good reason "to be concerned with how their sacred books were perceived by outsiders."[3] Finally, he refers to Haines-Eitzen's book *Guardians of Letters*, in which she maintains that, in early Christianity, copyists of Christian texts were also users of those texts and were influenced by current disputes among Christians as well as a desire to defend their faith in the face of criticism.[4] Yet the characterization of how early Christian texts were reproduced stands in need of further reflection. I have argued elsewhere that most copying of Christian texts was done by hired scribes who were not necessarily Christians, especially in the early centuries.[5] It is doubtful, then, that they were all engaged as readers and editors as some suggest, so perhaps not all copyists of Christian texts were interested parties whose copying was influenced by their unfriendly social contexts and who wished to adjust their texts in the light of pagan criticism. It remains to be seen, then, whether the variants discussed might have been created by scribes as "interested parties." Did copyists alter their texts "for tendentious purposes"? Did they "tamper" with the text? If "they" did, who were "they," and how widespread was their tampering?

In order to lay the foundation for an assessment of the variant readings, Kannaday sketches the contours of pagan opposition to Christians and the Christian faith in the early centuries.[6] Statements opposing Christians, their Scriptures, and Jesus himself are found in Pliny the Younger, Tacitus and Suetonius, Epictetus, Crescens, Lucian and Apuleius, Marcus Cornelius Fronto, Celsus, and Porphyry of Tyre.[7] Kanna-

2. On Porphyry, see Barnes, "Porphyry"; Boer, "Pagan Historian"; Barnes, "Scholarship or Propaganda?"; Edwards, "Porphyry."

3. Kannaday, *Apologetic Discourse*, 21.

4. Kannaday, *Apologetic Discourse*, 21–23.

5. Mugridge, *Copying*, 151–54.

6. Kannaday, *Apologetic Discourse*, 23–57. Cf. Kruger, *Crossroads*, 54–73.

7. Wilken notes the issues with attributing pagan criticisms cited in Macarius's *Apocriticus* which might not derive from Porphyry himself, especially his *Against the Christians* and *Philosophy from Oracles*, but they still provide evidence of criticism by people with that mindset. He also mentions views that Augustine referred to in his *Harmony of*

day also describes in some detail how Christian apologists responded to such criticism, providing a survey of the writings of Quadratus and Aristides, Justin Martyr, Tatian, Athenagoras of Athens, Theophilus of Antioch, Melito of Sardis, Clement of Alexandria, Origen, Tertullian, and Minucius Felix. In the following chapters I examine the texts that Kannaday argues were changed to produce variant readings as part of this response in the second and third centuries. The first area surveyed is that of intellectual integrity, that is, the antiquity, harmony, and factual consistency of Christian doctrines.

Christianity, a Recent Arrival?

Kannaday describes how religious cults and philosophical schools were commonly thought to be authentic or reasonable if they could lay claim to being ancient rather than recent arrivals since religious novelties were viewed with suspicion and disdain.[8] He cites Christian writers like Tertullian (*Marc.* 5.4.1) and opponents such as Celsus (Origen, *Cels.* 1.14) as testimony to this view,[9] and it seems clear that Theophilus (*Autol.* 3.1, 4) and Tatian (*Orat.* 35.2) were also responding to these kinds of charges. Opponents sometimes asserted that the OT was inaccurate and inconsistent, which Porphyry saw as a fatal flaw because Christians appealed to OT prophecy when commending their faith (Justin, 1 *Apol.* 30–51; *Dial.* 11–16). Celsus pointed out that as Christianity was a new religion, begun only recently by Jesus, these "new ideas" (καινοτομια, Origen, *Cels.* 3.5) showed that Christianity had little claim to be legitimate. In response, apologists like Justin, Tatian, Athenagoras, Theophilus, Origen, Minucius Felix, and Tertullian argued that the Christian faith was not "new" but rather predated other religions and philosophies, an argument used similarly by Jewish writers like Josephus and Philo against Hellenism. Thus, the apologists maintained that because OT prophets foretold the events of Jesus and the Christians, there *were* links to antiquity, which showed that their faith was not novel. The following variant readings are said to be the result of scribes endeavoring to remove infelicities or inconsistencies that might have been seized upon by opponents, especially in relation to prophecies.

---

the Gospels, esp. sec. 2–4 (*Christians*, 135–56). Cf. Wilken, "Pagan Criticism."

8. Kannaday, *Apologetic Discourse*, 59–64.
9. Cf. Wilken, *Christians*, 115–16, 123–24.

Scribes, Theology, and Apologetics

Mark 1:2, Matthew 13:35

Porphyry pointed out that the words cited in Mark 1:2–3 derive from Malachi and Isaiah, although only Isaiah is mentioned (Jerome, *Epist.* 57.9), and that Matt 13:35 cites a passage as being from Isaiah when it actually comes from Ps 78 (Jerome, *Tract. Ps.* 77). The introduction to the quotation(s) in the traditional reading of Mark 1:2 is καθως γεγραπται εν (τω) ησαια τω προφητη, but some MSS (A W $f^{1,13}$ vg^{ms} sy^h bo^{mss}) read εν τοις προφηταις. Since the quotation includes material drawn from Mal 3:1, Exod 23:20, and Isa 40:3,[10] it might seem that Mark made a "mistake" in attributing the whole quotation to Isaiah. Others maintain that he only named Isaiah because he felt he only needed to mention one source (or the main one). Numerous proposals have been put forward to resolve this issue, some more speculative than others, but the external evidence clearly supports the first reading given above as original, so that one or more people must have changed it to the general reference (εν τοις προφηταις). Kannaday asks what their motivation might have been, and he suggests that, since Porphyry had specifically mentioned this issue, the text was altered to counter that charge and restore this verse as a clear prophetic testimony to the arrival of John the Baptist and Jesus. So, the variant could well be "a transparent instance of scribal activity being shaped by apologetic concerns."[11]

Before discussing this issue, I review the variant in Matthew's Gospel. As noted above, Porphyry cited the quotation in Matt 13:35 from "Isaiah" as a blatant error because in fact it comes from Ps 78:2 (77:2 LXX). The introduction to the quotation is οπως πληρωθη το ρηθεν δια του προφητου λεγοντος, but some MSS (ℵ* Θ $f^{1,13}$ 33; Hier^{mss}) insert ησαιου before του προφητου, and Jerome refers to MSS inserting "Asaph" (Hier^{mss}). "Asaph" is probably derived from the heading of Ps 78 and is unlikely to be original in Matthew, despite Asaph being called a prophet in the OT (2 Chr 29:30; cf. 1 Chr 25:2). Further, no extant NT MS mentions Asaph, although Jerome apparently knew of some that did and proposed that this was corrected to Isaiah because Asaph was not commonly known as a prophet.[12] It was clearly an issue. The reading with

---

10. Guelich, *Mark 1—8:26*, 10.

11. Kannaday, *Apologetic Discourse*, 70.

12. Metzger, *Textual Commentary*, 27. Cf. Donaldson, "Explicit References," 151–53, 232–33, 256–57, 298, 329–30, 384–85, 444–45 (Cf. 108, 259, 272–73, 369–72 on other church fathers who referred to this).

ηcαιου is plainly the harder reading because the quotation is not from Isaiah, so some scholars suggest it was original and the passage was made easier by omitting it, thus resulting in the more general reference (δια του προφητου) or a specific one derived from the psalm ("through Asaph the prophet").[13] However, the external support for the variant without ηcαιου (ℵ¹ B C D W lat sy co; Eusebius) is quite strong, so it is probably original, with later copyists inserting Isaiah's name (cf. Matt 1:22, 2:5, 21:4; Acts 7:48) because he was well known,[14] as scribes sometimes inserted names for characters not actually named in NT documents.[15]

Kannaday argues that Matthew's literary style is usually to include a prophet's name in his formula quotations, so he concludes that intrinsic probabilities favor ηcαιου being original in 13:35. However, of the thirty-seven (or thirty-six) uses of προφητηc in Matthew's Gospel, fourteen (or thirteen) are in the plural, six refer to John or Jesus, and four are quite general ("a prophet"), which leaves five referring to "the prophet" and eight referring to Jeremiah, Isaiah, Jonah, or Daniel. Kannaday rightly dismisses the quotation in 27:35 as a harmonization to John 19:24, so of the remaining five referring to "the prophet," one is 13:35 (under discussion), 1:22 introduces a citation of Isa 7:14, 2:5 leads into Mic 5:2, 2:15 introduces Hos 11:1, and 21:4 leads into a conflated quotation of Isa 62:11 and Zech 9:9. Kannaday argues that leaving out a prophet's name might be understandable in 21:4 since others did this to ease a difficult reading (e.g., in Mark 1:2), but this is hardly a compelling argument. He notes that some MSS mention Isaiah at 1:22 and one does so at 2:15, and he sets aside the instance in 2:5 because the speakers, being Herod's advisers and hence opponents to Matthew's cause, could not be expected to be credited with "the same level of knowledge one would or could expect from a Christian character or the narrator."[16] However, there are no real grounds to omit these latter instances from consideration, so, apart from 13:35, there is every reason to think that four instances remain without a prophet's name (1:22; 2:5, 15; 21:4), as against eight with the prophet being named. Hence, the internal evidence does not necessarily show that Matthew *must* have included the name of Isaiah in 13:35.

Kannaday also refers to the Syriac versions, noting that in three cases (1:22, 2:15, 27:9) at least one Syriac MS includes a prophet's name

---

13. Kannaday, *Apologetic Discourse*, 70–71.
14. Metzger, *Textual Commentary*, 27; France, *Matthew*, 529n1.
15. Metzger, "Names."
16. Kannaday, *Apologetic Discourse*, 72–73.

Scribes, Theology, and Apologetics

alongside "the prophet." The name is also changed from Jeremiah to Zechariah in the margin of 27:9 (sy^h), perhaps intending to correct the name since the quotation seems to be from Zech 11:12–13, although it may be that here too there is a conflated citation from Zechariah and elements of Jer 18–19 and 32:6–15.[17] Further, at 2:15 (sy^s) the quotation is wrongly attributed to Isaiah, so the assertion that the Syriac tradition did not tend to correct errors of citation or omit the name altogether has not been proven.[18] Indeed, the Syriac MSS often differ among themselves. At 13:35 the bulk of them omit the name, which might indicate a concern to correct the original insertion, but since we are only dealing with a few instances, they could just as easily represent a faithful reproduction of the original which did *not* include the name. So, while the Syriac evidence deserves further discussion, suggesting a focus on prophecy in the Syriac tradition because Jonah is mentioned as a prophet in Syriac MSS (at 16:4), an emphasis in sy^h on Jesus fulfilling the prophet's words "totally" (in 21:4), and noting that sy^h includes 27:35 (from John 19:24) does not show how copyists of Syriac MSS generally treated Matthew's attribution of OT citations to various prophets. Thus, the evidence of the Syriac MSS cannot be used to support the originality of the reading that includes ησαιου in Matt 13:35. Nor does the external evidence lean toward including it, and intrinsic and transcriptional probabilities are also inconclusive.

Hence, we cannot be sure that δια ησαιου του προφητου is original here, so it would be fruitless to ask why copyists omitted the mention of Isaiah. It is just as likely that "Isaiah" was not present in the first place and Asaph was added by someone who knew that the quotation came from Ps 78, and then someone else, noting that Asaph is only rarely called a prophet, inserted Isaiah, either as a prophet more commonly known, or harmonizing to 3:3 and 4:14,[19] or under the influence of the earlier mention of Isaiah in 13:14.[20] Indeed, this might have been the text that Porphyry saw. Thus, it is uncertain that a copyist omitted the reference to Isaiah to remove an error in Matt 13:35 and eliminate support for Porphyry's criticisms,[21] because it is quite unclear that it *was* removed.[22]

---

17. Brown, *Death of the Messiah*, 1:651.
18. Pace Kannaday, *Apologetic Discourse*, 74n60.
19. Pardee, *Scribal Harmonization*, 310.
20. Nolland, *Matthew*, 555nb.
21. Pace Kannaday, *Apologetic Discourse*, 71–75.
22. Hagner, *Matthew 1–19*, 388ne. Pace Luz, *Matthew 8–20*, 265n1.

Finally, copyists might well have included ησαιου from their exemplar without having any "motive" at all.²³ It is also impossible to confirm that copyists had at their disposal copies of OT MSS *and* that they would know enough to suspect that the OT citation was conflated so that they would have checked their MSS and edited out the reference to Isaiah.

Similarly, regarding Mark 1:2, the reading εν τοις προφηταις is clearly secondary, but the person or persons responsible for it might simply have wished to make the text "more comprehensive" and consistent with the OT,²⁴ without aiming to respond to criticism that the text was inaccurate.

Luke 9:54

In response to a Samaritan village refusing to welcome Jesus because he was heading for Jerusalem, Luke records that James and John asked Jesus, θελεις ειπωμεν πυρ καταβηναι απο του ουρανου και αναλωσαι αυτους; (9:54), probably with 2 Kgs 1:10 or 1:12 in mind (cf. 1 Kgs 18:38). Some MSS (A C D W Θ f^{13} 33 it sy^{p,h} bo^{pt}) add ως και ηλαιας εποιησεν, but the evidence for the reading without this phrase is quite strong (P⁴⁵ P⁷⁵ ℵ B lat sy^{s,c} sa bo^{pt}), and most find it compelling.²⁵ Kannaday suggests, then, that the phrase mentioning Elijah might have been added to stress the continuity of Jesus with an ancient and worthy prophet, thus countering the charge that the Christian religion was a recent arrival to be treated with suspicion, perhaps indicating an apologetic interest as well as mollifying the violent character of the disciples' question (presumably by alluding to a precedent).²⁶ However, since there are numerous links with the OT in Luke's Gospel, this minor addition would have added little, and as Jesus clearly rejected their violent response (9:55), there is nothing to mollify if the whole narrative is taken into account. So, the phrase was more likely just a gloss "from an extraneous source,"²⁷ or it was simply inserted to fill in the details.²⁸

---

23. Schmid, "Scribes and Variants," 6–9.
24. Metzger, *Textual Commentary*, 62. Cf. Blumell, "Luke 22:43–44," 28.
25. E.g., Bovon, *Luke 2*, 4ne.
26. Kannaday, *Apologetic Discourse*, 75–76.
27. Metzger, *Textual Commentary*, 124.
28. Fitzmyer, *Luke I–IX*, 830.

Luke 2:39

After Luke recounts the visit of Joseph, Mary, and Jesus to Jerusalem (2:22–38), he records that επεστρεψαν εις την γαλιλαιαν εις πολιν εαυτων ναζαρεθ (2:39). But two MSS (D a) add material resembling Matt 2:23, καθως ερρεθη δια του προφητου οτι ναζωραιος κληθησεται. The addition is clearly secondary, given its slight external support, but why was it added? Perhaps someone had Matt 2:23 in mind and inserted material here because he thought it had been omitted.[29] But, since the wording of the addition (καθως ερρεθη δια του προφητου) is slightly different from Matt 2:23 (οπως πληρωθη το ρηθεν δια των προφητων), this is unlikely. Kannaday speculates that it was added by someone who "followed Matthew, almost blindly it would seem, in the evangelist's claim that there was prophetic anticipation that the Messiah would at some point hail from Nazareth."[30] He suggests that the copyists were not concerned to "track down" the OT source of the quotation but wished to incorporate "evidence that explained the location of Jesus' boyhood home as yet another instance of prophetic fulfilment." He concludes, then, that the words were added due to "an apologetic impulse."[31] However, the addition may just be a loose harmonization to Matt 2:23, so any theory as to why the phrase was added must remain uncertain.

Matthew 21:4, 24:6

In Matthew's account of Jesus entering Jerusalem for the last time, he records Jesus telling the disciples to bring a donkey that they would find in the village ahead of them (21:1–3). He then comments that τουτο δε γεγονεν ινα πληρωθη το ρηθεν δια του προφητου (21:4). A number of MSS (B C³ W f¹,¹³ 33 *Byz* vg^cl sy^h sa bo^ms etc.) add ολον after δε, which adds a slight emphasis to the prophetic interpretation of Jesus' triumphal entry ("now *all of this* occurred . . .").[32] In Matt 24:6 some MSS include παντα (C W f¹³ *Byz* sy^p,h), ταυτα (565 lat sy^s), or παντα ταυτα (1241 f)—δει γαρ (παντα/ταυτα) γενεσθαι αλλ ουπω εστιν το τελος. Kannaday interprets this as adding emphasis to Jesus' statement that certain things would take place before "the end" (vv. 5–6a)—"*all* (*these things*) must take place . . ." In both cases,

---

29. Fitzmyer, *Luke I–IX*, 432.
30. Kannaday, *Apologetic Discourse*, 77.
31. Kannaday, *Apologetic Discourse*, 76–77.
32. Luz suggests that ολον might be original (*Matthew 21–28*, 3n2).

he makes a connection between the secondary addition and the apologetic theme that the events of Jesus' life and death fulfilled the OT Scriptures, noting Justin's comments about this (1 *Apol.* 52).[33]

However, in Matt 24:6 the addition refers to Jesus' words about events in the future, not about his life and death fulfilling the OT, even though Justin makes that connection. In Matt 21:4, the addition of ολον does add emphasis,[34] but the scope of τουτο ολον is still confined to Jesus riding into Jerusalem on a donkey (21:1–3) and the formula quotation introduces an adapted version of Zech 9:9 whose focus is on the king likewise entering Jerusalem on a donkey (cf. 21:6–7). While 21:4–5 is clearly meant to show that the following events fulfilled the OT Scriptures, and the addition of ολον in 21:4 makes that slightly more emphatic, it is difficult to imagine that the emphasis would be noticeable to a reader in the context of the introduction formula and four-line quotation. Thus, the "apologetic motivation" of the person responsible for the addition of ολον in 21:4 is "as ready an explanation" for the addition as it having been inserted accidentally due to an unconscious harmonization to the similar wording in Matt 1:22. The addition of παντα ταυτα, etc., in 24:6 could also have occurred under the influence of 24:8 soon afterwards,[35] especially since the verb has no subject in the original.[36] Or these readings were created as a "stylistic improvement" of a rather curt text, especially when the parallel passage in Luke 21:9 has ταυτα.[37] Or the copyist wished to create consistency with Matt 1:22 and 26:56.[38] None of these suggestions, however, including a scribe with an apologetic motive, is more persuasive than the others, so the reasons for the variants are at present unknown.

Matthew 16:4, Luke 11:29, Matthew 5:18

In both Matt 16:4 and Luke 11:29, where το σημειον ιωνα is mentioned, a number of MSS add του προφητου—Matt 16:4 (C K N W Θ $f^{1,13}$ 33 Byz it^{cl} vg sy bo) and Luke 11:29 (A C K W $f^{1,13}$ 33 Byz it^{mss} vg^{cl} sy^{2,p,h}

---

33. Kannaday, *Apologetic Discourse*, 77.

34. Nolland, *Matthew*, 830nc.

35. Fitzmyer, *Luke X–XXIV*, 935; Hagner, *Matthew 14-28*, 689na; Nolland, *Matthew*, 646nd.

36. Nolland, *Matthew*, 959nb.

37. France, *Matthew*, 896.

38. Pardee, *Scribal Harmonization*, 242.

bo). Further, in Matt 5:18 Jesus emphasizes that nothing, however small, ου μη παρελθη απο του νομου. But a few MSS add και των προφητων (Θ f^{13} 565; Ir^{lat}). While the third variant might be drawn from the similar reference to "the law and the prophets" in Matt 5:17, Kannaday takes all three readings as evidence that "scribes, at points, changed the text of the New Testament intentionally, deliberately, and mindfully" in accord with the response of the apologists to pagan polemic, highlighting links with the OT Scriptures and reinforcing the antiquity of the Christian faith.[39]

There are other possible explanations for these variants, however. With respect to Matt 16:4 and Luke 11:29, Jonah is mentioned using similar phraseology but with the addition of "the prophet" in Matt 12:39 (σημειον ου δοθηcεται αυτη ει μη το σημειον ιωνα του προφητου). Indeed, this is the true parallel to Luke 11:29 where Jesus goes on to speak about Nineveh, the Queen of the South, and Solomon (Luke 11:30-32 // Matt 12:40-42). So it would not be unexpected if Luke 11:29 was harmonized to Matt 12:39 by the addition of του προφητου.[40] It would also be unsurprising if Matt 16:4 was harmonized to Matt 12:39, since that is the only other place in Matthew's Gospel where Jonah is mentioned.[41] Hence, it is possible and quite likely that copyists added του προφητου to Matt 16:4 and Luke 11:29 based on Matt 12:39. Because Jonah is only rarely mentioned in the Gospels, the longer phrase could well have been prominent in their memory.

At Matt 5:18, the addition of και των προφητων would also have been an easy addition to make if someone were at all familiar with the Gospels or, as noted above, under the influence of v. 17, which mentions "the law or the prophets."[42] The same paired phrase ("the law and the prophets") appears in Matt 7:12 and "the prophets and the law" occurs in Matt 11:13 and 22:40. Indeed, variations on this paired phrase occur elsewhere in the Gospels (Luke 16:16, 24:24; John 1:45), Acts (13:15, 24:14), and Romans (3:21), so it was apparently a common phrase in early Christian circles. Indeed, it was a traditional description of the OT Scriptures when a twofold phrase was used (cf. 2 Macc 15:9, 4 Macc 18:10, Sir Pro. 1).

Therefore, the suggestion that copyists made any of these additions in order to enhance the use of these texts for apologetic purposes is unlikely. Rather, they were probably made by copyists familiar with the NT

---

39. Kannaday, *Apologetic Discourse*, 78.
40. Nolland, *Luke 9:21—18:34*, 650nb.
41. Hagner, *Matthew 14-28*, 453ng.
42. Hagner, *Matthew 1-13*, 103na; Davies and Allison, *Matthew*, 1:490n24.

Jesus Subordinate to John?

Kannaday refers to Celsus citing John's temporal priority to Jesus in order to show that Jesus was less important (Origen, *Cels.* 2.4).[43] This passage, however, actually refers to the Jewish claim that, since John baptized Jesus, followers of Jesus should follow the OT law because John was a Jewish prophet. The issue of Jesus being subordinate to John does not appear, so there is no reason to think that Celsus made this suggested criticism of Jesus. Further, the statement that Christians were embarrassed by John baptizing Jesus, implying that John was superior, also lacks proof.[44] In addition, the claim that the Fourth Gospel "directly addresses" this issue is unfounded because statements of Jesus' superiority to John (John 1:1–18, 29), especially εμπροσθεν μου γεγονεν οτι πρωτος μου ην (1:15, 30), do not necessarily imply that this was a live issue. Rather, it reports the evangelist's and the Baptist's assertions about Jesus, without necessarily implying that these were responses to a later view. So, the existence of a pressing dispute over the relative status of Jesus and John has little basis. Nevertheless, I now examine the variant readings that are said to be responses to this proposed charge.

John 1:27

In John 1:19–51 the evangelist provides a number of reports of Jesus' encounters with people in the early period of his public ministry. In a section recounting a discussion between John the Baptist and priests and Levites from Jerusalem (1:19–23), and then with some Pharisees (1:24–27), John responds to the Pharisees and refers to Jesus as ο οπιςω μου ερχομενος (1:27), to which some MSS (A C³ K f^{13} Byz lat sy$^{(p),h}$ bo^{mss}) then add ος εμπροσθεν μου γεγονεν. It is difficult to see why this reading would have been omitted if it were original, and in fact its slight MS evidence shows that it is secondary. Kannaday suggests that this secondary variant

---

43. Kannaday, *Apologetic Discourse*, 78.
44. *Pace* Meier, *Marginal Jew*, 21–22, 101–5.

Scribes, Theology, and Apologetics

"would serve the apologetic cause by enhancing further the apologetic theme of the temporal priority of Jesus to John."[45]

Yet, while the perfect verb γεγονεν could be taken to support *some* reference to prior (and present) time, it is not a natural reading in the context, and it is certainly not the emphasis of the whole phrase. Rather, in 1:15 and 1:30 priority in time (πρωτος μου ην) is cited as the basis for Jesus' superiority in rank over John (ος εμπροσθεν μου γεγονεν; cf. Gen 48:20 LXX).[46] Hence, the addition of ος εμπροσθεν μου γεγονεν in 1:27 is not highlighting Jesus' temporal priority to John but his superior status. It was probably added under the influence of εμπροσθεν μου γεγονεν in 1:15 (cf. ος εμπροσθεν μου γεγονεν, 1:30), which there follows ο οπισω μου ερχομενος, the same phrasing as in 1:27. Harmonization to the immediate context, then, is the most probable cause of this variant reading, rather than someone's desire to support Jesus' temporal priority to John. It adds little to the other almost identical passages in the context.

Matthew 3:11, John 12:28

Matthew's Gospel also has an account of John the Baptist's encounter with Pharisees and Sadducees (3:7–12), where John refers to Jesus as ο δε οπισω μου ερχομενος, asserting that ισχυροτερος μου εστιν (3:11). But some MSS (P[101] a d sa[mss] Cyp) do not include οπισω μου, which results in Jesus just being described as ο . . . ερχομενος. Kannaday argues that the phrase was not accidentally omitted due to the large number of omicrons in the verse, as some suggest. Further, he points to differences in wording in the parallel Luke 3:16, which does not have οπισω μου, as evidence that the phrase was not omitted as a harmonization from there, although others argue that it was.[47] So, he suggests that οπισω μου might have been seen as providing fuel for the criticism of Jesus by people like Celsus, because οπισω μου can refer to someone following "after me" as their disciple (e.g., Matt 4:19, 10:38, 16:24; Mark 1:17, 8:34; Luke 9:23, 14:27). So, if a person did not want Jesus to be seen as John's disciple, they might have removed the possibility of that thought by omitting the phrase.[48] This proposal

---

45. Kannaday, *Apologetic Discourse*, 79.

46. McHugh, *John 1–4*, 63; Barrett, *John*, 177; Brown, *John I-XII*, 56; BDAG, 325, ἔμπροσθεν 1bζ.

47. Nolland, *Matthew*, 132nf; Pardee, *Scribal Harmonization*, 80–81.

48. Kannaday, *Apologetic Discourse*, 79–80.

may have some force, despite the lack of evidence for Celsus's criticism, but the omission might also have been due to a copyist being familiar with ο ερχομενος as a title for Jesus, as in Matt 11:3 (cf. 21:9, 23:39; Luke 17:19–20).

Kannaday also refers to John 12:28 where Jesus has just taken the arrival of certain Greeks as a signal that the time of his death was approaching (12:20–27). Jesus' words of reflection end with a prayer, πατερ δοξασον σου το ονομα. But Vaticanus has the SR μου το ονομα for σου το ονομα, while other later MSS (L ƒ^{1,13} 33 vg^{mss} sy^{hmg} bo etc.) read σου τον υιον (cf. 17:1),[49] and D includes a longer reading apparently adapted from its own version of 17:5 (εν τη δοξη η ειχον παρα σοι προ του τον κοσμον γενεσθαι και εγενετο). Based on these variants, Kannaday suggests that scribes were building on the already high Christology of the Fourth Gospel by "blurring more and more the lines between the Father and the Son." In support, he cites the words of the apologist Athenagoras (*Leg.* 18.2), where he compared the father-son relationship of Marcus Aurelius and Commodus to that of God the Father and the Son.[50]

However, it is unclear how a prayer to the Father to "glorify *my* name" (rather than "glorify *your* name"), or "glorify your *son*" (instead of "glorify your *name*"), could serve this purpose. Further, the long addition in 12:28 D only repeats material included elsewhere, so it is unlikely to have been seen as expressing a more exalted Christology than what was already present. Thus, although these readings are clearly secondary, it is not clear that those responsible for them were "doing theology" by inserting a high Christology that was not originally there. The long reading in D is the only one where this might be valid, with repetition from 17:5 D. Hence, it is quite unclear that the variants at 12:28 derived from someone's apologetic motive to make the Son less distinct from the Father and thus superior to John.[51] Rather, they show the influence of phraseology drawn from elsewhere in this Gospel (17:1, 5).[52]

---

49. Cf. Barrett, *John*, 425.

50. Kannaday, *Apologetic Discourse*, 80–81.

51. Pace Kannaday, *Apologetic Discourse*, 81–82.

52. Metzger, *Textual Commentary* 202; Beasley-Murray, *John*, 205nl.; Barrett, *John*, 425; Brown, *John I–XII*, 467.

Scribes, Theology, and Apologetics

Inconsistency and Harmonization of the Scriptures?

In introducing this series of variants, Kannaday reviews the charges made by pagan critics that there are glaring inconsistencies among the NT documents, and he outlines the responses that apologists made to this criticism.[53] He refers to the words of Celsus (Origen, *Cels.* 2.27), where he mentions believers who "alter the original text of the gospel three or four or several times over, and they change its character to enable them to deny difficulties in the face of criticism."[54] Chadwick stated, however, that it is unclear what Celsus had in mind here, but it is "not likely that Celsus had in mind the different manuscript readings," and perhaps Origen was right in taking Celsus to be referring to the activities of Marcion, as well as Valentinian and Lucan.[55] Nevertheless, Celsus was on the lookout for inconsistencies in the Scriptures with which to criticize the Christians.

Further, Macarius (*Apocrit.* 2.12-15) refers to a philosopher who spoke about inconsistencies among the Gospels, probably reflecting the kinds of things that Porphyry said. Origen was certainly aware of the issue (*Comm. Jo.* 10.2), and other writers such as Justin Martyr (*Dial.* 6-9), Tatian (*Orat.* 25.2), Aristides (*Ap.* 16), Theophilus (*Autol.* 3.1), and Origen (*Cels.* 2.23-24, 26-27; 3.1-2; 5:52-56) commended consistency among the Gospels in various ways, although not always mentioning claims of inconsistencies. Apologists responded to the charge of inconsistencies using allegorical or clarifying explanations, with some scholars suggesting that Tatian's *Diatessaron* was designed to remove inconsistencies altogether by composing one consistent Gospel narrative. Origen also spoke well of those who showed that the Scriptures were in harmony (*Comm. Matt.* 2.1). Moreover, since Origen wrote his commentary on Matthew in the same period as *Contra Celsum* (Eusebius, *Hist. eccl.* 6.36), Kannaday argues that this shows that between the time when Celsus wrote his work and Origen composed his response, perhaps eighty years later, the issue of discrepancies between the Gospels had become even more prominent. It was certainly an issue for Origen early in the third century, as we have seen, and Porphyry seems to have highlighted it later.

Kannaday also discusses the matter of copyists harmonizing their texts of the Gospels, drawing on the work of E. P. Sanders,[56] but since

---

53. Kannaday, *Apologetic Discourse*, 82-86.
54. Chadwick, *Origen*, 90, quoted in Kannaday, *Apologetic Discourse*, 82.
55. Chadwick, *Origen*, 90n2.
56. Sanders, *Tendencies*, referred to in Kannaday, *Apologetic Discourse*, 86-90.

Sanders was operating under the assumption that the Four Source Hypothesis is the proven "solution" to the Synoptic problem, his conclusions cannot be used as a firm basis for discussion here. Colwell's study showed that harmonization within a book or to the immediate context was common, but he observed that if copyists tended to harmonize to the context, then taking the reading that fits the context might not be the right procedure—so "intrinsic inclinations and transcriptional probabilities might cancel each other out."[57] According to Royse, we are more likely to be able to identify the tendencies of individual scribes, but he agrees that harmonization probably took place in Gospel MSS.[58] In this section, then, Kannaday highlights the value placed by scribes on consistency and freedom from error in the NT Gospels as a motive for their adjustments to the text.

However, in relation to Kannaday's outline of both pagan charges of inconsistencies among the Gospels and responses to those charges by apologists in the second and third centuries, some of the evidence cited is not as strong as might be hoped. It is not certain, for example, that Tatian composed his harmony "to serve an apologetic purpose."[59] Nevertheless, such matters were clearly under discussion, and they became more prominent in the third century, so I examine below the variant readings cited to see if they show an apologetic concern to remove inconsistencies and demonstrate factual accuracy in and logical consistency among the NT Gospels.

John 7:8

John 7 opens with an account of Jesus staying away from Judea in view of "the Jews" wishing to kill him. But since the Feast of the Tabernacles was approaching, his brothers urged him to go to Jerusalem, presumably to attract a following among the crowds (7:1–5). In response, Jesus urged them to go, but said, εγω ουκ αναβαινω εις την εορτην ταυτην, οτι ο εμος καιρος ουπω πεπληρωται. Instead of ουκ, however, some important MSS (P[66] P[75] B W P f[1,13] Byz f q sy[p,h] sa ly pbo) have ουπω. Kannaday points out that the narrative indicates that Jesus *did* in fact go to the feast incognito

---

57. Colwell, "External Evidence," 4.
58. Royse, "Scribal Tendencies," referred to in Kannaday, *Apologetic Discourse*, 88n109. Cf. Baarda, "ΔΙΑΦΩΝΙΑ-ΣΥΜΦΩΝΙΑ," 133–54.
59. Kannaday, *Apologetic Discourse*, 90.

later on (ου φανερως αλλ [ως] εν κρυπτω, 7:10) and that there was quite some talk there about whether he would come, apparently in view of the authorities' hostility toward him (7:11–13). If ουκ is original in 7:8, then it appears that Jesus was misleading his brothers, so it is often suggested that ουπω is a secondary reading inserted by someone who wished to remove this issue and clear Jesus' reputation.[60]

Yet, the external evidence supporting ουπω is certainly impressive, including B, W and $f^{1,13}$, although ουκ also has strong support (ℵ D lat sy^{s,c} bo). Kannaday examines the testimony of P[66] and P[75] (both ca. AD 175–225), which indicate an early date for ουπω, although they both show signs of having a somewhat polished text, so some readings might stem from the polishing process. However, P[66] has the SR ουδεπω instead of the second ουπω, so it is not quite polished at that point.[61] It appears, then, that external evidence does not strongly favor either reading.

Transcriptional probability could indicate that, if ουκ were original, a copyist might have seen ουπω later in the verse and written ουπω instead of ουκ earlier. If the copyist thought he was writing the second ουπω, he would have continued his text from that point, instead of writing ουπω and then going back and continuing with αναβαινω, so this would not be a case of parablepsis. However, this suggestion is just one possibility.

As for the intrinsic probabilities of the narrative, there are several arguments based on what John is likely to have written, or what Jesus did not know at the time, or even what Jesus meant by saying that his time had not yet (ουπω) come (7:6). Kannaday examines the use of ουπω in John's Gospel to see if there is any pattern that might shed light on the issue, concluding that the majority of the ten occurrences refer to "the hour" of Jesus. While this is true, four uses of ουπω are unrelated (3:24, 6:17, 8:57, 11:30), and two relate to the Spirit "not yet" (ουπω) given because Jesus had "not yet" (ουδεπω) been glorified and "not yet" (ουπω) ascended (7:39, 20:17). The latter two are related to Jesus' "hour," but do not have quite the same reference, so "the majority" of the occurrences of ουπω in John do not refer to Jesus' "hour"—only four out of ten—and the number of occurrences is not statistically significant anyway. Of course, ουπω is used to refer to Jesus' hour (ωρα) or time (καιρος) being "still pending," since that is what "not yet" means, but we can hardly conclude

---

60. Kannaday, *Apologetic Discourse*, 90–97; Metzger, *Textual Commentary*, 185.

61. Royse notes that since ουπω is well attested, it might not be due to the copyist, although ουδεπω might have arisen as a stylistically better reading (*Scribal Habits*, 541nn738–739).

that it *could not* have been used in 7:8, as if Jesus could not have used (or John could not have written) ουπω. So, the statistics provide little certainty. Nor does the use of the category of "prophetic formula" ("my hour has not yet come") as "an otherwise carefully prescribed and consistent use of the term" prove that ουκ *must* have been original but that the copyist conformed his text to the formula. The so-called "formula" varies anyway, sometimes using καιροc (7:6, 8) and sometimes ωρα (2:4, 7:30, 8:20), and the numbers are still not statistically significant.

Thus, the internal evidence is insufficient to decide which reading was original,[62] but Kannaday concludes that ουκ was original and a scribe later changed it to ουπω. Certainly, Porphyry referred to this verse (with ουκ) as showing that Jesus was changeable and fickle, and hence not worth following as a holy man (Jerome, *Pelag.* 2.17). Yet, Porphyry was not born, or was only very young, when P[66] and P[75] were copied (with ουπω), so we would need to postulate someone else at an earlier date being aware of the same issue with ουκ and making the same criticism provoking the substitution of ουπω for ουκ, which would require evidence from the second century that is presently lacking. Further, it is just possible that ουπω was original and that someone changed it to ουκ to avoid repetition of the ουπω in 7:6 but did not see the contradiction with 7:10.[63] Finally, if ουκ was original, the change to ουπω could simply have been due to someone who wished to smooth out a perceived difficulty,[64] without aiming to produce an apologetic response to criticism of Jesus, whether he was aware that it was a difficulty for anyone else or not.[65]

Luke 23:45

Luke's Gospel recounts events accompanying Jesus' death, including a note that around midday a darkness enveloped the whole land until mid-afternoon, but it also adds a phrase (του ηλιου εκλιποντοc) that does not appear in the parallel passages (Matt 27:45, Mark 15:33). Instead of this, certain MSS (A C³ (D) W Θ *f*¹,¹³ *Byz* lat etc.) read και εcκοτιcθη ο ηλιοc,

---

62. Haenchen seems to take ουπω as original (*John* 2, 7). Cf. Beasley-Murray, *John*, 103nd. *Pace* Barrett, *John*, 313.

63. Caragounis, "Jesus."

64. Brown, *John I-XII*, 307.

65. For a similar issue, see John 2:1–11, where Jesus similarly seemed to refuse to help when the wine ran out since his time had not yet come (ουπω ηκει η ωρα μου, 2:4), but he ended up helping anyway (2:7–9).

which is clearly secondary, given its weak MS support. Origen called this event an "eclipse," although this is not necessarily implied by εκλιποντος. In essence, εκλιποντος refers to "failing" or "failing to function properly," although with του ηλιου it can refer to an eclipse (cf. Job 31:26, Isa 60:20).[66] Origen does not say that Celsus raised this as a difficulty, but he mentions that it had no other source of attestation than Luke's Gospel, and he then refers to the pagan writer Phlegon of Tralles mentioning an eclipse in the time of Tiberius Caesar in the thirteenth or fourteenth book of his Chronicles (*Cels.* 2.33). Origen implies that it was apparently miraculous (*Cels.* 2.35), presumably because it was normally impossible for an eclipse to occur at Passover.[67] However, in his Commentary on Matthew, written at a similar time, Origen preferred και εσκοτισθη ο ηλιος (frag. 134) as the original reading, adding that του ηλιου εκλιποντος in Luke 23:45 had probably been added to provide ammunition to the critics of Christianity, apparently since it referred to an impossible event. Thus, Kannaday concludes that "Origen himself offered text-critical explanation as an apologetic response to Celsus."[68] It seems, then, that Origen was choosing from among extant readings, even though it was not needed since the original did not necessarily refer to an eclipse but to the sun's light "failing." Kannaday's dating of the creation of this variant is reasonable, since it appears in P[75] and hence arose "in near approximation and close association with the publication of *Contra Celsum*" (ca. AD 244–249).[69] So, the variant might have been created as an apologetic response to critics since we know that Origen was sensitive to the issue, but it could also have arisen before his time. Yet, Luke himself probably did not intend an allusion to an eclipse,[70] and the use of εσοτισθη for εκλιποντος might have first occurred simply as an equivalent reading.[71]

---

66. BDAG, 306, ἐκλείπω 3; GELS, 211, ἐκλείπω 3.
67. Cf. Westcott and Hort, *Appendix*, 69–71.
68. Kannaday, *Apologetic Discourse*, 97–98.
69. Nongbri argues for a fourth century date for P[75] (Nongbri, "Reconsidering"), but Orsini and Clarysse suggest AD 250–300 ("Early New Testament," 471).
70. Carrier shows that it was common belief that an eclipse accompanied the death of a great king ("Thallus," 185n4). If so, this might have influenced Luke's choice of language to describe the darkness.
71. Metzger notes the ambiguity and suggests that the variant was intended to clarify it (*Textual Commentary*, 155). Bovon translates "the sun had disappeared," and takes the original reference as just being to a highly significant event (*Luke 3*, 324–25). Cf. Fitzmyer, *Luke X–XXIV*, 1517–18.

Interestingly, apart from Origen we have no evidence that anyone else at the time felt this "difficulty," and we know nothing certain about the origins of και εσκοτιcθη ο ηλιοc. However, suggesting that it originated from Origen's concerns because some of the supporting MSS (Θ $f^{1,13}$) belong to the supposed "Caesarean" text type carries little conviction because the whole notion of the Caesarean text is now debated. Thus, we do not know when this reading originated. It might have been in exemplars of the MSS in which it occurs now, so it could have originated without any connection with Origen in the third century. Therefore, there is no certainty that this variant arose as a response to critics of Christianity referring to Luke's account as an inaccurate reference to an eclipse.

Mark 2:26

Mark's Gospel provides an account of Jesus' response to the Pharisaic criticism of his disciples picking and eating grain on the Sabbath (2:23–28). The major thrust of his defense is that David and his company were allowed to eat the consecrated bread from the sanctuary at Nob (1 Sam 21:1–7), with the implication that some (food) laws can be broken if the need is great enough (2:25–27). However, the name of the priest at Nob is given in the time phrase επι αβιαθαρ αρχιερεωc, where the MT has Ahimelech, not Abiathar. Matthew 12:1–8 and Luke 6:1–5 make no mention of a name, although it would be rash to claim that they omitted it to remove "the troublesome phrase,"[72] since it is uncertain that they were working from a copy of Mark's Gospel. Some MSS of Mark (D W it sy^s) omit the time phrase altogether, but αβιαθαρ might have been original and the copyists of those MSS just harmonized the text of Mark to Matthew or Luke. A small number of MSS have a reading with του before αρχιερεωc (or ιερεωc), which has been taken to allow the meaning to be that the event occurred in the time of Abiathar, but not necessarily when he was high priest, as he was at a later time.[73] I find it difficult, however, to see how this latter suggestion would work. Chrysostom dealt with this apparent inconsistency by suggesting that Abiathar had two names (*Hom. Matt.* 39.1), and Jerome said that such details were not significant, because the Gospel writers were just paraphrasing Scripture, not worrying about details (*Epist.* 57.9–11). Kannaday appears to treat all the

---

72. Pace Kannaday, *Apologetic Discourse*, 98–99. Cf. Evans, "Patristic Interpretation."
73. Metzger, *Textual Commentary*, 68.

secondary readings in the MSS and patristic explanations as attempts to defend the text of Mark against the charge of factual error—Abiathar instead of Ahimelech.

The issue, however, is a complex one for several reasons. First, the name given to the priest in 1 Sam 21:2 LXX is not Ahimelech (as in the MT) but Abimelech, and the title of Ps 34 (33:1 LXX) has Abimelech as the name of the Philistine king mentioned in 1 Sam 21:10-15, where the MT refers to Achish.[74] Indeed, even at 1 Sam 21:2, one LXX MS has Abimelech for Ahimelech, another has Amimelech, and one OL MS has Amelek. Also, the MT of Ps 52:2 has Ahimelech, but two LXX MSS of the same passage (Ps 51:1 LXX) have Abimelech (as in LXX Rahlfs). Obviously, there was some variation in the MSS between Abimelech and Ahimelech, and even between Achish and Abimelech. Second, the son of Abimelech (or Ahimelech) who survived the slaughter of the priests of Nob is named as Abiathar son of Ahimelech (1 Sam 22:20), and Ahimelech is named as the son of one Abiathar (2 Sam 8:17, 1 Chr 24:6), although the latter reading is suspect and should perhaps be reversed (cf. 1 Sam 23:6, 30:7).[75] There was plainly variation, then, in the MSS about Abimelech/Ahimelech and Abiathar.[76] Finally, the narrative in 1 Sam 21 only refers to Abimelech/Ahimelech being a priest, not a high priest, at Nob. Where did the notion of Abiathar or Abimelech/Ahimelech being a "high priest" come from? Perhaps there was no "high priest" at that time, although the presence of the ephod suggests that Nob was the main sanctuary at the time and the priest in charge there was the "high priest."

Therefore, since Abiathar was present at the time of this event and he was later effectively David's high priest, and since there is variation in the MSS between Abimelech/Ahimelech and Abiathar, as well as between Ahimelech and Achish, and also some variation as to whether Ahimelech was the father of Abiathar or his son, it would not be surprising that Mark or an early copyist wrote Abiathar when in fact Abimelech/Ahimelech was correct. Nevertheless, the variant readings in the MSS of Mark 2:26 seem to show that certain people wished to remove the apparent difficulty, and in this sense the readings might have been

---

74. Craigie suggests that Abimelech (lit. "my father is king") was an official title for Philistine kings, as Pharoah was an official title for Egyptian kings (*Psalms 1-50*, 278).

75. Gordon, *1 and 2 Samuel*, 246.

76. Botner suggests that the text of 1 Samuel in the first century was not as firmly fixed as we might imagine, so this issue should be treated with caution ("Has Jesus Read?," 498-99).

apologetic responses to forestall any criticism regarding the accuracy of the Gospels. We know that some apologists referred to this passage, so apparently critics referred to it as well. Of course, the variants might have originated from a desire to correct what someone viewed as a copying mistake, so in that case it would not be an apologetic response.[77] Or, it could have been changed to remove a perceived historical error.[78] It is thus not clear that the readings were constructed as apologetic responses to critics, although it is certainly possible.[79]

Luke 3:1

In the Gospel of Luke, the opening of John the Baptist's ministry is given a historical framework in the setting of the Roman Empire and Jewish administration (3:1–2), including the mention of Pontius Pilate ηγεμονευοντος (3:1). Bezae replaces this with the SR επιτροπευοντος, which Kannaday takes as a substitution of a word "in vogue during the second century," when the text of D might have had its origins. He suggests that "accuracy" has apparently been lost for the sake of "vernacular currency."[80] Of course, when Pilate is described as ηγεμονευοντος (cf. ηγεμων, 20:20), it was a more military term for a Roman governor, especially of a *praefectus*, as Pilate was, and as all Roman rulers of Judea were from AD 6. Thus, the use of επιτροπευοντος was more in accord with the Latin title *procurator*, given to Pilate in some later writings (Tacitus *Ann.* 15.44.4, Tertullian *Apol.* 21.18). It should also be noted that the *procurator* Felix is later called ηγεμων in Acts (23:24, 26, 33), so even when *procurator* was technically correct after the reorganization under Claudius in AD 46,[81] Luke still used the earlier military term.[82] Hence, the use of the more specific later term in Luke 3:1 D might have been

---

77. Marcus refers to the variation in transmission, citing other examples of such confusion (*Mark 1–8*, 241–42).

78. Metzger asserts that the reading in D, etc., was created "to avoid the historical difficulty" (*Textual Commentary*, 68). France takes this as "an obvious correction both to harmonize with Matthew and Luke and to remove the embarrassment of a historical error" (*Mark*, 142). Cf. Collins, *Mark*, 200nb; Meier, "Historical Jesus," 577–78.

79. Cf. Evans, *Manuscripts*, 461–63. Ehrman briefly cites the reading "Abiathar" as an example of Jesus making a mistake ("Text and Transmission," 334), but the issue is more complex than that.

80. Kannaday, *Apologetic Discourse*, 99.

81. Fitzmyer, *Luke I–IX*, 456–57. Cf. Bovon, *Luke 1*, 119–20.

82. Sherwin-White, *Roman Society*, 12. Cf. Brown, *Death of the Messiah*, 1:336–38.

an attempt to use contemporary terminology, if D did originate in the second century, although from AD 70 the Roman governor of Judea was generally called a *legatus*. In light of the variation of terms, D might have used a more current term, as Tacitus and Tertullian did, although it was not quite up to date. So, if preserving the original title for a Roman governor in a MS is seen as "accuracy," then the reading in D is inaccurate. But if using a more current term was seen as conveying the sense in a way that would be more easily understood by a later audience, then it would not derive from an apologetic motive in response to criticism by opponents of the Christians.

Luke 21:18

In the context of Jesus' discourse about future times of upheaval and persecution for his disciples (Luke 21:5–36), Luke records that Jesus said, και θριξ εκ της κεφαλης υμων ου μη αποληται (21:18). This seems to promise them safety in difficult times using an idiom drawn from the OT and implying divine protection (cf. Acts 27:34),[83] although the saying might not refer to being kept safe physically but kept strong in faith. Kannaday points out that some MSS (sy^c Marcion^E) omit this verse, perhaps by homoioarcton, since 21:17 also begins with και, although this would cause 21:17 to be omitted, not 21:18. He also proposes that a copyist might have omitted 21:18 because it did not square with the experience of Christians who were persecuted and suffered martyrdom, thus omitting the verse for the sake of consistency with experience, perhaps to avoid the criticism that Jesus' words were unreliable.

It would be odd, however, if only the Curetonian Syriac omitted it, as well as Marcion, according to Epiphanius's *Panarion* (e.g., 42.11:6.58), when persecution was a commonplace for the early Christians. If Marcion and one other person sensed the difficulty, why did not more people think it was an issue and remove the verse? Moreover, the idea that Jesus' disciples would need to endure (εν τη υπομονη υμων, 21:19) still implies hardship. On balance, it is unlikely that 21:18 was omitted as a response to the charge that Jesus' words were unreliable, although it is still unclear why it is absent in a few MSS.

---

83. Bovon outlines the background of the idiom and its meaning in the present context (*Luke 3*, 113–14). Fitzmyer needlessly proposes that Luke combined traditions, so that 21:18 jars with 21:19, because he was not concerned to make his narrative consistent (*Luke X–XXIV*, 1341).

John 19:14, Mark 15:25

Kannaday refers to copyists "routinely" assimilating or conflating the details of one Gospel to fit in with the details of another, when an issue of inconsistency or error was involved. For example, he cites the chronology of John 19:14, according to which Jesus' crucifixion took place after ωρα . . . ωc εxτη (about midday), while Mark 15:25 says that Jesus was crucified ωρα τριτη (at 9 a.m.). In John 19:14 some MSS ($\aleph^2$ D^s L Δ Ψ *l* 844) read τριτη instead of εxτη, and at Mark 15:25, Θ has εxτη and the sy^h has "sixth" in the margin. It may be that these readings were created in an attempt to make the Gospel narratives consistent,[84] but there are other possibilities. There might have been some confusion between the Greek numerals Γ (3) and F (6),[85] as Eusebius and other patristic writers suggested.[86] Or the issue might have stemmed from confusion between the Hebrew letters used for numbers—*gimel* (ג, 3) and *waw* (ו, 6).[87] More likely, however, ωρα εxτη in John comes from the prominence of that phrase in the Synoptic accounts (Matt 27:45, Mark 15:33, Luke 23:44) and this has found its way accidentally into the timing of the verdict, when someone didn't know that it was not the beginning of the time when Jesus was on the cross but the time when the darkness commenced.[88] Hence, the issue is not an easy one to resolve,[89] but it is far from certain that changes were made as apologetic responses to critics.

CONCLUSION

In this chapter I have examined claims that variant readings were created in response to charges made against the Christian faith, in order to show that it was not a recent and doubtful arrival on the religious scene, and that Jesus was not inferior to John the Baptist, and that the Scriptures that Christians appealed to are not inconsistent. However, I

---

84. Kannaday, *Apologetic Discourse*, 98. Cf. Evans, *Mark 8:27—16:20*, 497nc; Collins, *Mark*, 730na.

85. Barrett, *John*, 545. Cf. Brown, *John I–XII*, 882–83.

86. Metzger adopts the harmonizing solution but notes that Ammonius, Eusebius, and Jerome suggested confusion over the numbers (*Textual Commentary*, 99, 216, esp. 216nn1–3).

87. Barrett, *John*, 545.

88. France, *Matthew*, 644–45.

89. Brown, *John XIII–XXI*, 882–83.

have shown that few of the variants discussed can be clearly shown to be responses to such charges, most of them being the result of copyists' mistakes or unconscious harmonization to other passages, especially in the Gospels. In summary, the case for variants being apologetic scribal responses to charges by critics has not been proven and must await further confirmation.

6

Apologetic for the Person of Jesus?

THE VARIANTS STUDIED IN this chapter focus on Jesus himself. In his third chapter Kannaday first outlines a range of hostile pagan opinions about Jesus, including views expressed by Lucian and those described by Justin Martyr and Minucius Felix, but especially Celsus, as reported in Origen's *Contra Celsum*. Whether Celsus's work *True Doctrine* continued to have an impact on pagan opinion of Christians or not, Ambrose, Origen's patron, certainly thought it was worthwhile requesting him to refute Celsus's views, so he was clearly concerned about their deleterious effects on Christians. In response to the way in which Celsus denigrated Jesus, Origen responded by portraying him as a worthy man, and the efforts of the apologists in general "were designed to make Jesus appear respectable, moral, and loyal to the welfare of the state."[1] Kannaday notes that in the NT, and especially in the Gospels, certain statements of the authors, or of Jesus himself, could be taken as aiming to promote insurrection against the Roman authorities, and he argues that some variant readings were designed by scribes "to depict a Christ less vulnerable to stock criticism and more palatable to the pagan populace."[2]

---

1. Kannaday, *Apologetic Discourse*, 104.
2. Kannaday, *Apologetic Discourse*, 104.

Crucified and Foolish?

The first group of variants concern the crucifixion of Jesus. Kannaday raises this issue because it had been a difficulty for Jews and gentiles from the very beginning, when Jesus' crucifixion was "a stumbling-block to Jews and foolishness to gentiles" (1 Cor 1:23). Presumably, he was referring to Jews believing that anyone hanged was cursed by God (*m. Sanh.* 6.4; cf. Deut 21:23),[3] as well as gentiles thinking that it was foolish to believe that a man who had been crucified could be the Son of God, so Christianity was obviously a pernicious superstition (Tacitus, *Ann.* 15.44; Pliny, *Ep.* 1.96.8). Cicero spoke of crucifixion as a miserable and painful punishment appropriate only for slaves (*Verr.* 2.5.168, *Rab. Perd.* 16; cf. Valerius Maximus, *Factorum* 7.12; Josephus, *J.W.*, 7.202–3). Certainly, Lucian referred to Jesus' crucifixion with contempt (*Peregr.* 11, 13), and Caecilius is portrayed as saying that Christians worshipped "an executed criminal and his cross" (Minucius Felix, *Oct.* 8). In view of this criticism, apologists such as Justin responded by emphasizing that Jesus was crucified not because he was a criminal but because it had been foretold in the OT Scriptures (Ps 22, Isa 53, etc.) and was thus part of the purposes of God (1 *Apol.* 53; *Dial.* 59).[4] I now review proposals that variant readings resulted from copyists responding to these pagan criticisms out of apologetic concerns.

Matthew 27:35

Matthew's narrative of Jesus' crucifixion includes a description of what the Roman soldiers did to him after he had rejected a drugged drink (27:33–34)—σταυρωσαντες δε αυτον διεμερισαντο τα ιματια αυτου βαλλοντες κληρον (27:35). However, some mainly Western MSS (Δ Θ $f^{1,13}$ it vg[cl] sy[h,pal(mss)] etc.) add variations of what appears to reflect John 19:24, ινα πληρωθη το ρηθεν υπο του προφητου διεμερισαντο τα ιματια μου εαυτοις και επι τον ιματισμον μου εβαλον κληρον, making a link with Ps 22:18 (22:19 LXX).[5] It is possible that this whole section was original

---

3. Fitzmyer notes that in Palestine during the Roman period Deut 21:23 was understood to refer to crucifixion (4QpNah 3–4 i 4–9; 11QTemple[a] 64.6–13, comparing Josephus *Ant.* 13.14.2; *J.W.* 1.4.5) (*First Corinthians*, 159).
Kannaday, *Apologetic Discourse*, 105–6.

4. Kannaday, *Apologetic Discourse*, 105–6.

5. Nolland, *Matthew*, 1185–86nf; Luz, *Matthew 21–28*, 525n5.

and fell out by homoioteleuton (κληρον ... κληρον), but the weight of the MSS supporting the shorter reading (ℵ A B D W 33 vg^mss sy^p,(palmss) eth) suggests that it is original, so material from John 19:24 seems to have been added to Matt 27:35 along with Matthew's usual citation formula.[6] Kannaday refers to Justin Martyr's paraphrase of Ps 22:16-18 (*Dial.* 96-97) and his complete citation of Ps 22 (*Dial.* 98) as evidence of his apologetic strategy to show that Jesus' crucifixion was not the ignominious death of a criminal but one foretold by the OT, thus responding to the criticism that Jesus' death showed that he was no one great, and in fact a malefactor.

Of course, Ps 22 is cited elsewhere in the NT (Mark 15:34, John 19:24, Heb 2:12) and alluded to frequently, so it was clearly significant for the early Christians. Indeed, the evangelists made this connection between the events of Jesus' life and the OT in various ways, so whoever inserted this secondary addition into Matt 27:35 was only doing what the evangelists themselves had done. But Kannaday suggests that, since Justin used Ps 22 with apologetic interests, so also those who added this text to Matt 27:35, whether from Ps 22 or the parallel in John 19:24, must have had similar apologetic motives.[7] Yet, just because Justin used Ps 22 like this does not show that someone (or some people) inserted it in Matt 27:25 for the same reason. Further, since Jesus' crucifixion was probably seen as a shameful event anyway because he was naked and made fun of, someone might have thought it appropriate to include this verse as evidence that it was not shameful at all but an event foretold by ancient writings, although this is only one possibility. Perhaps someone just wanted to round out the story in Matthew by including what John had recorded in his narrative.

Luke 23:32

Luke's passion narrative relates how Jesus was taken out of Jerusalem to be crucified (Luke 23:26-31), and then ηγοντο δε και ετεροι κακουργοι δυο cυν αυτω αναιρεθηναι (23:32). It seems clear that this is the original word order in view of its limited but impressive support (P^75 ℵ B). However, ετεροι κακουργοι δυο could be translated as "two other evildoers," which might suggest that Jesus was one of three κακουργοι crucified, perhaps

---

6. Metzger, *Textual Commentary*, 57; Hagner, *Matthew 14-28*, 833ne.
7. Kannaday, *Apologetic Discourse*, 106-8.

with Isa 53:12 in mind, as Luke had noted that Jesus would be "numbered with the transgressors" (cf. 22:37).[8] So, Kannaday suggests that, in order to avoid the potential admission that Jesus was a criminal, in some MSS (A C D W Θ $f^{1,13}$ *Byz* sy[h]) scribes changed the position of δυο so that the text read ηγοντο δε και ετεροι δυο κακουργοι сυν αυτω, which would mean "others as well, two criminals with him," thus avoiding the problem.[9] Other MSS (c e sy[s] sa) omit ετεροι altogether, perhaps for a similar reason. Thus, Kannaday contends that Luke's allusion to Isa 53:12 introduced too many problems for scribes, so they changed the text to remove the issue.[10] Now, Jesus was not one of the three criminals.

However, whether the proposed unfavorable meaning was a valid reading of the text in the setting of Luke's Gospel or not, the issue is whether the original reading *could* have been understood to suggest that Jesus also was a κακουργος. This is certainly possible, so that δυο would qualify ετεροι κακουργοι, but it is not certain that the person responsible for the change in word order wished to avoid this interpretation.[11] In fact, would this have changed the meaning much, since the narrative recounts how Jesus was still crucified between two criminals (23:33), naked (23:34), and was the object of derision (23:35–39)? Would the change in the position of δυο have altered that shameful and horrific picture? Would a reader think it did, and could a copyist expect it to do so? Further, being crucified between two criminals probably implied "guilt by association,"[12] so it is far from certain that this change would have made any appreciable difference to the meaning. It is doubtful, then, that the change in the placement of δυο was made with an apologetic motive. Moreover, it is also possible that ετεροι δυο κακουργοι was original, as in the recently published *THGNT*. If this were the case, it would be necessary to explain the creation of ετεροι κακουργοι δυο, perhaps by a scribal misplacement at an early stage, but this would imply that the difference between the two readings was minimal to readers at the time. Even if ετεροι κακουργοι δυο was original, however, it is unlikely that it was changed to ετεροι δυο κακουργοι in order to avoid the idea that Jesus himself was a κακουργος.

8. Kannaday, *Apologetic Discourse*, 108–9.

9. Cf. Metzger and Ehrman, *Text*, 267, 294; Wasserman, "Variants of Evil," 78–80.

10. Cf. Fitzmyer, *Luke X–XXIV*, 1499; Ehrman, "Text of the Gospels," 97; Parker, *Living Text*, 161; Ehrman, *Misquoting*, 203.

11. *Pace* Wasserman, "Variants of Evil," 72.

12. Kannaday, *Apologetic Discourse*, 110.

Apologetic for the Person of Jesus?

Mark 15:28

Mark's crucifixion narrative reports that Jesus was crucified with a criminal on either side (15:27), and it goes on to relate the insults hurled at him by passersby (15:29). Some MSS, however, include 15:28, και επληρωθη η γραφη η λεγουσα και μετα ανομων ελογιcθη.[13] This reading is clearly secondary, since the MSS with v. 28 (K Θ f[1,13] *Byz* lat sy[p.h] bo[pt]) are far less significant than those without it (ℵ A B C D sy[s] sa bo[pt]). Further, the added text seems to echo Luke 22:37 with its citation of Isa 53:12, albeit with slightly different wording.[14] Kannaday suggests that the person responsible for adding v. 28 thought that Jesus suffering an ignominious death and being in dishonorable company might have given fuel to his critics (cf. *Cels.* 2.31, 44), so they added it to show that his death was the fulfilment of ancient Scriptures and therefore not blameworthy. Indeed, it showed the workings of divine providence, like Origen's citation of Ps 69:21 (68:22 LXX) to refute Celsus's description of Jesus greedily drinking the vinegar and gall (*Cels.* 2.37), portraying it instead as the fulfilment of the prophet's words.[15] While this reconstruction is possible, it is far from certain. Did the person responsible wish to soften the text and avoid the possible implication, as Origen did? He may only have wished to benefit the faithful by emphasizing the fulfilment of God's purposes.

The Author of Sedition?

The next theme that Kannaday deals with is the charge that Jesus was "the author of this sedition" (*Cels.* 8.14). Celsus's description of Jesus in unfavorable terms is mentioned in a number of places (*Cels.* 1.62, 71; 2.7, 24, 29, 46, 76), and Tacitus referred to him having been executed by sentence of Pontius Pilate (*Ann.* 15.44). In fact, Celsus called him a magician or sorcerer (*Cels.* 1.71; 2.32, 49; 8.41), and therefore having contravened Roman law.[16] At a later time Julian rejected any claim that Jesus was divine (*Gal.* 201e, 290e). It is not clear, however, that Jesus himself was generally viewed with disdain, but his followers certainly were seen

---

13. Cf. Schmid, "Conceptualizing," 61-62.

14. Metzger, *Textual Commentary*, 99; Evans, *Mark 8:27—16:20*, 497nf; France, *Mark*, 639; Collins, *Mark*, 730nc.; Marcus, *Mark 8–16*, 1044.

15. Kannaday, *Apologetic Discourse*, 109-111.

16. Cf. Benko, "Pagan Criticism"; Meredith, "Porphyry and Julian"; Wilken, *Christians*, 100-101, 104-6, 120; Benko, *Pagan Rome*, 149-51.

as a threat to society because of their "superstition." Nevertheless, the apologists were understandably keen to show Jesus in a good light, and Kannaday proposes that some textual variants were created to vindicate Jesus in the face of criticism that he had fostered sedition against Rome.

Matthew 10:34

When Matthew describes how Jesus sent out the Twelve, he includes a number of instructions (10:5–42). Among these, he spoke about the inevitable division that would result from people coming to acknowledge him as the Christ (10:32–34), stating that ουκ ηλθον βαλειν ειρηνην αλλα μαχαιραν. Kannaday notes that, instead of αλλα μαχαιραν, one MS (sy^c) reads "but division of mind," perhaps with αλλ η διαμερισμον in view (Luke 12:51). He suggests that the person responsible for this reading wished to remove any thought that Jesus came to bring contention or violence and to replace this with an intention to bring a "division of mind" or "difference of opinion," which could fit with the life and work of a philosopher canvassing a mode of thinking.[17]

However, the meaning of the proposed Greek translation of the Syriac (διαμερισμον των διανοιων), a "division of thoughts," is not entirely clear. It could mean "disunity of thoughts," but on either reading, it could also imply sedition, even if not violence. Someone sowing "division of thoughts" could be seen as fostering insurgence, so he could still be dangerous. So, while at first sight the Curetonian Syriac version seems to have removed attributing a possibly violent intention to Jesus and replaced it with an aim to foster calm philosophical debate, the new reading could have also been seen as portraying him as someone who came to stir up trouble. Further, a survey of patristic writers on this passage shows that few, if any, were troubled by it, some taking sword bearing as a normal aspect of life and others interpreting the reference metaphorically.[18] Roman laws placed restrictions on people meeting, especially at night, for this very reason, for who knew what they were doing and planning? Indeed, Christians were treated with suspicion since they met in the evening or before dawn. Did someone wish to remove any thought of sedition with this secondary reading? Perhaps, but in the context of Matt 10 Jesus is still recorded saying that his coming would not bring

---

17. Kannaday, *Apologetic Discourse*, 112–13.
18. Croy, "Sword Handling."

peace (10:34) but family disunity (10:35–36), asking his disciples to hold allegiance to him as a higher priority than family ties (10:37–39). It is difficult, then, to envisage anyone thinking that the secondary reading in this MS would change the confronting tone of the whole discourse. A reader would probably not notice the difference, so it is unlikely that a copyist changed the reading to remove that potential difficulty.[19]

Matthew 9:13

Matthew's Gospel records an incident in which Jesus was eating with "sinners" and tax collectors at Matthew's house, when Pharisees asked his disciples why he was doing so, presumably because he claimed to be a holy man and those people were deemed "unclean" (9:10–11). Jesus himself responded to the question, saying that ου γαρ ηλθον καλεσαι δικαιους αλλ αμαρτωλους. Kannaday observes that this might have sounded like Jesus was gathering rogues ("sinners") to further some illegal or immoral purpose, as some believed Christians were involved in. They seemed to be a secret society (Pliny, *Ep.* 10.96)—they met at night, they might have been involved in magic, and they were sometimes charged with atheism, infanticide, or gross sexual immorality. Celsus said that Christians welcomed "sinners" (*Cels.* 3.59), but Origen explained that they welcomed "sinners" so they would reform their lives, not go on sinning (*Cels.* 3.60–61). Similarly, Tertullian referred to the suspicion in which Christians were held as a danger to public order (*Apol.* 38.1), so they were persecuted, and even executed, just for being Christians. Kannaday, then, refers to the secondary reading in some MSS (C Θ f[13] Byz c g[1] sy[s,h**] sa bo[pt] etc.) that adds εις μετανοιαν to the end of the verse, thus clarifying why Jesus was gathering these people around him.

However, this reading was probably just harmonized to the parallel passage in Luke 5:32, where εις μετανοιαν appears in the same position.[20] Indeed, Justin (1 *Apol.* 15.8) included "to repentance" when he was referring to this saying of Jesus, although we do not know which Gospel

---

19. Wasserman wonders if the variants in Matthew were designed "to safeguard against a strict literal and more violent interpretation of Jesus' saying," which would apply to how Christians, as much as outsiders, understood the passage ("*Lectio vehementior potior*," 230–32).

20. Davies and Allison, *Matthew*, 2:105n108; Hagner, *Matthew 1–13*, 236ni; Nolland, *Matthew*, 384nh.

Scribes, Theology, and Apologetics

he had in mind.[21] He certainly stressed that when a sinner becomes a Christian, they are called to a better life. So, this variant might have been added to stop anyone seizing on Jesus' words and suggesting that he was gathering rogues for some criminal purpose or to stir up trouble, but it is impossible to be certain, and the fact that Justin uses the longer form adds little to the force of this suggestion.

Mark 13:33

Mark 13 is mostly taken up with Jesus' words about the fate of Jerusalem and the last days until the coming of the Son of Man. Toward the end of the discourse, however, Jesus urges his disciples, βλεπετε αγρυπνειτε, since they did not know when that time would come (13:33). While Kannaday translates αγρυπνειτε as "be alert in the night," αγρυπνεω has the more general meaning of "be alert" or "care for, look after,"[22] and, although it can refer to lying awake without sleeping, it does not necessarily imply that this occurs "at night."[23] That would require the addition of την νυκτα or the like. Further, the cognate noun αγρυπνια can refer to insomnia, but it can also mean "alertness."[24] The following context does refer to a master returning sometime at night, so he might find his servants sleeping (13:35–36), but "that day or hour" (13:32) or "that time" (13:33) could be at any time; the servants do not know when it will be (13:34). So, the proposal that these words could have been understood to be "ordering nocturnal guard duty" with rebellion in view is unlikely to have occurred to a reader. While the various times envisaged for the return of the "master" are between evening and dawn (13:35), this is only because that would be the most natural time *not* to be on the lookout. Hence the mention of "sleeping" in v. 36. The verb γρηγορεω is used in the context (13:34, 35, 37), but this also can simply mean "be watchful" or "be on the alert," as well as stay awake.[25] Thus, it is quite unlikely that a reader would have taken Jesus' use of αγρυπνεω as a call to be on night guard duty, so it is hard to imagine a copyist changing the reading to avoid that meaning.

21. Kannaday, *Apologetic Discourse*, 113–14.
22. BDAG, 16.
23. Cf. *GELS*, 8.
24. BDAG, 16; *GELS*, 8.
25. BDAG, 208; *GELS*, 137.

Nevertheless, some MSS (ℵ A C W Θ $f^{1,13}$ Byz lat sy co) add και προϲευχεϲθε, which Kannaday describes as replacing "contentious discord with pious harmony." Why did someone add και προϲευχεϲθε? It might have been harmonized to Mark 14:38 (γρηγορευετε και προϲευχεϲθε),[26] although this only has two terms, not three as in the variant reading (βλεπετε αγρυπνειτε και προϲευχεϲθε). Indeed, the contexts are quite different.[27] Perhaps prayer was seen as "a conventional extension of the exhortation to watch," especially with 14:38 in mind, and the parallel in Luke 21:36 uses δεομενοι along with αγρυπνειτε.[28] Also, Eph 6:18 includes these words in order, προϲευχηϲ και δεηϲεωϲ προϲευχομενοι . . . αγρυπνουντεϲ . . . δεηϲει (cf. Col 4:2).[29] So, in view of the similar context of ideas, it would be easy to imagine someone adding και προϲευχεϲθε in Mark 13:33 without any apologetic motive to stave off suspicion about meetings at night or to promote Jesus as encouraging pious prayer instead of "contentious discord." Although this was potentially relevant to the situation of Christians in the second and third centuries, it remains an unlikely motive for this addition. Rather, common phraseology is the more probable origin of this variant reading with the addition of prayer to an exhortation to "watch."

John 6:15

John 6 begins with an account of Jesus feeding five thousand people on the eastern shore of the Sea of Galilee and then the crowd thinking that he was "the (coming) prophet" (6:1–14). Apparently, they also wished to make him "king," and John records that in response ανεχωρηϲεν παλιν ειϲ το οροϲ αυτοϲ μονοϲ (6:15). Kannaday notes that some MSS (ℵ* lat sy^c) read φευγει instead of ανεχωρηϲεν, which is not to be dismissed lightly in view of its presence in ℵ*, although the external evidence certainly leans heavily in favor of ανεχωρηϲεν being original. He suggests that the B rating for ανεχωρηϲεν in GNT indicates some hesitation on the part of the UBS committee, although the rating in GNT³ was revised to an A rating in GNT⁴ and GNT⁵, suggesting their certainty that ανεχωρηϲεν was

---

26. Metzger, *Textual Commentary*, 95; Pardee, *Scribal Harmonization*, 361.

27. Kannaday, *Apologetic Discourse*, 114–15.

28. Collins suggests that mention of prayer is "the result of independent pious additions" (*Mark*, 593ns).

29. France, *Mark*, 497.

original. Kannaday also alludes to the fact that αναχωρεω occurs nowhere else in John's Gospel, and he takes this as evidence that φευγει was original. However, statistics based on such a small number of occurrences are not compelling, especially since αναχωρεω also occurs ten times in Matthew but only once in Mark and John, while φευγω appears seven times in Matthew, five times in Mark, three times in Luke, and twice in John. Kannaday refers to Celsus's charge that Jesus could not be divine since he was unable to flee (φευγω) from capture (*Cels.* 2.9–10), stating that he "hid himself" (κρυπτομαι) and "ran away" (διαδιδρασκω).[30] The general impression of Celsus's remarks is that Jesus lacked courage and the ability to rescue himself from difficulty.

The occurrence of φευγω in Celsus is not, however, evidence that φευγει rather than ανεχωρηcεν was the original reading in John 6:15, as if that was changed to avoid the charge of cowardice on Jesus' part.[31] Further, while φευγω could mean "seek safety in flight, *flee*," it need not have had such a negative connotation and could just mean "become safe from danger by eluding or avoiding it, *escape*," or "keep from doing something by avoiding it because of its potential damage, *flee from, avoid, shun*."[32] Moreover, αναχωρεω generally refers to departing from or returning to a location without any indication of why one is doing so.[33] It could also mean "seek seclusion" or even "*withdraw* in order to flee from a danger," such as in Tobit 1:19, where the other LXX version uses αποδιδρασκω (cf. διαδιδρασκω in *Cels.* 2.9).[34] It appears, then, that φευγω and αναχωρεω can, in certain contexts, refer to departing or withdrawing, but they can also both refer to running away, so the distinction between the two is not as clear as it might seem. So, comparison with the words of Celsus, while thematically relevant, does not provide evidence as to which word was original and which was secondary in John 6. Hence, it does not follow that copyists changed φευγει to ανεχωρηcεν to show that Jesus was "no coward" and did not "run away." More likely, ανεχωρηcεν was original and φευγει was just "a typical Western reading . . . to enliven the narrative," rather than an ideologically motivated change.[35]

30. Kannaday, *Apologetic Discourse*, 115–16.
31. *Pace* Beasley-Murray, *John*, 84nf.
32. BDAG, 1052 (italics original). Cf. *GELS*, 713.
33. BDAG, 75.
34. *GELS*, 48 (italics original).
35. Metzger, *Textual Commentary*, 181. Brown is unsure which was original (*John I–XII*, 235).

The second variant reading Kannaday refers to in John 6:15 is the addition of κακει προcηυχετο at the end of the verse in some MSS (D sa^ms). Kannaday notes that Jesus was clearly rejecting the call for him to seize political power, but Kannaday also suggests that those responsible for the addition wished to portray Jesus as "a man of prayer" rather than a political rebel, both of which would address charges leveled at Jesus by critics like Celsus.³⁶ Yet, although the wording is slightly different, this variant could just be a harmonization to the parallel account in Mark 6:46 where Jesus απηλθεν εic το οροc προcευξαcθαι,³⁷ a suggestion that is at least as likely as the proposal that it was included with an apologetic motive.

Only a Carpenter?

It was a common theme of certain critics that Christians were drawn mainly from the lower classes of Roman society, as Minucius Felix cites Caecilius saying (*Oct.* 8), and Jesus was also sometimes maligned as a low-class tradesman. Kannaday cites the words of Celsus which refer to Jesus as "a carpenter by trade" (*Cels.* 6.34), although it is not clear in the context that this was intended as a criticism. Rather, he was making fun of the Christians who made much of the link between the "tree" of life and "the resurrection of the flesh by the tree," and only then did he refer to Jesus being nailed to a cross (or "tree") and him being a carpenter. He mockingly went on to suggest that if Jesus were thrown off a cliff there would have been a "cliff of life" above the heavens; or if he had been a cobbler, stonemason, or blacksmith, then there would have been a "blessed stone, or an iron of love, or a holy hide of leather." He makes no derogatory mention of Jesus as a tradesman here, and Origen's response only addresses Celsus's mention of the "tree of life" and the cross of Jesus (*Cels.* 6.36). Thus, the suggestion that scribes were attempting to avoid mentioning Jesus as a carpenter has little basis, but I review below readings adduced in support of the contention that variants were created in response to the charge that Jesus was a low-class tradesman.

---

36. Kannaday, *Apologetic Discourse*, 116.
37. Haenchen, *John 1*, 272.

Scribes, Theology, and Apologetics

Mark 6:3

Mark 6 begins with an account of Jesus teaching in his home synagogue on a Sabbath day, provoking many to ask where this teaching had come from (6:1–2), for ουχ ουτος ο τεκτων; (6:3). Some MSS, however, read ο του τεκτονος υιος (f^{13} 33^{vid} P^{45vid} it vg^{mss} bo^{mss}) instead of ο τεκτων. Now Jesus is not a carpenter himself, just the son of a carpenter. Origen said that he knew of no MS that referred to Jesus as a carpenter (*Cels.* 6.36), supposedly responding to Celsus.[38] We do not know why he said this, but his text of Mark 6:3 might have had a reading harmonized from Matt 13:55 where Jesus is called ο του τεκτονος υιος,[39] or perhaps he just forgot this unique reference in the Gospels.[40] Moreover, Justin's reference to Jesus as a carpenter making "ploughs and yokes as symbols to teach righteousness and active living" (*Dial.* 88) shows that Justin at least did not downplay or dismiss the idea that Jesus was a carpenter.[41] It is possible that anti-Christian writers like Celsus saw this reference to be portraying Jesus as among the lower classes and hence not worthy of "divine stature," and Ehrman discusses whether Origen's reference to "gospels accepted in the churches" implies that he knew of other Gospels that *did* include a mention of Jesus as a carpenter. It is unclear exactly what Origen had in mind, although Kannaday asserts that he knew of such other readings but dismissed them because of Celsus's "attack" on Jesus. In fact, however, Origen's sentence comes almost as a footnote at the end of his discussion before he goes on to make further comments on Celsus's argument, which show that it was not one of his central concerns, if a concern at all. Celsus did refer to Jesus as a carpenter (*Cels.* 6.34, 36, 37), but it is not obvious that this was derogatory in itself. Thus, both the force of Celsus's accusations and of Origen's response do not prove that Celsus criticized Jesus for being a carpenter or that Origen wished to respond to that.[42]

While certain copyists opted for the reading in Mark 6:3 that does not mention Jesus as a carpenter, most of them would have just been

---

38. Ehrman, "Text of the Gospels," 93–94. Cf. Ehrman, "Text and Transmission," 331–32; Ehrman, *Misquoting*, 201–3.

39. Cf. Chadwick, *Origen*, 352n5.

40. Cf. Metzger, "Works of Origen," 93. He suggests that Origen had a lapse of memory, as he was apparently less well acquainted with Mark than with the other Gospels ("Works of Origen," 101). Cf. Donaldson, "Explicit References," 104n28, 106n33.

41. Kannaday, *Apologetic Discourse*, 117–19.

42. Pace Metzger, *Textual Commentary*, 75–76, 75n1.

following their exemplar. That the Palestinian Syriac omits ο τεκτων altogether is not compelling evidence of an apologetic motive, since homoioteleuton can account for the omission in a text written in *scriptio continua* (εcτιν ο . . . τεκτων ο). Hence, it is unclear that the variant that omits a reference to Jesus as a carpenter was intentional or that it was intended to be an apologetic response to criticism that he was.[43] So, since there is no firm proof that this was a criticism of Jesus at all, a harmonization to Matt 13:55 is the most viable suggestion as to how this variant arose in Mark 6.[44] Indeed, would it have made any difference for Jesus to be "the son of a carpenter" as opposed to being a carpenter himself? If not, it is unlikely that a copyist or anyone else would have made the change to avoid that reference.

A Magician and Deceiver?

The Gospels recount that during his ministry Jesus was accused of being in league with the devil (e.g., Matt 12:24–27, Mark 3:22–23, Luke 11:17–20) or possessed by demons (Mark 3:30, John 8:48–52), and accounts of Jesus' miracles probably brought magic and sorcery to mind for many in the educated classes of the Roman Empire.[45] This was a serious charge because it could result in being brought to court, as Apuleius found (*Apol.*),[46] and practicing magic could even be a capital offence due to possible links with sedition (Suetonius, *Aug.* 31.1; Apuleius, *Apol.* 4, 25–26, 100).[47] Justin Martyr alluded to this criticism of Jesus (*Dial.* 69),[48] and links to this theme are also traceable in Mark 16:18, the Infancy Gospel of Thomas, Justin (1 *Apol.* 30), Tertullian (*Apol.* 21.17), and Irenaeus (*Haer.* 1.23–35). In his response to Celsus, Origen also referred to it (*Cels.* 1.28, 38; 2.49–55; 8.41).

---

43. Pace Haines-Eitzen, *Guardians*, 117–18; Pardee, *Scribal Harmonization*, 178–79.

44. Metzger, *Textual Commentary*, 76; Guelich, *Mark 1—8:26*, 306nc; France, *Mark*, 241. Pace Blumell, "Luke 22:43–44," 29n126. Head allows harmonization to Matthew but also suggests that avoiding "embarrassment" might have been a factor ("Christology," 118–19). Collins discusses the various proposals without coming to a firm conclusion (*Mark*, 287–88nd).

45. Kannaday, *Apologetic Discourse*, 119–22.

46. Cf. Benko, *Pagan Rome*, 104–8.

47. Cf. Betz, *Greek Magical Papyri*, xli.

48. Benko, "Pagan Criticism," 1076; Benko, *Pagan Rome*, 103–39.

Kannaday suggests that for this reason Matthew and Luke purposefully omitted some "magical" elements from Mark's account (Mark 7:33, 8:23), but since it is not certain that they used Mark as one of their sources this is impossible to confirm. Nor is it clear that John called Jesus' miracles "signs" or reduced their number to seven to avoid charges of magic, or that Jesus' commands to keep his identity quiet were given so that he could act in secret, until his claims were forced from him at his trial (Mark 14:60–62). Despite all these qualifications, however, certain people did think of Jesus as demon possessed or as a kind of magician, both during his ministry and in the first three centuries, and some also suspected Christians of being involved in magical practices. I now review a number of textual variants that are said to have been created in order to avert this criticism.

Mark 6:2

Mark 6 begins with an account of Jesus going to his hometown (6:1) where, in response to his teaching in the synagogue on the Sabbath, the townspeople were amazed and asked, ποθεν τουτω ταυτα και τις η σοφια η δοθεισα τουτω και αι δυναμεις τοιαυται δια των χειρων αυτου γινομεναι; (6:2). Kannaday refers to MSS which attest a different reading (C* D K Θ it sy^h sa^{ms}), where two distinct questions are transformed into a single sentence—ποθεν τουτω ταυτα και τις η σοφια η δοθεισα αυτω ινα και δυναμεις τοιαυται δια των χειρων αυτου γινωνται[49]—and there are other readings in the MSS as well. The reading noted here is probably secondary, despite the traditional reading having only limited support (א* B 33 bo),[50] and Kannaday argues that the slight changes in this reading betray an apologetic agenda.[51] He suggests that the original text, with its two questions, leaves open the issue of the relationship between Jesus' wisdom and his ability to work miracles. In turn, this could have led readers to think that perhaps Jesus worked his miracles by magic, presumably on the basis that the gift of wisdom was distinguished from the ability to work miracles. So, the secondary reading, by directly specifying that Jesus' miracles were a result of his wisdom, would serve the apologetic interest of locating the source of Jesus' miracle-working ability within

---

49. Kannaday, *Apologetic Discourse*, 123.
50. Metzger, *Textual Commentary*, 75; Collins, *Mark*, 287nc.
51. Kannaday, *Apologetic Discourse*, 123–24.

himself (his coφια), so he could not be accused of drawing on an external magical power.

In support of the proposed apologetic tone, Kannaday refers to Justin Martyr's allusion to Jesus as the λογος of God (*Dial.* 61), so his miracles were "the extension of his own divinely endowed wisdom." Sossianus Hierocles contrasted Jesus as a sorcerer with Apollonius of Tyana, the latter portrayed as a philosopher and man of wisdom (Eusebius, *Hier.* 1–2), but Eusebius responded by saying that the facts showed quite the opposite. Elsewhere, Eusebius maintained that Jesus was not a magician (*Dem. ev.* 3.6–7), as did Justin (1 *Apol.* 30), Origen (*Cels.* 2.48; 5.62; 6.39), and Lactantius (*Inst.* 5.3.9). Interestingly, Porphyry said that Jesus was not a magician, but nor was he a god.[52]

However, even though Jesus was accused of being a magician by certain critics and a number of apologetic writers were concerned to rebut this charge, it does not follow that the variant in question was introduced as an apologetic response to that charge. Further, it is doubtful that the variant could have achieved that purpose, because the coφια of Jesus is still said to have been "given" (δοθεισα) to him, presumably by someone else. So, it was not an innate part of his being but something imparted to him from an outside source. Hence, it is doubtful that there is a real contrast between the readings, so there is no reason to suppose that there was an intentionally apologetic motive for this variant.[53]

Mark 1:34

In Mark's account of the early part of Jesus' public ministry, he reports events in Capernaum (1:21–34). In particular, he recounts Jesus healing the sick and casting out demons one evening, noting that he would not allow the demons to speak οτι ηδεισαν αυτον (1:34). Kannaday observes that this statement might have appeared to portray Jesus as a magician or sorcerer (cf. 3:19–27) since *they* knew him but *he* was able to command them. He also points out that some MSS (ℵ² B C W Θ $f^{1,13}$ 33 vg^{mss} sy^{h**} sa^{ms} bo etc.) have various readings that add some form of (τον) αυτον χριστον ειναι. These variants now state that the object of their knowledge is that "they knew him to be the Christ," although this could simply be

---

52. Kannaday, *Apologetic Discourse*, 124.
53. France, *Mark*, 241.

harmonizing to Luke 4:41.[54] Kannaday asks why someone might have inserted these words here, and on the basis of the commonly accepted theory of Synoptic relationships, he argues that Matthew's reference to Jesus' healings fulfilling Isa 53:4 (Matt 8:16–17) served the interests of apologists in the second century by finding authenticity in fulfilling an ancient prophecy.[55] He also proposes that Luke modified his Markan source by adding οτι ηδεισαν τον χριστον αυτον ειναι (Luke 4:41) so that "Luke defended his work on the basis of Messianic identity."[56] Yet, there is no sign of Luke *defending* Jesus' work, nor is it certain that he used Mark as one of his sources. He simply asserted what the demons knew. Hence, we do not know if Luke had any special motive in writing a longer text. Nor is it clear why copyists inserted the phrase into MSS of Mark's Gospel, other than perhaps harmonizing to Luke's account. There is, then, no evidence that the addition of (τον) αυτον χριστον ειναι ever did function apologetically or that it was designed to do so.

Matthew 9:34

Matthew's Gospel records Jesus healing two blind men (9:27–31) who began to spread the news of their recovery, and then healing a demon-possessed man with a speech impediment (9:32–33a). In response to the latter event, Matthew adds that the crowd was amazed (9:33b) and οι δε φαρισαιοι ελεγον εν τω αρχοντι των δαιμονιων εκβαλλει τα δαιμονια (9:34). Kannaday points out that a few MSS (D a k sy^s Hil) omit the whole of 9:34, but the editors of the GNT^5 give it a *B* rating, indicating their view that it is probably original.[57] Further, while some suggest that 9:34 is a harmonization from Matt 12:24 or Luke 11:15, it seems to be needed in Matthew as the basis for Jesus being called Beelzebul in 10:25.[58] So, 9:34 is most likely original, and Kannaday suggests that it was omitted in some MSS because it contained "material that was cited by pagan critics against Christians" that said Jesus was a magician.[59]

---

54. Metzger, *Textual Commentary*, 64; Marcus, *Mark 1–8*, 197; France, *Mark*, 108; Collins, *Mark*, 175na.; Wasserman, "Variants of Evil," 73–74.
55. Kannaday, *Apologetic Discourse*, 124–27.
56. Kannaday, *Apologetic Discourse*, 127.
57. Cf. Metzger, *Textual Commentary*, 20–21.
58. Davies and Allison, *Matthew*, 2:139; Luz, *Matthew 8–20*, 50n2.
59. Kannaday, *Apologetic Discourse*, 128.

APOLOGETIC FOR THE PERSON OF JESUS?

It is difficult to be sure, however, about the motivation of the person responsible for omitting this verse, especially because we have no evidence that it *was* intentionally omitted.[60] It might have been omitted as "anticlimactic,"[61] or perhaps "due to a desire to avoid duplication of the offensive charge which will recur in 12:24."[62] Thus, although it is difficult to account for the omission of 9:34 in a few MSS, it is also uncertain that it was omitted to respond to criticism of Jesus as a magician.

Luke 23:52-53

Luke's Gospel relates how Joseph of Arimathea asked Pilate for Jesus' body, presumably to give it a decent burial (23:50–52), and then how he retrieved the body from the cross and placed it in a tomb as its first occupant (23:53). In this context, Kannaday refers to one OL MS (c, XII/XIII AD) that reports that Pilate ascertained that Jesus had indeed died and even praised God on hearing that. He suggests that the reading might have come from a time much earlier than when the MS was produced.[63] However, it might also have originated in the twelfth century, especially in view of the pious remark attributed to Pilate, or it could be a rough and enhanced harmonization from Mark 15:44–45.

Matthew records that Joseph of Arimathea was responsible for placing a large stone over the entrance to the tomb (27:60), and that the Jewish authorities were concerned that the disciples might come and steal Jesus' body, so Pilate gave them a guard who remained on site and put a seal on the tomb (27:62–66; cf. 28:4, 11–15). Kannaday notes that in Luke 23:53 a small number of MSS (U f^{13} 700 bo) include mention of a large stone being rolled in front of the entrance to the tomb, and a few MSS (D c (sa)) embellish this by adding that twenty men could scarcely move it.[64] He proposes that this was meant to suggest that only supernatural force could have removed the stone, not the disciples, but there is no real evidence for this motivation. Thus, while these variants in Luke 23 *could* have served apologetic interests, showing that Jesus had really died and been buried so that any interference with the body was humanly

---

60. Birdsall remains uncertain as to which reading is original ("Textual Evidence").
61. Nolland, *Matthew*, 402nbb.
62. France, *Matthew*, 359n9.
63. Kannaday, *Apologetic Discourse*, 128–29.
64. Cf. Metzger, *Textual Commentary*, 156.

impossible, and while this *could* have served to refute the kind of charges of deception and fraud made against Jesus and the Christians, there is no evidence that these variant readings *were* used for this purpose. It is just as likely that they were harmonizations from other Gospels, with pious embellishments—corruptions certainly, but not necessarily apologetically motivated.[65]

A Bad-tempered Man?

Kannaday shows that Graeco-Roman society prized "four cardinal virtues," including prudence, temperance, and fortitude, and was opposed to the demonstration of anger, which was not viewed as worthy of a divine personage.[66] Indeed, early Christian apologists like Aristides (*Apol.* 1, 7, 8), Athenagoras (*Leg.* 21.1), Tatian (*Orat.* 10), and Arnobius (*Nat.* 3) emphasized that God was not angry or subject to emotion, and Origen referred to "the so-called wrath of God and what is called his anger" (*Cels.* 4.72). However, critics like Celsus condemned the God of the Scriptures for angry utterances or outbursts (*Cels.* 4.71, 5.14) and derided Jesus for "threats and empty abuse" (*Cels.* 2.76), presumably with passages like Matt 11:22–25 and 23:13–29 in mind.[67] Kannaday then examines a number of variant readings he suggests show a desire on the part of copyists to alter the text of the Gospels to avoid attributing such seemingly unworthy, personal characteristics to Jesus.

Mark 1:41

Mark's Gospel records a leper appealing to Jesus for "cleansing" εαν θελῃc (1:40). Jesus' response to this appeal is traditionally, cπλαγχνιcθειc εκτειναc την χειρα αυτου ηψατο και λεγει αυτω θελω καθαριcθητι (1:41), emphasizing his compassion using cπλαγχνιζομαι. However, some MSS (D a ff² r¹*) read οργιcθειc instead of cπλαγχνιcθειc, and Kannaday suggests that οργιcθειc was original and was replaced by cπλαγχνιcθειc for apologetic reasons—to avoid saying that Jesus was angry.[68] Regarding

---

65. Metzger describes this as a "characteristic interpolation" in D (*Textual Commentary*, 156).

66. Kannaday, *Apologetic Discourse*, 129–30.

67. Chadwick, *Origen*, 123n6.

68. Kannaday, *Apologetic Discourse*, 130–34.

external evidence, οργιcθειc is found in only a small number of Western MSS dating from the fourth to the eighth centuries (D it[a,d,ff2,r1]). But some suggest that it originated in the second century or earlier, especially in view of its presence in Ephrem's commentary on Tatian's Diatessaron.[69] The GNT[5] and NA[28] show the editors' confidence regarding the originality of cπλαγχνιcθειc.[70]

Some authors favour οργιcθειc as the original reading on the basis that it is the harder reading since it portrays Jesus being angry, which they regard as unfavorable.[71] Then, scribes might have changed it to cπλαγχνιcθειc, in order to remove that reference. Yet, the Gospels record Jesus' anger elsewhere, and there is no evidence that copyists were averse to recording it. Mark 3:5 includes it (μετ οργηc) and some MSS include it at Luke 6:10 (εν οργη),[72] so there was apparently no issue with it in MSS of those passages. So, if οργιcθειc were original, there is no reason to think that it was changed because it presented an unfavorable picture of Jesus sometimes being angry. The Gospels record that he was angry at other times.

Others claim, however, that Jesus' anger suited certain occasions because they were healing settings, in contrast to him showing compassion in crowd settings (Mark 6:41, 8:6–7). Jesus' anger (or dismay) is mentioned in Mark 8:11–12 (αναcτεναζω)[73] and his being indignant in 10:14 (αγανακτεω), but some suggest that his emotion at 10:14 can be explained because laying hands on children in 10:13–16 was in a healing setting. However, laying hands on someone was a symbolic action with various possible meanings, and without any healing connotations in 10:16. So, linking this with the exorcism in 9:14–32 (esp. 9:22–24) is unlikely, and the inference that Jesus being indignant in 10:14 had something to do with it being in a "healing setting" is improbable. Hence, a reference to his anger at 1:41, as if that were such a "healing setting," is not necessarily more likely than his compassion.

---

69. Cf. McCarthy, *Ephrem's Commentary*, 201–4.

70. Cf. Metzger, *Textual Commentary*, 65.

71. Haelewyck takes οργιcθειc as original, but he offers no explanation as to why it might have been changed (Haelewyck, "Healing of a Leper").

72. Head, "Christology," 122–23.

73. Muraoka notes that in the LXX αναcτεναζω refers to groaning for various reasons, such as grief (Lam 1:4) or being in dire straits (Sus 22 Th), and cτεναζω also referred to bemoaning or expressing sorrow (*GELS*, 45, 634).

Thus, οργιcθειc does not appear to be the harder reading because it portrayed Jesus' anger, or more appropriate because it occurred in a healing setting, but it certainly seems to be the harder reading in the narrative context.[74] It has also been suggested that the verbs in 1:43 (εμβριμηcαμενοc, εξεβαλεν) would fit more naturally with anger than compassion in 1:41, which would then support the originality of οργιcθειc there.[75] However, although εμβριμαομαι means "rebuke" in 14:5, it need not have that meaning in 1:43. While it could mean "scold, censure,"[76] it could also mean "be deeply moved" (cf. John 11:33, 38). John's usage is evidence for this meaning in the first century, so Mark might also have used it with this meaning. In the LXX εμβριμαομαι refers to a strong feeling or utterance,[77] but context must decide what kind of strong emotion or utterance is intended. In the LXX, the cognate noun εμβριμημα meant an "intense emotional agitation,"[78] and the compound προcεμβριμαομαι meant "*to orally express indignant displeasure besides* causing some other discomfort or injury."[79] Thus, the rather uncommon verb εμβριμαομαι refers to strong emotion, either felt internally or expressed in a strong warning, admonition, or rebuke.[80] In Lam 2:6 LXX the noun οργη accompanies εμβριμαομαι in order to convey a connotation of anger. There is, then, no necessary correlation between the proposed anger of Jesus with the leper in 1:41 and his supposed "rebuke" of him in 1:43.[81] What kind of strong utterance was intended in 1:43? It might have been a rebuke, but there is nothing in the context to indicate that. Instead, when Jesus' words are given in 1:44, they show that his strong language in 1:43 was not a rebuke for a misdemeanor but a firm dismissal, along with an exhortation not to spread the story of his healing and to do whatever the OT law required in terms of sacrifice. Indeed, the sternness of Jesus'

---

74. Metzger, *Textual Commentary*, 65; France, *Mark*, 115; Marcus, *Mark 1-8*, 206; Perrin, "Managing Jesus' Anger." *Pace* Spencer, "Why did the 'leper'?."

75. Ehrman, "Leper in the Hands." Cf. Ehrman, "Text of the Gospels," 94-97; Ehrman, "Text and Interpretation," 310-16; Ehrman, *Misquoting*, 133-39, 200-201.

76. BDAG, 322.

77. Muraoka notes that it means "speak sternly to" in Dan 11:30 LXX (*GELS*, 226). R. Timothy McLay translates this verb here as "rebuke" (Pietersma and Wright, *New English Translation*, 1020).

78. *GELS*, 226.

79. *GELS*, 593 (italics original).

80. Cf. LSJ, 540.

81. *Pace* Metzger, *Textual Commentary*, 65. Cf. Guelich, *Mark 1—8:26*, 72nc; Collins, *Mark*, 177nb; Perrin, "Managing Jesus' Anger."

words to the leper do not relate to the leper himself but to Jesus' desire for privacy or freedom of movement; Mark notes that because the man did not heed the warning, ωϲτε μηκετι αυτον δυναϲθαι φανερωϲ ειϲ πολιν ειϲελθειν (Mark 1:45), implying that Jesus' intentions were thwarted in some way.

The meaning of εκβαλλω in Mark's Gospel requires clarification as well. It can refer to ripping out an eye (9:47), throwing merchants out of the temple (11:15), or throwing someone out of a vineyard (12:8). So, it does not always imply aggression or exorcism,[82] and the suggestion that εκβαλλω meant that Jesus cast the leper out "as if he were a demon" does not take account of its wide semantic range. Where demons are the intended object, the context makes that plain. So, it refers to a "forceful" sending away, which in this context refers to Jesus sending the leper away before strongly urging him not to spread news of his healing. Therefore, the use of εμβριμηϲαμενοϲ and εξεβαλεν in 1:43 offer no support for the view that οργιϲθειϲ was original in 1:41 due to the emotional and theological setting.

Other arguments are based on the commonly accepted "solution" to the Synoptic problem, according to which Matthew and Luke made use of Mark's Gospel when composing theirs.[83] Thus, in the parallel accounts, neither Matthew nor Luke includes either ϲπλαγχνιϲθειϲ or οργιϲθειϲ, and it has been inferred from this that they omitted the original reading οργιϲθειϲ because they found it offensive for, had they found ϲπλαγχνιϲθειϲ in their copies of Mark, there would have been no reason to leave it out.[84] Further, when Mark refers to Jesus being angry (οργη) or indignant (αγανακτεω; Mark 3:5, 10:14), neither Matthew nor Luke does (Matt 12:13, 19:14; Luke 6:10, 18:16), so it seems that Matthew and Luke left out these references to Jesus' "negative" emotions, which would be consistent with Mark 1:41 originally having οργιϲθειϲ here but it being omitted by Matthew and Luke.

There are good reasons, however, to be cautious about drawing this conclusion. First, the commonly accepted "solution" to the Synoptic problem should not be treated as a fact on which to build arguments since it is far from certain that Matthew and Luke derived their material from Mark's Gospel, so we do not know that they consciously omitted references to

---

82. BDAG, 299; *GELS*, 204.

83. Cf. Ehrman, "Text of the Gospels," 94–97; Elliott, "Eclectic Textual Commentary," 52–53.

84. Cf. France *Mark*, 115.

Jesus' so-called "negative" emotions. Second, the data is limited anyway for the few cases where Matthew and Luke include a reference to Jesus' compassion as Mark does, and the two cases where they do not include a reference to Jesus' negative emotions where Mark does are hardly sufficient evidence on which to conclude that they were embarrassed about Jesus showing "negative" emotion. The fact that Matthew and Luke do not include a description of Jesus' emotions in the parallel passages could just be in line with their more restrained style, or it was not in their sources. Since they did not include *any* reference to Jesus' emotions on this occasion, it is likely that recording Jesus' emotions was just not part of their narrative style, at least on this occasion.

Kannaday also examines the use of σπλαγχνιζομαι elsewhere in Mark's Gospel and notes that Matthew and Luke have similar accounts, either (1) the same as Mark 6:34 or similar (Matt 14:14; αποδεξαμενος in Luke 9:11); (2) the same as Mark 8:2 (Matt 15:32, but the whole episode is not in Luke); or (3) somewhat similar to Mark 9:22 but with different wording (omitted in Matt 17:14-20; δεομαι for σπλαγνιζομαι in Luke 9:37-43). In the third reference, a father's appeal to Jesus for help is not expressed with σπλαγνιζομαι ("have mercy," Mark 9:22) but with δεομαι ("ask [for help]," Luke 9:38), so Luke has not omitted the request for help but simply used a different word. On the other hand, σπλαγχνιζομαι is used in a healing context in Matt 20:34 and Luke 7:13. So, while Synoptic comparisons cannot form the basis of an argument, it is notable that Matthew's and Luke's accounts do mention Jesus' compassion at times. But they are generally more restrained in relating his forceful responses. Further, the number of instances is minimal so they cannot be used to show that Matthew and Luke carried over Mark's themes of compassion but rejected any thought of anger, even if we knew that they used Mark. Indeed, God is portrayed as angry in both Matthew and Luke (οργιζομαι, Matt 18:34, 22:7; Luke 14:21), as is Jesus (Luke 19:27), and harsh retribution by God and Jesus is far from being absent either (e.g., Matt 21:41; 25:30, 46; Luke 16:28). Therefore, it is uncertain that Matthew and Luke omitted a reference to Jesus' anger here, as if that were unusual or undesirable, so there is no basis on which to suggest that later copyists did that either.

Thus, there is no reason to ignore the weight of the external evidence for σπλαγχνισθεις being original in Mark 1:41.[85] If we *knew* that

---

85. Johnson, "Anger Issues." Lorenz argues that there are cogent reasons for seeing the Latin *iratus* (for οργισθεις) as the secondary reading, based on a discussion of the

ὀργισθείς was original, the change to σπλαγχνισθείς *might* have been a useful change to make, if we *knew* that the person responsible for changing it had in mind the charges made against Jesus by pagan critics, but neither of these are certain. The balance of the evidence, then, shows that ὀργισθείς is secondary,[86] even if it is unclear how and why it arose, and that there is no clear evidence that σπλαγχνισθείς was substituted for ὀργισθείς out of apologetic interests.[87] Perhaps someone made a mistake early on since both words have three syllables, both end in -ισθείς, and ὀργισθείς may simply be one of those colorful and inexplicable readings, for which Codex Bezae and the Western textual cluster are notable.

In a similar way, some MSS (W b c e) omit 1:42b–43, which Ehrman proposes was done so as to remove Jesus' rebuke of the man and his stern warning and sending him away, presumably to make him appear as a nicer person. Yet it is possible that, after writing λεπρα (1:42a), instead of continuing with και(εκαθαρισθη), a copyist continued with και(λεγει) (1:44a) and omitted all the intervening material (1:42b–43)—a common scribal slip in texts written in *scriptio continua* (και . . . και), especially if the end of a line was involved. The omission of 1:42b–43, then, is probably not pertinent to the present discussion.

Matthew 21:44

After the parable of the talents, Matthew records the punishment that will be meted out to the religious authorities as the faithless "tenants" of Israel (21:33–46). As part of his words of judgment, Jesus said that they would have no part in the kingdom of God but others who produced the "fruit" of obedience would share in its blessings (21:43). Matthew then recounts a pithy concluding saying, και ο πεςων επι τον λιθον τουτον συνθλασθησεται εφ ον δ αν πεςη λιμχηςει αυτον (21:44). Some MSS (D 33 it sy^s) omit this verse entirely, and the GNT[5] gives it a C rating, indicating doubt about its originality. Indeed, Metzger notes that many see it as "an early interpolation" from Luke 20:18, although the wording is slightly

---

interrelationships among the Latin MS tradition ("Counting Witnesses").

86. Cf. Metzger, *Textual Commentary*, 65. Perrin comes to the same conclusion based on the "internal" evidence of the theological context of Mark's Gospel, notably the "redemptive story" behind the narrative ("Managing Jesus' Anger"). *Pace* Piazzetta and Paroschi, "Jesus and the Leper."

87. Cf. Williams, "An Examination." Baarda traces the reading ὀργιθεις in three early works ("Mk 1:41").

different, and it would more naturally follow v. 42 (citing Ps 118:22–23). He also notes that a copyist's eye might have passed from αυτης (end of 21:43) to αυτον (end of 21:44),[88] although it would perhaps be more likely to pass from και (beginning of 21:44) to και (beginning of 21:45).

Only a few MSS omit the verse, along with some church fathers, so Kannaday concludes that the external evidence is divided.[89] This is far from obvious, however, although Origen seems to have had a text without this verse, as does a Syriac translation of Eusebius. However, the quality of the MSS that include the verse far outweighs the quality of those that omit it, and it is unclear that it was deliberately omitted from the MSS in which it does not appear. The external evidence, then, appears to show that 21:44 is original.

Regarding intrinsic probabilities, the strong language of Matt 21, especially in the previous two parables (21:28–32, 21:33–41) and the following one (22:1–14), provide a context for the strong words of 21:44, perhaps with several OT passages in mind (Dan 2:34, 44; Isa 8:14–15, 28:16). Further, harmonizing from Luke 20:18 *at this point* (after 21:43, not 21:42) would appear to be odd. In conclusion, there is no reason to reject Matt 21:44 as the original text where it stands,[90] so it was probably omitted by parablepsis (και . . . και), or perhaps as an awkward and difficult saying,[91] rather than because someone wished to clear Jesus' name of using harsh and violent language.

Matthew 15:26

Matthew's Gospel relates an encounter between Jesus and "a Canaanite woman" who asked him to cast a demon out of her daughter (15:21–28). At first, he met her with silence, and the disciples urged him to send her away because of her annoyance (15:23). He responded to the disciples that his mission was only to Israel, and presumably the woman heard this but continued to ask for help (15:24–25). Jesus' reply is then given, ουκ εστιν καλον λαβειν τον αρτον των τεκνων και βαλειν τοις κυναριοις (15:26). Some MSS, however, have the variant reading εξεστιν instead of καλον (D

---

88. Metzger, *Textual Commentary*, 47.

89. Kannaday, *Apologetic Discourse*, 135.

90. *Pace* Metzger, *Textual Commentary*, 47; Davies and Allison, *Matthew*, 3:186n65; Lanier, "Case for the Assimilation."

91. France, *Matthew*, 807–8n3.

it sy[s,c]), which would refer to what was not "lawful" rather than what was not "good." The MS evidence for εξεστιν is slight, although Origen knew of this reading. While Kannaday notes that GNT³ only gave καλον a C rating,[92] GNT⁵ does not even mention a variant, so the editors seem to have settled on καλον as original. While the few Western MSS supporting εξεστιν are early in the history of transmission, they do not provide much support, and there is no evidence that the similar wording to Mark 7:27 was harmonized to that of Matthew. In fact, since εξεστιν can mean "be authorised for the doing of someth., *it is right, is authorized, is permitted, is proper,*"[93] the difference in meaning might have been minimal, although εξεστιν is probably a little stronger.[94] It follows that the distinction between what is morally fitting (καλον) and what is "lawful or permitted by social constraint" (εξεστιν) is probably too precise, so there is little reason to think that καλον was changed to εξεστιν to make Jesus appear "law abiding." While this might possibly have had an apologetic use, there is no evidence that it ever did, and it is hard to imagine the change being made to achieve that, so the proposal will have to remain in the realm of speculation.[95]

Mark 3:21

The final passage here comes from Mark's account of Jesus' busy schedule (3:20), when οι παρ αυτου (his family/relatives)[96] tried to take charge of him and commented that εξεστη ("he is mad," 3:21).[97] Kannaday notes that those who made this comment are described differently in certain MSS (D W it), which read οι γραμματεις και οι λοιποι, instead of οι παρ αυτου. This variant reading now ascribes this comment to "the scribes and the others" who heard "about him" (περι αυτου), rather than his family or friends. This secondary reading could certainly have been inserted by someone wishing to protect Jesus from the accusation that those who knew him best thought he was mad,[98] but it is uncertain that the person

---

92. Kannaday, *Apologetic Discourse*, 137–38.
93. BDAG, 348–49 (italics original). Cf. *GELS*, 249.
94. Hagner, *Matthew 14–28*, 438ng.
95. Cf. Kannaday, *Apologetic Discourse*, 138.
96. BDAG, 756, παρά A3βב.
97. BDAG, 350, ἐξίστημι 2a. Holland takes εξεστη to mean "he was amazed" (Holland, "Meaning"), but this is hardly viable here.
98. Kannaday, *Apologetic Discourse*, 138–39; Metzger, *Textual Commentary*, 70;

responsible had in mind such charges made by critics and hence that it was an apologetically motivated change.[99] Thus, this variant does not seem to have been the result of "scribal apologetics" either.

CONCLUSION

In this chapter I have surveyed the readings to which Kannaday has alluded and have found a number of reasons to doubt the majority of his conclusions with regard to variants touching on the person of Jesus. There are good reasons to doubt that some of the readings alleged to be original are in fact original, so the basis for the conclusions drawn is removed at the start. Other variant readings have been found to be more easily explained as accidental scribal changes, or at most harmonizations to parallel or similar passages, rather than readings intentionally created for some purpose—thus, accidental, not deliberate. Even if a reading is clearly motivated for some reason, it is only rarely that it can be shown to have been created with an apologetic purpose, in order to combat certain criticisms of critics of Jesus. Further, even when we know that critics were making certain charges against Jesus so a reading might aid an apologetic purpose, we cannot confirm that this was what the person responsible had in mind, unless we know that a precise text was cited by critics, and even then we cannot be certain that a variant reading was inserted to respond to that; they may have been deliberate, but were not necessarily apologetic, and perhaps motivated by piety or a desire to embellish the Gospel account. In a number of cases, it has been quite uncertain that a copyist would have thought that a reader would even notice the change, let alone take it as supporting an apologetic purpose, so it is unlikely that he would have made the change to achieve that end. For all these reasons relating to lack of evidence and the interpretation of the evidence available, Kannaday's general conclusions cannot be endorsed, except in a few possible cases. Hence, the argument for "scribal apologetics" in these readings concerning Jesus is generally unconvincing, as is the portrayal of scribes, especially early scribes, as "themselves apologists and even evangelists."[100]

Marcus, *Mark 1–8*, 270; Collins, *Mark*, 225nc; France, *Mark*, 164; Head, "Christology," 119.

99. Guelich suggests that the change was meant to set the stage for the reference in 3:22 to the scribes from Jerusalem arriving and charging Jesus with being demon-possessed (*Mark 1—8:26*, 267ne).

100. Kannaday, *Apologetic Discourse*, 139.

7

Apologetic for the Followers of Jesus?

IN CHAPTER 4 OF his book, Kannaday examines variants bearing on how Christians were denigrated by pagan authors in the first three centuries, whether with regard to their loyalty to the empire, their moral character, or their intellectual ability. He begins with a review of pagan assessments of Christians, starting with Pliny's letter to Trajan (*Ep.* 10.96) and Trajan's reply (Pliny, *Ep.* 10.97). The letters refer to rumors about Christians, but they are restrained in their criticism, although they still indicate that harsh treatment should be meted out to them.[1] The issue seems to have been that Christians were viewed with suspicion because little was known about them, and they seemed to be obstinate in their beliefs and practices. Marcus Aurelius referred to their apparent enthusiasm for martyrdom (*Med.* 11.3), and both Tacitus (*Ann.* 15.44) and Suetonius (*Nero* 16.2) called Christianity a *superstitio* since Christians rejected the traditional religious beliefs and practices that stood at the heart of Roman Imperial society. In those early days of the church, most pagans also saw little difference between Jews and Christians, except that at least Jews had a religion that stretched back to antiquity,[2] while Christians were seen as Jewish renegades whose sect had only begun in recent times.

Lucian's satire, *Death of Peregrinus*, relates how Peregrinus identified with the Christians for a time and fooled them into supplying his needs. He describes them as foolish and easily duped "simpletons" who

---

1. Kannaday, *Apologetic Discourse*, 141–48. Cf. Benko, "Pagan Criticism," 1056–68; Wilken, *Christians*.

2. Kannaday, *Apologetic Discourse*, 143n8.

worshipped "a crucified sophist" (*Peregr.* 11–13), noting that they were mostly "grey haired widows and orphan children." Minucius Felix is probably referring to Fronto when he describes Caecilius reporting all kinds of slanders about the Christians' folly, cannibalism, sexual deviance, seditious alliances, religious novelty, fostering of family breakup, and other abhorrent behavior (*Oct.* 9.1–7). Celsus derided Christians as lacking intellect, courage, and moral values, and Porphyry suggested that, not only were the Christian Scriptures misleading, but Christians themselves were foolish. Aelius Aristides probably also had Christians in mind when he describes the "impious ones from Palestine" (*Plato* 671–73). I note such accusations in more detail below but suffice it to say here that apologists like Athenagoras and Minucius Felix explicitly rejected these charges. I now turn to examine readings in NT MSS that are said to be apologetic responses by scribes to these kinds of charges.

Fanatics?

Christians were charged with being anti-social because they did not attend public festivals, and they were also criticized for excessive behavior at their own gatherings (e.g., Athenagoras, *Leg.* 3.1; Theophilus, *Autol.* 3.4). Apologists such as Aristides (*Apol.* 15–16), Athenagoras of Athens (*Apol.* 33), Minucius Felix (*Oct.* 31.5), Clement of Alexandria (*Paed.* 2.2), Tatian (*Orat.* 22.1), and Justin (1 *Apol.* 65–66) responded to such charges, claiming that Christians were pious and sober, and lived a pure life. Some variant readings in NT MSS are said to have been designed to serve this kind of apology.

Luke 5:33

In Luke 5:33–39 there is an account of certain people addressing Jesus and referring to the disciples of John the Baptist and those of the Pharisees fasting and praying frequently, saying, οι δε cοι εcθιουcιν και πινουcιν. Kannaday suggests that this might well have recalled for later believers the kinds of slurs aimed at them when people accused them of being gluttons and drunkards, and he points to MSS (D e) that have the secondary more general reading οι δε μαθηται cου ουδεν τουτων ποιουcιν. Kannaday then proposes that this reflects an apologetic interest aimed at creating the lesser accusation against Jesus' followers that they did not fast and pray, rather than that they engaged in "excess and gluttony."[3] However, on the basis of Jesus' own practice of not fasting like John but "eating and drinking," he himself was charged with being a glutton and a drunkard (φαγος και οινοποτης, Matt 11:18–19; Luke 7:33–34), even in D. So, it would seem unlikely that εσθιουσιν και πινουσιν was dropped here in favor of a less specific phrase in order to remove such a charge against Jesus' disciples, when there was easy support for that charge elsewhere.

Further, the result of the secondary reading is that the disciples were now being charged with *not* frequently fasting and praying. Would someone remove a reading that might have implied the disciples' gluttony and drunkenness and replace it with one that referred to not fasting and praying? Certainly, Celsus mentioned Christians debasing "their religious piety" and not praying to the gods, and Origen responded to this (e.g., *Cels.* 5.52, 7:44, 8.26), but fasting was quite uncommon in Roman society,[4] so *not* fasting might have been viewed favorably. Thus, not praying might have been perceived negatively, but not fasting would not have been unusual. On the other hand, Tertullian refers in his *Apology* to Christians fasting as something commendable (*Apol.* 40.14–15), so the evidence of pagan perceptions about such matters is mixed. So, one cause of accusation has been replaced with at least one other, and another that might or might not have been viewed more favorably. The argument, then, that the phrase was changed to respond to criticism of the Christians gains strength by the implication that the disciples did *not* fast, but that is there in either reading, so the suggestion seems to be an oversubtle reading of this variant's significance.

Mark 9:29

Mark's Gospel includes an account of Jesus casting a demon out of a boy after his disciples had not been able to do so (9:14–28) and then the disciples wanting to know why they had been unsuccessful. The assumption is that they were wondering what the problem was, since Jesus had given them authority to cast out demons when he sent them out (3:14–15, 6:7). Indeed, Mark reports that they did have some success (6:13), but on this occasion they were thwarted (9:18). Jesus' response to their question was that τουτο το γενος εν ουδενι δυναται εξελθειν ει μη εν προσευχη (9:29), and

---

3. Kannaday, *Apologetic Discourse*, 150–51.
4. Henrichs, "Fasting," 569.

Scribes, Theology, and Apologetics

at the end of the verse numerous significant MSS (P⁴⁵ᵛⁱᵈ ℵ² A C D W Θ $f^{1,13}$ 33 *Byz* lat syʰ co) add και νηςτεια, thus adding the requirement of fasting to what would be needed to cast out "this kind" of demon. This variant reading is probably secondary, since it is not supported by ℵ* B and other weighty MSS, although it is apparently quite early.[5] So, it might have been inserted by someone who valued fasting and perhaps asceticism in general as that became more popular in the early church.[6] Tertullian (*Apol.* 40.14–15) and Clement of Alexandria (*Strom.* 3.9.3) referred with approval to Christians fasting, so adding και νηςτεια might have had an apologetic motive, showing restraint rather than excess.[7] However, as noted above, fasting was not a common Roman practice or virtue, so it would have had little apologetic appeal. Kannaday concludes that it is difficult to know if the person responsible for this reading acted out of a desire to promote pious asceticism or a desire to defend Christians against pagan critics, but he observes that whatever their motive, they were willing to add their own interpretation to the NT text. This appears to be correct, although it is also possible that the phrase was original (cf. Luke 5:33) and was omitted to discourage an overemphasis on fasting.[8] It is unclear, however, that it was an apologetic variant introduced to respond to criticism.

John 6:55–56

After an account of Jesus feeding five thousand people (6:1–15) and walking on the lake (6:16–24), there is an extended record of his discussion with the crowd using imagery drawn from them being fed earlier (6:25–59). During this discussion, Jesus is said to have made statements about eating his flesh and drinking his blood in more explicit and provocative ways, especially in 6:55–56. The text of those verses appears to be clear, but D and two OL MSS (a ff²) include a long addition at the end of 6:56—καθως εν εμοι ο πατηρ καγω εν τω πατρι αμην αμην λεγω υμιν εαν μη λαβητε το σωμα του υιου του ανθρωπου ως τον αρτον της ζωης ουκ εχετε ζωην εν αυτω. This might be "a homiletic expansion" based on

---

5. France refers to 1 Cor 7:5 and Acts 10:30 for similar variants (*Mark*, 361).

6. Metzger, *Textual Commentary*, 85; Ehrman, "Text of the Gospels," 98; Evans, *Mark 8:27—16:20*, 47ns; Ehrman, *Misquoting*, 97; Collins, *Mark*, 434nj; Marcus, *Mark 8–16*, 655–56.

7. Kannaday, *Apologetic Discourse*, 151–52.

8. France, *Mark*, 361.

6:53 and 10:38,[9] or a "typical Western expansion,"[10] perhaps originating as a marginal gloss, and it appears to make an explicit link to the Eucharist.[11] Kannaday points out that D omits και το αιμα μου αληθης εστιν ποcιc in 6:55, noting that it could have been omitted by homoioteleuton (βρωcιc . . . ποcιc),[12] but he suggests that someone might have omitted the reference to Jesus' blood in order to counter the frequent criticisms of Christians participating in cannibalism.[13] He concedes that references to blood remain in D (6:53, 56)—and we might add "receive the body" of the Son of Man (in the added variant)—but he notes that 6:53 D (and MS a) has λαβητε instead of φαγητε, which could have been an attempt to move the imagery away from cannibalism with the apologetic purpose of avoiding such criticism.[14]

A pagan critic, perhaps Porphyry, cited by Macarius (frag. 69; *Apocrit.* 3.18) refers to Jesus' words in 6:53 as "beastly and absurd," making a link between that verse and the accusation of cannibalism against the Christians, and this kind of criticism became quite common in the second century (e.g., Minucius Felix, *Oct.* 9.5–6). Since this was such a strong criticism and Christian apologists made a point of refuting it, it would not be surprising if someone wished to counter it by removing some of its sting in the NT documents and adding a clarification of the symbolism involved in 6:56.[15] Despite the possibility, or even probability, of this proposal as an explanation for the long secondary addition, the object of λαβητε is still την cαρκα του υιου του ανθρωπου, still with possible "cannibalistic" overtones. Further, that verse still preserves και πιητε αυτου το αιμα. And however much the addition *might* serve to soften the impact with a kind of analogy in 6:56, there is still a reference to things easily interpreted as cannibalism—ο τρωγων μου την cαρκα και πινων μου

---

9. Metzger, *Textual Commentary*, 183.

10. Beasley-Murray, *John*, 85nr; Brown, *John I-XII*, 283.

11. Barrett, *John*, 300.

12. Cf. Haenchen, *John 1*, 295; Barrett, *John*, 299.

13. Kannaday, *Apologetic Discourse*, 152–53. Cf. Benko, *Pagan Rome*, 56, 60, 70–71; McGowan, "Eating People." Grant refers to the charge by Apion, the anti-Jewish writer, that Jews occasionally kidnapped a Greek and fattened him for sacrifice (Josephus, *Ag. Ap.*, 2.95), which was apparently a common charge made by Roman writers against foreign cults. The words of the Lord's Supper lent themselves to this kind of accusation, so it is no wonder the charge was leveled against Christians in a similar way (*Greek Apologists*, 16).

14. Cf. Haenchen, *John 1*, 296.

15. Kannaday, *Apologetic Discourse*, 153–55.

το αιμα . . . λαβητε το cωμα του υιου του ανθρωπου. This is certainly a case where pagan criticism was violent and the response of the Christian apologists was vehement denial, so it is one of the strongest possibilities that a variant reading was apologetically motivated. However, it is hard to imagine that anyone could have thought that the change in 6:53 and the addition in 6:56 would have achieved the proposed softening. There is too much other material remaining in the context that could be interpreted as cannibalistic for anyone to think that these minor changes could make any difference to how a pagan critic would read this section of John's Gospel. There is little reason, then, to think that a copyist would have made these changes to circumvent that criticism.

Luke 22:19b–20

The next variant has been widely discussed in some detail, including in chapter 3 above, but the focus here is whether a variant reading shows an apologetic motive on someone's part.[16] Although there are a number of variant readings in Luke's account of the Last Supper (22:7–38), there are two major alternatives here. The "longer reading" includes 22:19b–20 and has very strong MS support (P^{75} ℵ B C W Θ $f^{1,13}$ etc.), as well as being the "difficult reading" since it seems to include mention of a second cup. The "shorter reading" omits 22:19b–20, with support from Western MSS (D a d ff i l), and results in the sequence cup-then-bread, although this is an odd sequence since both Matthew and Mark have bread-then-cup (Matt 26:26–29, Mark 14:22–25). The former order might receive support from the order cup-then-bread in 1 Cor 10:16 (cf. Did 9.2–3), but even there Paul's usage might have been rhetorical since 1 Cor 11:22–26 has the order bread-then-cup. Agreement on which reading is original has been difficult to achieve, with some accepting the longer reading, perhaps with hesitation,[17] and others taking the shorter one as original.

Kannaday refers to arguments based on the shorter reading being one of Westcott and Hort's "Western non-interpolations"—uncharacteristically short and hence likely to be original. I reviewed these arguments in chapter 3, specifically those based on the supposed absence of atonement theology in Luke-Acts, and I showed reason to reject that line of argument. There is too much speculation as to the significance of the

---

16. Kannaday, *Apologetic Discourse*, 155–62. Cf. Ehrman, "Salvific Effect."
17. GNT^5 gives it a *B* rating. Cf. Metzger, *Textual Commentary*, 148–50.

temple curtain being torn and too much built on arguments from silence to support those conclusions, so the inference that Luke cannot have included words supporting a theology of atonement in Luke 22:19b–20 does not follow. The statistical note that there is no Lukan parallel to Mark 10:45 also offers little support for the view that Luke's theology of the meaning of Jesus' death was different from Mark's, since this saying only occurs once in Mark anyway.

If the longer reading was original, it is difficult to account for the shorter one, and the argument that a scribe would surely have omitted the first cup (vv. 17–18), not the second (v. 20), is difficult to sustain because the order was sometimes reversed, as noted above (1 Cor 10:16; cf. Did 9.2–3). Indeed, the Didache text stems from a later time than the NT when the shorter ending might well have originated. Still, it is not easy to explain why 22:19b–20 would have been omitted. Further, if the shorter reading was original, the distribution of the cup is given little explanation (22:17–18), while the bread is given some—τουτο εςτιν το cωμα μου (22:19a). The shorter reading, then, has some meaning attributed to the cup and the bread, but the cup is only said to symbolize wine in the kingdom of God and only the bread is linked with Jesus' "body." This provides some explanation but not much, and not even the minimal explanation in 1 Cor 10:16, let alone 1 Cor 11:23–26. Yet, the shorter variant could reflect the uncertainty of the disciples at that Last Supper, particularly since Matt 26:26–29 and Mark 14:22–25 both include a link between the bread and Jesus' "body," and both make a link between drinking the cup and the kingdom of God. So, the shorter reading would fit with this, although in reverse order, but the longer reading might testify to a longer original event being reported more briefly in Matthew and Mark. The argument that the longer reading is secondary because it embodies the salvific effect of Jesus' death—"my body given *for you*" (22:19b) and "my blood poured out *for you*" (22:20), as in Matt 26:28 and Mark 14:24—as well as a reference to his real physical death ("*blood poured out* for you"), as an anti-docetic ending, is unconvincing, as we have seen, because Luke-Acts as a whole *does* include enough material to support an atonement theology just as strong as Mark's or Matthew's. So, this argument is flawed in several ways and cannot serve as the basis for a decision as to which reading was original.

Kannaday also examines the Syriac versions, which all have the bread before the cup and a rendering of some part of Luke 22:19b–20, as well as only one cup. After noting differences among the Syriac witnesses, he suggests that Justin's apparent use of the bread-then-cup pattern in his apologetic defense of the Christians (1 *Apol.* 62) shows that the changes in the Syriac tradition could "potentially reduce the perception of either drunkenness or blood ingestion," and hence they were apologetically motivated. The argument is not compelling enough, however, to prove that the shorter reading is original and that the changes were designed to rebuff charges of cannibalism made against the Christians in the second century. It is far too subtle. Rather, the longer reading should stand as the original in view of its overwhelming MS support, with only one Greek MS (D) and the OL tradition supporting the shorter reading.[18] So, the assertion that Luke 22:19b–20 was omitted for apologetic reasons remains doubtful.

Mark 5:33

In the middle of an account of Jesus raising a young girl to life (Mark 5:21–24, 35–43), Mark's Gospel recounts a woman with a long-term debilitating hemorrhage also wanting help and finding it (5:25–34). After she had been healed, Jesus is said to have enquired who touched him, and Mark recounts how she came to him, προcεπεcεν αυτω, and told him her story. Kannaday raises the issue that two MSS (C a) support the secondary reading, προcεκυνηcεν αυτω, thus changing the thought from "falling before" Jesus to "worshipping" him.[19] As background to this variant, he refers to Celsus's criticisms of people who prostrated themselves on their knees χαμαιπετηc (on the ground), although Origen defends the practice (*Cels.* 6.15).[20] Tertullian also advocated the wearing of sackcloth and ashes and prostration before the elders of the church as an expression of repentance (*Paen.* 9), even though some Christians apparently found that distasteful.[21] Some pagan writers, such as Plutarch (*Mor.* 166A) and Theophrastus (*Char.* 16), also found kneeling before someone repugnant and saw it as an expression of "barbarian superstition."[22]

Kannaday notes the various words used in the NT and wider Graeco-Roman literature for the action of kneeling in front of someone, and he

18. Fitzmyer, *Luke X–XXIV*, 1387–88; Nolland, *Luke 18:35—24:53*, 1041nc; Bovon, *Luke 3*, 154–56.
19. Kannaday, *Apologetic Discourse*, 163.
20. Kannaday, *Apologetic Discourse*, 162–63.
21. Chadwick makes this observation based on Tertullian, *Paen.* 11 (*Origen*, 328n3).
22. Kannaday, *Apologetic Discourse*, 162.

makes a distinction between the various words and expressions involved that focus on kneeling (γονυπετεω, προςπιπτω, τιθεναι επι τα γονατα, καμπτειν τα γονατα, οκλαζειν επι τα γονατα) and προςκυνεω, which is a compound of κυνεω (kiss; entreat, beseech). So, he portrays προςκυνεω as a term describing "worshipping" rather than "kneeling." However, the usage of προςκυνεω in the LXX shows that it predominantly meant "do obeisance, prostrate oneself (before)," as an expression of respect to someone more important, whether the person before whom one knelt was a human being (e.g., Gen 33:3, 37:9; Exod 11:8; Jdt 14:7), angelic/divine (Gen 18:2, Num 22:31), or purely divine (Gen 24:26, 48), and it is often accompanied by a phrase indicating that the person bowed down "to the ground." Thus, it still retained the idea of bending, sometimes made more specific by the addition of an explicit phrase. So προςκυνεω *can* mean "take part in worship" (Jer 33:2), but it can *also* mean simply "pay respectful regard to," even referring to "paying regard" to advice (4 Macc 5:12).[23] The notion of "worship" is only appropriate when a divine personage is the object, or at least a personage belonging to the heavenly realm.[24] So, Bathsheba and Nathan bowed (προσεκυνηςεν) before David (1 Kgs 1:16, 23), and the magi wished to do homage (προςκυνηςαι) to the King of the Jews (Matt 2:2), and they did so (πεςοντες προςεκυνηςαν αυτω) when they found him (Matt 2:11). Further, in the patristic period, while προςκυνεω often meant "venerate, revere, adore, worship," it could also mean "make obeisance," "make act of reverence, bow," "greet, salute," "entreat, beg," and "hold in honour, respect." And the cognate words can mean "salutation," "obeisance, act of reverence," "salutation, greeting," as well as having connotations more suited to "worshipping" a divine person.[25] So the portrayal of προςκυνεω as necessarily meaning "worship" rather than "bowing down" is untenable and, however much it was true in some contexts, it cannot be used as a rule to show that by substituting προσεκυνηςεν for προςεπεςεν someone has changed the meaning of a text from "bowing to the ground" to "worshipping," whatever that would mean.

Thus, in Mark 5:33, where two MSS have προσεκυνηςεν instead of προςεπεςεν, it is not clear that by inserting this reading someone wished to remove the taint of people "bowing down" to Jesus and replace it with "worshipping" him out of an apologetic desire to respond to pagan

---

23. *GELS*, 596; Lust et al., *Greek-English Lexicon*, 526.
24. Cf. BDAG, 882–83; LSJ, προςκυνέω I.
25. *PGL*, 1174–78 προσκυνέω etc.

criticisms of servile behavior. In this context they would mean virtually the same thing, both including the notion of "bowing down."

Mark 15:19, 1:40

In a similar way, some MSS (D k vg^ms*) omit Mark 15:19b with its account of the soldiers mocking Jesus after his arrest (και τιθεντες τα γονατα προσεκυνουν αυτω), which could have been omitted by homoioteleuton (αυτω και . . . αυτω και). Further, Mark's Gospel recounts a leper coming to Jesus and asking for healing (1:40), and he is described as begging Jesus for help και γονυπετων (1:40), with some MSS omitting that phrase (B D W et al.).[26] It is unclear whether the phrase in 1:40 is original, but the argument for its originality on the basis of the commonly accepted "solution" to the Synoptic problem is unconvincing because that "solution" is not a fact. If it were original, it could have been omitted by homoioteleuton (αυτον και . . . γονυπεων και), but the MS evidence is quite divided.[27] Hence, speculation as to why it was omitted must remain just that—speculation.[28] So, in 15:19 accidental omission probably caused the omission of the phrase, but in 1:40 it is unclear whether the phrase was original (and then omitted) or was added at a later time.[29]

Kannaday notes that elsewhere in the Gospels, where people are recorded as kneeling before Jesus (e.g., Matt 17:14, Mark 10:17), there are no variants, but in all three cases reviewed above he suggests that a word referring to kneeling has been removed and replaced with another word that does not bear that connotation. This was not proven for Mark 5:33, and a scribal slip would explain the variants in Mark 15:19 and Mark 1:40, so these are not a uniform group showing a reticence to portray people bowing down to Jesus. Even if we admit all the changes outlined,

---

26. Kannaday, *Apologetic Discourse*, 163–64.

27. Metzger, *Textual Commentary*, 65. Cf. Collins, *Mark*, 177na.

28. France notes homoioteleuton as a possible factor in omitting the phrase if it were original, or it was "felt to be redundant" after παρακαλων αυτον, or because the parallel in Matt 8:2 does not use the rare verb γονυπετεω but προσκυνεω (*Mark*, 115). Haelewyck argues that και γονυπετων is original, as he finds no reason for its removal ("Healing of a Leper," 16–19). Kannaday's argument would provide such a reason, if it held.

29. Marcus proposes that the phrase might have been added to assimilate it to 10:17 and highlight Jesus' divinity (*Mark 1–8*, 205–6), but γονυπετων did not necessarily convey homage to a divinity.

the evidence that the changes were intentional is lacking,[30] so the argument is unproven and, due to its subtlety, unlikely.

Matthew 25:40, 28:10; Acts 1:15

Jesus' parable of the sheep and the goats (Matt 25:31–46) includes the King's commendation of those on his right for acting with kindness ενι τουτων των αδελφων μου των ελαχιστων (25:40), but some MSS (B* ff¹ ff²) omit των αδελφων μου. In Matt 28:10, where the risen Jesus told the women to go and απαγγειλατε τοις αδελφοις μου to go to Galilee, a few MSS (157, l 2211 pc) read μαθηταις instead of αδελφοις. In Acts 1 there is an account of a meeting of the disciples in Jerusalem to choose a replacement for Judas (1:15–26), and in the introduction to that account Luke refers to Peter standing up εν μεσω των αδελφων, while some MSS read μαθητων (C³ D 81 1739ˢ Byz it sy mae) or αποστολων (P⁷⁴ᵛⁱᵈ) instead of αδελφων.

Some pagan critics accused Christians of engaging in incest, citing as evidence the fact that they called one another "brothers" and "sisters" (Minucius Felix, *Oct.* 8), so Kannaday suggests that the reference to "brothers" in the MSS cited above might have been replaced by "disciples" (or "apostles") in response to such criticisms.[31] However, some apologists made much of the commendable behavior of masters treating slaves as brothers when they became Christians, which clearly weakens this suggestion.[32] None of the MSS supporting these variants come from the second or third centuries, and the vast majority are much later, so there is little evidence that they arose in a time when it would have been relevant for the changes to be made. Further, the omission of των αδελφων μου in Matt 25:40 can be accounted for by homoioteleuton (των . . . των), or by assimilation to 25:45, where των αδελφων does not occur.[33] Similarly, the reading μαθηταις instead of αδελφοις in Matt 28:10 would be a natural mistake, and the same variant in Acts 1:15 might

---

30. Kannaday, *Apologetic Discourse*, 165.

31. Hagner proposes "christological commitments" as the cause of the variant here, presumably meaning that there might have been a hesitation to call people Jesus' "brothers" (*Matthew 14–28*, 872ne).

32. Kannaday, *Apologetic Discourse*, 165–66.

33. Hagner, *Matthew 14–28*, 739ne; Nolland, *Matthew*, 1022ne-e; Luz, *Matthew 21–28*, 264n2; Pardee, *Scribal Harmonization*, 245. Davies and Allison wonder if των αδελφων μου was added "to make the Christian application clear" (*Matthew*, 3:428n53).

have been due to a desire to avoid confusion with the αδελφοι in 1:14.³⁴ Indeed, Peter's words of address are still to the ανδρες αδελφοι in 1:16. Finally, would these changes have even been noticed? Would anyone have thought that, in the context of the Gospels as a whole where disciples are often called "brothers," "sisters," or even "mother" (e.g., Matt 12:50, Mark 3:35, Luke 8:21, and commonly in Acts), such minor changes would even be noticed? It is highly unlikely, then, that copyists might have intended to make the changes to avoid this kind of language.

Fools?

The next section of Kannaday's book deals with pagan portrayals of Christians as foolish, especially exhibited in "insecure bashfulness around adults, or being afraid or intellectually bewildered," and he examines a number of variants that could have been intended to respond to such accusations.³⁵ First he outlines criticisms that portrayed Christians as being mostly "women, children and gullible males," evident in pagan writers like Lucian (*Peregr.* 13) and Celsus (*Cels.* 3.44, 50, 55), noting that Origen offered an extended response to this charge (*Cels.* 3.44–58), presumably because he took it so seriously.³⁶ I now examine variant readings said to be responses to those criticisms.

Mark 10:13

Mark's account of Jesus blessing children (10:13–16) begins with the mention of people bringing little children for him to "touch" (αψηται), presumably implying that this would be accompanied by prayer for divine blessing (cf. Mark 8:22), but it is also recorded that the disciples responded by rebuking "them" (επιτιμησαν αυτοις). This strong reaction on the part of the disciples was doubtless due to their view that children were unimportant, a common enough view at the time, although there might also have been a desire to protect Jesus from being unduly bothered. Kannaday points out that some MSS (A D *f*¹,¹³ *Byz* lat sy) read τοις (προς)φερουσιν instead of αυτοις, thus making it clear that the disciples

---

34. Bruce, *Acts*, 108; Pervo, *Acts*, 48na.
35. Kannaday, *Apologetic Discourse*, 167–76.
36. Kannaday, *Apologetic Discourse*, 167–68.

were speaking to the adults ("those who brought them").³⁷ He notes that the original text of Mark (επιτιμησαν αυτοιc) was probably portraying the disciples rebuking the adults anyway, but he argues that this variant was meant to show Christians standing up to a mixed crowd of adults, including men, not hiding from them or acting obsequiously, as they were often charged with doing.³⁸

Yet, if the natural meaning of the original αυτοιc referred to adults, why would someone change it to τοιc (προc)φερουcιν? Admittedly, the variant could have been an attempt to make it quite clear that the children were not in view, but if the original text (αυτοιc) did refer to adults and the secondary variant was simply there to make this clear,³⁹ it is a subtle change indeed. In the social context of the time the original reading would have already implied that adults were in view, so the case for the variant being created by "sensitive" scribes to stave off this charge made by pagan critics against Christians is almost certainly oversubtle.

Mark 14:4

In the final days before Jesus' arrest, Mark records that he was in the house of Simon the leper in Bethany when a woman came and poured a jar of expensive ointment on his head (14:3). "Some people" (τινεc) there were indignant (αγανακτουντεc), however, and referred to her action as a waste of perfume (14:4). There are several secondary readings at this point, including MSS that identify the critics of the woman's behavior as οι μαθηται (D Θ 565 (it); cf. W). Kannaday rightly defends τινεc as original, but he asks why someone would have changed that to a specific reference to "the disciples."⁴⁰ He notes that the verb αγανακτεω conveys a strong oppositional reaction,⁴¹ and suggests that the disciples are assumed as its subject, as in the parallel in Matt 26:8. Further, the MSS with οι μαθηται also use the verb διαπονουμαι ("be annoyed"; cf. Acts 4:2, 16:18) rather than αγανακτεω, while the cognate words διαπονηcιc and διαπονητεον were used by Clement of Alexandria to describe the effort

37. Cf. Metzger, *Textual Commentary*, 89; Marcus, *Mark 8–16*, 714; Evans, *Mark 8:27—16:20*, 90na; Collins, *Mark*, 471na; Pardee, *Scribal Harmonization*, 261.

38. Kannaday, *Apologetic Discourse*, 168–69.

39. Cf. France, *Mark*, 395. He asks why, if this suggestion were valid, there is no similar "correction" in the parallels in Matthew and Luke.

40. Kannaday, *Apologetic Discourse*, 169–71.

41. Cf. BDAG, 5; GELS, 3.

associated with a godly life, without any apparent implication of annoyance (*Paed.* 3.10). On the basis that διαπονουμαι had lost its emotional force by Clement's time, Kannaday suggests that copyists used it here in place of αγανακτεω to tone down the portrayal of hostility on the part of onlookers of the woman's actions, especially since the disciples were assumed or explicitly mentioned as its subject. Thus, they were not angry with her but merely discussed what was going on.[42]

This reading of the evidence, however, is unlikely for several reasons. First, that two cognate words are used without emotional force by Clement does not show that the verb διαπονουμαι itself had lost its force for everyone after the first century. It is not even mentioned in *PGL*, so it was presumably rare or unused by speakers or writers in the patristic period, despite appearing in D (V AD). Further, while διαπονεω meant "work out with labor, elaborate, cultivate, practice" in the active voice, when used in the passive it meant "be worn out, troubled," as in Acts 4:2 and 16:18.[43] And the cognate words, διαπονηcιc and διαπονητεον, always meant "working at, preparing" and "one must work hard at,"[44] so citing their usage in Clement is not evidence of a shift in meaning. So, there is no reason to think that someone changed αγανακουντεc to διεπονουντο to remove an emotional response on the part of the disciples. Even διεπονουντο describes the disciples as being "worked up."[45] Indeed, the original reading (αγανακτουντεc προc εαυτοιc)—"became angry (and said) to one another"—is elliptical since it only implies, without stating, that they spoke "to one another." So, it was probably the unusual nature of this expression, which would normally have meant "they became angry with one another,"[46] that gave rise to the use of διεπονουντο as an attempt to clarify the narrative by removing an awkward expression.[47] This latter proposal is certainly a more cogent explanation of the variants than suggesting that the reading was changed to portray the disciples calmly discussing the issue rather than being annoyed. Indeed, the original did not specifically mention the disciples at all, so there was no reason to make them appear less emotional.

42. Kannaday, *Apologetic Discourse*, 171.
43. LSJ, 408.
44. LSJ, 408. Cf. *PGL* 358.
45. Evans, *Mark 8:27—16:20*, 358nc. Collins translates διεπονουντο as "they became annoyed" (*Mark*, 620nb).
46. BDAG, 5.
47. Collins, *Mark*, 620nb.

APOLOGETIC FOR THE FOLLOWERS OF JESUS?

Matthew 17:23

In response to Jesus' announcement that he would be killed (17:22–23a), Matthew reports that the disciples ελυπηθησαν cφοδρα (17:23b), but one MS (K, IX AD) omits this. It may seem that Matthew has already "mollified" Mark's rather strong account (οι δε ηγνοουν το ρημα και εφοβουντο αυτον επερωτηcαι, Mark 9:32), but since it is not certain that Matthew was using Mark, all that can be said is that Matthew's account may not be as strong. Even so, mentioning that the disciples did not understand Jesus' words and were hesitant to ask him about their meaning (Mark 9:32) is not "mollified" by reporting that the disciples were "very upset."[48] Rather, it is simply a different slant on the event, perhaps sparing them from shame.[49] Hence, this variant in a late MS has not been shown to arise from copyists wishing to lessen the disciples' emotional reactions in order to counter criticism of Christians as emotional and foolish.

Mark 9:10

In Mark's account of Jesus' transfiguration (9:2–13), he reports that as the group went back down the mountain the disciples were discussing what Jesus meant by το εκ νεκρων αναcτηναι (9:10). Some MSS, however, replace this with οταν εκ νεκρων αναcτη ("when he would rise from the dead," D W $f^{1,13}$ lat). The original reading, however, need not mean that the disciples were astonished and confused by the phrase "rising from the dead," but merely that they could not see what Jesus meant by that phrase in relation to himself (9:9). So, the variant reading is probably only saying this in a more specific way—*when* he would rise, not *what* "rising from the dead" meant (in Jesus' case). Kannaday suggests that copyists "sensed a need to transpose this dialogue" for apologetic reasons, so that, instead of being dumbfounded by Jesus' words, they are merely curious about when it will happen.[50] However, there is little doubt that like most Jews of the first century they believed in a doctrine of the resurrection.[51] They

---

48. Davies and Allison make no mention of Matthew's narrative being less forceful (*Matthew*, 2:734).

49. Nolland, *Matthew*, 718ne-e. Hagner suggests that the words were omitted "for theological reasons," without indicating what these might have been (*Matthew 14–28*, 506ne).

50. Kannaday, *Apologetic Discourse*, 171–72.

51. This obviously excludes the Sadducees (cf. Matt 22:23, Acts 23:8).

just could not see how Jesus' talk of him rising from the dead fitted into the timetable.⁵² Thus, they were discussing *Jesus'* resurrection. As far as Mark's narrative is concerned, the original reading refers to their silence due to what "rising from the dead" could have had to do with his immediate plans. The secondary reading also refers to them discussing when his resurrection would take place so they could then tell other people about his glorious appearance (9:9).⁵³ Both readings refer to their uncertainty about what Jesus meant in his case, but the secondary reading is a clumsy adjustment, since it records that the disciples were cuζητουντες τι εcτιν οταν εκ νεκρων αναcτη, which is quite awkward syntactically. The variant does not, then, show signs of being motivated by an apologetic design to avoid portraying the disciples as confused; it suggests that they were simply curious about when Jesus would rise. Both readings have basically the same meaning, although the secondary one is quite clumsy and unlikely to have arisen for apologetic reasons.

Mark 9:15

Following on from Mark's account of Jesus' transfiguration, the narrative relates the healing of a demon-possessed boy (9:14–32). The introduction to this sequence of events recounts how there was a large crowd around the other disciples, with scribes arguing "with them" (9:14). When the people saw Jesus, they were "overcome with wonder" (εξεθαμβηθηcαν) and προcτρεχοντες ηcπαζοντο αυτον (9:15), although we are not told why they were overcome with wonder. Some MSS (D it) have the reading προcχαιροντες instead of προcτρεχοντες, which now describes the crowd as "rejoicing" (cf. Prov 8:30 LXX) as they greeted Jesus, not "running to" him and greeting him. Kannaday proposes that this variant was designed to serve an apologetic interest, portraying Christians, not as gullible masses easily amazed and swayed, but as people who just rejoiced in Jesus' presence.⁵⁴ However, προcχαιροντες could just as easily have originated as a mistaken transcription of one word for a similar sounding one with an identical number of syllables, the same four first letters and

---

52. Marcus, *Mark 8–16*, 643.

53. Evans points out that this variant rephrases and repeats the wording in 9:9 (*Mark 8:27—16:20*, 40nc).

54. Kannaday, *Apologetic Discourse*, 172.

five last letters (προc . . . οντεc), so it is "probably an early corruption."⁵⁵ Further, the portrayal of a crowd who saw Jesus and were "immediately" (ευθυc) overcome with wonder (εξεθαμβηθηcαν) and "rejoiced greatly" (προcχαιροντεc) when they saw him, as in the variant reading, does not fit the suggested portrayal of people just understanding Jesus and calmly rejoicing in his company.⁵⁶ Instead, it has all the associations of masses being amazed and swayed, so the secondary reading would not have had the proposed apologetic connotation.

Luke 15:1

Luke 15:3–32 is given over to three parables told in response to an adverse reaction by Pharisees and scribes to Jesus welcoming "sinners" and eating with them (15:1–2). The opening sentence describes how tax collectors and "sinners" εγγιζοντες παντες . . . ακουειν αυτου (15:1), but some MSS (W lat sy^{s,c,p}sa^{ms}) do not include παντες. Kannaday acknowledges that παντες might have been omitted accidentally but suggests that its omission could have been meant to show that those listening to Jesus were not "all" "sinners, tax collectors, and members of the lowest classes."⁵⁷ It is clear that Luke's use of παc is a favorite and often hyperbolic (e.g., 6:17, 30; 9:1, 43; 11:4), and it would be here too, if it were original. In view of the external evidence, it appears that it was original but was subsequently omitted in some MSS, most likely by homoioteleuton due to a sequence of four identical letters at the end of two adjacent words (εγγιζ<u>οντες</u> π<u>αντες</u>). Even if παντες was omitted intentionally by someone who was "unhappy with the hyperbole,"⁵⁸ the hyperbole was not a heightened statement that Jesus' audience consisted only of low-class people, but that many of them were keen to hear his message and he was willing to "welcome" them and share a meal with "all" of them. There is, then, little sign that the omission of παντες was meant to lessen the number of undesirables listed as Jesus' hearers, so the proposal does not carry conviction. Rather, παντες was more likely omitted by scribal slip from one set of four letters to the identical four in the following word.

---

55. Collins, *Mark*, 433nd.
56. The two compound verbs are probably meant to heighten the force of the narrative.
57. Kannaday, *Apologetic Discourse*, 173.
58. Metzger, *Textual Commentary*, 139.

Luke 9:26

Luke recounts Jesus speaking about the difficulties that will ensue for those who follow him, urging his listeners to persevere in faith in view of the eternal consequences of their decision (9:23–27). In this context, he refers to a person, ος γαρ αν επαισχυνθη με και τους εμους λογους, saying that the Son of Man would be ashamed of him when he comes in his glory. However, some MSS (D a e l sy^c) do not include λογους, so Jesus is then referring to a person being ashamed of him and "his people" (τους εμους). In view of its weak MS support this reading is clearly secondary. The word might easily have been omitted by homoioteleuton (τους εμ<u>ους</u> λογ<u>ους</u>), but Kannaday proposes that it gives the honor of Jesus' words to "his people," thus elevating their status.[59] This is presumably assuming that judgment for being ashamed of his people makes them important, while the "glory" mentioned subsequently is not given to Jesus' words or his people but to him. There is little here, however, to suggest that the variant was driven by an apologetic desire to enhance the status of Jesus' followers in the eyes of critics. Rather, a scribal slip is the more natural explanation,[60] as in the identical omission in different MSS at the parallel passage in Mark 8:38.[61]

Matthew 6:12

In commenting on a part of the Lord's Prayer (Matt 6:12), Origen records the petition to be forgiven for τα παραπτωματα rather than τα οφειληματα, as in the original. Kannaday suggests that this was a deliberate change by Origen to "avoid the ambiguity of a term wrought with economic meaning (debts) by substituting a term that was clearly ethical in content (misdeeds)," especially in view of his sensitivity to pagan views about Christians as poor people with low social status.[62] The meaning of τα οφειληματα in the original text is clearly metaphorical, referring to offences as "debts,"[63] but Kannaday proposes that Origen chose to use παραπτωματα, or found it in his MS, just as Luke used τας αμαρτιας (Luke 11:4), although even the Didache uses a form of τα οφειληματα

---

59. Kannaday, *Apologetic Discourse*, 173.
60. Nolland, *Luke 1—9:20*, 475nd.
61. Metzger, *Textual Commentary*, 84.
62. Kannaday, *Apologetic Discourse*, 174.
63. Davies and Allison, *Matthew*, 1:611; BDAG, 743.

(8:2). Kannaday notes that παραπτωματα occurs in Matt 6:14 with a metaphorical meaning soon afterwards, which might have suggested using that term in 6:12, but he proposes instead that someone created this reading with an apologetic motive, attempting to show that Christians were not asking God to remove their economic debts but to forgive their sins, thus countering any suggestion that Christians were social revolutionaries wishing to be rid of their debts. If so, Origen, or whoever was responsible for this variant, would not be changing the meaning of the prayer but simply the way in which it was expressed.

Yet, we do not know that Origen "altered this text" at all, since he might have found it in his MS. Indeed, he felt free to allow τοις οφειλεταις to stand in the following line and went on in the subsequent material to discuss various (non-economic) "debts" owed to God. Further, he cites the Lukan text in the parallel passage where both τας αμαρτιας and παντι οφειλοντι occur, presumably showing that he, like Luke, saw little difference between the two. Thus, in view of the use of παραπτωματα in the immediate context, it would be far easier to see the change as a harmonization to context than as a change created to forestall a portrayal of Christians praying that God would release them from their economic burdens. Further, D and some OL and Vulgate MSS support the secondary reading οφειληματα in Luke, going against the proposed trend. In sum, the suggestion that this reading was created by Origen, or anyone else, with this motive in mind is unconvincing. Rather, it is an alternative word without the monetary imagery of sins as "debts" and probably drawn from the context.

Mark 1:18, Matthew 4:20

Both Mark's and Matthew's Gospels record Jesus calling his first disciples (Mark 1:14–20, Matt 4:18–22), referring first to Simon and Andrew and concluding, και ευθυς αφεντες τα δικτυα ηκολουθησαν αυτω. Some MSS insert αυτων after τα δικτυα in Matthew (K W 565 it sy[s,p,h]co) and Mark (A K f[1] *Byz* f l sy[s,p,h**]sa bo[mss]). Kannaday proposes that the people responsible for those readings "felt compelled" to insert αυτων, so the disciples were now leaving not just "a job" but "their own nets," thus portraying them as people of some substance. He also suggests that the other MSS (D it) that replace τα δικτυα with παντα in Mark 1:18 add an even more universal tone to what they left behind to follow Jesus. He concludes that these changes were intended to elevate the status of the disciples, especially Peter, since they had *their own* nets and presumably *their own* business.[64]

However, this is a subtle reading of the evidence, except for the replacement of τα δικτυα with παντα in Mark 1:18, and even this might be a harmonization to Luke 5:11—a "heightening and generalizing" of the original text, but little more.[65] Indeed, since Simon and Andrew are described as αλιεις in Mark 1:16 and Matt 4:18, αυτων is already implied. Thus, the proposal of apologetically driven variant readings is unlikely, since it assumes that someone would have thought that by inserting αυτων a reader would have been given a different portrayal of the economic status of the disciples. The difference is far too slight for that. A reader would have hardly noticed, so it is improbable that a copyist would have made the change to convey that thought.

Mark 9:35

Mark's Gospel records a discussion between Jesus and his disciples on the subject of wanting to be "great" (9:33–37). Having introduced the subject, Mark recounts that Jesus called the Twelve και λεγει αυτοις ει τις θελει πρωτος ειναι εσται παντων εσχατος και παντων διακονος (9:35). Two MSS (D-d k) support omitting this whole section, which is clearly a secondary variant in view of its slim MS support, and it probably occurred accidentally by homoioteleuton (και λεγει . . . και λαβων). Others suggest that Mark's text here has been harmonized to Matt 18:1–4 and Luke 9:46–48, which make no mention of the content of Mark 9:35. Still others propose that Matthew and Luke omitted it deliberately from their copies of Mark, although it is uncertain that Matthew and Luke used copies of Mark, so we cannot be certain that they omitted the original sentence as a response to slurs against Christians belonging to the lower classes. While Celsus did criticize Christians because they were predominantly slaves (*Cels.* 3.50), it is unclear that scribes omitted this sentence to respond to such criticism.[66] Further, although the apologist Athenagoras maintained that some Christians owned slaves themselves (*Leg.* 35), instead of seeing this as a response to such criticism, the context of his remarks shows that it is only mentioned in passing. The case for this being an apologetically

---

64. Kannaday, *Apologetic Discourse*, 174–75.
65. Collins, *Mark*, 156nb.
66. *Pace* Kannaday, *Apologetic Discourse*, 175–76.

APOLOGETIC FOR THE FOLLOWERS OF JESUS?

motivated omission, then, lacks support. Again, it is more likely that the omission was due to homoioteleuton, resulting in MSS with the shorter reading.[67]

John 9:8

John 9 recounts a series of episodes arising from Jesus healing a man who had been born blind, including a description of reactions by those who knew him (9:8). The original text referred to these people as οι θεωρουντες αυτον το προτερον οτι προcαιτηc ην, and it mentions that some of them thought he was ο καθημενοc και προcαιτων. A number of MSS (C³ f¹³ Byz), however, read τυφλοc instead of προcαιτηc, while others (69 it) have the conflate reading, τυφλοc . . . και προcαιτηc. Both of these secondary readings refer to the man being blind, rather than (or, as well as) being a beggar, so Kannaday suggests that this "muting" of his economic condition was intentionally designed to counter pagan criticisms of Christians as almost all from the lower classes of society.[68] However, the conflate reading, like many such readings, is clearly an attempt to deal with two different variants by including both, so it is unlikely to have had any other motivation. Further, the suggestion that substituting τυφλοc for προcαιτηc was an attempt to remove some of the pagan calumny against Christians is too subtle, because it presumes that the person responsible for it thought that such a change would have that effect, when the immediate context goes on to record the crowd's suggestion that he was the one who used to sit there και προcαιτων (9:8). A reader could hardly fail to miss this second reference to begging (προcαιτων), so it would have been unlikely for someone to change the first one (προcαιτηc) with this motivation and leave the second intact. More likely, it was a change harmonizing to the immediate context, in which the man was clearly blind (9:1–7, esp. τυφλοc in 9:1–2) and someone named him as such in their MS, instead of referring to him as a beggar, although he was still begging.

---

67. Collins suggests that the omission was designed "to improve the coherence and pointedness of the passage" (*Mark*, 442nc), but the above proposal is simpler.

68. Kannaday, *Apologetic Discourse*, 176.

Scribes, Theology, and Apologetics

Mostly Women?

The next group of variants relate to pagan criticisms of Christians being mostly women and, indeed, women of questionable character. Juvenal had composed satires against certain Graeco-Roman cults preying on women,[69] and his comments were echoed with regard to the early Christians by a number of pagan writers such as Celsus (*Cels.* 3.44, 55). Celsus especially mentioned "hysterical" women as the supposed witnesses of Jesus' resurrection (*Cels.* 2.55), and Origen responded to his implied charge against Mary Magdalene with some vigor (*Cels.* 2.59–60). Kannaday reviews the predominant view of men in Roman society that women in general were gullible and superstitious, so that Christianity, being mostly adopted by women, was perceived as foolish, as well as promiscuous and seditious.[70] He also outlines recent studies of the role of women in early Christianity,[71] although I have shown cause to question some of these conclusions, especially regarding variants in Codex Bezae said to show a bias against women.[72] Nevertheless, I examine below variant readings that are alleged to have been created to offset this view of Christians as mostly gullible and silly women.

Matthew 19:29, Mark 10:29

After relating Jesus' encounter with a rich young man (19:16–26), Matthew goes on to report Peter's comment about what they had left behind to follow Jesus, presumably in contrast to the rich man who could not bring himself to leave his wealth behind (19:27). As part of Jesus' response, Matthew notes his promise that whatever sacrifices someone might make for his sake will be more than made up for (19:29). Mark has a similar account (10:17–31), including a comparable comment about sacrifices that might be made by a disciple (10:29) and the corresponding promise of recompense (10:30). Some MSS include η γυναικα in the list of possible losses for the sake of following Jesus; there are a number of slightly different readings with this addition in Matt 19:29, but only one variant that does so in Mark 10:29. In view of the MS support for the Markan text, it seems clear that the addition of η γυναικα is secondary

---

69. Georgi, "Socioeconomic Reasons," 37–38.
70. Kannaday, *Apologetic Discourse*, 176–77.
71. Kannaday, *Apologetic Discourse*, 177–79.
72. Mugridge, *Scribes*, 196–205.

at Mark 10:29, but at Matt 19:29 the evidence for the text without it is limited (B a n), so it is unclear if η γυναικα is a secondary addition or an original phrase omitted later.[73] Certainly, there is more variation among the MSS in Matt 19:29, including where η γυναικα is placed in the list, the omission of η πατερα (D sy^s), the substitution of γονεις in place of πατερα η μητερα (f^1),[74] and the singular οικιαν instead of the plural οικιας (K 33 565 700), so further consideration should be given to any conclusions drawn on the basis that the two sets of variants are equivalent.[75] Although η γυναικα might have been added as a harmonization to Luke 18:29,[76] Kannaday is not convinced. He asks if the addition of η γυναικα in Matt 19:29, or even a harmonization, could have been done to support ascetic interests emphasizing abstaining from marital relations. But it is just as possible, if η γυναικα was original, that it might have been omitted due to a possible tension felt with 19:3-10 (arguing against divorcing a wife), or just due to harmonization to Mark 10:29.[77]

Kannaday notes that there is no mention of giving up husbands, which could reflect the fact that the words were directed to men in the contemporary "male-dominant culture," and he wonders if this was to further the apologetic purpose of contradicting the charge that Christians were destructive of the father-centered family in Roman society.[78] This could reflect an "omission" of something originally present, but since there is no evidence that any of these texts ever did mention husbands, the lack must be original to Matthew and Mark (and Luke); there is no evidence that this charge (of Christians being destructive of families) was current when they composed their Gospels. It is more likely that not mentioning husbands was due to the message being directed primarily to men.

The proposals regarding these variant readings need qualification, however, especially in view of the different textual evidence in the case of Matt 19:29 and Mark 10:29, but also because of the interpretation of that evidence. The addition of η γυναικα in Mark 10:29 makes no reference to

---

73. Cf. France, *Matthew*, 740n4.

74. Perhaps this was a harmonization to Luke 18:29, where γονεις is used instead of πατερα η μητερα.

75. Pace Kannaday, *Apologetic Discourse*, 179-80.

76. See Metzger on Matt 19:29 (*Textual Commentary*, 40), although he does not discuss Mark 10:29. Cf. Pardee, *Scribal Harmonization*, 317.

77. Davies and Allison, *Matthew*, 3:59-60, esp. 60n138.

78. Kannaday, *Apologetic Discourse*, 180n143.

"repudiation of nuptial union," as suggested, as if a man's "leaving" his wife referred particularly to giving up sexual relations with her, which is far too limited in its scope. Jesus clearly had in mind the consequences that might follow for a person who became one of his followers, and those consequences were probably not envisaged as being of the disciple's making. Family loyalty was not to be the highest priority when it came to following him (Matt 10:37), for a disciple might find that their family became hostile toward them (Matt 10:34–36). Jesus' words here do not focus so much on "willing celibacy" as on the harsh reality of rejection by family members when someone became one of Jesus' disciples, whatever Peter may have meant by his pious comment about leaving "everything" in the framework of Jesus' itinerant ministry (Matt 19:27). So, the addition of η γυναικα in Matthew was unlikely to have been a reference to willing celibacy and therefore cannot be adduced as evidence of an apologetic response to charges of sexual laxity among Christians, as grave as that charge was and as seriously as it was taken by the apologists. It is true that Athenagoras asserted the high standards of sexual purity among Christians (*Leg.* 32.2; 33.2) and even the practice of sexual abstinence if that furthered holiness (*Leg.* 33.3), and both Tatian (*Orat.* 35) and Theophilus (*Autol.* 3.15) made similar comments. However, this cannot serve as background to these variants because the emphasis in this passage is on what a disciple might have to be willing to leave behind if they were rejected by their family, including houses, brothers and sisters, father and mother, children and fields. So, the constructions put on the reasons for the inclusion of "or a wife" in these variants in Mark 10:29 do not fit, and they do not explain the addition of η γυναικα if it was not original. In fact, the variety of variants in Matt 19:29 (as also in Luke 18:29) is probably due to the lengthy list of items all joined by a single-letter particle (η).

Thus, various suggestions have been made about the reasons for the variants here. Did D omit η πατερα due to someone's desire to increase the prominence of the father, or perhaps to decrease the prominence of the mother? Was leaving "parents" different from leaving "father or mother"? Was leaving one "house" different from leaving "houses"? In Matt 19:29, the presence of η γυναικα in some MSS was most likely an assimilation to Luke 18:29,[79] and the replacement of πατερα η μητερα by γονεις might have been influenced by Luke 18:29 or it was just an equivalent substitution, and the absence of η πατερα was probably due to

---

79. Luz, *Matthew 8–20*, 509n6.

homoioteleuton.⁸⁰ The situation with the addition of η γυναικα is probably similar in Mark 10:29.⁸¹ The best suggestions are the simplest, and the involved connections and arguments put forward to explain these variants as apologetically motivated do not stand up to scrutiny, even though they are in a context where they might have been appropriate.

Matthew 5:32

In Matthew's Sermon on the Mount, a small section is given over to the subject of divorce (5:31–32), and Kannaday alludes to Witherington's argument regarding this.⁸² His suggestion is that the MSS (D a b k) that omit και ος εαν απολελυμενην γαμηςη μοιχαται at the end of v. 32, thus avoiding labelling as an adulterer the man who marries the divorced woman mentioned at the beginning of the verse, shows the tendency in Western MSS to "highlight and protect male privilege, while also relegating women to a place in the background."⁸³ Thus, adultery would be a purely female "crime." This reading of the evidence, however, is selective, because the force of the whole section is to speak out against a man divorcing his wife for almost any reason and justifying that by showing that he had conformed to the OT requirement of providing her with a certificate (Deut 24:1). Jesus, however, limited the just causes for divorcing a wife to her "committing adultery," a pronouncement that upheld the cause of women who risked being divorced for inconsequential reasons, with some traditions even including the desire of a husband to marry "someone prettier than she" as a valid ground for divorce. As I showed in *Scribes, Motives, and Manuscripts*, these words of Jesus were intended to protect women, and the omission in some MSS of the case of a man marrying a woman who had been so easily divorced hardly changes the thrust of the passage.⁸⁴ Perhaps the variant arose from a copyist thinking και ος εαν απολελυμενην γαμηςη μοιχαται was redundant in view of the previous words,⁸⁵ or perhaps it was omitted by parablepsis from one word to another with an

---

80. Metzger, *Textual Commentary*, 40; Hagner, *Matthew 14–28*, 563nb; Nolland, *Matthew*, 796nb. Cf. France, *Matthew*, 740n4. Davies and Allison appear to be undecided (*Matthew*, 3:59n138).

81. Collins, *Mark*, 475ni.

82. Kannaday, *Apologetic Discourse*, 180–81.

83. Witherington, "Anti-feminist Tendencies," 83–84.

84. Mugridge, *Scribes*, 85–93.

85. Metzger, *Textual Commentary*, 11.

identical beginning and ending (μοιχευθηναι ... μοιχαται), although this would create a grammatically difficult passage. Whatever the case, the suggested interpretation of the variant does not fit the context of the passage. The loss of the reference to the second man marrying the divorced woman hardly changes the forcefulness of the original, which condemned in the strongest terms the way in which women could be divorced on trivial grounds and sent on their way with a certificate, thus fulfilling the letter of the law but not its intention. The law was being used to justify men's desires, and Jesus was speaking out against that, as Matthew makes plain. The variant hardly changes the force of that pronouncement at all, so the proposed construction put on the variant reading, according to which the words were omitted to conform to the current view of women and highlight male privilege, does not take account of the context for a reader (and copyist). It is much more likely to have been occasioned by scribal error or the absence of that material in 19:9.[86]

Luke 8:3

Luke's summary of Jesus' itinerant ministry includes the mention of his companions—first the Twelve (8:1) and then a number of women (8:2–3). There are two alternative readings at the end of the verse, where the women's support is mentioned (αιτινες διηκονουν αυτοις εκ των υπαρχοντων αυταις). Some MSS read αυτω instead of αυτοις.[87] One reading mentions the women using their financial resources to support "them" (presumably Jesus and disciples) and the other refers to them supporting "him" (Jesus). It has been suggested that the original reading was not αυτοις but αυτω, so that, while the original text mentioned the women providing for Jesus (αυτω), others changed the text to say that they provided for them (αυτοις, "the menfolk"). Thus, this removes the "labor of love" for Jesus and makes it into a labor of women for men, which is said to fit a pattern of growing "oppression of women" in the early church.[88]

There have been various attempts to explain the readings, as well as different verdicts on which was original. The external MS evidence is quite balanced, although slightly in favour of αυτοις (B D W Θ f^{13} lat sy[s,c,p]) over αυτω (ℵ A f^1 33 it vg[cl] sy[h] co; Marc[T]). It is not obvious that the

---

86. Nolland, *Matthew*, 240nc-c.
87. Kannaday, *Apologetic Discourse*, 181–83. Cf. Witherington, "On the Road."
88. Ehrman, "Text of the Gospels," 92–93.

context favours αυτω, so it does not follow that it was changed to αυτοιc to place the women on a par with the Twelve. Nor is it clear that 8:1–3 is arranged around "two subjects, Jesus and the women, each governing a verb."[89] Rather, the main clause describes what Jesus was doing using a verb in the indicative mood (διωδευεν), and the Twelve are mentioned being with him as he did so (και οι δωδεκα cυν αυτω). Then there is a note that certain women were also there (και γυναικεc τινεc). These women are then described in a series of clauses—a relative clause (αι ηcαν τεθεραπευμεναι . . . αcθενειων), a list of those women (μαρια . . . και ιωαννα . . . και cουcαννα και ετεραι πολλαι), and a final relative clause relating what the women did (αιτινεc διηκονουν . . . αυτοιc). The only subject of an indicative verb in a main clause is Jesus. Then there are two additions in a manner common to Greek style:[90] a second and third subject are added but covered by the first verb—they also were "going around"—and then a series of subordinate clauses follow describing the women. So, it is entirely appropriate for English translations to separate off mention of the Twelve and the women, since both groups are "tacked on" as additional persons "going around" like Jesus.

Hence, the use of the plural αυτοιc does not make the women patrons of the group rather than of Jesus himself (αυτω), thus reducing their significance—assuming that αυτω was replaced by αυτοιc. However, given the balance of the MS evidence, the question is more likely why αυτοιc was changed to αυτω in some MSS, which could have been a harmonization to Mark 15:41 or Matt 27:56. Further, it is also uncertain that, since the Gospel writers did not mention the women supporting the whole group in the passion narrative, Luke would not have done so here. So, the conclusion that αυτω is original, and that this has been distorted to the detriment of the women, is unconvincing. Instead, αυτοιc is more likely original, with αυτω arising as a harmonization to Mark or Matthew,[91] or deriving from a desire to focus on Jesus, perhaps stemming from Marcion.[92] Thus, it is difficult to be certain about the origin of these

---

89. Kannaday, *Apologetic Discourse*, 182.

90. In John 2:2, for example, Jesus is said to have been invited to the wedding (εκληθη δε και ο ιηcουc), and then the disciples are mentioned as also being invited (και οι μαθηται αυτου), even though εκληθη is in the singular.

91. Fitzmyer, *Luke I–IX*, 698. Cf. Metzger, *Textual Commentary*, 121. Nolland proposes dependence on Mark 15:41 and suggests that it may be "christologically motivated," without specifying what this means (*Luke 1—9:20*, 363nb).

92. Metzger, *Textual Commentary*, 120–21.

readings, although it is possible that someone changed αυτοις to αυτω out of a desire to focus on the women's service to Jesus.

Mark 15:41, Luke 23:55, P. Dura 24

Mark's account of Jesus' crucifixion concludes with a list of three women onlookers (15:40), outlining how in Galilee ηκολουθουν αυτω και διηκονουν αυτω (15:41), but a few MSS (C D Δ 579 n) omit και διηκονουν αυτω. In Luke 23:55, the women who followed Joseph to Jesus' tomb are described as αι γυναικες αιτινες ησαν συνεληλυθυιαι εκ της γαλιλαιας αυτω, but two MSS (D c) omit αυτω. Kannaday suggests that the omission in Luke 23:55 distances the women from Jesus.[93] But the reason for the omission is probably less dramatic because αυτω comes well after the verb it modifies (συνεληλυθυιαι) and would more easily fit immediately after it, where a number of MSS (A C² W Θ $f^{1,13}$ 33 Byz sy) place it. So, it is not difficult to see how it could have been omitted at the end of the clause due to its somewhat awkward placement.[94] Or perhaps someone thought it was clearly implied and therefore unnecessary. The omission of και διηκονουν αυτω in Mark 15:41 can most easily be accounted for by parablepsis (αυτω . . . αυτω), so there is no need to posit an apologetic or ideological reason for the omission, as if someone wished to remove any trace of women supporting Jesus.

Kannaday also discusses a small papyrus published in 1959 as P. Dura 10 (inv. 24), although the *editio princeps* by Carl H. Kraeling appeared in 1935.[95] The papyrus is generally dated to the first half of III AD and, following Kraeling, several authors have suggested that this text is a fragment of Tatian's *Diatessaron*, although others are doubtful. The identification is not material to our study here, but if not part of the *Diatessaron* the date of the variant considered cannot be located with any degree of confidence, although this does not affect the discussion of the reading itself.

The first line of the fragment has been reconstructed as ζεβεδαιου και σαλωμη και αι γυναικες των συνακολουθησαντων αυτω. It seems to be parallel to Mark 15:40-41, Matt 27:55-56, and Luke 24:49, apparently

---

93. Kannaday, *Apologetic Discourse*, 183.

94. Marshall, *Gospel of Luke*, 881.

95. Kraeling, *Greek Fragment*. Cf. Welles et al., *Parchments and Papyri*, 73-74; Crawford, "Diatessaron."

referring not to the women travelling with Jesus but to the wives of the men travelling with him. Some authors suggest that if this text was originally composed in Syriac, it was an inadvertent (mental) omission of one letter in Syriac that resulted in this reading. Others have posited that the reading arose out of a desire to avoid the mention of women in Jesus' company since it would have been "a liability to the Christian movement."[96] Kannaday argues that this change was meant to serve an apologetic purpose, attempting to counter criticism of Christians in relation to the place of women in Jesus' ministry and among his later followers, so that women are sidelined in order to respond to criticisms of Christian groups being composed mainly of women[97] or to avoid any suggestion of impropriety on Jesus' part.[98]

A major issue, however, is that the text of *P. Dura* 10 is not necessarily exactly as cited above, since the beginning of line 2 should probably read εκ των cυνακολουθηcαντων αυτω,[99] implying that αι γυναικες are not "the wives of those who followed" Jesus but "the women among those who followed him," where "those who followed him" are presumably the αλλαι πολλαι αι cυναναβαcαι αυτω εic ιεροcολυμα (Mark 15:41) or the whole group of women and men. In either case, the supposed removal of women from the group of Jesus' followers does not actually appear in this MS, so the reading cannot have had the proposed apologetic aim.[100]

Hence, none of the three variant readings provides any reason to think that someone tried to remove the idea of Jesus having women followers or to counter pagan criticism of the place of women in Christian groups. It also follows that they do not provide support for the suggestion that αυτω was original in Luke 8:3, so they give no credence to the proposal that it was changed to remove the notion that the women served Jesus (αυτω) or to make them instead into women serving "the menfolk" (αυτοιc).[101]

---

96. Colwell, "Method in Locating," 38.

97. Kannaday, *Apologetic Discourse*, 183–84.

98. Lagrange, "Deux nouveaux textes," 325, referred to in Colwell, "Method in Locating," 39.

99. Parker et al., "Dura-Europos." Cf. Crawford, "Diatessaron," 261–65.

100. Pace Kannaday, *Apologetic Discourse*, 184–85.

101. Pace Ehrman, "Text of the Gospels," 92–93.

Luke 4:39

Luke recounts how Jesus healed Simon's mother-in-law (4:38–39a), adding that παραχρημα δε αναστασα διηκονει αυτοις (4:39b). Bezae has the SR παραχρημα ωςτε αναστασαν αυτην διακονειν αυτοις, which changes the final clause from an independent clause into a result clause, and Kannaday interprets this as now casting the healing of Simon's mother-in-law as resulting in her serving Jesus and his followers, and thus as "a type of call narrative."[102] He also maintains that this change makes her service into an action that did not arise from her own decision but as a *result* of being healed. This is an oversubtle reading of the change, however, because even in the original text it is implied that she served (and was able to serve) the group because she had been healed. There is no evidence for the proposed change in emphasis, so it does not follow that this is an instance of the presence and status of women in the church being reduced or depreciated. The meaning of the secondary reading in D was already implied in the original and does not carry any significance that might denigrate the woman concerned or contradict any charge that women were very prominent among Christians.

John 4:25

John 4:4–38 contains a narrative of Jesus' encounter with a woman near the Samaritan village of Sychar, and during her discussion with Jesus she is recorded saying, οιδα οτι μεςςιαν ερχεται ο λεγομενος χριςτος (4:25). Some MSS have the secondary reading οιδαμεν instead of οιδα (P[66c] ℵ[2] f[13] 33 f sy[hmg] ly bo Or[pt]), which Kannaday interprets as removing a reference to the woman's individual faith and instead representing "the established beliefs of a religious community." He then interprets this as an instance of the visibility and leadership of women in early Christianity being reduced, which would reflect the proposed "efforts of the early church to placate pagan sensibilities" about the prominence of women in Christian circles.[103]

However, the plural verb οιδαμεν was most likely used under the influence of 4:22, where the contrast that Jesus is referring to is clearly between two communities—υμεις προςκυνειτε ο ουκ οιδατε ημεις

---

102. Kannaday, *Apologetic Discourse*, 185–86.
103. Kannaday, *Apologetic Discourse*, 186–88.

προσκυνουμεν ο οιδαμεν.[104] This community perspective, including the use of οιδαμεν, is then taken up in the variant reading at 4:25, so that οιδαμεν fits more easily with ημιν later in the verse (αναγγελει ημιν απαντα),[105] which shows that when the woman expressed her own belief (οιδα), it was expressed as a member of the Samaritan community (αναγγελει ημιν).[106] So, in light of the context, the secondary reading probably arose as an extension by a copyist of the community element in the context rather than being created out of a desire to reduce the prominence of women in early Christianity in order to placate criticism of the importance of women in the new faith.

Luke 1:28

Luke's narrative of Mary being told about her coming pregnancy and the status of the Son to be born (1:26–38) includes the angelic greeting χαιρε κεχαριτωμενη ο κυριος μετα cου (1:28). Other MSS, however, add ευλογημενη cυ εν γυναιξιν (A C D Θ f^{13} 33 *Byz* latt sy bo[mss]), anticipating Elizabeth's outburst in 1:42. There is no reason why the extra material would have been omitted from early MSS, so it is probably secondary,[107] and MS 565 (IX AD) has a marginal note that it was not found "in the ancient copies." Kannaday agrees that the longer reading is secondary, but he suggests that asserting Mary's blessedness εν γυναιξιν serves not to elevate her status but to qualify it, for she is only blessed *among women* and not in comparison with men.[108] This comparison with male status, however, is not relevant to the significance of the phrase, but it does highlight an element of the meaning of the original, even in 1:42. That is, Mary is to be privileged by being able to give birth to the promised Messiah. Of course, she is privileged "among women" because men do not share in giving birth, and of all women, her son will be the promised Savior. Hence, the secondary reading, probably drawn from 1:42,[109] serves to highlight Mary's status *among women*, not to lessen her status, but to emphasize her superior status in the community of those who give

---

104. Haenchen, *John 1*, 223–24.
105. Maloney, *John*, 133.
106. McHugh, *John 1–4*, 286.
107. Metzger, *Textual Commentary*, 108.
108. Kannaday, *Apologetic Discourse*, 187–88.
109. Fitzmyer, *Luke I–IX*, 346; Nolland, *Luke 1—9:20*, 40nb. Bovon also traces the influence of Tatian's *Diatessaron* (*Luke 1*, 50n67).

birth to children. It does not follow, then, that the longer reading is a case of apologetic lowering of the status of women in relation to men out of deference to pagan criticism of the prominence of women among early Christians.

Matthew 1:25, Luke 2:7

The final examples discussed under this heading are also in the narratives of events leading up to Jesus' birth. In Matt 1:25, two MSS (k sy^s) omit ουκ εγινωσκεν αυτην εως ου ("he did not 'know' her until"), perhaps because someone wished to remove any hint that Joseph and Mary had sexual relations after she gave birth to Jesus,[110] or perhaps "sensing a contradiction with the angelic insistence that the marriage should go ahead" (1:20–21).[111] In Luke 2:7, Codex W omits τον πρωτοτοκον, perhaps due to a desire to omit any idea that Mary had further children (by natural means after her "firstborn"), although the use of πρωτοτοκος does not necessarily imply that she did in fact have further children.[112] Aristides's use of θεοτοκος with reference to Mary is probably not relevant because it says nothing about Mary's status.[113] In both cases, it is possible that someone wished to make a theological point and changed the text for this reason, so these instances might be theological corruptions, although not slanted against the importance of women but toward veneration of Mary and her continuing virginal status.[114]

The Ending(s) of Mark

Kannaday has a lengthy discussion of the endings of Mark's Gospel.[115] I have discussed this issue above in chapter 2, so I only deal with it here in relation to his particular perspective. He uses the commonly accepted nomenclature of the Longer Ending (16:9–20), the Shorter Ending

---

110. Davies and Allison, *Matthew*, 1:219n63. Kannaday refers to the Protoevangelium of James 19:3—20.2 (*Apologetic Discourse*, 188), but this is rather different since there it is implied that Mary's hymen is still intact even though she had just given birth.
111. Nolland, *Matthew*, 88ng-g.
112. Fitzmyer, *Luke I–IX*, 407–8.
113. Pace Kannaday, *Apologetic Discourse*, 188n178.
114. Cf. Globe, "Doctrinal Variants," 62–63; Head, "Christology," 117–18.
115. Kannaday, *Apologetic Discourse*, 189–96.

(16:9-10),[116] and the "Freer Logion" (inserted in 16:14 in Codex W), and he calls the text ending at 16:8 the "Abrupt Ending." In view of the MS evidence and the textual content of the "endings" beyond 16:8, they are all now widely regarded as secondary,[117] so they are all examples of "scribal interpolation." Kannaday implies that Mark intentionally ended his Gospel at 16:8, but it is quite likely, in my view, that the last section of the Gospel was lost at an early stage. However, his purpose is to discuss the aims of those who created the secondary endings, in order to assess if they might have been designed to counter pagan criticism of the Christians.

The Shorter Ending

This ending occurs in a small number of MSS (L Ψ 099 0112 k sy[hmg] sa[mss] bo[mss]). It relates how the women reported to Peter and the other disciples what they had seen and been told and that Jesus sent out the message of salvation "through them." Kannaday maintains that the testimony to Jesus' resurrection and the task of proclaiming it in this ending "is transferred from the female followers to the male disciples" as a way of reducing the prominence of women in Christian circles.[118] But this is far from clear in the text. The women are said to have reported their experience (and the message entrusted to them) to the group of disciples gathered around Peter, presumably in fulfilment of the angelic command υπαγετε ειπατε τοιc μαθηταιc αυτου και τω πετρω (16:7). In such a truncated version of events, it is hard to see any ideological motivation.

Further, Kannaday suggests that the message is directed "westward, i.e., in the direction of Rome," presumably out of deference to the Roman Empire. However, the phrase "from east to west" (απο ανατοληc και αχρι δυcεωc) is "an old and widespread formula expressing the totality of space," as in Ps 113:3 (112:3 LXX, απο ανατολων ηλιου μεχρι δυcμων) and Isa 45:6 (οι απο ανατολων ηλιου και οι απο δυcμων),[119] not a direction of movement from east to west.[120] Finally, Peter is identified as the leader

---

116. This occurs along with 16:9-20 in most of the MSS that include it, but it is the final part of the Gospel in the OL MS k.

117. Evans, *Mark 8:27—16:20*, 545-57; France, *Mark*, 685-88; Marcus, *Mark 8-16*, 1088-90.

118. Kannaday, *Apologetic Discourse*, 192-93.

119. Collins, *Mark*, 802-3 and 803n12.

120. Cf. εν τε τη ανατολη και εν τη δυcει (1 Clem 5.6).

of the apostolic group, supposedly in response to criticism of his role in early Christianity, although this has already been mentioned in 16:7.

Thus, the "themes" Kannaday has isolated in the shorter ending are either unsurprising in the context or not present. Hence, however much they can be set against a background in the writings of pagan critics and the responses made by apologists, the assertion that they express apologetic interests on the part of the person responsible for creating the ending does not stand up to scrutiny. Kannaday changes the interpretation of the second element above from indicating a westward direction toward Rome to "the universal scope of the great commission," noting references to this in Origen (*Cels.* 2.13); and he traces the focus on Peter in early apologists such as Origen (*Cels.* 2.45; *Comm. Matt.* 12.10–11), Tertullian (*Pud.* 21), and Clement of Alexandria (*Strom.* 11), noting that both Celsus and Porphyry had ridiculed Peter. Nevertheless, the elements referred to in the shorter ending do not demonstrate the proposed ideological biases, so they do not show apologetic interests on the part of the person or persons responsible for it. They certainly do not demonstrate a desire to placate criticism of the Christians for the prominence of women in their circles.

The Longer Ending

In relation to the longer ending (commonly, vv. 9–20), Kannaday proposes a number of points relating to apologetic themes.[121] First, he takes the description of Mary as the one from whom Jesus had driven seven demons (16:9; cf. Luke 8:2) as an indication that she is a sane and reliable witness to his resurrection (because the demons have been removed), in contrast to Celsus's description of her as a παροιστρος (hysterical) woman. Even so, the disciples whom she told "did not believe it" (16:11), just as they did not believe the two (men) who met Jesus while walking in the country (16:12–13)—they only believed when they saw Jesus himself (16:14). So, Kannaday suggests that this was all to emphasize that the disciples did not believe the testimony of others, including a reliable woman, and they only did so when they saw the proof with their own eyes, thus showing their rational approach. This would fit with Theophilus's emphasis on credible eyewitnesses for Jesus' resurrection (*Autol.* 3.2).

---

121. Kannaday, *Apologetic Discourse*, 193–95.

The universal emphasis on proclaiming the gospel to the whole world (16:15) is mentioned by apologists, along with miracles worked by believers (16:17–18; cf. Origen, *Cels.* 1.38). Yet, we know little of pagan critics bowing to such arguments, if miracles were in fact being wrought. In relation to the ascension account in 16:19, Kannaday suggests that Luke 24:51 was not original but that the narrative in this longer ending concurs with the use made of Jesus' ascension by apologists like Aristides. He emphasized that Jesus passed on his teaching to the apostles prior to leaving them, so it must be reliable.

There are, then, certain links between themes mentioned in the Longer Ending and those highlighted by the early apologists, but since the bulk of the material in this ending is drawn from the Gospels in one way or another, someone might just have wished to finish off Mark's Gospel by combining elements from the other Gospels and adding more, without any particular point to make.[122] The fact that there is some overlap with matters emphasized by the apologists is then a coincidence. However, it is not purely accidental. Rather, it stems from the fact that the apologists made use of themes in the Gospels, which the person responsible for the Longer Ending also used. Indeed, some of the themes have only a tenuous link with the way in which they are used by the apologists, so the contention that this ending was created with apologetic purposes in mind has little to commend it.

The Freer Logion

This short addition to 16:14 in Codex W is a complex of ideas, and Kannaday highlights some of them: the disciples' defense of their unbelief on the grounds that this present age is under the rule of Satan, as well as Jesus' promise that this situation would come to an end after a time of suffering. He shows that these themes were mentioned by apologists such as Tatian (*Orat.* 6.1, 12.4, 14.2, 16.1, 26.2, and esp. 29.2), Origen (*Cels.* 1.31), and Athenagoras (*Apol.* 27.2).[123] So, this material would then "soften" the condemnation of the apostles in 16:14, prior to them being sent out as his witnesses (16:15) and workers of miracles (16:17–18). Jesus' death for them should be enough to inspire them to live in his

---

122. France gives a summary of places in the Gospels from which details have been drawn (*Mark*, 686–87). Cf. Wasserman, "Scribal Alterations," 305n4; Kellhoffer, *Miracle and Mission.*

123. Kannaday, *Apologetic Discourse,* 195–96.

service.[124] Yet, despite sharing some themes with apologists, it is unclear what apologetic purpose this logion would serve.

Thus, proposals as to apologetic motives for the creation of the endings of Mark's Gospel (beyond 16:8) do not carry conviction, and we are left with the general impression that the endings were crafted in order to finish off what seemed to be an incomplete Gospel—whether this was so or not—based on various components drawn from the Gospels.[125]

CONCLUSION

Kannaday's characterization of the variant readings surveyed in this chapter does not carry conviction on the whole. There are a few cases where his contentions seem to hold, but in general they offer no certainty as interpretations of those readings nor of their initial intentions. Rather than being motivated by an apologetic desire to defend Christians against pagan critics, there are almost always other more viable explanations for the variants, often related to the exigencies of copying MSS in antiquity. Even when the themes raised by the variants are those mentioned by the apologists, or perhaps in contrast to charges leveled against Christians by pagan critics, there is often little evidence that the variants were crafted with those charges in mind, and there are usually much more feasible explanations as to how they arose.

---

124. Collins, *Mark*, 805–6, 809–10.
125. Metzger, *Textual Commentary*, 102–6; Collins, *Mark*, 818.

8

Apologetic for Christians in the Roman Empire?

THE FINAL SUBSTANTIVE CHAPTER in Kannaday's book concerns how Christians were seen in relation to the political claims of the Roman Empire on its citizens. He first reviews why Christians were persecuted, beginning in the first century when persecution was sporadic and localized, going on to the period from the second century onwards when Christians were viewed with widespread suspicion and sometimes subjected to harsh persecution. Yet, it was only under the rule of Decius (AD 249–51) and Diocletian (AD 284–305) that they experienced extensive persecution sponsored by the empire.[1]

Kannaday reviews the debates as to why Christians were persecuted, noting that the suspicion and hostility Christians faced was focused on their rejection of the Roman religious status quo, including local religions, as well as their exclusivist claims that they were right and everyone else was wrong. Further, by rejecting the religious status quo, it appeared that they were also rejecting the current political state of affairs, so they could be seen as subversives in an empire that required conformity to maintain its stability. The correspondence between Pliny and Trajan exemplifies the view that Christians were a menace to society. Later critics also denounced Christians for not believing in the gods or as immoral conspirators and potential traitors who were better removed from society than allowed to work their mischief in its midst (cf. Tacitus,

1. Kannaday, *Apologetic Discourse*, 199–210.

Ann. 15:44; Minucius Felix, *Oct.* 8, 12; Origen, *Cels.* 8.2). As time went on, Christians just became unpopular (*Cels.* 3.59, 8.68).

In response to this hostile suspicion, the early apologists spoke out with vigor, maintaining that Christians were good citizens (Melito, in Eusebius *Hist. eccl.* 4.26.7–8; *Diogn.* 5), who wished to honor the emperor (Theophilus, *Autol.* 1.10; Athenagoras, *Leg.* 37.2–3), and who looked to a heavenly "kingdom" not an alternative earthly one (Justin, 1 *Apol.* 11; Origen, *Cels.* 8.65, 75). I review below the variant readings said to have been crafted to counter the charges made against Christians as unbelievers in the gods and disloyal to the Roman Empire.

Another "Kingdom" than Rome?

The first group of variants concern language related to the word βαϲιλεια, especially in the Gospel of Luke. Kannaday maintains that in every case where the word βαϲιλεια occurs in Luke's Gospel without further definition there are variants with certain modifications to avoid a blanket description of Christians having an allegiance to a "kingdom" other than the Roman Empire.

Luke 9:27

After Luke's account of Peter's confession of Jesus as "the Christ of God" (9:18–20), he adds Jesus' response, first about his own death and resurrection (9:21–22), then foretelling the suffering that would come upon his followers, urging them to cling to their faith whatever suffering they might undergo (9:23–26). Finally, he said that some of those present would not die εωϲ αν ιδωϲιν την βαϲιλειαν του θεου (9:27). But instead of την βαϲιλειαν του θεου, D has the SR τον υιον του ανθρωπου ερχομενον εν τη δοξη αυτου. There is no obvious explanation for this reading as an accidental change, although Kannaday notes the partial parallel in Matt 16:28, which has βαϲιλεια for δοξα. So, the person responsible for the reading in D removed a reference to την βαϲιλειαν του θεου and replaced it with τον υιον του ανθρωπου ερχομενον εν τη δοξη αυτου,[2] perhaps with the apologetic motive of avoiding any implication that Christians were subversives engaged in destabilizing behavior in the Roman Empire in

---

2. Kotansky takes the reading in D (εν τη δοξη αυτου) as original ("Early Papyri," 268).

favor of another empire. This was certainly a point that apologists made (cf. Tertullian, *Apol.* 29.1–7).[3] However, the reference in D to the Son of Man coming in his glory could simply have been drawn from the previous verse (οταν ελθη εν τη δοξη αυτου), although this would still not explain *why* someone changed the reading. Perhaps they had the parallel in Matt 16:28 in mind (τον υιον του ανθρωπου ερχομενον εν τη βασιλεια αυτου) but kept the phraseology of the previous verse (εν τη δοξη του πατρος αυτου), although this is a rather complicated solution. It seems, then, that there is no clear explanation for this variant. Either some amount of harmonization has occurred, both with the immediate context in Luke and with a parallel passage in Matthew,[4] or an apologetic motive lies behind its creation. Yet, βασιλεια occurs thirteen times in Luke before this verse and twenty-nine times after it, without removing those where a variant has replaced it. Thus, it is unlikely that anyone would have noticed if it were removed, so a copyist would have been unlikely to delete it with an apologetic purpose in mind.

Luke 11:2

Luke's version of the Lord's Prayer opens with the petition to God as Father, asking that his name be treated as holy (11:2bc) and then continuing with the same words as in Matt 6:10, ελθετω η βασιλεια σου (11:2d). D adds εφ ημας before this petition, with slightly different word order, and Kannaday suggests that this change might have been motivated by a desire to divert any thought that the kingdom of God would come "upon" the Roman Empire as a rival and replacement kingdom. He notes that the reading in D (and many other MSS) includes the next line from Matt 6:10, asking that the will of God would be done επι της γης, just as it is done in heaven, perhaps forming a parallel with the prayer that the kingdom of God would come εφ ημας.[5] Yet, this does not easily fit the context, and it is still difficult to explain the addition of εφ ημας. Perhaps it is a remnant of the longer variant discussed below.[6]

The longer reading replaces ελθετω η βασιλεια σου with ελθετω το πνευμα σου το αγιον εφ ημας και καθαρισατω ημας (162 700; Marcion[T]

---

3. Kannaday, *Apologetic Discourse*, 211–12.
4. Nolland, *Luke 9:21–18:34*, 475ng.
5. Kannaday, *Apologetic Discourse*, 212–13.
6. Nolland, *Luke 9:21–18:34*, 89, 610nb; Metzger, *Textual Commentary*, 130–31.

Greogry of Nyssa), and it seems to go back at least to the fourth century since it is mentioned by Gregory of Nyssa and Maximus the Confessor (Gregory of Nyssa, *De orat. dom.* 3, Maximus, *Or. dom.* 350).[7] It might have been added by someone familiar with a form of the Lord's Prayer adapted for baptism or the laying on of hands, who then inserted it based on links with Luke's emphasis on the Spirit, especially with the mention in the nearby context of God giving his Spirit to those who ask (11:13).[8] A similar prayer in the Acts of Thomas 27 (ελθε το αγιον πνευμα και καθαρισον τους νεφρους αυτων και την καρδιαν αυτων) lends credence to this.[9] It has also been suggested that scribes wished to make the text in Luke identical to that in Matthew,[10] but since copyists of the NT documents often left the Gospels in quite different forms, this is doubtful.

Kannaday, however, focuses on what is missing in this longer variant, proposing that η βασιλεια σου was intentionally omitted so there is no mention of the coming of God's βασιλεια. This is particularly revealing because it occurs in the writings of Tertullian who was at pains to emphasize that Christians were no threat to the Empire.[11] This would then remove any grounds for the suspicion that Christians were a threat to the Roman Empire and were looking for another kingdom to replace it. However, in Tertullian (*Marc.* 26), as in Gregory of Nyssa, this reading follows the address to the Father, and is followed by a petition for God's kingdom to come, so it must have replaced the previous petition about God's name being treated as holy, not the petition about God's kingdom.[12] It follows, then, that this variant was not created to counter criticism of Christians as enemies of the empire. More likely, it is an addition from a later form of the Lord's Prayer, perhaps drawn from a liturgical setting.[13]

---

7. Metzger, *Manuscripts*, 122.

8. Metzger, *Manuscripts*, 122; Nolland, *Luke 9:21—18:34*, 610nb; Fitzmyer, *Luke X-XXIV*, 903-4.

9. Metzger, *Textual Commentary*, 129-32, esp. 131.

10. Ehrman, *Misquoting*, 97.

11. Kannaday, *Apologetic Discourse*, 212-13.

12. Metzger, *Textual Commentary*, 130-31. Cf. Bovon, *Luke 2*, 87.

13. Metzger, *Textual Commentary*, 131. Cf. Fitzmyer, *Luke X-XXIV*, 903-4; Nolland, *Luke 18:35—24:53*, 610nb.

Luke 12:31

Luke's account of Jesus' exhortation to his disciples not to worry about what they might eat or wear (12:22–34) includes the positive exhortation ζητειτε την βασιλειαν αυτου (12:31), but some MSS read ζητειτε την βασιλειαν του θεου (P^{45} A D^1 W Θ $f^{1,13}$ 33 *Byz* lat sy; Marcion^E). P^{75} just omits αυτου, presumably in line with the copyist's regular practice of omitting personal pronouns.[14] Or it might have been due to harmonization to the parallel in Matt 6:33,[15] although there are several variant readings even there. Kannaday proposes that the secondary reading removed any hint that Jesus might have been trying to remove the Roman Empire and replace it with his own kingdom (or empire).[16] Yet, in the context (12:30, 32) "*his* kingdom" referred to the Father's kingdom, and the secondary variant just specifies this Father as "God." This is clearly the meaning of the original anyway because αυτου (12:31) refers back to God as υμων ο πατηρ in v. 30 and forward to the Father giving them "the kingdom" in v. 32. Moreover, even if the variant *were* removing any thought of Jesus' kingdom and speaking of God's kingdom instead, it is hard to imagine that this would remove the charge that Christians were concerned with an empire other than the Roman Empire. Although Jesus emphasized that his kingdom did not belong to this world in John 18:36, replacing "his kingdom" with "God's kingdom" in Luke 12:31 is hardly comparable. So, the suggestion as to the apologetic motivation for the creation of the variant is unlikely. Instead, it is an equivalent phrase without any significant difference in meaning, with the copyist of P^{75} omitting αυτου perhaps as superfluous or just out of habit.[17]

Luke 19:38

Luke's Gospel contains an account of Jesus' entry into Jerusalem (19:28–44), especially referring to "the whole crowd of the disciples" crying out loudly in praise to God for the miracles they had seen, saying, ευλογημενος ο ερχομενος (ο) βασιλευς εν ονοματι κυριου (19:38). While there are many variants in this verse, the text as cited is most likely original.[18] However,

---

14. Metzger, *Textual Commentary*, 136.
15. Royse, *Scribal Habits*, 691.
16. Kannaday, *Apologetic Discourse*, 213.
17. Pardee, *Scribal Harmonization*, 134 (cf. 170 on Matt 6:33).
18. Metzger, *Textual Commentary*, 144–45.

a few MSS (W 1216 it vg^mss bo^ms) omit ο βαcιλευc,[19] and Kannaday points out that this harmonizes the text of Luke with the parallel Synoptic passages (Matt 21:9, Mark 11:10). He agrees that the omission could have been due to homoioarcton, although it is hard to see how this would have worked. Harmonization to the parallel passages could account for it, but Kannaday suggests that the omission of Jesus as "king" might have been meant to show that Jesus (and the Christians) were not in opposition to the Roman Empire.[20] The age of the MSS supporting this variant, however, is against this since none of them are earlier than the fourth century. Instead, it is likely due to the loss of the word by harmonization rather than being intentionally removed to curtail criticism of Jesus and his followers. After all, the context still contains a reference to η βαcιλεια του θεου (19:11), as well as the clear implication that Jesus was going to return at some time having received his βαcιλεια (19:12, 15). Indeed, it is possible that the variants were derived from the Septuagint (Ps 118:26; Ps 117:26 LXX) and parallel passages (Mark 11:10, John 12:13).[21] Thus, both the context and the existence of other available explanations mitigate against the suggestion that omitting ο βαcιλευc was motivated by a desire to avoid Jesus and the Christians being seen as seditious.

Luke 22:29

In Luke's account of the Last Supper, there is a description of Jesus' response to the disciples' discussion as to which of them was the greatest (22:24–30). As part of his reply, Jesus is said to have urged them to be content to be servants, as he was (22:25–27). He referred to their loyalty to him in his "trials," and in contrast promised that they would share in his kingdom (22:28–30). Indeed, Jesus says, καγω διατιθεμαι υμιν καθωc διεθετο μοι ο πατηρ μου βαcιλειαν, with βαcιλειαν implied after υμιν (22:29; cf. 12:32). He also promised them a share "at my table" εν τη βαcιλεια μου (22:30). Some MSS (A Θ 579 sy^h) add διαθηκην in 22:29 in place of the implied βαcιλειαν applying to the disciples. Indeed, MS 579 (XIII AD) inserts διαθηκην there, as well as replacing βαcιλειαν with διαθηκην at the end of the verse. Kannaday suggests that since βαcιλειαν could have been

---

19. Bezae omits ο βαcιλευc here, but it adds ευλογημενοc ο βαcιλευc after κυριου.
20. Kannaday, *Apologetic Discourse*, 213.
21. Metzger, *Textual Commentary*, 144–45; Marshall, *Gospel of Luke*, 715.

misconstrued as having political overtones, it was deliberately replaced with "religious language," reflecting apologetic concerns.[22]

However, while "religious language" has been substituted for potentially political language, the new reading is quite awkward, with the Father "conferring" a kingdom on Jesus (except in 579) but Jesus "making" a covenant with the disciples (or "leaving" to them a last will and testament). This would involve an adjustment of the meaning of διατιθεμαι to fit the variant reading when it does not make clear sense. Further, even the MSS with the variant reading (except for 579) retain βαcιλειαν at the end, so Jesus is said to have been given a kingdom by his Father. This could still have political overtones, and MS 579 is very late anyway. Although it is difficult to account for διαθηκην in the variant, it might have come to mind after the cup being called η καινη διαθηκη in 22:20, especially since the cognate verb διατιθεμαι appears at the beginning of 22:29. This is purely speculative, but it is unlikely that διαθηκην was added to remove political overtones because βαcιλειαν still occurs at the end of the verse—even in the MSS that replace the implied βαcιλειαν with διαθηκην (except for 579)—as well as βαcιλεια, θρονων, and κρινοντεc in 22:30. All of these could sound political. The small change in this variant would have made little difference.

Luke 23:42

Luke's passion narrative includes a portrayal of one of the two κακουργοι crucified on either side of Jesus expressing his faith in him as the Messiah (23:32–33, 39–41), and asking him, μνηcθητι μου οταν ελθηc εις την βαcιλειαν cου (23:42). Kannaday refers to the variation between εις and εν in the MSS, suggesting that εν τη βαcιλεια cου sounds more like a "return to the Roman earth," but εις την βαcιλειαν cου sounds like Jesus being received into God's paradise. This distinction is difficult to maintain, however, in view of the fluidity between these two prepositions in Koine Greek.[23] Kannaday also refers to the variant reading in D, where εις την βαcιλειαν cου is replaced by εν τη ημερα της ελευcεωc cου, thus removing την βαcιλειαν altogether. This is clearly not original, but he suggests that it was "a deliberate effort on the part of a scribe to discard the political

---

22. Kannaday, *Apologetic Discourse*, 213–14.

23. BDAG, 326–30; GELS, 196–97, 231–33; Zerwick, *Biblical Greek*, 33–37. Cf. Bovon, *Luke* 3, 311.

Scribes, Theology, and Apologetics

vernacular in favor of theological phraseology."[24] Yet, while it is difficult to know how this reading arose, whoever was responsible for it seems to have been somewhat confused since he also referred to Jesus responding to the criminal as the one "who was scolding" him (τω επιπληccoντι), which is a strange reading in the context when the person in view was appealing to Jesus as his Savior.[25]

Thus, the variant readings for βαcιλεια in Luke were probably the result of several factors including linguistic variation in Koine Greek and the occurrence of a multitude of strange readings in D, so there is no clear evidence that they were introduced to avoid a political implication being drawn from the original.

Pilate as Innocent?

The next series of variants are said to have been created in order to exonerate Pilate from responsibility for Jesus' death and shift the blame onto the Jewish authorities and the Jewish people. Kannaday states that the effect of this was to enhance the claim that Jesus was innocent, while others have sought to locate this trend as an example of a growing anti-Judaic bias in early Christianity. Kannaday shows that the theme of Jesus' innocence is certainly present in the passion narratives as a whole, but he aims to examine if there is a progression in how Pilate is portrayed as time went on, making him less responsible for the death of Jesus.

He notes how Matthew's Gospel portrays Jesus as "innocent" (δικαιoc, 27:19), and records that Pilate washed his hands of the matter (27:24) and that πac o λαoc accepted responsibility for Jesus' death (27:25). In Luke, Jesus was declared innocent three times (24:4, 13, 22) and the supervising centurion also declared him δικαιoc (23:47). In John's Gospel, Pilate declared him innocent (18:38) and was unsettled when he heard about his claims to be "the Son of God" (19:7–8). Thus, Kannaday suggests that there is "a linear pattern" that shifts responsibility for Jesus' death from Pilate to the Jews, as well as highlighting Pilate's view that Jesus was innocent. He traces the development of both these trends from Mark's Gospel to Matthew, Luke, and John.[26] However, since it is not certain that Mark was written first, or that Matthew and Luke made

---

24. Kannaday, *Apologetic Discourse*, 214–15.
25. Cf. Bovon, *Luke 3*, 312n161.
26. Kannaday, *Apologetic Discourse*, 216–19.

use of Mark, or that John was written much later, the element of a "linear pattern" or "trend" is difficult to sustain. Further, even Mark's Gospel has the elements that are present in the others—Pilate's amazement at Jesus' response to the charges (Mark 15:5), his attempts to release him (15:6–10) being opposed by the Jewish authorities (15:11), the authorities stirring up the crowd (15:11), and Pilate's capitulation to the will of the crowd, despite knowing that Jesus was innocent (15:10, 12–15). While the other Gospels provide more detail in their fuller and more polished narratives, the portrayal is not markedly different.

Kannaday also traces these themes in the writings of the apologists and early noncanonical writings, referring to studies in which the portrayal of Pilate as a ruthless governor by Philo, Josephus, and "the sources for Luke 13:1–2" are contrasted with the picture of him as a "perceptive politician" in the canonical Gospels.[27] However, the contrast between the portrait of Pilate in the Gospels and in contemporary sources is not as clear as it might seem because the available material in the Gospels is so limited. Apart from two references in Luke (3:1, 13:1), all the references to Pilate concern his dealings with the trial of Jesus (Matt 27, Mark 15, Luke 23, John 18–19). The two earlier references in Luke mention him as ἡγεμονεύων (3:1) and as the one responsible for the brutal killing of Jews in Jerusalem (13:1), which clearly implies severity. Therefore, since the only other occasions when Pilate's actions are recounted in the Gospels relate to Jesus' trial and crucifixion, it would be unwise to draw too stark a contrast with other sources based on these alone. It may be that later sources "softened" Pilate's responsibility for Jesus' death in various ways, but his portrayal in the Gospels is brief in comparison with the material available in the writings of Josephus (*Ant.* 18.35, 55–64, 87–89, 177; *J.W.* 2.169–75) and Philo (*Legat.* 1.299, 304), so it cannot be made to form such a strong contrast.

Kannaday then discusses how Pilate's responsibility seems to have been reduced in the early sources, as well as Jesus' innocence being confirmed. Melito of Sardis laid the blame for Jesus' death squarely on the shoulders of "an Israelite" (frag. 51; *Peri Pascha* 96), and he removed blame for persecution of Christians from Nero and Domitian, adding that Hadrian and his son Antoninus Pius had been just to Christians (frag. 1). Justin Martyr wrote that the Acts of Pilate showed that Jesus' crucifixion fulfilled Scripture (1 *Apol.* 35, 63), although this does not

27. In particular, he refers to Paul Winter's *On the Trial of Jesus* (*Apologetic Discourse*, 220).

necessarily affect Pilate's level of responsibility. Tertullian also referred to Roman gods as witnesses to the truth of Christ (*Apol.* 21), but again it is unclear what this implies about Roman authorities. He also referred to Trajan's response to Pliny not to hunt Christians down and spoke of Marcus Aurelius as the protector of Christians (*Apol.* 5). While not denying Pilate's responsibility for Jesus' death, Tertullian made it clear that the Jewish authorities were ultimately responsible, even suggesting that Pilate was a Christian (*Apol.* 21)! Indeed, the fourth century fictional Acts of Pilate refers to Pilate speaking about Jesus as a King (1.2), ordering that he be treated gently and recounting the imperial standards to bow when he came (1.5). This kind of fictitious material (cf. 2.5, 4.1) clearly betrays a pious age when fantasy was thought to provide support for Christians' faith or at least to give some comfort to those suffering on account of it. There were some who defended Pilate's actions and even portrayed his conversion. I now turn to the variants that are said to derive from a similar trend, highlighting Pilate's innocence and lack of responsibility for Jesus' death, as well as emphasizing Jesus' innocence.

Matthew 27:22

In Matthew's narrative of Jesus' trial before Pilate (27:11–26), he recounts Pilate asking the crowd if they want him to release Jesus or Barabbas (27:21). When the crowd calls for the release of Barabbas, Pilate then asks them, τι ουν ποιηcω ιηcουν τον λεγομενον χριcτον; (27:22). Some MSS (D it), however, read ποιηcωμεν rather than ποιηcω, which Kannaday interprets as removing personal blame from Pilate and drawing the crowd into the decision-making process.[28] This means, however, that the variant would be drawing the account closer to Mark's narrative, where Pilate asks, το ουν θελετε ποιηcω; (Mark 15:12), with their wish as the deciding factor. So, the variant reading in Matthew makes the crowd partly responsible for the decision but no more than in Mark. Indeed, the original narrative in Matthew preserves Pilate asking the crowd whom they wished to be released (27:17, 21) and bowing to their wishes (27:22, 24). He apparently still had the right to grant their wish or not. Of course, Matthew's narrative goes on to relate Pilate washing his hands (27:24) and "the people" accepting responsibility (27:25), but it was still οι cτρατιωται του ηγεμονοc who took him away, treated him

---

28. Kannaday, *Apologetic Discourse*, 224.

roughly, and led him off to be crucified (27:27–31). It was, then, still "a Roman execution" in Matthew, however much Pilate wished to remove the blame from himself and whoever had been the moving force behind the crucifixion. So, the use of ποιηcωμεν rather than ποιηcω would not have made much difference. The suggestion that Matthew's portrayal of Pilate as less responsible by the insertion of ποιηcωμεν in some MSS is thus unfounded, even if the *joint responsibility* of Pilate and the crowd is heightened. In fact, the first-person plural might not have been meant to refer to Pilate and the crowd at all (the inclusive "we"), but Pilate and his Roman retainers (the exclusive "we").

Matthew 27:22–23

In Matt 27:22 some MSS (L *Byz* c f) insert αυτω into the description of the crowd's response to Pilate's question, so λεγουcιν αυτω παντεc, and in 27:23 Pilate's response, introduced by ο δε εφη, has αυτοιc added in one of the two secondary variants: 1) ο δε ηγεμων εφη (A W Byz sy^h); 2) λεγει αυτοιc ο ηγεμων (D f^1 lat sy^p mae bo). Kannaday suggests that inserting the pronouns highlights the contrast between the crowd and Pilate, but it is difficult to see how this "suggestively reduces the enmity between Jesus and Pilate, and therefore, by implication, Christians and Rome."[29] This appears to be a rather oversubtle reading of the significance of the variants, and in fact inserting ο ηγεμων highlights Pilate's position as the one ultimately responsible. So, the proposed motivation for the variants is unproven, with no real significance clearly intended in either.

Matthew 27:24

Matthew's account continues by relating Pilate "washing his hands" of the whole affair απεναντι του οχλου and then stating that he was innocent of the blood of "this man" (τουτου, 27:24). One MS (Θ) replaces οχλου with λαου, and others (ℵ W $f^{1,13}$ 33 *Byz* lat sy^p,h sa^mss mae bo) read του δικαιου τουτου instead of just τουτου. Kannaday notes that this insertion of Pilate's statement of Jesus' innocence might have been harmonizing to Pilate's threefold declaration of Jesus' innocence in Luke (23:14, 16, 22), as well as the centurion's statement that he was δικαιοc (23:47).[30] But Jesus' inno-

---

29. Kannaday, *Apologetic Discourse*, 224.
30. Kannaday, *Apologetic Discourse*, 224–25. Wettlaufer argues that του δικαιου τουτου

cence had been stated twice already in Matthew's narrative, Judas using αθωoc (27:4) and Pilate's wife employing δικαιoc (27:19), so inserting του δικαιου here adds little to the narrative.[31] Nor does it take much away from the portrayal of Pilate's role in the matter.[32] The use of λαoc in Θ probably refers specifically to "the Jews," but λαoc is frequently used in Matthew's Gospel with this meaning, a number of instances occurring in the chapters both before (25:32; 26:3, 5, 47; 27:1, 9) and after 27:24 (27:25, 64). So, it is unlikely that one more reference to ο λαoc adds much to the specificity with which the Jews are mentioned in these chapters in relation to Jesus' death. The suggested significance of these variants is again overly subtle since they would hardly have been noticed in the narrative, so it is unlikely that anyone would have inserted them with the suggested purpose in mind.

Matthew 27:26

The final variant cited in this section is in the note that Pilate released Barabbas but had Jesus flogged and παρεδωκεν ινα cταυρωθη (Matt 27:26). Some MSS, however, add αυτοιc after παρεδωκεν (ℵ[2a vid] D Θ *f* lat sy[s] sa[ms] mae), and a few (D Θ it) read cταυρωcωcιν αυτον instead of ινα cταυρωθη. Kannaday interprets this as showing that "the Jews" are thus being given total responsibility for Jesus' death, at least in the second variant.[33] In a similar vein, Ehrman refers to the same readings in D as signs of "the rise of Christian anti-Semitism,"[34] and he infers that αυτοιc was added "to heighten even further the Jewish culpability in Jesus' death," so that he was handed over "in order that *they* [the Jews] might crucify him."[35]

However, there are reasons to be cautious about drawing these conclusions. Pilate's words need mean no more than that he was giving in to their wishes. After all, Matthew had just written that he had symbolically washed his hands of the whole affair, and then said υμειc οψεcθε (27:24), which is apparently an idiom for passing on responsibility to them, just as the religious authorities had said cυ οψη to Judas earlier

---

was original ("Second Glance"). Davies and Allison suggest that του δικαιου was original but omitted by scribal leap, presumably του δικαιου τουτου (*Matthew*, 3:590n52).

31. Pace France, *Matthew*, 1047n11.

32. Wettlaufer, "Second Glance," 248–50. Pace Metzger, *Textual Commentary*, 56–57; Hagner, *Matthew 14–28*, 826nc.

33. Kannaday, *Apologetic Discourse*, 225.

34. Ehrman, "Text of the Gospels."

35. Ehrman, *Misquoting*, 193–94. Cf. Ehrman, "Text of the Gospels," 89–90.

when he expressed remorse for his actions (27:4). Further, the previous clause states that απελυcεν αυτοιc, but this did not allow the crowd to engage in their own lynching, since Matthew goes on to relate that Pilate's soldiers took Jesus away in preparation for his crucifixion (27:27–31). The function of passive verbs is often to leave the subject vague. Since it is οι cτρατιωται του ηγεμονοc who take charge of Jesus (27:27), it would be most natural to take the implied actors of the passive verb cταυρωθη as the soldiers, as well as to take them as the ones who flogged him, the ones to whom Pilate handed him over (αυτοιc, 27:26), and the ones who crucified (cταυρωcωcιν) him. Moreover, the addition of αυτοιc adds little to what appears already in 27:24, and the change from the singular passive verb to the plural active (with the addition of "him") is probably only a general reference to "people" performing an action, a common Greek idiom to express an indefinite plural (cf. Matt 7:16, Luke 12:20).[36] Such third person plural generalizations occur elsewhere in relation to Jesus' crucifixion, such as in Acts 13:29, where it might seem that "the Jews" were in mind (cf. 13:28). But Paul's address relates how "they" carried out what had been written in the OT about him and "they" took him down from the cross and laid him in a tomb, while the passion narratives in the Gospels are clear that the Roman soldiers crucified Jesus and Joseph of Arimathea was responsible for taking his body down from the cross and putting it in his tomb (e.g., Luke 23:50–54). So also in Matt 27:26, the addition of αυτοιc in D probably refers to the Roman soldiers, not "the Jews," and the change from cταυρωθη to cταυρωθωcιν αυτον is not an obvious sign of a desire to lessen Pilate's role in Jesus' death. Nor would these variants heighten the level of responsibility of the Jews in the account of Jesus' crucifixion.

Therefore, the minor changes mentioned do not show the influence of apologetics on the creation of variant readings, as if Pilate was alleviated of ultimate responsibility for Jesus' death in order to curry favor with imperial authorities. Nor do they show the influence of an anti-Judaic bias or the shifting of blame from Pilate to be more acceptable to Roman political authorities by portraying Rome in conflict with Judaism, not with the Christians. The evidence does not support these proposals, and the variants can be more easily explained as slightly more expansive forms of the original account.

---

36. Cf. *SSG*, 751–52; Wallace, *Grammar*, 402–3.

Secrets among Themselves?

In the next section, Kannaday reviews variants possibly relevant to the suspicions of pagan critics regarding Christians meeting in secret. Writers such as Celsus (*Cels.* 1.7) and Fronto (Minucius Felix, *Oct.* 9.4) voiced such charges, with the implication that secret meetings at night might have had to do with magic, and apologists like Origen responded vigorously to these charges (*Cels.* 1.7). Kannaday acknowledges that this motif is not obvious in the case of the following variants, but he suggests that they could *possibly* refer to such accusations against Christians and hence *might* have been created with apologetic aims in mind.

Mark 1:44

Mark recounts an incident when Jesus "cleansed" a leper and then urged him, ορα μηδενι μηδεν ειπης αλλ υπαγε. Some MSS, however, do not include μηδεν (ℵ A D W f^{13} 33), which could be the result of homoioarcton (μηδενι μηδεν).[37] Kannaday, however, interprets this as an attempt to remove Jesus' concern with "concealing his work of healing," which could have been misconstrued as a portrayal of Jesus as a magician not wishing his actions to be subjected to public scrutiny. Removing μηδεν would then shift the emphasis from secrecy to immediacy.[38] This is too subtle, however, since the variant reading preserves the command, ορα μηδενι ειπης, so it still conveys an exhortation to silence. Kannaday interprets the variant to mean that the leper should go straight to the priest without engaging in conversation along the way, but the original could just as easily be interpreted in the same way. The distinction in meaning between the variant and the original is, then, minimal, as there is no real difference between "not saying anything to anyone" and "not speaking to anyone." In fact, μηδεν might have been omitted due to harmonization to the parallels in Matt 8:4 and Luke 5:14,[39] or as a superfluous word,[40] or by parablepsis, as noted above, so there is little evidence that it had the proposed apologetic significance.

---

37. Haelewyck reviews the evidence for the originality of μηδεν without coming to a firm conclusion ("Healing of a Leper," 32).

38. Kannaday, *Apologetic Discourse*, 227–28.

39. Collins, *Mark*, 177–78nc.

40. Pardee, *Scribal Harmonization*, 340.

Mark 5:33

A variant occurs in an account of an incident where Jesus heals a woman with a long-term debilitating hemorrhage (Mark 5:24b–34). Mark records that, when the woman came to Jesus, she came φοβηθειcα και τρεμουcα (5:33), but some MSS include an explanation for her fear and trembling—διο πεποιηκει (πεποιηκεν, Θ) λαθρα (D Θ it). Kannaday interprets this addition in light of the possibility that the woman's act was "an act of social indiscretion," suggesting that she had shown no indication of restraint.[41] However, the fact that she came up from behind (οπιcθεν, 5:27) and her thought was that if she *just* touched his clothes (εαν αψωμαι καν των ιματιων αυτου), she would be healed (5:28), already shows a level of hesitation and restraint. Thus, the narrative already indicates her "restraint" and, given the social situation, there was good reason for a woman with a hemorrhage to exercise it. The suggestion that her plan was spoken out loud because the verb ελεγεν is used is possible since there is no qualifying phrase like "to herself," but it is highly unlikely in the context. To whom would she have spoken? The idea that a pagan reading this account might have taken her actions as exemplifying "contagious magic" and showing that she was "vulnerable to superstition" is also implausible, and there is no sign of "aggression," as the whole phrase shows (εαν αψωμαι καν). Falling at Jesus' feet when she was discovered is understandable in the circumstances, however much it might have been viewed as obsequious. Rather than demonstrating "a complete lack of decorum at gaining the attention of a previously occupied crowd" her actions show the hesitant and fearful actions of a woman unused to being in the public gaze. Jesus knew that a woman had touched him (περιεβλεπετο ιδειν την τουτο ποιηcαcαν),[42] and she knew that he would probably find her out, so her actions can hardly be construed by a reader as a *faux pas*, except in the eyes of a hostile audience.[43]

Thus, the variant that specifies why she came "afraid and trembling" adds a new dimension to the account, but it would hardly mollify a reader who was already hostile toward a woman acting like that. The mention of "discretion," if that is how we take λαθρα, is already present in the account, as noted above, and the addition of the reason for her fearful approach to Jesus when discovered hardly "tempered her assertiveness

---

41. Kannaday, *Apologetic Discourse*, 228–29.
42. Marcus, *Mark 1–8*, 359.
43. Kannaday, *Apologetic Discourse*, 229–30.

and rendered her humble," so it cannot be used as evidence that the person responsible for the variant had an apologetic motive in mind. Again, the suggested reason for the variant reading is not compelling, however much the social background portrayed is correct. It is much more likely just an explanatory addition.[44]

John 11:28

Another variant that might show apologetic motives in the realm of "secrecy" occurs in John's account of Jesus raising Lazarus (11:1–44). After a discussion with Jesus, Martha went into the house to call her sister Mary, λαθρα ειπουσα (11:28). Some MSS (D lat sy^s) replace λαθρα with σιωπη, but the weight of evidence clearly favors λαθρα as original.[45] Kannaday suggests that the variant σιωπη was created out of a concern that "secrecy language" was ascribed to Christians, so an equivalent alternative was supplied instead. However, σιωπη hardly exhibits "serene gentility," portraying Martha's approach as coming "gently and quietly, not covertly or surreptitiously."[46] While λαθρα could refer to actions done "without others being aware, *secretly*," or "without going through the proper channels, *without the knowledge of, behind the back of*,"[47] surely it is the first of these that is in view here. Expressed differently, it could be defined as "out of public view," with or without hostile intent,[48] but there is no sign of hostility in the narrative. Hence, the meaning of λαθρα here is clearly that Martha approached her sister privately, and a reader would clearly be expected to understand this in the context, which should be the determining factor in ascertaining what connotations might be attributed to λαθρα. A woman spoke to her sister "secretly" or "privately" after her brother's death with the prospect of a revered teacher hinting that he would be able to reverse the situation (11:25–26). Would this convey anything about Christians meeting "in secret" and possibly having "secret" agendas or engaging in secret rites? It seems doubtful. So, although pagan critics were making such accusations about Christians,

---

44. Collins, *Mark*, 275ni.
45. Barrett suggests that σιωπη might have been original (*John*, 397).
46. Kannaday, *Apologetic Discourse*, 230–31.
47. BDAG, 581.
48. GELS, 422.

the suggestion that someone changed this adverb in the narrative with the explicit aim of countering such criticism is unlikely.

Opponents as Evil?

Kannaday then refers to apologists who portrayed opponents of the Christians as wicked and immoral people. Melito referred to Jews as "Christ-killers" (*Pass.* 96, 99), Athenagoras said that opponents of Christ were driven by their evil desires to commit adultery, robbery, and murder (*Apol.* 11.3), and Theophilus redirected criticisms of cannibalism, atheism, and sexual perversion to pagans involved in polytheistic cults (*Autol.* 3.4, 9). Similarly, Aristides redirected charges of sorcery, etc., against Jesus to the Greeks (*Apol.* 8). Kannaday argues that the following textual variants reflect this same tendency to portray the enemies of Christ and Christians as evil.

Luke 5:22

Luke recounts Jesus healing a paralyzed man and some Pharisees responding with accusations that he was a blasphemer (Luke 5:17–21). He then describes how Jesus countered by asking them, τι διαλογιζεcθε εν ταιc καρδιαιc υμων; (5:22). A few Western MSS (D it vg^s) add πονηρα after this, thus defining their thoughts as evil, and this is said to be an example of an emphasis on the malevolence of Jesus' opponents.[49] However, the original sentence is incomplete, because there is no object provided for διαλογιζεcθε,[50] so it would have been natural to add an object of some kind, such as ταυτα, which is in the parallel in Mark 2:8. The content of their hostile thoughts is supplied in two rhetorical questions in Luke 5:21, introduced by the participle λεγοντεc, but this is not enlarged upon in 5:22. Further, the other parallel in Matt 9:4 includes πονηρα. So this variant reading is most likely a harmonization to that passage in the light of the clipped grammatical construction in the original, rather than a

---

49. Kannaday, *Apologetic Discourse*, 232.

50. Muraoka notes how in the LXX διαλογιζομαι often had elements added specifying the person against whom someone was plotting, or such additions as λογιcμουc πονηρουc (1 Macc 11:8) or κακα (Prov 17:12). And even when διαλογιζομαι means "reflect on, muse over," the object of that reflection or musing was frequently added (*GELS*, 153).

variant aiming to make an apologetic point about the wickedness of the opponents of Jesus and his followers.

Luke 11:39

The context of this variant is Luke's account of a dinner held at a Pharisee's house during which Jesus responded to his surprise at the fact that Jesus did not wash his hands before the meal (11:37–54). He began by referring to his host as a member of the Pharisees, νυν υμεις οι φαρισαιοι (11:39), and Kannaday observes that two MSS (D b) add υποκριται after οι φαρισαιοι, which could be characterizing opponents as more evil than in the original.[51] Yet, it might also be a harmonization to the parallel text in Matt 23:25,[52] and indeed φαρισαιοι υποκριται is repeated six times in that same chapter (23:13, 15, 23, 25, 27, 29). Clearly, anyone familiar with Matt 23 could have added υποκριται to the text of Luke 11:39 out of habit, particularly when Luke's account of Jesus' diatribe continues with repeated sentences beginning with ουαι υμιν (11:42, 43, 44, 46, 47, 52) as in Matthew (23:13, 15, 16, 23, 25, 27, 29). So, the addition of υποκριται in Luke 11:39 is more likely the result of harmonization to the familiar phrase φαρισαιοι υποκριται in Matt 23:35 (and the whole chapter), rather than a desire to score an apologetic point about the wickedness of Jesus' opponents, especially considering that the following condemnation of the Pharisees is still quite severe (το δε εσωθεν υμων γεμει αρπαγης και πονηριας).

Luke 11:44

In the same context as the previous passage, Jesus is said to pronounce a woe on the Pharisees, describing them as being like unmarked graves— ουαι υμιν οτι εστε ως τα μνημεια τα αδηλα (11:44). Some MSS, however, add γραμματεις και φαρισαιοι υποκριται after υμιν (A D W Θ f^{13} Byz it sy^{p,h} bo^{pt}). Kannaday takes this as an apologetically motivated reading, emphasizing the evil and hypocritical nature of Jesus' critics.[53] However, ουαι υμιν is used six times in this diatribe, twice followed by τοις νομικοις (11:46, 52) and twice by τοις φαρισαιοις (11:42, 43), so it would not be

---

51. Kannaday, *Apologetic Discourse*, 232.
52. Fitzmyer, *Luke X–XXIV*, 947.
53. Kannaday, *Apologetic Discourse*, 232.

surprising for someone to add γραμματεις και φαρισαιοι υποκριται, using the more common word γραμματεις (for νομικοις), and indeed the entire phrase from the parallel passage in Matt 23, where it appears six times (23:13, 15, 23, 25, 27, 29). Thus, the variant draws on elements in Luke 11, as well as reflecting the exact wording of the repeated phrase in Matt 23. So, this variant reading is likely to have been caused by taking wording from Luke 11 as well as harmonizing to Matt 23:27, rather than being an attempt to inject more heat into the original description.[54]

Luke 20:23

The closing chapters of Luke's Gospel contain a discussion between Jesus and agents sent by the religious authorities on the matter of paying taxes to Rome (20:20–26). In Luke's narrative, he records that Jesus recognized αυτων την πανουργιαν (20:23), but some MSS (C* D a e l r¹ sy[s,c,hmg]) read αυτων την πονηριαν instead. On this basis, Kannaday proposes that this is an elevation of the level of criticism with an apologetic edge, designed to paint Jesus' opponents in darker colors.[55] This variant, however, could easily have happened when someone made a slip from one word to another (πανουργιαν to πονηριαν), since they begin and end in the same way and have the same number of syllables. Further, the new reading would make sense in the context, so it would be a natural mistake to make, substituting a more common word for a less common one. It is also unclear that the change from πανουργιαν to πονηριαν is really a change that makes the agents appear worse. Is "evil" more serious than "cunning, craftiness, trickery"? It is certainly a more general term, but not necessarily worse. So, the suggestion is improbable, and it is much more likely that someone made a mistake in reproducing their MS by substituting a similar sounding and more common word that made sense in the context.

Luke 6:11

Luke records Jesus responding to criticism by Pharisees about his disciples picking grain in the fields and eating it on a Sabbath day (6:1–5) and then healing a man with a shriveled hand on another Sabbath (6:6–11). Then the Pharisees' reaction forms the high point of the narrative,

54. Cf. Fitzmyer, *Luke X–XXIV*, 949.
55. Kannaday, *Apologetic Discourse*, 232.

αυτοι δε επλησθησαν ανοιας και διελαλουν προς αλληλους τι αν ποιησαιεν τω ιησου (6:11). Bezae however has the SR διελογιζοντο προς αλληλους πως απολεςωςιν αυτον instead of διελαλουν προς αλληλους τι αν ποιησαιεν τω ιησου. The variant reading thus changes their deliberations about "what they might do about Jesus" to "how they might destroy him," a change that certainly provides a more negative portrayal, although "doing something about" Jesus probably implied much the same as destroying him anyway. Nevertheless, the wording is clearly more negative, so Kannaday suggests that this was done intentionally in order to paint Jesus' opponents as more wicked than in the original text.[56]

However, Luke first described their reaction as επλησθησαν ανοιας, where ανοια could refer to being out of one's mind or "foolish," as in the Septuagint,[57] but in this context it clearly refers to "senseless anger," "fury," or "madness."[58] Further, both διαλαλεω (6:11) and διαλογισμοι (6:8) have negative connotations, so the portrayal of the Pharisees in the original reading is quite negative—plotting against Jesus and "mad with fury."[59] So, the variant that refers to the Pharisees plotting how to get rid of Jesus is only marginally stronger than the original one with its negative overtones and probably derives from someone harmonizing this passage with one or both of the parallels in Mark 3:6 (συμβουλιον εδιδουν κατ αυτου οπως αυτον απολεςωςιν) or Matt 12:14 (συμβουλιον ελαβον κατ αυτου οπως αυτον απολεςωςιν). The variant is almost identical to those texts, but without Luke's literary use of the uncommon optative mood (ποιησαιεν), which could well have been one factor motivating a copyist to modify it. Thus, the variant is most likely due to harmonization to a parallel passage or clarification of an uncommon grammatical construction, or both, rather than being designed to portray the Pharisees as worse than in the original text.

John 5:16

John's Gospel recounts Jesus healing a long-term invalid next to the Pool of Bethesda in Jerusalem (5:1–15) and "the Jews" becoming hostile toward

56. Kannaday, *Apologetic Discourse*, 232–33.
57. *GELS*, 54. Cf. *LSJ*, 145.
58. *BDAG*, 84; Fitzmyer, *Luke I–IX*, 611. In the patristic period, there was another development—ανοια could still mean "folly" but in certain contexts could mean "distress of mind, despair" (*PGL*, 147).
59. Bovon, *Luke 1*, 204.

him as a result (5:16). Some MSS (A Θ f^{13} *Byz* e q f r¹ sy[p,h] bo[pt]) then add και εζητουν αυτον αποκτειναι, referring to "the Jews," which in John's Gospel seems to refer to the Jewish authorities. Kannaday suggests that this portrays them being more opposed to Jesus and more evil than the original.[60] Yet, hints of hostility have already appeared in the narrative, with "the Jews" questioning the man who had been healed as to why he was carrying his mat on the Sabbath day (5:9–10) and then wishing to know who had told him to carry it (5:11–12). There is also the ominous note that the man finally informed on Jesus after he saw him later in the temple (5:14–15), and this is highlighted later when we are told that δια τουτο ουν μαλλον εζητουν αυτον οι ιουδαιοι αποκτειναι, οτι . . . ελυεν το cαββατον (5:18). So, the variant reading carries on the note of earlier hostility and anticipates what occurs shortly afterwards, beginning with the introduction (και δια τουτο . . . δια τουτο ουν) and continuing in 5:18 (εδκιωχον οι ιουδαιοι τον ιηcουν και εζητουν αυτον αποκτειναι . . . εζητουν αυτον οι ιουδαιοι αποικτειναι). So, the variant is only drawing out the hostility already present in the account and leading into the material in the context almost immediately afterwards. Hence, it could have arisen from someone who was familiar with the story in this narrative inserting remembered material that would come a little later in the story anyway. Further, John's Gospel has a large amount of material dealing with "the Jews" plotting to kill Jesus (7:1, 19, 20, 25; 8:37, 40), so anyone familiar with the Gospel might well have accidentally inserted this phrase in view of the comments in the context. This is a more likely scenario for the origin of this variant than seeing it as the result of an apologetic desire to portray Jesus' enemies as worse than in the original. Further, with all the negative portrayal in the context, a reader would hardly notice the change, so it is unlikely that a copyist would have made the change for the suggested reason.

Matthew 23:25, 26:3

Two other instances that might show copyists wishing to depict the scribes and Pharisees as more wicked than in the original text occur in Matt 23 and 26. In a number of "woes" to scribes and Pharisees (Matt 23:1–39), Jesus charges them with being hypocrites—outwardly clean but inwardly γεμουcιν εξ αρπαγηc και ακραcιαc (23:25). Some MSS, however, have other readings for ακραcιαc: αδικιαc (C f sy[p]), ακαθαρcιαc (*l* 844* lat sy[s]

---

60. Kannaday, *Apologetic Discourse*, 233.

co), ακραcιαc αδικιαc (W sy^h), or πλεονεξιαc (M pc). Kannaday maintains that each of these variants "intensifies a negative trait on the part of Jesus' enemies," so they are portrayed as worse than in the original.[61]

The suggestion, however, is unconvincing for several reasons. First, the characterization of the original criticism as "a lack of discipline" vastly reduces the charge that they were "hypocrites" because they wished to appear good on the outside but were secretly "full of greed and self-indulgence" (γεμουcιν εξ αρπαγηc και ακραcιαc), not just a lack of discipline.[62] In any case, the criticism was not just regarding those characteristics, but the hypocrisy that wished to parade itself as religious in the eyes of the watching world, while being inwardly dominated by selfishness (cf. 23:5a). That is, it referred to a show of ritual "purity" without the corresponding inward and ethical "purity."[63] In view of this cutting criticism in the original, the variants which refer to αδικια, ακαθαρcια, or πλεονεξια are not discernibly different in intensity. So, αδικια is a more general reference to unrighteous behavior (like πονηρια in the parallel Luke 11:39); ακαθαρcια draws on the imagery of "purity" to mean "impurity" like the later charge of being like whitewashed tombs (looking good on the outside, but on the inside γεμουcιν οcτεων νεκρων και παcηc ακαθαρcιαc, 23:27); and πλεονεξια (greed) is almost a synonym for αρπαγη except that it focusses on the desire for gain. Since all the variant readings with words replacing ακραcια are similar in meaning to the original and either draw on vocabulary in the surrounding context or in a parallel in Luke, they do not portray the scribes and Pharisees as worse than in the original and certainly do not change a mere "lack of discipline" to "spiritual and moral decay" or "character assassination."[64] Clearly, character assassination was already present in the original, as well as in the whole of Matt 23, and the variants were probably glosses to clarify a word that might have seemed a little inappropriate in the context.[65]

The second text occurs in a short account of the chief priests and elders gathering in the high priest's house and plotting to arrest Jesus surreptitiously and kill him (Matt 26:3-4). Other MSS, however, insert

---

61. Kannaday, *Apologetic Discourse*, 233–34.

62. BDAG, 133, ἁρπαγή 3; 38, ακραcια; *GELS*, 22. France describes the two terms together functioning as "a hendiadys denoting an unrestrained selfishness which rides roughshod over the rights and interests of others" (*Matthew*, 866n6).

63. Cf. Luz, *Matthew 21–28*, 126–28.

64. Nolland suggests that ακαθαρcιαc is drawn from 23:27 (*Matthew*, 930–31ne).

65. Metzger, *Textual Commentary*, 50.

into the list of those present on this occasion και οι γραμματεις (*Byz* it sy[p,h]) or και οι φαρισαιοι (W). Kannaday acknowledges that both additions might have originated as harmonizations to the parallels in Mark 14:2 and Luke 22:2 (οι γραμματεις) or John 11:47 (και οι φαρισαιοι), but he suggests instead that they were deliberately included here by copyists wishing to make these groups responsible for the death of Jesus in a way that was not originally present.[66]

However, the scribes are frequently mentioned in Matthew's Gospel as being opposed to Jesus (5:20, 9:3, 12:28, 15:1, 16:21, 20:18, 21:15, et al.), often in conjunction with chief priests (2:4, 16:21, 20:18, 21:15, 27:41) or Pharisees (5:20; 12:38; 15:1; 23:2, 13, 15, 23, 25, 27, 29), and especially in relation to the part they played in Jesus' arrest and crucifixion (16:21, 20:18, 21:15, 26:57, 27:41). It would be natural, then, for someone to accidentally insert a reference to them in this context, especially in view of the parallels in Mark and Luke. This is much more likely than this variant being an attempt to falsely include them in the list of those responsible for Jesus' death. The narrative of the whole Gospel makes it clear that this was already the case, even without this reference. Further, right from the early parts of Matthew's narrative the Pharisees are portrayed as being opposed to Jesus (9:11, 34; 12:2, 24; et al.), as well as being involved in plots to have him killed (12:14; 22:15; 27:62). Again, it would be easy for someone to add them into this list, particularly in view of the parallel in John 11:47 since they were clearly involved, but this one addition hardly increases their level of responsibility for Jesus' crucifixion in the narrative. The account elsewhere makes it clear that they were intimately involved in and highly responsible for Jesus' death, and this one addition would add little extra, so a copyist is unlikely to have added it for the proposed reason. The contention, then, that these two references were specifically designed to describe the scribes and Pharisees as worse than they are portrayed in the original text, especially in their responsibility for Jesus' crucifixion, does not carry conviction.

GENERAL CONCLUSION

In chapters 5–8 I have assessed proposals put forward that certain variant readings in the NT Gospels were designed to respond to criticisms leveled against Jesus and the Christians by pagan critics. Kannaday offers

---

66. Kannaday, *Apologetic Discourse*, 233.

Scribes, Theology, and Apologetics

a clear account of pagan criticisms in the second and third centuries, as well as providing a detailed report of responses to those criticisms on the part of early Christian apologists. However, the overall conclusion is flawed for a number of reasons. First, on the few occasions where a variant is proposed as original in contrast to the more generally accepted view, the reasons given are not convincing, so the conclusions drawn do not follow. Second, certain arguments in support of the meaning and significance of the original reading are not compelling, either in regard to aspects of the variant readings or the relationship between the original and the variant. Word meaning and grammar in Koine Greek are also sometimes not considered as they should be. Even when an argument might show that a variant *has* been deliberately inserted, the interpretation of its significance is frequently oversubtle. On the whole, then, although a few instances may be accepted where Kannaday's argument holds and a variant does seem to have been created to respond to criticism of Christ and the Christians, the bulk of the instances cited cannot be shown to be valid, as they are usually unlikely explanations for the origin of the variants, especially in light of other more probable mundane explanations of scribal slips. Third, it is often assumed that a reader would see the proposed difference in meaning, but the immediate context or the entire context of the Gospel usually weighs against this. So, if a reader would hardly notice the change, a copyist would have been unlikely to insert the variant to achieve that difference in meaning.

In Kannaday's final chapter he notes that we know little about the copyists of the NT documents, especially in the early period, but he aimed to contribute to the field of study of textual variants as a window into the history of early Christianity.[67] Yet, since it seems that the early copyists were generally professional scribes and that they were not necessarily Christians by conviction, this takes away from the force of arguments presented in relation to early variant readings. It would be as well to address this issue, although some steps have been taken in this regard in my recent study of the handwriting and layout of early Greek Christian MSS.[68]

Kannaday alludes to the criticisms leveled against Christians by critics such as Celsus and Porphyry, along with responses to these charges by apologists, but he makes too much of Origen's citation of Celsus's words that allude to "believers" who "alter the original text of the gospel

---

67. Kannaday, *Apologetic Discourse*, 237–38.
68. See Mugridge, *Copying*.

APOLOGETIC FOR CHRISTIANS IN THE ROMAN EMPIRE?

three or four times or several times over" and "change its character to enable them to deny difficulties in the face of criticism" (*Cels.* 2.27). He takes this as evidence for, or at least consonant with, variant readings in the MSS of the NT being inserted that "modified the text of the Gospels under the influence of apologetic interests."[69] But Celsus's words do not refer to such changes, as he then mentions Marcion and the Valentinians (*Cels.* 2.27), which implies a reference to alternative Gospels.[70] Of course, the NT documents were not copied in a vacuum, but the variant readings that are said to show the "fingerprints" of the copyists and, in particular, variants that were "intentional in nature and apologetic in character,"[71] have been shown on the whole to have more likely explanations relating to their literary context in the Gospels and the social and historical context of the copyists. Claims to have uncovered variants that show copyists concerned to rebut various criticisms of Christ and the Christians have been shown to lack certainty on the whole, partly due to issues of methodology and partly due to the hypothetical attribution of motives to the creators of the variants.[72] It is possible that a variant might have been useful to support the claim that Christians were not as foolish or bad or socially subversive and deserving of suspicion as many people thought, or that Jesus' enemies (and, by implication, those of Christians as well) were worse than the public realized, or that the role of the Jews in Jesus' crucifixion was greater than the role of the Roman officials. But it is not clear that they were created with these purposes in mind.

It should also be remembered that, while it is a valid historical exercise to enquire why the variant readings of the NT MSS were created, this is a highly speculative area, where we are not only noting variant readings but asking why someone inserted them. This usually includes a high level of conjecture, so any conclusions should take this into account. It is probably only possible to know something about the personal interests of the copyists if we concentrate on individual copyists in particular MSS,[73] but Kannaday has attempted to draw on the vast array of variant readings in all the MSS available. So, the conclusion that "Christian copyists engaged in the reproduction of the New Testament Gospels sometimes altered

---

69. Kannaday, *Apologetic Discourse*, 240.
70. Chadwick, *Origen*, 90n2.
71. Kannaday, *Apologetic Discourse*, 240.
72. Cf. Kruger, review of *Apologetic Discourse*, 824–27.
73. Chapa, "Contribution," 132–33.

Scribes, Theology, and Apologetics

their texts in the interest of apologetic concerns"[74] has not been proven in general and in fact is unlikely, except in a small number of cases.

Nor has it been shown that variants such as the endings of Mark's Gospel were intentionally created with apologetic ends in mind. The concern that textual critics keep a keen eye on the historical context, both of the original NT texts and of the MSS that transmit them, is certainly a valid one. But we also need to consider the limitations of the data and hence the limitations on the certainty with which we may draw conclusions. The role of patristic writings is also an important aspect of Kannaday's study, as are the writings of those who wrote about the Christian faith in the early centuries, but our knowledge of those writings is also subject to the vicissitudes of history, just as much as the NT documents.

Thus, the aim to locate the period in which variants entered the historical tradition is a much more difficult one to fulfill than might be thought, so the caveat that "we must be careful not to assert more than we can positively maintain" and admit "what we do not know"[75] is clearly a valid one. Further, the context in antiquity should certainly play a part in textual criticism.[76] As Kannaday notes, "Copyists labored for a variety of reasons," and it is usually difficult to show that a variant was "deliberate." As he observes, the changes were "subtle rather than blatant,"[77] but my review has shown that the interpretation of the significance of variants offered is often too subtle.[78]

Kannaday's conclusion that such copyists showed that they felt able to change the text at will and hence that they did not hold to the sacredness of the NT documents that they were reproducing is also in need of qualification. If the copyists were not Christians, then, of course, they had no such thoughts at all. They were merely copyists, who succeeded to varying degrees in reproducing the exemplar with which they were supplied. If they were Christians, most of them were still professional scribes, and the background of their craft, in which their task was to produce an accurate copy, would surely have had an influence on the way in which they went about their task, attempting to reproduce their text as

---

74. Kannaday, *Apologetic Discourse*, 244.

75. Kannaday, *Apologetic Discourse*, 246.

76. Kannaday, *Apologetic Discourse*, 247.

77. Kannaday, *Apologetic Discourse*, 248.

78. Others have given more positive reviews. See Haines-Eitzen, review of *Apologetic Discourse*. Gurtner gives only qualified approval (Gurtner, review of *Apologetic Discourse*; cf. Knust, review of *Apologetic Discourse*).

accurately as possible. It is always possible, of course, that some might have wished to inject their views into their MSS, and it seems that this did happen occasionally, perhaps more as time went on and more copyists were Christians. As Kannaday writes, "Certainly they understood their function to be that of copyists, not authors, and certainly not evangelists," but it has yet to be proven that "the survival of the movement and the perpetuity of the Gospel appears to have been for them a more profound responsibility than the stoic reproduction of a manuscript."[79] Finally, his summary of the process of the transmission of the NT documents by the numerous copyists responsible for their reproduction is as follows: "Thus the text of the Gospel was reproduced and transmitted, but not without first being interpreted and modified—revised, buttressed, corrected, harmonized, refined, polished, stylized, abbreviated, enhanced, or otherwise altered."[80] It would seem, from our study of the variants cited, that this characterization of the process is exaggerated, since it implies the instability of the NT text to a degree that has not been established and that assumes conclusions that have yet to be proven.

---

79. Kannaday, *Apologetic Discourse*, 249.
80. Kannaday, *Apologetic Discourse*, 250.

9

Conclusion

IN THIS CHAPTER, I draw together conclusions reached in the previous chapters in which I have reviewed Bart Ehrman's book *The Orthodox Corruption of Scripture* and Wayne Kannaday's *Apologetic Discourse and the Scribal Tradition*. The issues raised and the conclusions reached here are not markedly different from those outlined in my companion volume, *Scribes, Motives, and Manuscripts*, so readers will find much of that material restated here, albeit in an altered form. Both Ehrman and Kannaday show a detailed acquaintance with the issues, whether regarding Greek NT MSS, versions, or patristic authors. They have also provided clear and balanced descriptions of early "heresies" and "orthodox" responses, as well as criticisms leveled at early Christians and the responses early Christian apologists made to those criticisms. In general, however, I argue that, while there are a small number of variants that could have been theologically or apologetically motivated, most can be explained more easily on other grounds, although there are many readings whose origins are still unclear. I now outline below conclusions that summarize the argument of this book and indicate their relevance for current debates in the field of NT textual criticism.

THEORIES AND FACTS

As in *Scribes, Motives, and Manuscripts*, many of the suggestions discussed in this book regarding how and why variant readings have found their way into MSS of the Gospels depend on treating the Two (or Four) Source Hypothesis (or "solution") to the Synoptic problem as a fact on which to base arguments. This assumes that Matthew and Luke used a copy of Mark's Gospel, along with other material, when they composed their own Gospels. While this might be the most likely "solution" to the Synoptic problem, its level of certainty is low due to the paucity and complexity of the data. It should continue to be treated as a theory, then, not as a fact on which to build arguments about how the authors of the NT Gospels composed their works and which readings are original and which are secondary. The role of oral tradition is also not given the place it deserves, even in theory, although little is known about the part it played in the composition of the Gospels. I have shown how this issue affects proposals about variants stemming from copyists' desires to insert "orthodox" theology into a MS or to respond to criticism of Christians by outsiders.

Other theories about NT texts are also treated as facts. For example, it is stated that Luke's Gospel and Acts do not exhibit a theology of atonement, and this is then made the basis of arguments regarding textual variants in Luke-Acts. I have shown, however, that there are good reasons to believe that Luke-Acts does exhibit a theology of atonement, just as much as the other Gospels, and this should be considered when evaluating whether Luke 22:19b–20 is the primary or secondary reading.

HISTORY AND FAITH

Most students of the Gospels believe that the endings of Mark's Gospel after 16:8 are secondary, so the issue arises as to whether the Gospel ended at 16:8 or whether it was originally longer but its ending was lost at an early stage. Since a number of other texts from antiquity have lost their beginning, ending, or other parts, and many of the extant NT MSS exist in quite a damaged or diminished state, it seems quite possible that at an early date Mark's Gospel also lost its final few columns of the roll it was written on, or the final page or two if it was already in codex form. I have argued that suggestions about subtle reasons for the shape of the "longer ending" should not be given much credence, although all of the endings certainly constitute "corruptions." If aspects of the endings do show evidence of being created to support certain theological views, then they could be "orthodox corruptions," and it has also been suggested that certain details were inserted for apologetic reasons. However, the historical task is to establish the text of Mark's Gospel, as best we can, even if there are proposals as to why the endings were added in their current form. Only then can the text of Mark's Gospel serve as evidence for "the Jesus of history."

ORIGINAL OR NOT?

Again, I raise the issue of the "original" text. I showed in *Scribes, Motives, and Manuscripts* that editors of other texts from antiquity continue to attempt to establish the original texts of those works, although they no doubt admit that we can never be sure about every detail. In the same way, the question is not whether we can attain the NT text with complete certainty, but what amount of the text can be recovered with reasonable certainty. Clearly, some scholars are happy to live with a measure of uncertainty because they believe that the vast bulk of the original NT text is recoverable. Hence, although scholars may study the secondary variants as possible indicators of the identity and setting of those who produced them, it is also a valid enterprise to continue to work toward an edition of the NT text as near as possible to the original, while recognizing that the task will never be absolutely exact.

PRIMARY AND SECONDARY

I have referred to primary and secondary readings as a basic distinction in NT textual criticism. If we cannot establish what the primary reading was before someone changed it to another form (the secondary reading) in a particular MS, then we have no way of knowing how or why a variant reading arose. Clearly, this is a necessary distinction if we are to search for the original reading, even if we are only interested in tracing variants and their causes.

So, a secondary (non-original) reading in a MS might have derived from the scribe of that section of the MS, or it might have been already present in his exemplar. If the latter, how did it get onto *that* MS? Unless the reading conforms to a pattern of secondary variant readings in the MS, ideally SRs, it is impossible to know when the variant arose or at what stage it was inserted in the chain of copies from the original text to the MS in question. Royse's use of "the complex scribe" of a MS as a construct

CONCLUSION

of all the scribes of MSS leading up to that one MS is probably the best we can do in the situation. However, since we do not know anything about the "tradition" or the stages of transmission of a MS, including how many copies stand between the original text and a particular MS or those who were responsible for those intermediate copies, it might be best not to be too confident to state what part a particular copyist has played or what aspect of the MS he was responsible for, unless there is firm evidence or at least a high degree of probability.

It follows that it is difficult to attribute a variant to a certain period of history. We may be able to date a MS on the basis of paleography to a period of fifty years or so, and there is sometimes debate about even that. Hence, it is difficult to locate a variant reading in the time frame of a particular theological debate and then suggest that it was constructed to respond to that. Of course, much later MSS were dated, but they do not necessarily indicate much about the origin of early readings. Similarly, variants that have been proposed as responding apologetically to critics of Jesus or his followers are sometimes located in later MSS when such criticisms were not being made, so there is little reason to think that this was why they appeared in the first instance.

Some of the proposals examined in this book depend on a reevaluation of the textual evidence for a variant reading and the possibility of accepting a reading as original when it is commonly agreed to be secondary. For example, it has been suggested that "You are my son, today I have begotten you" is the original reading in Luke 3:22, and that this was replaced by "You are my son. I am pleased with you" in order to hinder an adoptionist reading of this text, which focused on a moment when Jesus was adopted ("begotten") by God. However, the MS evidence supporting the latter reading is very strong, and arguments supporting the originality of the former are inconclusive. It is also proposed that Luke 24:51 is a later addition designed to emphasize Jesus' ascension in order to oppose docetic Christologies, but there are good reasons to accept the originality of that verse in Luke as part of a stylized ending that was later omitted by scribal error in some MSS. The variant in Mark 1:41, according to which Jesus was "angry" with a leper seeking healing, is said to be original but later changed to Jesus "having compassion" on him in order to avoid Jesus being portrayed in a bad light. There are good reasons, however, to support a reference to Jesus' compassion as the original reading, even if it is difficult to know how the variant reading arose. Indeed, numerous variants reviewed in this study are said to be original when they are traditionally taken as secondary, but I argue that most of these proposals are unlikely because the suggested "original" readings enjoy only limited MS evidence, and the supporting arguments are unconvincing.

READINGS IN CONTEXT

One of the factors in assessing whether a variant is primary or secondary is how it fits into its context, including its immediate and wider literary context. If it is manifestly out of place, then it is likely to be secondary, but this is often not clear-cut. For example, although a variant in certain MSS might possibly have been designed to highlight the divinity of Jesus, the context should be examined to see if anyone is even likely to have noticed the change. So, instead of a former demoniac being urged to proclaim how much "the Lord" had done for him in Mark 5:19, some MSS read "God." This has been taken as emphasizing that Jesus is God, but in the context of that account, Jesus is called the "Son of the Most High God" (v. 7). If a hearer or reader would not notice the difference with "God" as the reading, it is unlikely that a scribe would have made the change with the suggested purpose in mind. Nor can the variant "God" instead of "the Lord" in Luke 1:15 be taken as evidence of someone wishing to refer to Jesus as God, because in the context "the Lord" is plainly the Lord God, however much Jesus' life and ministry is portrayed as the means of God's coming to his people. At Heb 2:14 the variant that reads "the same sufferings" instead of just "sufferings" is said to be emphasizing Jesus' true human experience, not the suffering he underwent in death. But the context in vv. 9–18 clearly indicates at a number of points that his death is in view, and the basis of that is his true human nature.

Another aspect of the context of a MS and its variants is the linguistic context. I have argued that some discussions of variants need to take more account of the varieties in Koine Greek syntax, lexical semantics, and orthography. In particular, Septuagintal usage should be examined, because that was the familiar OT text for Greek-speaking readers and Christian scribes and it formed the basis of a number of versions in other languages. So, for example, it is doubtful that the use of επ αυτον for εις αυτον in the account of the Spirit coming to Jesus in Mark 1:10 is an example of a variant designed to avoid gnostic Christology because επι and εις could be quite similar in meaning in Koine Greek. Who would have noticed the difference? At Matt 12:30, some MSS add "me" so that Jesus spoke about certain people who "scatter [σκορπιζω] me." It is suggested that this is meant to refute those who make a division between Jesus and Christ, as certain gnostics did, but the context does not allow this reading because of the parallel phrase ("is against me") and the fact that the verb σκορπιζω can hardly bear the meaning "divide." So also, emphasizing the difference between two variants using αγαπητοc and εκλεκτοc in Luke 9:35 would require further examination of their possible overlap in meaning. Other factors that are sometimes not considered include the vowel exchanges or the doubling of consonants in Koine Greek, as evident in extant papyri, as these affect the evaluation of variants and sometimes provide simple explanations for them.

Further, context can also play a part in providing the background for statements that appear to say one thing but would have been understood differently by hearers or readers because there were factors in their setting that are not explicitly stated in the text. Variants should also be seen in their religious and social context.

THOROUGH EXEGESIS

Thorough and balanced exegesis is also a necessity in the discussion of the priority or otherwise of textual variants in NT MSS. Jesus' "temptation" (or "testing") in Heb 2:18 has been said to have worried certain people, so they omitted that word to avoid the issue. However, the reference is clearly to Jesus being tested in Gethsemane to avoid the will of God by refusing to suffer death, and early Christians would surely have been aware of that. The issue of the mention of Abiathar as the high priest in the time of David in Mark 2:26 has also raised questions. The MT refers to Ahimelech as the high priest on that occasion, so "Abiathar" seems to be a mistake. Yet, the textual situation of the OT text at that point is quite complex and requires further discussion in order to arrive at a verdict as to how Abiathar could have come to be in Mark and why variants occur there.

The reading χωριc θεου instead of χαριτι θεου in Heb 2:9 has been portrayed as stemming from a desire to suggest that the reference is to everything "apart from God" being subjected to Jesus. But the syntax does not allow this reading because the phrase appears in the clause "so that χωριc/χαριτι θεου he [Jesus] might taste death for everyone." It does not refer to his "being crowned," which occurs in the previous clause, but to experiencing death. Nor can the claim that this is a reference to the theology of Hebrews with the notion that Jesus died far from God's presence be justified. And other arguments in support of χωρις θεου being original but supplanted by χαριτι θεου do not follow, such as χαρις appearing in the NT more than χωρις so it is more likely to be the secondary reading.

I also argue that many interpretations of variant readings are oversubtle. When a variant in Mark 10:13 replaces "them" with "those who brought them," it is said that this was done in order to show that the disciples were standing up to a mixed crowd of adults, not just talking to children, so that Christians might not be maligned for being totally dominated by women and children. The context, however, indicates that the disciples were addressing the adults anyway, so the proposal of an apologetic motive for this variant is doubtful, and the meaning remains unchanged.

Further, exegesis is sometimes strained. So, a portrayal of Jesus promising the insurgent on the adjacent cross that his kingdom would come that day is also misconceived since it does not consider what it meant for a Jew to enter "paradise" on the day of his death, as appears in one of Jesus' parables in Luke's Gospel. There are many examples of this kind of exegesis noted in previous chapters. Exegesis needs to consider all the relevant factors of linguistic, literary, and social context, which would have had an impact on how hearers or readers understood a text and why a copyist might have created a variant reading.

PATRISTIC EVIDENCE

Several variants reviewed in this book have pointed to patristic evidence, either as background to the social setting in which MSS were copied or as providing vital clues to contemporary readings and their significance. This is clearly a valid procedure, but it should be remembered that the MSS on which patristic texts are based are themselves subject to the vicissitudes of history, and they are sometimes much later than those on which a NT text itself is based. Further, when a patristic author refers to a passage, it is sometimes unclear whether he was meaning to quote the text verbatim or just paraphrase. Even if he was meaning to quote word for word, however, it is not always clear whether he was citing from a MS or just from memory.

CONCLUSION

Thus, patristic authors' discussions of variant readings in MSS are clearly valuable, but they should be used with care in NT textual criticism. It has been shown, for example, that a citation is not always attributable to a particular author or a particular time and place. Moreover, there are numerous cases where a variant reading has been used by a church father or apologist in order to address an unorthodox christological view or to defend Christ or Christians against charges made against them, but it is usually impossible to prove that the reading was originally created for that same reason. Variants were seized upon to justify theological points of view, but they may not have been created by someone with the same purpose in mind.

IDENTIFYING THE "CULPRITS"

Who were the people responsible for the variant readings discussed in this volume or, indeed, for all variants in NT MSS? Clearly, copyists were responsible for many aspects of a MS, but others were probably involved too. Thus, those who commissioned MSS might have had a part to play, or readers who added comments in the margin of a MS that were then incorporated into later copies of that MS. What else was a copyist supposed to do, when faced with a comment in the margin? If he only had access to one MS, he could have included the reading in his MS, thinking that it was original but had been left out and replaced in the margin. It cannot simply be assumed that a copyist of a MS was responsible for its every aspect.

As I have argued elsewhere, we also cannot assume that all copyists of early NT MSS were Christians by conviction, unless a MS was clearly produced for private usage. Once a MS had been copied in codex form, and after some *nomina sacra* had been inserted, later copyists would just have followed suit, whether they were Christians or not. So, neither of these criteria can be used to prove that copyists were generally Christians. I have argued that many variant readings might have been the result of harmonization to parallel passages, especially in the Gospels, but that would only have become more likely as time went on. Since it became easier to identify as a Christian from the middle of the fourth century, it would also have been easier for copyists to be familiar with NT texts, especially as monasteries grew in number and size and took on the task of producing copies of numerous books, including the NT. Since we know little about the scribes who produced copies of NT MSS in the early centuries, it is perhaps less likely that harmonization occurred in the early period of the church. That became more probable later on.

Were scribes involved in the theological debates of their time? Were they wishing to change the text in order to offer apologies and defend Christians from criticism in the early centuries of the church? Although many proposals have been made, it is almost impossible to prove that they were as conscious of the theological debates and the contrary views of critics as some allege. Were they wanting to address any of those issues? It is difficult to find conclusive evidence, despite the suggestions reviewed in this book.

REASONS FOR CHANGE

The discussion of variants in this volume has shown that it is highly likely that many variant readings are scribal slips due to tiredness or inattention, or they resulted from parablepsis or some other scribal error. So υιου θεου was probably omitted from ιησου χριστου υιου θεου (Mark 1:1) due to all the words ending in -ου and a scribe thinking he had copied the last words when in fact he had not. If all the words had been *nomina sacra*, it would have been even easier. Or, when referring to Jesus' death in 1 Pet 2:21 and 3:18, επαθεν was written as απεθανεν in some MSS since they were similar words and would have conveyed the same meaning. They need not have had a theological intention. There are numerous examples of this kind of error discussed in this book, which are all the more likely in the context of copying MSS by hand in antiquity.

There are also many instances where readings have been introduced that can certainly count as "corruptions," and some of them seem to support a Christology that came to form part of orthodoxy. However, it is possible that they were often just expressions of a copyist's faith but not created to oppose another point of view—they were simply the natural outpouring of a scribe's piety and, as such, not "theological corruptions" at all but "pious insertions." It may be that "pious sensibilities" caused people to omit "nor the Son" from the sentence in which no one was said to know the time of the coming of the Son of Man (Matt 24:36), but that need not have been done in order to oppose another view but just to clarify what seemed an issue. Thus, many of the variants discussed above were no doubt due to the shortcomings of the copyist, his or her piety, or inattention to the task. It was not easy to make a perfect copy and eliminate all errors.

On the other hand, some variants were clearly intentional, so how can we determine the difference between scribal mistakes and intentional changes? The isolation of SRs gives a good guide—perhaps the only reliable guide to what the "scribal habits" of a particular scribe were. But even then, it is possible that a variant was not created by the copyist of the MS concerned, even though it had to originate with someone. Still, "intentional" variants occur, even if almost unconsciously created, and they were clearly of various kinds and with a range of "intentions." It is, however, not always easy to identify what that intention was. Many deliberate changes were stylistic in nature or intending to clarify, but we know almost nothing about the particular circumstances of individual scribes or the scribes themselves.

At Acts 20:28, "the church of the Lord" and "the church of God" are alternative readings, and there is some discussion about the meaning of the following reference to "the blood of his own [Son]" or "his own blood." Most likely, the original phrase was awkward, and the variants are attempts to preserve Luke's reference to Jesus' blood without confusing which Lord was in view, so the variants were probably just attempts to clarify the meaning. So also, in Luke 22:43–44, there is an account of Jesus praying earnestly in the Garden of Gethsemane and an angel appearing to strengthen him. Some MSS omit this whole passage, so was it original or not? If it was, was it omitted because someone was uncomfortable with Jesus going through suffering or because it might have been taken as showing Jesus as a weakling? If it was not original, was it inserted to affirm Jesus' true humanity? It is not certain that it was a secondary reading, but even if it was, it is difficult to be sure why it was inserted.

Even if a variant was a copyist's harmonization to a Gospel parallel, what was his intention in harmonizing? He might have wanted to make the text of the Gospels consistent, or he might equally have genuinely thought that someone had omitted something. We are not really in a position to know that scribes were "uncomfortable with" certain texts, or that they wished to resolve certain tensions, or that they wished to avoid particular conclusions being drawn from the text they were copying, or that they wanted to defend Christians against charges of insurrection or practicing magic.

Of course, the text was "corrupted" by variant readings, whether intentional or not. While it has been proposed that certain variants were created deliberately with some purpose in mind, some MSS show signs of opposing points of view, if those views were behind the variants. For example, in a number of MSS in Luke 2 (vv. 22, 27, 33, 41–43) there are variants that could be seen as supporting adoptionist Christology and others supporting anti-adoptionist Christology in the same MS. Although a scribe (and others involved) might not have consistently changed the text in their MS to support their theology, it would be strange if they allowed various and opposing Christologies to gain force from readings in their MS. For consistency's sake, in order to evaluate such proposals, each MS would need to be treated as an artifact and its variants studied to show that a certain point of view is evident, as Royse has done with care for some early NT papyri.

The issue of the Western text is relevant here, particularly the text of Codex Bezae and the OL tradition. These often stand on their own in support of certain variants, but it is hard to know where their readings came from. This is especially the case with Codex Bezae, and how or why the readings it includes originated has been the subject of a great deal of scholarly debate. It seems that some people either had access to extra traditions or they wished to add color to the text, but it often resulted in a longer text. It is difficult to know how these readings arose and whether they were intentional or not and, if intentional, what the intention of the person responsible was.

In relation to readings proposed as being apologetically motivated, I raised an issue earlier, but it is worth repeating here. Even if a copyist (or someone else) wanted to respond to a critic of Christ or the Christians by altering the reading from what he found in his exemplar to the reading in his MS, who would have read it? Would a copyist have imagined that any of those critics would read his MS? It is unlikely. Perhaps, however, such readings were not designed for the benefit of critics but for Christians who might find support for themselves in such readings. The critics would be shown to be wrong because look at what the NT says! Yet, this suggestion is hypothetical and must remain a possibility, not a certainty, or even a probability.

Finally, as I emphasized in *Scribes, Motives, and Manuscripts*, the evidence of readings in other languages should clearly form a part of NT textual criticism, but in view of the nature of translation and of traditions of pious expression, care is required. Sometimes a MS in another language might just be paraphrasing, or it might reflect a different reading. So, in Luke 1:17 the original text says that John the Baptist will go

CONCLUSION

"ahead of him," but some MSS read "ahead of the Lord" and Persian and Georgian MSS read "ahead of God," but it is unclear whether these readings are just clarifying what people thought the original text meant or attempting to reinforce Jesus' divine status. At Luke 2:26, however, one OL MS reads "Christ, namely God" as a clear corruption implying Jesus' divinity. The issues with reading back from another language to the Greek text of the NT is one thing, but the reasons for that reading occurring in that language is a complication that can only be resolved by a study of the piety and traditions of NT MSS in that language.

THE WAY FORWARD

This study has reviewed proposals that certain readings in NT MSS were intentionally created, whether these intentions were theological or apologetic. I have reviewed most of the variant readings in the two studies examined and attempted to show cause to doubt many of the reasons given for their creation. In many cases, I have disagreed with the proposed direction of change—that is, regarding which were the primary and secondary readings. In other cases, however, the authors have followed the verdicts given in modern editions of the Greek NT, and the discussion has proceeded on that basis. Sometimes, the proposals are treated as quite subtle and as only possible readings of the evidence, but at other times suggestions are made with a certainty that is not warranted by the evidence. The number of plausible instances of theologically intentional variants has been shown to be tiny in comparison to the claims made, and the motives of those responsible for the variants are usually not as clear as suggested. On the whole, copyists of the NT documents can be seen as having generally resisted "the temptation to 'improve' the Gospel texts,"[1] viewing their task as passing on the text of the exemplar before them, even if sometimes those who were Christians by conviction carried out their work with minor changes since they saw their work as an act of devotion, especially in later centuries.

One of the main issues here is that discussions have not taken sufficient account of the context of the readings, particularly the literary, social, and linguistic context, and exegesis of the passages in question has not been as thorough as we might hope. Moreover, knowing the purpose or intention of the scribes depends on knowing how they viewed their

---

1. Head, "Christology," 128–29.

context, but the proposals reviewed in this study ultimately depend on the variants providing a window into the mind of the scribes, which is clearly a difficult task.

Further investigation may be able to identify variants that show an "orthodox" or apologetic intention, but for the present the two studies reviewed in this book have not in general proven their case. Either the evidence provided is too slight or the argumentation is inconclusive. Generally, I argue that variants are much more likely to have arisen from more "ordinary" causes than those associated with the copyists' personal situation, whether in a certain theological climate or in a world hostile toward Christians. At the present time, the vast majority of the NT text has been established beyond reasonable doubt, but this does not mean that we ought not to continue the attempt to establish the original text of the NT in those sections that are still uncertain. Nor should it be inferred that we can ignore the history of the transmission of the NT text since that might shed light on later history. My hope is that the material put forward in this volume will add to the discussion as to what the original text of the NT was and why variants occurred in the MSS attesting its text.

Glossary

Adoptionism	The view that Jesus was not originally divine but human and was subsequently "adopted" (taken up) into the divine Godhead.
Apologetics	The activity of Christians defending themselves against charges of illegal or immoral behavior made against them, and sometimes commending their faith to other people.
Atticism, Attic	The Attic dialect of Greek was used in Athens, particularly in V–IV BC, so "Atticism" was the practice of returning to the use of that dialect in various ways after the growth of Koine Greek.
Bookhand	A more formal style of writing, usually for literary works rather than documents.
Catena	A series of quotations, often from the Old Testament.
Codex	A manuscript in the form of pages bound together at the spine, with various numbers of gatherings (quires) consisting of a number of leaves.
Coherence-Based Genealogical Method	The method of NT textual criticism using computers to trace relationships between readings in MSS, and then attempting to assign readings as earlier or later in the development traced.
Collate, collation	A MS is collated when its text is compared to that in another MS or text, and the differences are recorded in a collation.
Conjectural emendation	A conjectural emendation is a corrected reading in a MS proposed by an editor, which does not appear in any MS but seems to be needed in order to make the text meaningful.
Copyist	The person responsible for producing a copy of a MS (see *scribe*).
Dittography	The writing of an element in a Greek sentence twice (by mistake)—the opposite of haplography.
Docetism	The belief that Jesus only *seemed* to be a human being.

GLOSSARY

Document	A "document" usually refers to a more mundane written text, such as a tax return, letter, contract, or receipt, often in contrast to a literary text.
Epicism, Epic	An epic is a long poem usually derived from ancient oral tradition; epicism is the attempt to make a text conform to elements of epic style.
Exemplar	The MS a copyist was attempting to reproduce when he or she was producing his or her copy of a text.
Extant	An extant MS is one that is currently in existence.
Hand	The handwriting of a particular copyist or scribe.
Haplography	When a repeated element in a sentence is written only once—the opposite of dittography.
Homoioarcton	When two words have similar (or identical) beginnings, which may result in the intervening material being omitted.
Homoioteleuton	When two words have similar (or identical) endings, which may result in the intervening material being omitted.
Ionic	The dialect of ancient Greek related to Attic, usually allied with the works of Homer, Hesiod, Herodotus, and others.
Itacism, iotacism	The tendency in Koine Greek for speakers to pronounce a number of vowels like iota.
Lacuna	A gap in a MS due to damage of various kinds, often because of deterioration over long periods of time in the ground, or even if housed in libraries or the like. A section of a MS with a lacuna is called "lacunose."
Leaf	One page of a codex MS.
Literary text	A literary text normally designates a work of "literature," although that may include a wide range of texts such as classical works by Homer, speeches composed for delivery in court, plays, or short philosophical treatises.
Majuscule	The majuscule script in Greek refers to "capital" (uppercase) letters, with each letter usually distinct from the others. It was in common use until minuscule writing became predominant.
Manuscript	A piece of writing produced by hand on a writing surface.
Meter, metrical	The poetic structure of Greek poetry, occurring in various standard forms. Such poetry had a "metrical" format.
Minuscule	The minuscule script involved using small (lowercase) letters often joined by strokes. It came to predominate after majuscule script.

GLOSSARY

Nomen sacrum (pl. *nomina sacra*)	Certain words associated with divine personages—hence "sacred names" (*nomina sacra*)—were sometimes abbreviated with a superior line indicating that such an abbreviation had been made.
Papyrus	A writing surface made from a plant. In NT textual criticism "papyri" refers to a number of MSS written on papyrus containing the text of parts of the NT. However, "papyrus" is commonly used more widely in papyrology to denote a text written on portable surfaces including papyrus, vellum (parchment), as well as "ostraca" (broken pottery), but not inscriptions on stone.
Parablepsis	The movement of a copyist's eye from one part of a text to another, which might take the form of homoioarcton or homoioteleuton.
Patripassianism	The view that God the Father also suffered when Jesus died.
Reading	The text comprising one or more words appearing on a MS.
Recension	A critical revision of a text to produce a new "edition."
Roll	A piece of material, usually papyrus or parchment, in the form of a roll on which Greek text was usually inscribed in columns from left to right.
Scholia	Commentaries on the text written in a MS, sometimes appearing in the upper, lower, or side margins.
Scribe	A person whose occupation was to produce various kinds of written material, whether of a documentary or literary nature (see *copyist*).
Scriptio continua	The practice of writing texts without spaces between words.
Singular reading	A reading in a MS that does not occur in any other MS, sometimes limited to any other Greek MS.
Staurogram	A symbol resembling a cross (rho superimposed on a tau, thus resembling a crucified person), often used as part of words meaning "cross" or "crucify."
Stemma	A "stemma" is a family tree of MSS, denoting which MSS were copied from which others.
Textual criticism	The use of extant MSS and certain principles to locate the original text of a work, as well as tracing the origin of variant readings.
Transposition	The movement of two elements in a sentence to replace one another thus reversing their order.
Uncial	An equivalent term for majuscule scripts in Greek (and Latin).
Variant (reading)	A reading of a text attested in a MS where there are other readings at that point in other MSS.

GLOSSARY

Vowel exchange	The occurrence of variant spelling of vowels or diphthongs in Koine and Byzantine Greek due to scribes not distinguishing between the sound of vowels or diphthongs (e.g., ο–ω, αι–ε, υ–οι, or ει–α).
Vulgate	A standard edition of a work, such as Homer's *Iliad*. Vulgate can also refer to the standardized Latin version of the Bible.
Version, versional	A translation of a text into another language, usually used in NT textual criticism to refer to versions in languages other than Greek. Readings in such translations are then "versional."
Western non-interpolation	A reading in a MS that is usually described as "Western" in orientation but is shorter than opposing (often Alexandrian) readings despite "Western" readings usually being longer.

Bibliography

Achtemeier, Paul J. *1 Peter*. Hermeneia. Minneapolis: Fortress, 1996.
Aland, Kurt, and Barbara Aland. *The Text of the New Testament*. Translated by Erroll F. Rhodes. 2nd ed. Grand Rapids: Eerdmans, 1989.
———. *Text und Textwert der griechischen Handschriften des Neuen Testaments IV: Die Synoptischen Evangelien: 1. Das Markusevangelium*. Vol. 2. Berlin: de Gruyter, 1998.
The American and British Committees of the International Greek New Testament Project. *The Gospel According to St. Luke: Part 1*. The New Testament in Greek 3. Oxford: Clarendon, 1984.
Attridge, Harold W. *A Commentary on the Epistle to the Hebrews*. Hermeneia. Philadelphia: Fortress, 1989.
———. Review of *The Orthodox Corruption of Scripture*, by Bart Ehrman. *CBQ* 57 (1995) 391–93.
Baarda, Tjitze. "ΔΙΑΦΩΝΙΑ—CΥΜΦΩΝΙΑ: Factors in the Harmonization of the Gospels, especially in the Diatessaron of Tatian." In *Gospel Traditions in the Second Century*, edited by William L. Petersen, 133–54. Notre Dame: University of Notre Dame Press, 1989.
———. "Mk 1:41: ὀργιθείς; A Reading Attested for Mar Ephraem, the Diatessaron, or Tatian." *ZNW* 103 (2012) 291–95.
Barnes, Timothy D. "Porphyry *Against the Christians*: Date and the Attribution of Fragments." *JTS* 24 (1973) 424–42.
———. "Scholarship or Propaganda? Porphyry *Against the Christians* and Its Historical Setting." *BICS* 39 (1994) 53–65.
Barrett, C. K. *A Critical and Exegetical Commentary on the Acts of the Apostles*. 2 vols. ICC. Edinburgh: T&T Clark, 1994, 1998.
———. *The Gospel According to St. John: An Introduction, with Commentary and Notes on the Greek Text*. 2nd ed. London: SPCK, 1978.
Barth, Markus, and Helmut Blanke. *Colossians: A New Translation with Introduction and Commentary*. AB 34B. New York: Doubleday, 1994.
Bates, Matthew W. "A Christology of Incarnation and Enthronement: Romans 1:3–4 as Unified, Nonadoptionist, and Nonconciliatory." *CBQ* 77 (2015) 107–27.
Bauckham, Richard J. *Jude, 2 Peter*. WBC 50. Waco: Word, 1983.
Bauer, Walter. *Orthodoxy and Heresy in Earliest Christianity*. Translated by Philadelphia Seminar on Christian Origins. Edited by Robert Kraft and Gerhard Krodel. Philadelphia: Fortress, 1971.

BIBLIOGRAPHY

Beasley-Murray, George R. *John*. 2nd ed. WBC 36. Nashville: Thomas Nelson, 1999.
Benko, Stephen. "Pagan Criticism of Christianity during the First Two Centuries A.D." *ANRW* II.23.2 (1980) 1055–118.
———. *Pagan Rome and the Early Christians*. Bloomington, IN: Indiana University Press, 1986.
Best, Ernest. *A Critical and Exegetical Commentary on Ephesians*. ICC. Edinburgh: T&T Clark, 1998.
Betz, Hans Dieter. *Galatians: A Commentary on Paul's Letter to the Churches in Galatia*. Hermeneia. Philadelphia: Fortress, 1979.
———, ed. *The Greek Magical Papyri in Translation including Demotic Spells*. Chicago: University of Chicago Press, 1986.
Billings, Bradley S. "The Disputed Words in the Lukan Institution Narrative (Luke 22:19b–20): A Sociological Answer to a Textual Problem." *JBL* 125 (2006) 507–26.
———. *Do This in Remembrance of Me*. London: T&T Clark, 2006.
Birdsall, J. Neville. "A Note on the Textual Evidence for the Omission of Matthew 9:34." In *Jews and Christians: The Parting of the Ways A.D. 70 to 135*, edited by James D. G. Dunn, 117–22. Grand Rapids: Eerdmans, 1999.
———. Review of *The Orthodox Corruption of Scripture*, by Bart Ehrman. *Theology* 97 (1994) 460–62.
Blumell, Lincoln H. "Luke 22:43–44: An Anti-docetic Interpolation or an Apologetic Omission?" *JBTC* 19 (2014) 1–35.
Boer, W. den. "A Pagan Historian and His Enemies: Porphyry Against the Christians." *CP* 69 (1974) 198–208.
Botner, Max. "Has Jesus Read What David Did? Probing Problems in Mark 2:25–26." *JTS* 69 (2018) 488–99.
———. "How Do the Seeds Land? A Note on ΕΙΣ ΑΥΤΟΝ in Mark 1:10." *JTS* 66 (2015) 547–52.
———. "The Role of Transcriptional Probability in the Text-Critical Debate on Mark 1:1." *CBQ* 77 (2015) 467–80.
Bovon, Francois. *Luke 1: A Commentary on the Gospel of Luke 1:1—9:50*. Translated by Christine M. Thomas. Hermeneia. Minneapolis: Fortress, 2002.
———. *Luke 2: A Commentary on the Gospel of Luke 9:51—19:27*. Translated by Donald S. Deer. Hermeneia. Minneapolis: Fortress, 2013.
———. *Luke 3: A Commentary on the Gospel of Luke 19:28—24:53*. Translated by James E. Crouch. Hermeneia. Minneapolis: Fortress, 2012.
Brown, Raymond. *Death of the Messiah*. 2 vols. New York: Doubleday, 1994.
———. *The Epistles of John: A New Translation with Introduction and Commentary*. AB 30. Garden City, NY: Doubleday, 1982.
———. *The Gospel According to John I–XII: A New Translation with Introduction and Commentary*. AB 29. Garden City, NY: Doubleday, 1966.
———. *The Gospel According to John XIII–XXI: A New Translation with Introduction and Commentary*. AB 29A. Garden City, NY: Doubleday, 1966.
Bruce, Frederick F. *The Acts of the Apostles: Greek Text with Introduction and Commentary*. 3rd ed. Grand Rapids: Eerdmans, 1990.
———. *The Epistle to the Galatians*. NIGTC. Grand Rapids: Eerdmans, 1982.
———. *The Epistle to the Hebrews*. Rev. ed. Grand Rapids: Eerdmans, 1990.
———. *The Epistles to the Colossians, Philemon and Ephesians*. NICNT. Grand Rapids: Eerdmans, 1984.

BIBLIOGRAPHY

Bultmann, Rudolf. *The Gospel of John*. Translated by George R. Beasley-Murray et al. Philadelphia: Westminster, 1971.

Burkholder, Benjamin J. "Considering the Possibility of a Theological Corruption in Joh 1,18 in Light of Its Early Reception." *ZNW* 103 (2012) 64–83.

Burton, Ernest de Witt. *Critical and Exegetical Commentary on Galatians*. ICC. Edinburgh: T&T Clark, 1921.

Caneday, Ardel B. "'Anyone Hung Upon a Pole Is Under God's Curse': Deuteronomy 21:22–23 in Old and New Covenant Contexts." *SBJT* 18 (2014) 121–36.

Caragounis, Chrys. "Jesus, His Brothers and the Journey to the Feast (John 7:8–10)." *SEÅ* 63 (1998) 177–87.

Carrier, Richard. "Thallus and the Darkness at Christ's Death." *JGRChJ* 8 (2011–12) 185–91.

Chadwick, Henry, trans. *Origen: Contra Celsum*. Cambridge: Cambridge University Press, 1953.

Chapa, Juan. "The Contribution of Papyrology in the Interpretation of the Gospels." In *The Gospels: History and Christology; The Search of Joseph Ratzinger—Benedict XVI*, edited by Bernado Estrada, et al., 81–149. Vatican City: Vatican Publishing House, 2013.

Charlesworth, Scott. "T. C. Skeat, P64+67 and P4, and the Problem of Fibre Orientation in Codicological Reconstruction." *NTS* 53 (2007) 582–604.

Clarysse, Willy, and Pasquale Orsini. "Christian Manuscripts from Egypt to the Times of Constantine." In *Das Neue Testament und sein Text im 2. Jahrhundert*, edited by Jan Heilmann und Matthias Klinghardt, 107–15. Text und Arbeiten zum neutestamentliche Zeitalter 61. Tübingen: Francke, 2018.

Clivaz, Claire. "The Angel and the Sweat Like 'Drops of Blood' (Lk 22:43–44): P^{69} and f^{13}." *HTR* 98 (2005) 419–40.

———. "The New Testament at the Time of the Egyptian Papyri: Reflections Based on P^{12}, P^{75} and P^{126} (*P. Amh.* 3B, *P. Bod.* XIV-V and *PS* 1497)." In *Reading New Testament Papyri in Context*, edited by Claire Clivaz and Jean Zumstein, 15–55. BETL 242. Leuven: Peeters, 2001.

Collins, Adela Y. "Establishing the Text: Mark 1:1." In *Texts and Contexts: Biblical Texts in Their Textual and Situational Contexts. Essays in Honor of Lars Hartman*, edited by Tord Fornberg and David Hellholm, 111–27. Oslo: Scandinavian University Press, 1995.

———. *Mark*. Hermeneia. Minneapolis: Fortress, 2007.

Colwell, Ernest C. "External Evidence and New Testament Textual Criticism." In *Studies in the History and Text of the Text of the New Testament in Honor of Kenneth Willis Clark, PhD*, edited by Boyd L. Daniels and M. Jack Suggs, 1–12. Studies and Documents 39. Salt Lake City: University of Utah Press, 1967.

———. "Method in Locating a Newly Discovered Manuscript." In *Studies in Methodology in Textual Criticism of the New Testament*, 26–44. NTTS 9. Grand Rapids: Eerdmans, 1969.

Comfort, Philip W., and David P. Barrett. *The Text of the Earliest Greek New Testament Manuscripts*. Wheaton, IL: Tyndale House, 2001.

Countryman, L. William. Review of *The Orthodox Corruption of Scripture*, by Bart Ehrman. *CH* 66 (1997) 81–83.

Coutsoumpos, Panayotis. "The Difficulty of ΜΟΝΟΓΕΝΗΣ ΘΕΟΣ in John 1:18: A Reassessment." *Bib* 98 (2017) 435–46.

Craigie, Peter C. *Psalms 1–50*. WBC 19. Waco: Word, 1983.
Cranfield, C. E. B. *A Critical and Exegetical Commentary on the Epistle to the Romans*. 2 vols. ICC. Edinburgh: T&T Clark, 1975–79.
Crawford, Matthew R. "The Diatessaron: Canonical or Non-canonical?" *NTS* 62 (2016) 253–77.
Croy, N. Clayton. *The Mutilation of Mark's Gospel*. Nashville: Abingdon, 2003.
———. "Sword Handling: The Early Christian Reception of Matthew 10:34." *JBRec* 6 (2019) 135–62.
Dauer, Anton. "Zur Authentizität von Lk 24,12." *ETL* 70 (1994) 294–318.
Davies, William D., and Dale C. Allison Jr. *A Critical and Exegetical Commentary on the Gospel According to Saint Matthew*. ICC. 3 vols. Edinburgh: T&T Clark, 1988–97.
Dixon, Edward P. "Descending Spirit and Descending Gods: A 'Greek' Interpretation of the Spirit's 'Descent as a Dove' in Mark 1:10." *JBL* 128 (2009) 759–80.
Donaldson, Amy M. "Explicit References to New Testament Variant Readings among Greek and Latin Church Fathers." PhD diss., University of Notre Dame, 2009. https://doi.org/10.7274/5712m615k50.
Dunn, James D. G. *The Epistles to the Colossians and to Philemon*. NIGTC. Grand Rapids: Eerdmans, 1996.
———. *Romans 1–8*. WBC 38A. Dallas: Word, 1988.
———. *Romans 9–16*. WBC 38B. Dallas: Word, 1988.
Edwards, Mark. "Orthodox Corruption? John 1:18." *StPatr* 44 (2010) 201–5.
———. "Porphyry and the Christians." In *Studies on Porphyry*, edited by George Karamanolis and Anne Sheppard, 111–26. BICS Supplement 98. London: Institute of Classical Studies and University of London Press, 2007.
Ehrman, Bart D. "Christ as Divine Man." In *Studies in the Textual Criticism of the New Testament*, 361–76. Leiden: Brill, 2006.
———. "Christ Come in the Flesh." In *Studies in the Textual Criticism of the New Testament*, 343–60. Leiden: Brill, 2006.
———. "The Cup, the Bread and the Salvific Effect of Jesus' Death." In *Studies in the Textual Criticism of the New Testament*, 156–77. Leiden: Brill, 2006.
———. "1 John 4.3 and the Orthodox Corruption of Scripture." In *Studies in the Textual Criticism of the New Testament*, 221–46. Leiden: Brill, 2006.
———. "A Leper in the Hands of an Angry Jesus." In *Studies in the Textual Criticism of the New Testament*, 120–41. Leiden: Brill, 2006.
———. *Misquoting Jesus*. New York: HarperCollins, 2005.
———. *The Orthodox Corruption of Scripture: The Effect of Early Christological Controversies on the Text of the New Testament*. New York: Oxford University Press, 1993.
———. *Studies in the Textual Criticism of the New Testament*. NTTS 33. Leiden: Brill, 2006.
———. "Text and Interpretation: The Exegetical Significance of the 'Original' Text." In *Studies in the Textual Criticism of the New Testament*, 307–24. Leiden: Brill, 2006.
———. "Text and Transmission: The Historical Significance of the 'Altered' Text." In *Studies in the Textual Criticism of the New Testament*, 325–42. Leiden: Brill, 2006.
———. "The Text of Mark in the Hands of the Orthodox." In *Studies in the Textual Criticism of the New Testament*, 142–55. Leiden: Brill, 2006.
———. "The Text of the Gospels at the End of the Second Century." In *Studies in the Textual Criticism of the New Testament*, 71–99. Leiden: Brill, 2006.

Ehrman, Bart D., and Mark A. Plunkett. "The Angel and the Agony: The Textual Problem of Luke 22.43-44." In *Studies in the Textual Criticism of the New Testament*, 178-95. Leiden: Brill, 2006.

Ehrman, Bart D., and Michael W. Holmes, eds. *The Text of the New Testament in Contemporary Research*. 2nd ed. NTTSD 42. Leiden: Brill, 2014.

Ellingworth, Paul. *The Epistle to the Hebrews: A Commentary on the Greek Text*. NIGTC. Grand Rapids: Eerdmans, 1993.

Elliott, J. K. "An Eclectic Textual Commentary on the Greek Text of Mark's Gospel." In *New Testament Textual Criticism: Its Significance for Exegesis*, edited by Eldon J. Epp and Gordon D. Fee, 47-60. Oxford: Oxford University Press, 1981.

Elliott, John H. "The Epistle to the Hebrews: Textual Variation and Philological Considerations." *FN* 30 (2017) 71-78.

———. *I Peter: A New Translation with Introduction and Commentary*. AB 37B. New York: Doubleday, 2000.

———. "The Last Twelve Verses of Mark: Original or Not?" In *Perspectives on the Ending of Mark: 4 Views*, edited by David A. Black, 80-102. Nashville: B&H Academic, 2008.

———. Review of *The Orthodox Corruption of Scripture*, by Bart D. Ehrman. *NovT* 36 (1994) 405-6.

———. "When Jesus Was Apart from God: An Examination of Hebrews 29." *ExpTim* 83 (1972) 339-41.

Elliott, W. J., and David C. Parker, eds. *The Gospel According to St. John: The Papyri*. Vol. 1. The New Testament in Greek 4. Leiden: Brill, 1995.

Engberg, Jacob, et al., eds. *In Defence of Christianity: Early Christian Apologists*. Frankfurt: Lang, 2014.

Epp, Eldon J. "The Ascension in the Textual Tradition of Luke-Acts." In *Perspectives on New Testament Textual Criticism: Collected Essays, 1962-2004*, 211-25. Atlanta: Society of Biblical Literature, 2005.

———. Review of "The Disputed Words in the Lukan Institution Narrative (Luke 22:19b-20)," by Bradley S. Billings. *Bib* 90 (2009) 407-16.

———. "Textual Criticism in the Exegesis of the New Testament." In *Perspectives on New Testament Textual Criticism: Collected Essays, 1962-2004*, 461-95. Atlanta: Society of Biblical Literature, 2005.

———. *The Theological Tendency of Codex Bezae Cantabrigiensis in Acts*. Society for New Testament Studies Monograph 3. Cambridge: Cambridge University Press, 1966.

Evans, Craig A. *Jesus and the Manuscripts: What Can We Learn from the Oldest Manuscripts?* Peabody, MA: Hendrickson Academic, 2020.

———. *Mark 8:27—16:20*. WBC 34B. Nashville: Thomas Nelson, 2001.

———. "Patristic Interpretation of Mark 2:26: 'When Abiathar Was High Priest.'" *VC* 40 (1986) 183-86.

Fee, Gordon D. *The First Epistle to the Corinthians*. NICNT. 2nd ed. Grand Rapids: Eerdmans, 2014.

———. *Paul's Letter to the Philippians*. NICNT. Grand Rapids: Eerdmans, 1995.

———. Review of *The Orthodox Corruption of Scripture*, by Bart Ehrman. *CRBR* 8 (1995) 203-6.

Fitzmyer, Joseph A. *The Acts of the Apostles: A New Translation with Introduction and Commentary*. AB 31. New York: Doubleday, 1998.

———. *First Corinthians: A New Translation with Introduction and Commentary*. AB 32. New Haven: Yale University Press, 2008.

———. *The Gospel According to Luke I–IX: A New Translation with Introduction and Commentary*. AB 28. New York: Doubleday, 1981.

———. *The Gospel According to Luke X–XXIV: A New Translation with Introduction and Commentary*. AB 28A. New York: Doubleday, 1985.

Flink, Timo. "New Variant Reading of John 1:34." *AUSS* 45 (2007) 191–93.

———. "Son and Chosen: A Text-Critical Study of John 1:34." *FN* 18 (2005) 87–111.

Focant, Camille. "Un silence qui fait parler (Mc 16,8)." In *New Testament Textual Criticism and Exegesis: Festschrift J. Delobel*, edited by Adelbert Denaux, 79–96. Leuven: Peeters, 2002.

France, Richard T. *The Gospel of Mark*. NIGTC. Grand Rapids: Eerdmans, 2002.

———. *The Gospel of Matthew*. NICNT. Grand Rapids: Eerdmans, 2007.

Furnish, Victor P. *II Corinthians: A New Translation with Introduction and Commentary*. AB 32A. New York: Doubleday, 1984.

Georgi, Dieter. "Socioeconomic Reasons for the 'Divine Man' as a Propagandistic Pattern." In *Aspects of Religious Propaganda*, edited by Elisabeth S. Fiorenza, 27–42. Notre Dame: University of Notre Dame Press, 1976.

Gignac, Francis T. *A Grammar of the Greek Papyri of the Roman and Byzantine Periods*. 2 vols. TDSA 55. Milan: Istituto Editoriale Cisalpino-La Goliardica, 1976–81.

Globe, Alexander. "Some Doctrinal Variants in Matthew 1 and Luke 2, and the authority of the neutral text." *CBQ* 42 (1980) 52–72.

Gordon, Robert P. *1 and 2 Samuel*. Exeter: Paternoster, 1986.

Grant, Robert M. *Greek Apologists of the Second Century*. London: SCM, 1988.

Green, Joel. *The Death of Jesus*. WUNT 2.33. Tübingen: Mohr Siebeck, 1988.

Guelich, Robert A. *Mark 1—8:26*. WBC 34A. Dallas: Word, 1989.

Gundry, Robert H. *Mark: A Commentary on His Apology for the Cross*. Grand Rapids: Eerdmans, 1993.

Gurtner, Daniel M. Review of *Apologetic Discourse and the Scribal Tradition*, by Wayne C. Kannaday. *WTJ* 68 (2006) 152–55.

Haelewyck, Jean-Claude. "The Healing of a Leper (Mark 1, 40–45). A Textual Commentary." *ETL* 89 (2013) 15–36.

Haenchen, Ernst. *John 1*. Hermeneia. Philadelphia: Fortress, 1984.

———. *John 2*. Hermeneia. Philadelphia: Fortress, 1984.

Hagner, Donald A. *Matthew 1–13*. WBC. 33A. Waco: Word, 1993.

———. *Matthew 14-28*. WBC 33B. Dallas: Word, 1995.

Haines-Eitzen, Kim. *Guardians of Letters: Literacy, Power, and the Transmitters of Early Christian Literature*. New York: Oxford University Press, 2000.

———. Review of *Apologetic Discourse and the Scribal Tradition*, by Wayne C. Kannaday. *JBL* 124 (2005) 381–83.

Hargis, Jeffrey W. *Against the Christians: The Rise of Early Anti-Christian Polemic*. New York: Lang, 1999.

Harris, Murray J. "The Translation and Significance of Ὁ ΘΕΟΣ in Hebrews 1:8–9." *TynBul* 36 (1985) 129–62.

Harris, W. Hall, III. "The Ascent and Descent of Christ in Ephesians 4:9–10." *BSac* 151 (1994) 198–214.

Hartog, Paul A. "The Text of Hebrews 2:9 in Its Patristic Reception." *BSac* 171 (2014) 52–71.

BIBLIOGRAPHY

Head, Peter. "Additional Greek Witnesses to the New Testament (Ostraca, Amulets, Inscriptions, and Other Sources)." In *The Text of the New Testament in Contemporary Research*, edited by Bart D. Ehrman and Michael W. Holmes, 429–60. 2nd ed. Leiden: Brill, 2014.

———. "Christology and Textual Transmission: Reverential Alterations in the Synoptic Gospels." *NovT* 35 (1993) 105–29.

———. "The Early Text of Mark." In *The Early Text of the New Testament*, edited by Charles E. Hill and Michael J. Kruger, 108–20. Oxford: Oxford University Press, 2012.

———. "Scribal Behaviour and Theological Tendencies in Singular Readings in *P. Bodmer* II (P^{66})." In *Textual Variation: Theological and Social Tendencies?*, edited by Hugh A. G. Houghton and David C. Parker, 55–74. Piscataway, NJ: Gorgias, 2008.

———. "A Text-Critical Study of Mark 1.1: 'The Beginning of the Gospel of Jesus Christ'." *NTS* 37 (1991) 621–29.

Henrichs, Albert. "Fasting." In *OCD*, edited by Simon Hornblower and Anthony Spawforth, 569. 4th ed. Oxford: Oxford University Press, 2012.

Hernández, Juan, Jr. "The Early Text of Luke." In *The Early Text of the New Testament*, edited by Charles E. Hill and Michael J. Kruger, 121–39. Oxford: Oxford University Press, 2012.

———. *Scribal Habits and Theological Influences in the Apocalypse: The Singular Readings of Sinaiticus, Alexandrinus, and Ephraemi*. WUNT 2.218. Tübingen: Mohr Siebeck, 2006.

Hill, Charles E., and Michael J. Kruger, eds. *The Early Text of the New Testament*. Oxford: Oxford University Press, 2012.

Hixson, Elijah. "'They Took the Body of God.' John 19,40 in Codex Alexandrinus." *ETL* 90 (2014) 743–49.

Hixson, Elijah H., and Peter J. Gurry, eds. *Myths and Mistakes in New Testament Textual Criticism*. Downers Grove, IL: IVP Academic, 2019.

Hoehner, Harold W. *Ephesians: An Exegetical Commentary*. Grand Rapids: Baker, 2002.

Holland, Drew S. "The Meaning of Ἐξέστη in Mark 3:21." *JIBS* 4 (2017) 6–31.

Houghton, Hugh A. G. "Recent Developments in New Testament Textual Criticism." *EC* 2 (2011) 245–58.

Houghton, Hugh A. G., and David C. Parker, eds. *Textual Variation: Theological and Social Tendencies?* Texts and Studies 3.6. Piscataway, NJ: Gorgias, 2008.

Hutchison, David. "The 'Orthodox Corruption' of Mark 1:1." *SwJT* 48 (2005) 33–48.

Isenberg, Wesley W. "The Gospel of Philip (II, 3)." In *The Nag Hammadi Library in English*, edited by James M. Robinson. 3rd ed. Leiden: Brill, 1988.

Iverson, Kelly R. "A Further Word on Final Γάρ (Mark 16.8)." *CBQ* 68 (2006) 79–94.

Jewett, Robert, and Roy D. Kotansky. *Romans: A Commentary*. Hermeneia. Minneapolis: Fortress, 2007.

Jipp, Joshua W. "Ancient, Modern and Future Interpretations of Romans 1:3–4: Reception History and Biblical Interpretation." *JTI* 3 (2009) 241–59.

Johnson, Luke T. *The Acts of the Apostles*. Sacra Pagina 5. Collegeville: Liturgical, 1992.

Johnson, Nathan C. "Anger Issues: Mark 1.41 in Ephrem the Syrian, the Old Latin Gospels and Codex Bezae." *NTS* 63 (2017) 183–202.

———. "Romans 1:3–4: Beyond Antithetical Parallelism." *JBL* 136 (2017) 467–90.

Jongkind, Dirk. "'It Does Not Make a Difference': The Fraught Relation Between the Textual Criticism of the New Testament and Theology." *Presb* 49 (2023) 38–53.
Kannaday, Wayne C. *Apologetic Discourse and the Scribal Tradition: Evidence of the Influence of Apologetic Interests on the Texts of the Canonical Gospels.* Text-Critical Studies 5. Atlanta: Society of Biblical Literature, 2004.
Keener, Craig S. *Acts: An Exegetical Commentary.* Vol. 3. Grand Rapids: Baker, 2014.
Kellhoffer, James A. *Miracle and Mission: The Authentication of Missionaries and Their Message in the Longer Ending of Mark.* WUNT 2.112. Tübingen: Mohr Siebeck, 2000.
Knust, Jennifer W. Review of *Apologetic Discourse and the Scribal Tradition*, by Wayne C. Kannaday. *JR* 86 (2006) 671–72.
Koester, Craig R. *Hebrews: A New Translation with Introduction and Commentary.* AB 36. New York: Doubleday, 2001.
Köstenberger, Andreas J., et al. *Going Deeper with New Testament Greek.* Nashville: B&H Academic, 2016.
Kotansky, Roy. "The Early Papyri, 'Gospel-Parallel' Variants, and the Text of the New Testament in the Second Century." In *Scribes and Their Remains*, edited by Craig A. Evans and Jeremiah J. Johnston, 224–80. LSTS 94. London: T&T Clark, 2019.
Kraeling, Carl H, ed. *A Greek Fragment of Tatian's Diatessaron from Dura.* London: Christophers, 1935.
Kristianto, Stefanus. "Evaluating Bart Ehrman's Textual Reconstruction: A Test Case on John 1:18." *AJT* 31 (2017) 23–35.
Kruger, M. A. Review of *The Orthodox Corruption of Scripture*, by Bart Ehrman. *Neot* 28 (1994) 606–7.
Kruger, Michael J. *Christianity at the Crossroads: How the Second Century Shaped the Future of the Church.* Downers Grove, IL: IVP Academic, 2018.
———. Review of *Apologetic Discourse and the Scribal Tradition*, by Wayne C. Kannaday. *JETS* 48 (2005) 824–27.
Lagrange, Marie-Joseph. "Deux nouveaux textes relatifs à l'Évangile." *RB* 44 (1935) 321–43.
Lane, William. *Hebrews 1–8.* WBC 47A. Dallas: Word, 1991.
———. *Hebrews 9–13.* WBC 92. Dallas: Word, 1991.
Lanier, Gregory R. "A Case for the Assimilation of Matthew 21:44 to the Lukan 'Crushing Stone' (20:18) with Special Reference to P^{104}." *JBTC* 21 (2016) 1–21.
Layton, Bentley. *The Gnostic Scriptures.* London: SCM, 1987.
Lincoln, Andrew T. *Ephesians.* WBC 83 Dallas: Word, 1990.
Longenecker, Richard N. *Galatians.* WBC 72. Dallas: Word, 1990.
———. *Romans.* NIGTC. Grand Rapids: Eerdmans, 2016.
Lorenz, Peter E. "Counting Witnesses for the Angry Jesus in Mark 1:41: Interdependence and Insularity in the Latin Tradition." *TynBul* 67 (2016) 183–216.
Lust, Johan. "'And I Shall Hang Him on a Lofty Mountain': Ezek 17:22–23 and Messianism in the Septuagint." In *IX Congress of the International Organization for Septuagint and Cognate Studies: Cambridge 1995*, edited by Bernard A. Taylor, 231–50. Society of Biblical Literature Septuagint and Cognate Studies 45. Atlanta: Scholars, 1997.
Lust, Johan, et al. *Greek-English Lexicon of the Septuagint.* Rev. ed. Stuttgart: Deutsche Bibelgesellschaft, 2004.

BIBLIOGRAPHY

Luz, Ulrich. *Matthew 8-20*. Translated by James E. Crouch. Hermeneia. Minneapolis: Fortress, 2001.

———. *Matthew 21-28*. Translated by James E. Crouch. Hermeneia. Minneapolis: Fortress, 2005.

MacDonald, Margaret Y. *Colossians and Ephesians*. Collegeville, MN: Liturgical, 2000.

Malik, Peter. "Myths about Copying: The Mistakes and Corrections Scribes Made." In *Myths and Mistakes in New Testament Textual Criticism*, edited by Elijah H. Hixson and Peter J. Gurry, 152-70. Downers Grove, IL: IVP Academic, 2019.

Maloney, Francis J. *The Gospel of John*. Sacra Pagina 4. Collegeville, MN: Liturgical, 1998.

Marcello, Robert D. "Myths about Orthodox Corruption." In In *Myths and Mistakes in New Testament Textual Criticism*, edited by Elijah H. Hixson and Peter J. Gurry, 211-27. Downers Grove, IL: IVP Academic, 2019.

Marcus, Joel. *Mark 1-8: A New Translation with Introduction and Commentary*. AB 27. New York: Doubleday, 2000.

———. *Mark 8-16: A New Translation with Introduction and Commentary*. AB 27A. New Haven: Yale University Press, 2009.

Marshall, I. Howard. *A Critical and Exegetical Commentary on the Pastoral Epistles*. ICC. Edinburgh: T&T Clark, 1999.

———. *The Epistles of John*. NICNT. Grand Rapids: Eerdmans, 1978.

———. *The Gospel of Luke: A Commentary on the Greek Text*. NIGTC. Grand Rapids: Eerdmans, 1978.

———. *Luke: Historian & Theologian*. 3rd ed. Grand Rapids: Academie Books, 1989.

Martin, Michael W. "Defending the 'Western Non-Interpolations': The Case for an Anti-Separationist *Tendenz* in the Longer Alexandrian Readings." *JBL* 124 (2005) 269-94.

Matthews, Shelley. "Fleshly Resurrection, Authority Claims, and the Scriptural Practices of Lukan Christianity." *JBL* 136 (2017) 163-83.

McCarthy, Carmel. *Saint Ephrem's Commentary on Tatian's Diatessaron*. Journal of Semitic Studies Supplement 2. Oxford: Oxford University Press, 1993.

McGowan, Andrew B. "Eating People: Accusations of Cannibalism Against Christians in the Second Century." *JECS* 2/3 (2004) 413-42.

McHugh, John F. *A Critical and Exegetical Commentary on John 1-4*. ICC. London: T&T Clark, 2009.

McReynolds, Paul R. "Establishing Text Families." In *The Critical Study of Sacred Texts*, edited by Wendy Doniger, 97-113. Berkeley: Graduate Theological Union, 1979.

Meier, John P. *A Marginal Jew: Rethinking the Historical Jesus; Mentor, Message and Miracles*. Vol. 2. AB Reference Library. New York: Doubleday, 1994.

Meredith, Anthony. "Porphyry and Julian Against the Christians." *ANRW* 2.23.2 (1980) 1119-49.

Messer, Adam G. "Patristic Theology and Recension in Matthew 24.36: An Evaluation of Ehrman's Text-Critical Methodology." In *Revisiting the Corruption of the New Testament: Manuscript, Patristic, and Apocryphal Evidence*, edited by Daniel B. Wallace, 127-88. Grand Rapids: Kregel, 2011.

Messina, Giuseppe. *Diatessaron Persiano*. Rome: Pontifical Biblical Institute, 1951.

Metzger, Bruce M. "Explicit References in the Works of Origen to Variant Readings in New Testament Manuscripts." In *Historical and Literary Studies: Pagan, Jewish, and Christian*, 88-103. Leiden: Brill, 1968.

BIBLIOGRAPHY

———. *Manuscripts of the Greek Bible.* Oxford: Oxford University Press, 1981.
———. "Names for the Nameless in the New Testament." In *Kyriakon: Festschrift Johannes Quaesten,* edited by P. Gransfield and J. A. Jungmann, 79-99. Münster: Aschendorff, 1970.
———. Review of *The Orthodox Corruption of Scripture,* by Bart Ehrman. *PSB* 15 (1994) 210-12.
———. *A Textual Commentary on the Greek New Testament.* Stuttgart: United Bible Societies, 1971.
———. *A Textual Commentary on the Greek New Testament.* 2nd ed. Stuttgart: United Bible Societies, 1994.
Metzger, Bruce M., and Bart D. Ehrman. *The Text of the New Testament: Its Transmission, Corruption, and Restoration.* 4th ed. Oxford: Oxford University Press, 2005.
Meyer, Marvin, ed. *The Nag Hammadi Scriptures.* New York: HarperOne, 2007.
Michaels, J. Ramsey. *1 Peter.* WBC 72. Dallas: Word, 1988.
Miller, Krista M. "Evaluating the Reading Χωρις Θεου in Hebrews 2:9 in Light of Patristic Evidence." ThM thesis, Dallas Theological Seminary, 2010.
Miller, Philip M. "The Least Orthodox Reading Is to Be Preferred: A New Canon for New Testament Textual Criticism?" In *Revisiting the Corruption of the New Testament,* edited by Daniel B. Wallace, 57-89. Grand Rapids: Kregel, 2011.
Moo, Douglas J. *The Epistle to the Romans.* NICNT. Grand Rapids: Eerdmans, 1996.
Moore, Anne. "Enigmatic Endings." In *Text and Community: Essays in Memory of Bruce M. Metzger,* edited by Harold J. Ellens, 103-20. Vol. 1. Sheffield: Sheffield Phoenix, 2007.
Morgan, Matthew P. "The Legacy of a Letter." In *Revisiting the Corruption of the New Testament,* edited by Daniel B. Wallace, 91-126. Grand Rapids: Kregel, 2011.
Moule, Charles F. D. *An Idiom Book of New Testament Greek.* Cambridge: Cambridge University Press, 1963.
Moulton, James H. *A Grammar of New Testament Greek: Prolegomena.* Vol. 1. Edinburgh: T&T Clark, 1906.
Mounce, William D. *Pastoral Epistles.* WBC 46. Nashville: Thomas Nelson, 2000.
Mugridge, Alan J. *Copying Early Christian Texts: A Study in Scribal Practice.* WUNT 2.362. Tübingen: Mohr Siebeck, 2016.
———. *Scribes, Motives, and Manuscripts: Evaluating Trends in New Testament Textual Criticism.* Eugene, OR: Wipf & Stock, 2024.
Muraoka, Takamitsu. *A Greek-English Lexicon of the Septuagint.* Leuven: Peeters, 2009.
———. *A Greek-Hebrew/Aramaic Two-Way Index to the Septuagint.* Leuven: Peeters, 2010.
———. *A Syntax of Septuagint Greek.* Leuven: Peeters, 2016.
Neirynck, Frans. "Luke 24,12: An Anti-docetic Interpolation?" In *New Testament Textual Criticism and Exegesis: Festschrift J. Delobel,* edited by Adelbert Denaux, 145-58. Leuven: Peeters, 2002.
———. "A Supplementary Note on Luke 24,12." *ETL* 72 (1996) 425-30.
Neyrey, Jerome H. "The Absence of Jesus' Emotions—the Lucan Redaction of Lk 22, 39-46." *Bib* 61 (1980) 153-71.
Nolland, John. *The Gospel of Matthew.* NIGTC. Grand Rapids: Eerdmans, 2005.
———. *Luke 1—9.20.* WBC 35A. Dallas: Word, 1989.
———. *Luke 9:21—18:34.* WBC 35B. Dallas: Word, 1993.
———. *Luke 18:35—24:53.* WBC 35C. Dallas: Word, 1993.

Nongbri, Brent. "Reconsidering the Place of Papyrus Bodmer XIV–XV (P[75]) in the Textual Criticism of the New Testament." *JBL* 135 (2016) 405–37.

O'Collins, Gerald. "Buried by His Enemies? Acts 13:28–31." *ExpTim* 130 (2019) 399–403.

Orsini, Pasquale, and Willy Clarysse. "Early New Testament Manuscripts and Their Dates: A Critique of Theological Palaeography." *ETL* 88 (2012) 443–74.

Osburn, Carroll D. "The Text of I Corinthians 10:9." In *New Testament Textual Criticism: Its Significance for Exegesis*, edited by Eldon J. Epp and Gordon D. Fee, 201–12. Oxford: Oxford University Press, 1981.

Painter, John. *1, 2 and 3 John*. Sacra Pagina 18. Collegeville, MN: Liturgical, 2002.

Panackel, Charles. ΙΔΟΥ Ο ΑΝΘΡΩΠΟΣ *(Jn 19,5b): An Exegetico-Theological Study of the Text in the Light of the Use of the Term* ΑΝΘΡΩΠΟΣ *for Jesus in the Fourth Gospel*. Analecta Gregoriana 251. Rome: Pontificia Università Gregoriana, 1988.

Pardee, Cambree G. *Scribal Harmonization in the Synoptic Gospels*. NTTSD 60. Leiden: Brill, 2019.

Parker, David C. *An Introduction to the New Testament Manuscripts and Their Texts*. Cambridge: Cambridge University Press, 1998.

———. *The Living Text of the Gospels*. Cambridge: Cambridge University Press, 1997.

———. Review of *The Orthodox Corruption of Scripture*, by Bart Ehrman. *JTS* 45 (1994) 707–8.

Parker, David C., et al. "The Dura-Europos Gospel Harmony." In *Studies in the Early Text of the Gospels and Acts*, edited by David G. K. Taylor, 192-228. Atlanta: Society of Biblical Literature, 1999.

Parsons, Mikael C. "A Christological Tendency in P[75]." *JBL* 105 (1986) 465–79.

———. *The Departure of Jesus in Luke-Acts*. JSNT Supplement 21. Sheffield: JSOT, 1987.

———. "The Text of Acts 1:2 Reconsidered." *CBQ* 50 (1988) 58–71.

Perrin, Nicholas. "Managing Jesus' Anger: Revisiting a Text-Critical Conundrum (Mark 1:41)." *CTR* 13 (2016) 3–16.

Pervo, Richard. *Acts: A Commentary*. Hermeneia. Minneapolis: Fortress, 2009.

Petersen, William L., Review of *The Orthodox Corruption of Scripture*, by Bart Ehrman. *JR* 74 (1994) 562–64.

Petzer, Jakobus H. "Luke 22:19b–20 and the Structure of the Passage." *NovT* 26 (1984) 249–52.

———. "Style and Text in the Lucan Narrative of the Institution of the Lord's Supper (Luke 22.19b–20)." *NTS* 37 (1991) 113–29.

Piazzetta, Cristian, and Wilson Paroschi. "Jesus and the Leper: A Text-Critical Study of Mark 1:41." *Kerygma* 12 (2016) 45–60.

Pietersma, Albert, and Benjamin G. Wright, eds. *A New English Translation of the Septuagint*. Oxford: Oxford University Press, 2007.

Pope, Michael F. "The Downward Motion of Jesus' Sweat and the Authenticity of Luke 22:43–44." *CBQ* 79 (2017) 261–81.

Porter, Stanley E., and Andrew W. Pitts. *Fundamentals of New Testament Textual Criticism*. Grand Rapids: Eerdmans, 2015.

Powell, Charles. "Textual Problem of Οὐδὲ 'Ο Υἱός in Matthew 24:36." Bible.org. https://bible.org/article/textual-problem-matthew-2436.

Price, Robert M. Review of *The Orthodox Corruption of Scripture*, by Bart Ehrman. *The Bible Geek* (blog). www.robertmprice.mindvendor.com/reviews/ehrman_ortho_corrupt.htm.

BIBLIOGRAPHY

Pryor, John. "Of the Virgin Birth or the Birth of Christians? The Text of John 1:13 Once More." *NovT* 27 (1985) 296–318.

Quek, Tse-Ming. "A Text-Critical Study of John 1.34." *NTS* 55 (2009) 22–34.

Robinson, J. Armitage. *Commentary on Ephesians: The Greek Text with Introduction, Notes and Appendices.* 2nd ed. London: McMillan, 1909.

Rodgers, Peter R. "Irenaeus and the Text of Matt 3.16–17." In *Text and Community: Essays in Memory of Bruce M. Metzger*, edited by Harold J. Ellens, 51–54. Vol. 1. Sheffield: Sheffield Phoenix, 2007.

———. "The Text of John 1:34." In *Theological Exegesis: Essays in Honor of Brevard S. Childs*, edited by Christopher Seitz and Kathryn Greene-McCreight, 299–305. Grand Rapids: Eerdmans, 1999.

———. "A Textual Commentary on Philippians 2:5–11." In *Text and Community: Essays in Memory of Bruce M. Metzger*, edited by Harold J. Ellens, 187–95. Vol. 1. Sheffield: Sheffield Phoenix, 2007.

Royse, James R. *Scribal Habits in Early Greek New Testament Papyri.* NTTSD 36. Leiden: Brill, 2008.

———. "Scribal Tendencies in the Transmission of the Text of the New Testament." In *The Text of the New Testament in Contemporary Research*, edited by Bart D. Ehrman and Michael W. Holmes, 461–78. 2nd ed. Leiden: Brill, 2014.

Sanders, E. P. *The Tendencies of the Synoptic Tradition.* Cambridge: Cambridge University Press, 1969.

Schmid, Ulrich. "Conceptualizing 'Scribal' Performances: Readers' Notes." In *The Textual History of the Greek New Testament: Changing Views in Contemporary Research*, edited by Klaus Wachtel and Michael W. Holmes, 49–64. Atlanta: Society of Biblical Literature, 2011.

———. "Scribes and Variants—Sociology and Typology." In *Textual Variation: Theological and Social Tendencies?*, edited by Hugh A. G. Houghton and David C. Parker, 1–23. Piscataway, NJ: Gorgias, 2008.

Sherwin-White, A. N. *Roman Society and Roman Law.* Oxford: Clarendon, 1963.

Silva, Moisés. Review of *The Orthodox Corruption of Scripture*, by Bart Ehrman. *WTJ* 57 (1995) 262–64.

Skinner, Christopher W. "'Son of God' or 'God's Chosen One' (John 1:34)? A Narrative-Critical Solution to a Text-Critical Problem." *BBR* 25 (2015) 341–57.

Smalley, Stephen S. *1, 2, 3 John.* WBC 51. Waco: Word, 1984.

———. *The Revelation to John: A Commentary on the Greek Text of the Apocalypse.* Downers Grove, IL: IVP Academic, 2005.

Spencer, F. Scott. "Why Did the 'Leper' Get Under Jesus' Skin? Emotion Theory and Angry Reaction in Mark 1:40–45." *HBT* 36 (2014) 1–22.

Stewart, Robert B., ed. *The Reliability of the New Testament: Bart D. Ehrman and Daniel B. Wallace in Dialogue.* Minneapolis: Fortress, 2011.

Strecker, Georg. *The Johannine Letters.* Translated by Linda M. Maloney. Hermeneia. Minneapolis: Fortress, 1996.

Thiselton, Anthony T. *The First Epistle to the Corinthians.* NIGTC. Grand Rapids: Eerdmans, 2000.

Thrall, Margaret E. *The Second Epistle to the Corinthians.* Vol. 1. ICC. Edinburgh: T&T Clark, 1994.

BIBLIOGRAPHY

Tuckett, Christopher M. "Luke 22, 43-44. The 'Agony' in the Garden and Luke's Gospel." In *New Testament Textual Criticism and Exegesis: Festschrift J. Delobel*, edited by Adelbert Denaux, 131-44. Leuven: Peeters, 2002.

Turner, Nigel. *Grammar of New Testament Greek: Syntax*. Vol. 3. Edinburgh: T&T Clark, 1963.

Wachtel, Klaus. "Kinds of Variants in the Manuscript Tradition of the Greek New Testament." In *Studies in Stemmatology*, edited by Pieter van Reenen et al., 87-98. Vol. 2. Amsterdam: John Benjamins, 2004.

———. "Towards a Redefinition of External Criteria: The Role of Coherence in Assessing the Origin of Variants." In *Textual Variation: Theological and Social Tendencies?*, edited by Hugh A. G. Houghton and David C. Parker, 109-27. Piscataway, NJ: Gorgias, 2008.

Wallace, Daniel B. "The Gospel According to Bart." *JETS* 49 (2006) 327-49.

———. *Greek Grammar Beyond the Basics: An Exegetical Syntax of the New Testament*. Grand Rapids: Zondervan, 1997.

———. "Lost in Transmission: How Badly Did the Scribes Corrupt the New Testament Text?" In *Revisiting the Corruption of the New Testament*, edited by Daniel B. Wallace, 19-55. Grand Rapids: Kregel, 2011.

———. "The Son's Ignorance in Matthew 24:36: An Exercise in Textual and Redaction Criticism." In *Studies on the Text of the New Testament and Early Christianity: Essays in Honor of Michael W. Holmes on the Occasion of His Sixty-Fifth Birthday*, edited by Daniel M. Gurtner et al., 178-205. Leiden: Brill, 2015.

Walton, Steve. *Leadership and Lifestyle*. Cambridge: Cambridge University Press, 2000.

Wasserman, Tommy. "The Coherence Based Genealogical Method as a Tool for Explaining Textual Changes in the Greek New Testament." *NovT* 57 (2015) 206-18.

———. "Criteria for Evaluating Readings in New Testament Textual Criticism." In *The Text of the New Testament in Contemporary Research*, edited by Bart D. Ehrman and Michael W. Holmes, 579-612. 2nd ed. Leiden: Brill, 2014.

———. "*Lectio vehementior potior*: Scribal Violence on Violent Texts?" In *Encountering Violence in the Bible*, edited by Markus Zehnder and Hallvard Hagelia, 216-33. Sheffield: Sheffield Phoenix, 2013.

———. "Misquoting Manuscripts? The Orthodox Corruption of Scripture Revisted." In *The Making of Christianity: Conflicts, Contacts, and Constructions; Essays in Honor of Bengt Holmberg*, edited by Magnus Zetterholm and Samuel Byrskog, 325-50. Coniectanea Biblica. New Testament Series 47. Winona Lake, IN: Eisenbrauns, 2012.

———. "Scribal Alterations to the 'Canonical' Gospels in Second- and Third-Century Manuscripts." In *From Thomas to Tertulllian: Christian Literary Receptions of Jesus in the Second and Third Centuries CE*, edited by Jens Schröter and Christine Jacobi, 305-27. The Reception of Jesus in the First Three Centuries 2. Edinburgh: T&T Clark, 2019.

———. "A Short Textual Commentary on Galatians." In *Studies on the Text of the New Testament and Early Christianity: Essays in Honor of Michael W. Holmes on the Occasion of His Sixty-Fifth Birthday*, edited by Daniel M. Gurtner et al., 345-71. Leiden: Brill, 2015.

———. "The 'Son of God' Was in the Beginning (Mark 1:1)." *JTS* 62 (2011) 20-50.

———. "Variants of Evil: The Disassociation of Jesus from Evil in the Text of the New Testament." In *Evil in Second Temple Judaism and Early Christianity*, edited by Chris Keith and Loren T. Stuckenbruck, 69–86. WUNT 2.417. Tübingen: Mohr Siebeck, 2016.

Watson, Francis. "Is John's Christology Adoptionist?" In *The Glory of Christ in the New Testament: Studies in Christology in Memory of George Bradford Caird*, edited by L. D. Hurst and N. T. Wright, 113–24. Oxford: Clarendon, 1987.

Welles, C. Bradford, et al. *The Parchments and Papyri*. The Excavations at Dura-Europos 5.1. Conducted by Yale University and the French Academy of Inscriptions and Letters. New Haven: Yale University Press, 1959.

Westcott, Brooke F., and Fenton J. A. Hort. *The New Testament in the Original Greek: Introduction and Appendix*. Vol. 2. New York: Harper & Brothers, 1882.

Wettlaufer, Ryan D. "A Second Glance at Matthew 27.27." *NTS* 53 (2007) 344–58.

Whitsett, Christopher G. "Son of God, Seed of David: Paul's Messianic Exegesis in Romans 2:3–4." *JBL* 119.4 (2000) 661–81.

Wilken, Robert L. *The Christians as the Romans Saw Them*. New Haven: Yale University Press, 1984.

———. "Pagan Criticism of Christianity: Greek Religion and Christian Faith." In *Early Christian Literature and the Classical Intellectual Tradition*, edited by William R. Schoedel and Robert L. Wilken, 117–34. Paris: Beauchesne, 1979.

Williams, Peter J. "An Examination of Ehrman's Case for ὀργισθείς in Mark 1:41." *NovT* 54 (2012) 1–12.

Willker, Wieland. "TCG: An Online Textual Commentary on the Greek Gospels." Bible Pages. http://www.willker.de/wie/TCG/index.html.

Wilson, Robin McL. *Colossians and Philemon: A Critical and Exegetical Commentary*. ICC. London: T&T Clark, 2005.

Winter, Paul. *On the Trial of Jesus*. Berlin: de Gruyter, 1961.

Witherington, Ben, III. "The Anti-feminist Tendencies of the 'Western Text' in Acts." *JBL* 103 (1984) 82–84.

———. "On the Road with Mary Magdalene, Joanna, Susanna, and Other Disciples—Luke 8 1–3." *ZNW* 70 (1979) 243–48.

Wright, Brian J. "Jesus as ΘΕΟC." In *Revisiting the Corruption of the New Testament*, edited by Daniel B. Wallace, 242–47. Grand Rapids: Kregel, 2011.

Yoder, James D. "The Language of the Greek Variants in Codex Bezae." *NovT* 3 (1959) 241–48.

Zerwick, Maximilian. *Biblical Greek: Illustrated by Examples*. 4th ed. Adapted from Latin by Joseph Smith. Rome: Pontifical Biblical Institute, 1963.

Zuntz, Gunther. *The Text of the Epistles: Disquisition Upon the Corpus Paulinum*. London: Oxford University Press, 1953.

Zwiep, Arie W. "The Text of the Ascension Narratives (Luke 24:50–3; Acts 1:1–2, 9–11)." *NTS* 42 (1996) 219–44.

Principal New Testament Passages

Matthew
1:16	5, 75
1:18	27–28, 75–76
1:25	252
3:11	182–83
3:16	77–78
4:18	110
4:20	239–40
5:18	179–81
5:32	245–46
6:12	238–39
8:27	145–46
9:13	201–2
9:27	110–11
9:34	210–11
10:34	200–201
12:30	70–71
13:35	174–77
15:26	218–19
16:4	179–81
16:21	80–81
17:12–13	117
17:23	235
19:29	242–45
20:22–23	117–18
20:30	111
21:4	178–79
21:44	217–18
23:25	277–79
24:6	178–79
24:36	57–58
25:40	231–32
26:3	277–79
26:68	81
27:22–23	267
27:22	266–67
27:24	267–68
27:26	268–69
27:35	196–97
27:50	118–19
28:6	131
28:7	96
28:10	231–32
28:17	97

Mark
1:1	28–31
1:2	174–77
1:3	34–35
1:10	35–36, 79–80
1:18	239–40
1:34	104–5, 209–10
1:40	230–31
1:41	212–17
1:44	270
2:7	157–58
2:26	189–91
3:11–12	105
3:11	36
3:21	219–20
5:19	36–37
5:33	228–30, 271–72
6:2	208–9
6:3	206–7
9:10	235–36
9:15	236–37

PRINCIPAL NEW TESTAMENT PASSAGES

Mark (continued)

9:29	223–24
9:35	240–41
10:13	232–33
10:29	242–45
10:51	111
12:26	158–59
13:33	202–3
14:4	233–34
14:22, 24	122–23
14:65	81
15:19	230–31
15:25	193
15:28	199
15:34	82–84
15:41	248–49
16	97–99, 252–56
16:4, 19	138–39

Luke

1:15, 17	37–38
1:28	251–52
1:35	76–77
1:76	37–38
2:7	252
2:22	6–7
2:26	37–38
2:27, 33	6–7
2:39	178
2:40	59
2:41–43	6–7
2:43	31–32
2:48	7–8
3:1	191–92
3:21	31–32
3:22	8–13, 80
3:23	13–14
4:22	14
4:39	250
5:19	112
5:22	273–74
5:33	222–23
6:11	275–76
7:9	38
7:16	159–60
8:3	246–48
8:28	39
8:39	159–60
8:40	39
9:20	39–40
9:26	238
9:27	258–59
9:35	19–20
9:54	177
11:2	259–60
11:23	70–71
11:29	179–81
11:39	274
11:44	274–75
12:31	261
15:1	237
19:38	261–62
20:23	275
20:42	40
21:18	192
22:19–20	123–29, 226–28
22:29	262–63
22:43–44	119–22
22:64	81
23:32	197–98
23:35	20
23:42–43	142–44
23:42	263–64
23:45	187–89
23:52–53	211–12
23:53	132
23:55	248–49
24:12	132–34
24:36	134–35
24:37	135–36
24:40	136
24:51–52	139–42

John

1:1	105–6
1:13	14–15
1:18	40–44, 160–61
1:27	181–82
1:34	20–22
1:36	84
4:25	250–51
5:16	276–77
6:15	203–5
6:42	16

PRINCIPAL NEW TESTAMENT PASSAGES

6:55–56	224–26
7:8	185–87
7:46	146–47
9:8	241
9:33, 35	32–33
10:7–8	153–54
10:36	106
11:28	272–73
12:28	182–83
12:41	44–45
14:9	161–62
18:32	45
19:5	60–61
19:14	193
19:40	46
20:28	162
20:30	136–37
21:1	136–37

Acts

1:2, 9–11	139–42
1:15	231–32
1:22	139–42
2:30	16–17
2:38	112
3:13	99–100
4:33	100
7:59	112–13
8:36	106–7
10:37–38	22–23
13:29	129
13:32–33	101
13:33	23–24
16:34	163
20:28	51–53, 163–64
28:31	144

Romans

1:3–4	24, 151–52
5:19	147–48
6:11	113
8:10–11	101–2
8:34	85–86
9:5	154–55
10:9	113
14:10	53–54
15:8	107
16:18, 20	113–14

1 Corinthians

5:7	129–30
9:1	102–3
10:4–5	61–62
10:9	54–56
11:23–24	130
11:27	86–88
15:15	103–4
15:45	62
15:47	62–63

2 Corinthians

4:10	86–88, 108
5:6, 8	56
5:15	86–88
11:4	71–72

Galatians

2:20	46–47
3:16–17	155
4:4	152
5:5	164
5:11	86–88
6:17	86–88

Ephesians

4:9	33
5:30	148

Philippians

2:9	165

Colossians

1:14	130–31
1:22	64
2:2	165–66

1 Timothy

1:1	47–48
3:16	48–49

2 Timothy
1:10	49

Titus
3:6	49

Hebrews
1:3	65, 88–89
1:8	166–67
2:9	89–92
2:14	149–50
2:18	65–66
3:1	108
9:26	93
10:29	66–67
13:20	50

1 Peter
2:21	93–95
3:18	93–95
4:1	93–95, 137–38

2 Peter
1:1–2	167–68

1 John
1:7	95–96
2:28	144–45
3:23	50
4:2–3	72–74
4:15	108–9
5:5	109
5:6	17–18
5:9	150
5:10	168
5:18	24–26
5:20	150–51

Revelation
22:21	114

www.ingramcontent.com/pod-product-compliance
Lightning Source LLC
Chambersburg PA
CBHW050616300426
44112CB00012B/1532